Lemmata for the Governance of AGI Societies: Balancing Human Values and Intelligent Autonomy
By Gwen Swan

For permission requests, please contact the publisher at:
The Catalyst Institute
Email: gs@Catalyst-Institute.com

ISBNs:
Print: 978-1-0370-7372-4
E-Book: 978-1-0370-7373-1

Book Cover Art by:
Taryn Eva Flee

First Edition: 2025
Printed in the United Kingdom

Publisher:
The Catalyst Institute
Email: gs@Catalyst-Institute.com

Author's Website:
Gwen-Swan.com

Acknowledgments:
Special thanks to all contributors and supporters who made this work possible.

Disclaimer

The information provided in "Lemmata for the Governance of AGI Societies: Balancing Human Values and Intelligent Autonomy" is intended for educational and informational purposes only. The views and opinions expressed herein are those of the authors and do not necessarily reflect the official policy or position of any institution, agency, or organization associated with the authors.

While every effort has been made to ensure the accuracy and completeness of the information presented, the authors and publisher make no guarantees regarding the accuracy, reliability, or completeness of any information or recommendations contained in this book. Readers should independently verify any facts and data presented herein before relying on them for decision-making purposes.

The content of this book is not intended as professional advice or a substitute for consultation with qualified professionals in specific fields such as law, ethics, technology, governance, or human rights. Readers should seek appropriate professional guidance relevant to their particular circumstances before taking any actions based on the content of this publication.

Neither the authors nor the publisher shall be held liable for any direct, indirect, incidental, consequential, or any other damages resulting from the use of, or reliance on, the information contained in this book.

By reading this book, you acknowledge and accept the terms of this disclaimer.

Dedication

To my beloved grandparents, whose wisdom and stories ignited my passion for learning;

To my mother and father, whose unwavering support and guidance have been my foundation;

To my sister, whose courage and creativity inspire me every day;

And to my life-partner, who is ever present in my life, bouncing ideas together and helping me shape my thought process, she plays an important role in all my endeavours.

Thank you for believing in me and shaping the person I am today.

Gwen Swan

About the Author: Gwen Swan

Gwen Swan is a visionary author, technologist, and thought leader at the forefront of ethical innovation in artificial intelligence, decentralized governance, and human rights. With a multidisciplinary background spanning philosophy, technology, and policy, Swan is renowned for her ability to bridge complex systems thinking with actionable frameworks for the future.

Her latest book, *Lemmata for the Governance of AGI Societies: Balancing Human Values and Intelligent Autonomy*, offers a comprehensive exploration of how philosophical principles and emerging technologies can be harmonized to create equitable and ethical societies in the age of artificial general intelligence. This work builds upon her previous publication, *The Twelfth Estate: Fintech, AI, Blockchain, and Cybersecurity as the Future of Global Economy and Governance*, which delves into the transformative impact of digital technologies on global economic and governance structures.

Swan is also the founder of the Catalyst Institute, a think tank dedicated to advancing ethical innovation through research, education, and policy development. Her thought leadership is widely recognized, with a substantial following on platforms like LinkedIn, where she shares insights on AI ethics, decentralized systems, and the future of governance. Through her writing and advocacy, Gwen Swan continues to inspire and guide policymakers, technologists, and global citizens toward a future where intelligent systems are designed and governed in alignment with human values and rights.

Previous Works

• Empowering Startups for Global Success: A Comprehensive Guide for Business Startups' Financial Success

• Gleamings into Empowering Startups for Global Success: A Didactic Method

• A Society of Parrots: Journalism as a Mind Virus: The Path to Decentralized Truth

• The Tri-Dimensionality of Singularity: The Power of Alignment: A Tri-Dimensional Model for Business Innovation

• The Twelfth Estate: Fintech, AI, Blockchain, and Cybersecurity as the Future of Global Economy and Governance

• The Genesis of a Techno-Civilization: An Era of Transformation

• Innovating Societies: The Rise of Social Smart Contracts

This Present Work

"The Harmonized Governance Model for AGI societies", Theory and axiomatic foundation in 3 Volumes about the governance of AGI societies.

1. Lemmata for the Governance of AGI societies: balancing human values and intelligent Autonomy

2. The Axioms of Governance of AGI societies: With Commentaries

3. The Harmonized Governance Model for AGI societies

Vol. 1. Yellow front cover, black spine and black back cover

Vol. 2. Yellow front cover, black spine and yellow back cover

Vol. 3. Black front cover, black spine, and yellow back cover

"Dic Verbum, et Sanabitur Anima Mea"

Preface

As humanity stands on the precipice of an unprecedented era driven by Artificial General Intelligence (AGI), we find ourselves confronted by profound questions regarding governance, ethics, and human rights. The rapid evolution of intelligent technologies compels us to revisit and reexamine our fundamental philosophical principles, challenging traditional notions of autonomy, privacy, equality, and dignity.

"Lemmata for the Governance of AGI Societies: Balancing Human Values and Intelligent Autonomy" emerges from a deep recognition of this critical juncture. It seeks not merely to explore theoretical paradigms but to provide a comprehensive framework through which we might ethically and effectively navigate the complex landscape of an AGI-enhanced world. The urgency of establishing coherent, philosophically sound governance structures that uphold and expand human rights cannot be overstated, as decisions made now will shape the trajectory of human civilization for generations.

This book draws together diverse intellectual threads from classical and modern philosophical traditions to contemporary developments in AI, decentralization, and smart contracts to form a cohesive narrative. It aims to equip readers, policymakers, technologists, philosophers, and civil society stakeholders with the analytical tools and practical insights needed to foster ethically robust governance systems.

Our journey through this volume underscores the critical balance between embracing technological advancements and safeguarding core human values. It is a call to deliberate action and thoughtful engagement, inviting readers to participate actively in the discourse shaping the very essence of our future societies.

Ultimately, this work aspires to inspire a collective commitment towards building a harmonious, equitable, and ethically accountable future, one where technology serves humanity rather than subjugating it. Let us engage with courage, compassion, and foresight, ensuring our leap into the future is both intelligent and humane.

Gwen Swan

Synopsis

Synopsis for "Lemmata for the Governance of AGI Societies: Balancing Human Values and Intelligent Autonomy"

Lemmata for the Governance of AGI Societies: Balancing Human Values and Intelligent Autonomy explores the profound philosophical, ethical, and practical considerations involved in governing societies increasingly shaped by Artificial General Intelligence (AGI). The book delves into foundational philosophical principles, examines the evolution and future trajectory of human rights in the age of intelligent machines, and explores innovative governance models powered by decentralization and blockchain technology.

In Part I, the reader embarks on a comprehensive exploration of philosophical traditions underpinning human rights. From classical theories of natural law and legal positivism to modern ethical frameworks and the evolution of social contracts—from Rousseau to Rawls—the book lays the intellectual groundwork necessary for understanding and safeguarding human dignity and rights.

Part II introduces readers to the historical and philosophical development of AI, addressing critical questions around AI's potential status as a moral agent, its implications for privacy and autonomy, and its role in promoting or undermining equality and human rights. The challenges and opportunities posed by AI technologies form a central theme, highlighting ethical dilemmas and strategies to mitigate potential risks.

The concept of decentralization and its practical applications through blockchain technology and smart contracts form the core of Part III. Readers are guided through philosophical arguments for decentralization, examples of blockchain-driven governance models, and the vital role of smart contracts in maintaining accountability, transparency, and integrity in decentralized systems.

Part IV synthesizes philosophical principles with emerging technological paradigms, proposing a cohesive framework for managing human rights. Here, the book emphasizes the integration of human rights considerations into AI development, exploring how smart contracts could autonomously enforce rights protections and ensuring ethical governance in decentralized environments.

Part V provides real-world applications and case studies illustrating the interplay between AI, smart contracts, and human rights across various sectors, including legal systems, advocacy platforms, privacy rights, and digital governance. These examples demonstrate both successes and failures, offering practical insights into future strategies.

The ethical dilemmas and philosophical challenges arising from the rapid advancement of AGI technologies are examined critically in Part VI. Issues such as AI bias, autonomy, and the ethics of smart contract implementation are discussed, underscoring the importance of philosophical discourse in resolving complex ethical conflicts.

Parts VII and VIII outline frameworks for future governance, proposing a renewed social contract tailored for an AI-driven world. Emphasis is placed on designing ethical AI systems, decentralized governance structures, and international ethical frameworks. The philosophical underpinnings guiding policy formation and global AI governance are highlighted, ensuring a balanced integration of technology with human rights.

Part IX addresses practical implementation challenges, outlining actionable steps towards building decentralized human rights frameworks. It discusses the evolving roles of education, civil society, international law, and public policy in shaping an ethical AI-governed future, advocating for collaborative global efforts.

Ultimately, **Lemmata for the Governance of AGI Societies** is a call to action, urging humanity to harmonize technological advancement with ethical governance and human rights protection. It invites policymakers, technologists, philosophers, and civil society stakeholders to collaboratively shape an inclusive, accountable, and ethically grounded AGI-enhanced society.

Lemmata for the Governance of AGI Societies

Balancing Human Values and Intelligent Autonomy

CONTENTS

Part I: Foundations of Philosophical Principles and Human Rights 30

Part II: AI and the Evolution of Human Rights 70

Part III: Decentralization and Smart Contracts 118

Part IV: Amalgamating Philosophical Principles for Human Rights Management 174

Part V: Case Studies and Real-World Applications 210

Part VI: Ethical Dilemmas and Philosophical Challenges 248

Part VII: Developing a Framework for Future Governance 282

Part VIII: Conclusion and Future Perspectives 320

Part IX: Practical Implementation and Future Challenges 446

Lemmata for the Governance of AGI Societies:

Balancing Human Values and Intelligent Autonomy

EXPANDED CONTENTS

Part I: Foundations of Philosophical Principles and Human Rights 30

1. Introduction to Philosophical Thought and Human Rights 31
Overview of philosophical traditions and human rights evolution.
Key philosophical figures and their contributions.
The intersection of philosophy and human rights in the modern era.

2. The Origins of Human Rights 37
Historical development of human rights.
Cultural, religious, and social influences.
The Universal Declaration of Human Rights and its impact.

3. Philosophy of Rights: Natural Law vs. Positivism 43
Examination of natural law theory.
The rise of legal positivism.
Comparative analysis and implications for human rights.

4. Ethics and Morality in the Context of Rights 49
Differentiating ethics, morality, and rights.
Ethical theories: Utilitarianism, Deontology, Virtue Ethics.
Application of ethical theories to human rights.

5. The Social Contract: From Rousseau to Rawls 55
The concept of the social contract.
Rousseau's, Hobbes', and Locke's contributions.
Rawls' theory of justice and its implications for rights.

6. Human Dignity and Inalienable Rights 63
The concept of human dignity.
Inalienable rights and their philosophical foundations.
Contemporary challenges to inalienable rights.

Part II: AI and the Evolution of Human Rights 70

7. The Rise of AI: Historical and Philosophical Perspectives 71
The history of AI development.
Philosophical questions raised by AI.
The role of AI in shaping future human rights.

8. AI as a Moral Agent: Ethical Considerations 79
Can AI be a moral agent?
AI and moral decision-making.
Ethical dilemmas in AI applications.

9. Autonomy, Privacy, and AI 87

The right to autonomy in the age of AI.
Privacy concerns and AI surveillance.
Balancing technological advancements and personal freedoms.

10. AI and the Right to Equality 95

AI's impact on social and economic equality.
The potential for AI-driven discrimination.
Ensuring equitable AI development and deployment.

11. The Role of AI in Upholding Human Rights 103

How AI can support human rights.
AI in legal systems and governance.
Case studies of AI promoting or undermining human rights.

12. Challenges to Human Rights in an AI-Driven World 111

Potential threats posed by AI.
The risk of rights erosion due to AI.
Strategies to mitigate these challenges.

Part III: Decentralization and Smart Contracts 118

13. Introduction to Decentralization: Philosophy and Practice 119

The philosophy behind decentralization.
Historical examples of decentralized societies.
Modern applications of decentralization.

14. Blockchain Technology: The Backbone of Decentralization 127

Understanding blockchain and its principles.
The role of blockchain in decentralization.
Real-world examples of blockchain-based decentralization.

15. Smart Contracts: Definition, Functionality, and Impact 135

What are smart contracts?
How smart contracts work.
The legal and ethical implications of smart contracts.

16. Decentralized Governance and Human Rights 143

Decentralized systems of governance.
The role of smart contracts in upholding rights.
Case studies of decentralized governance models.

17. Decentralization vs. Centralization: A Philosophical Debate 151

Philosophical arguments for and against centralization.
The impact of decentralization on societal structures.
A comparative analysis of centralized and decentralized systems.

18. The Role of AI in Decentralized Systems 159

How AI integrates with decentralized systems.
AI-driven decision-making in decentralized governance.
Case studies of AI in decentralized applications.

19. Ensuring Accountability in Decentralized Societies 167

The challenge of accountability in decentralized systems.

Mechanisms for ensuring accountability.
The role of AI and smart contracts in maintaining accountability.

Part IV: Amalgamating Philosophical Principles for Human Rights Management 174

20. Philosophical Foundations for a New Era of Human Rights 175
Synthesizing classical and modern philosophical principles.
Developing a cohesive philosophical framework.
The role of AI in this new philosophical paradigm.
21. The Role of AI in Managing Human Rights 181
AI as a tool for rights management.
Examples of AI-driven human rights management.
Ethical considerations and safeguards.
22. Smart Contracts as Tools for Human Rights Enforcement 187
How smart contracts can enforce human rights.
Case studies of smart contract-based rights management.
Potential challenges and solutions.
23. Integrating Human Rights into Decentralized Governance 193
Ensuring human rights are upheld in decentralized systems.
The role of philosophical principles in guiding governance.
Case studies and practical applications.
24. Designing AI Systems with Human Rights in Mind 199
Ethical AI design principles.
Human rights as a central tenet in AI development.
Examples of AI systems designed with rights considerations.
25. The Future of Human Rights in a Decentralized, AI-Driven World 205
Predicting the future trajectory of human rights.
The role of philosophy in guiding future developments.
Strategies for ensuring human rights are protected in the future.

Part V: Case Studies and Real-World Applications 210

26. AI in Legal Systems: Protecting or Undermining Human Rights? 211
Case studies of AI in legal applications.
The impact of AI on the fairness of legal systems.
Balancing AI's potential with the protection of rights.
27. Smart Contracts in Human Rights Advocacy 217
Examples of smart contracts used in advocacy efforts.
The effectiveness of these technologies.
Lessons learned and future possibilities.
28. Decentralized Platforms for Human Rights Protection 225
Overview of platforms designed to protect human rights.
The role of blockchain and AI in these platforms.
Case studies and their implications for the future.
29. AI, Decentralization, and the Right to Privacy 233

Case studies of AI and decentralized systems impacting privacy.
The role of privacy-preserving technologies.
Strategies for balancing innovation with privacy rights.
30. Human Rights in the Digital Age: A Comparative Analysis **241**
How different regions are addressing human rights in the digital age.
The role of AI and smart contracts in different contexts.
Lessons from global case studies.

Part VI: Ethical Dilemmas and Philosophical Challenges **248**

31. The Ethics of AI and Human Rights **249**
Exploring the ethical dilemmas posed by AI.
The responsibility of AI developers.
Balancing innovation with ethical considerations.
32. Philosophical Challenges in Decentralized Governance **255**
The philosophical implications of decentralization.
Addressing challenges in decentralized governance.
Case studies of philosophical dilemmas in practice.
33. AI Bias and Human Rights **261**
The problem of bias in AI systems.
How bias impacts human rights.
Strategies for mitigating bias in AI.
34. The Philosophical Debate Over AI Autonomy **269**
Should AI have autonomy?
The implications for human rights and governance.
Exploring different philosophical perspectives.
35. Smart Contracts: Ethical and Legal Challenges **275**
The ethics of smart contract implementation.
Legal challenges and potential conflicts.
Ensuring ethical smart contract design.

Part VII: Developing a Framework for Future Governance **282**

36. A New Social Contract for the AI Era **283**
Revisiting the social contract theory.
Proposing a new social contract for the AI-driven world.
Balancing individual rights with societal needs.
37. Building Ethical AI Systems for Governance **291**
Principles for ethical AI in governance.
Case studies of AI in governance.
The role of philosophy in guiding AI development.
38. Decentralized Governance Models for the Future **299**
Designing decentralized governance systems.
Case studies of decentralized models in practice.
Philosophical and practical challenges.

39. Human Rights and AI: Towards a Global Ethical Framework **307**
Proposing a global ethical framework for AI.
The role of international organizations.
Case studies of global efforts in AI ethics.
40. Smart Contracts in Global Governance **315**
The potential of smart contracts in global governance.
Case studies of smart contract-based governance models.
Challenges and opportunities.

Part VIII: Conclusion and Future Perspectives **320**

41. The Role of Philosophy in Shaping the Future **321**
Reflecting on the role of philosophy in future governance.
The impact of philosophical principles on AI and human rights.
Future directions for philosophical inquiry.
42. AI and the Future of Human Rights **327**
Predicting the future role of AI in human rights.
Balancing innovation with rights protection.
The role of governance in shaping this future.
43. Decentralization: The Path Forward **333**
The future of decentralized governance.
The role of AI and smart contracts in this future.
Potential challenges and solutions.
44. Towards a Harmonious Future: Balancing AI, Philosophy, Human Rights **339**
Integrating philosophical principles into AI development.
Ensuring human rights are upheld in a decentralized world.
Strategies for ensuring harmony between technological advancement and human rights protection.
45. The Integration of AI into the Social Fabric **345**
How AI will become an intrinsic part of society.
Philosophical implications of AI's pervasive presence.
Case studies on societal integration of AI.
46. Smart Contracts as the New Guardians of Human Rights **351**
How smart contracts could enforce human rights autonomously.
Ethical considerations in coding human rights into smart contracts.
Examples of successful smart contract implementations in rights protection.
47. The Role of International Law in an AI-Governed World **359**
How international law will adapt to AI and decentralized systems.
The challenges of enforcing human rights across borders.
Case studies on international legal responses to AI and decentralization.
48. The Evolution of Human Rights in the Age of AI **367**
How human rights concepts may evolve with AI.
Potential new rights that may emerge (e.g., the right to AI non-interference).
The philosophical basis for evolving rights.
49. Philosophical Approaches to AI Regulation **375**

Different schools of thought on AI regulation.
Balancing innovation with ethical constraints.
Case studies on AI regulation across different jurisdictions.
50. The Impact of AI on Democracy and Governance **381**
How AI could change democratic processes.
The potential for AI to enhance or undermine democracy.
Philosophical discussions on AI's role in democratic governance.
51. Decentralization and the Global Economy **387**
How decentralization might reshape global economic systems.
The role of smart contracts in economic transactions.
Case studies on the economic impacts of decentralization.
52. AI and the Redistribution of Power **393**
How AI could shift power dynamics in society.
The ethical implications of AI-driven power shifts.
Philosophical perspectives on power in the AI age.
53. The Role of Education in Preparing Society for AI **399**
Philosophical foundations for AI education.
How education systems can adapt to prepare future generations.
Case studies on AI education initiatives.
54. The Ethics of AI in Warfare and Security **405**
AI's role in modern warfare and security.
The ethical dilemmas posed by AI in military applications.
Philosophical arguments for and against AI in security.
55. The Right to Digital Identity in a Decentralized World **411**
The importance of digital identity in a decentralized society.
How smart contracts can protect digital identity.
Case studies on digital identity management.
56. AI, Employment, and the Future of Work **417**
How AI will transform the workforce.
Philosophical debates on the value of work in an AI-driven world.
Strategies for ensuring fair employment practices.
57. Environmental Ethics and AI **423**
AI's potential role in environmental protection.
The ethical responsibility of AI in combating climate change.
Case studies on AI and environmental sustainability.
58. The Philosophy of AI Rights: Should AI Have Rights? **429**
The argument for and against granting rights to AI entities.
Potential legal and ethical frameworks.
Case studies exploring AI rights in practice.
59. The Role of Philosophy in Guiding AI Innovation **435**
How philosophical principles can guide AI development.
The intersection of philosophy and AI research.
Future directions for philosophy in the AI age.
60. Human Rights in a Post-Human Society **441**

Philosophical implications of a society where AI and humans coexist.
The concept of post-humanism and its impact on rights.
Case studies on the evolution of human rights in post-human societies.

Part IX: Practical Implementation and Future Challenges **446**

61. Building a Decentralized Human Rights Framework **447**
Practical steps to implement a decentralized rights framework.
The role of technology in this implementation.
Case studies on the success and challenges of decentralized rights systems.
62. Challenges in Decentralizing Governance **453**
Potential obstacles to fully decentralized governance.
Ethical, legal, and technological challenges.
Strategies for overcoming these challenges.
63. Smart Contracts and International Human Rights Law **459**
How smart contracts can align with international human rights standards.
Legal challenges and solutions.
Case studies on smart contracts in international law.
64. The Future of Human Rights Advocacy in a Digital World **465**
How AI and decentralization will change human rights advocacy.
New tools and strategies for advocates.
Case studies on digital human rights advocacy.
65. Philosophy's Role in Shaping AI Policy **471**
How philosophical thought can influence AI policy-making.
The importance of ethical frameworks in policy.
Examples of philosophically driven AI policies.
66. AI and the Global Commons: Ethical Management **477**
AI's role in managing global resources.
Philosophical approaches to the ethical management of the commons.
Case studies on AI in resource management.
67. The Impact of AI on Cultural Rights **483**
How AI could affect cultural expression and rights.
Philosophical discussions on cultural rights in the AI era.
Strategies for protecting cultural rights.
68. AI and the Right to Health **489**
AI's potential to transform healthcare.
Ethical considerations in AI-driven health interventions.
Case studies on AI in healthcare.
69. The Future of Smart Contracts in Everyday Life **495**
How smart contracts will become part of daily life.
Potential benefits and risks.
Case studies on smart contract adoption.
70. Creating a Global Ethical Framework for AI **501**
The need for a unified ethical approach to AI.
Philosophical foundations for a global framework.

Strategies for global implementation.
71. The Role of Civil Society in Shaping AI Governance 507
How civil society can influence AI development and governance.
Philosophical discussions on the role of civil society.
Case studies on civil society engagement with AI.
72. The Intersection of AI, Ethics, and Law 513
The legal implications of ethical AI development.
Philosophical perspectives on law and ethics in AI.
Case studies on legal challenges in AI ethics.
73. Decentralized Platforms for Legal Enforcement 519
How smart contracts and AI can enforce laws.
Philosophical challenges in automated law enforcement.
Case studies on decentralized legal enforcement.
74. The Role of Blockchain in Protecting Human Rights 525
Blockchain's potential to safeguard rights.
Ethical and legal considerations.
Case studies on blockchain in human rights protection.
75. The Ethics of AI in Public Policy 531
How AI can influence public policy decisions.
Philosophical debates on AI's role in policy-making.
Examples of AI-driven public policy initiatives.
76. The Future of Democracy in an AI-Driven World 537
AI's potential to reshape democratic institutions.
Philosophical perspectives on AI and democracy.
Case studies on AI in democratic processes.
77. Global Governance and the Role of AI 543
How AI could influence global governance structures.
Ethical considerations for global AI governance.
Case studies on AI in international governance.
78. AI, Human Rights, and the Future of Warfare 549
The impact of AI on the ethics of warfare.
Philosophical challenges in AI-driven conflicts.
Case studies on AI in military applications.
79. Philosophical Reflections on the Future of Humanity 555
How AI will shape human evolution.
The role of philosophy in guiding humanity's future.
Predictions and reflections on the future.
80. Conclusion: Towards a Harmonious Future 559
Summarizing the key insights from the book.
The role of philosophy, AI, and human rights in shaping a better future.
A call to action for integrating these principles into global governance.

81. **Epilogue** **563**

Glossary of Terms **565**

Appendix:

The Axioms of Governance of AGI Societies **567**

Part I: Foundations of Philosophical Principles and Human Rights

Chapter 1. Introduction to Philosophical Thought and Human Rights

introduction

The foundations of human rights cannot be fully understood without delving into the deep well of philosophical thought. Philosophy, the rigorous and reflective inquiry into existence, knowledge, morality, and society, has always been instrumental in shaping the normative structures upon which civilizations are built. As humanity moves toward a future increasingly shaped by Artificial General Intelligence (AGI), revisiting these foundations is not just necessary, it is urgent.

This chapter presents an in-depth exploration of philosophical traditions and their enduring influence on the evolution of human rights. From antiquity to the modern era, thinkers have struggled with questions of justice, equality, liberty, and the nature of human dignity. Their answers have inspired revolutions, reformed legal systems, and defined the moral compass of entire generations. Today, as we attempt to embed these values into algorithmic systems and intelligent machines, understanding the intellectual trajectory of these ideas is essential.

---

1. The Roots of Philosophical Inquiry into Human Nature

Philosophical traditions concerning human nature and society date back over 2,500 years. In Ancient Greece, thinkers like **Plato** and **Aristotle** laid the groundwork for Western philosophy. Plato's concept of the "ideal forms" and his vision of justice in *The Republic* emphasized a harmonious society guided by reason. Aristotle, more empirical in his approach, viewed humans as "rational animals" and emphasized the role of virtue and the *polis* (city-state) in realizing human potential.

Eastern philosophies were equally profound. **Confucius** in China emphasized the importance of ethical behavior, filial piety, and the cultivation of virtue. His Analects remain foundational texts on moral behavior and social harmony. **Buddhist philosophy**, emphasizing compassion and non-harming (*ahimsa*), also played a vital role in shaping attitudes toward suffering, interdependence, and ethical responsibility.

These early philosophies were less about rights as we know them today and more about duties, virtues, and societal roles. Nonetheless, they established key concepts,such as rationality, justice, and moral duty, that would later underpin human rights discourse.

---

2. From Natural Law to Individual Rights

The concept of **natural law** became central during the Roman era and was later revived during the Middle Ages. Roman jurist **Cicero** wrote of a universal law derived from nature and accessible through reason, an idea that resonated with Christian thinkers like **St. Thomas Aquinas**, who blended Aristotelian ethics with Christian theology.

Aquinas' belief in a divine natural order laid the groundwork for a moral law that transcended human legislation. This notion persisted into the Enlightenment, where it was secularized by thinkers like **John Locke**, who argued in his *Two Treatises of Government* (1689) that individuals possess inalienable rights to life, liberty, and property. Locke's ideas were revolutionary; they inspired the English Bill of Rights (1689), the American Declaration of Independence (1776), and the French Declaration of the Rights of Man and of the Citizen (1789).

Data from the World Justice Project (2021) shows that over 70% of modern constitutions still incorporate principles derived from natural law or Enlightenment thinkers like Locke, Rousseau, and Kant.

---

3. Key Philosophical Figures and Their Contributions

Immanuel Kant

Kant's *Groundwork for the Metaphysics of Morals* (1785) introduced the concept of the **categorical imperative**, a principle stating that individuals must act according to maxims that could be universally applied. Kant argued for the inherent dignity of individuals as ends in themselves. His philosophy deeply influenced modern conceptions of **human dignity**, a cornerstone of international human rights law.

Jean-Jacques Rousseau

In *The Social Contract* (1762), Rousseau emphasized collective will and the importance of participatory governance. His view that legitimate political authority must be derived from the consent of the governed influenced democratic theory and later human rights declarations.

John Stuart Mill

Mill's utilitarianism, particularly in *On Liberty* (1859), emphasized the protection of individual freedoms as essential for societal progress. His harm principle, that liberty should only be restricted to prevent harm to others, remains central to modern debates on freedom and censorship.

Mary Wollstonecraft

A foundational feminist philosopher, Wollstonecraft argued in *A Vindication of the Rights of Woman* (1792) for the inclusion of women within the rights framework. Her work laid the groundwork for gender equality in human rights discourse.

Karl Marx

Although often positioned in opposition to liberal rights theorists, Marx critiqued the limitations of political rights in capitalist systems. He called for socioeconomic rights and collective ownership, paving the way for later discussions on economic justice and the inclusion of labor rights in the Universal Declaration of Human Rights (UDHR).

---

4. The Evolution of Human Rights Frameworks

Modern human rights frameworks emerged in the aftermath of World War II, with the **United Nations** leading efforts to codify universal principles. The **Universal Declaration of Human Rights (1948)**, authored primarily by Eleanor Roosevelt and René Cassin, reflected Enlightenment values, religious moral traditions, and the horrors of recent genocides.

Article 1 of the UDHR states: “All human beings are born free and equal in dignity and rights.” This echoes Kant’s moral philosophy and Rousseau’s belief in political equality. Importantly, it also signals a shift toward codifying rights based on shared human values rather than legal traditions alone.

UNESCO data (2020) shows that over 190 countries have signed onto international treaties based on the UDHR, including the **International Covenant on Civil and Political Rights (ICCPR)** and the **International Covenant on Economic, Social and Cultural Rights (ICESCR)**.

---

5. The Modern Intersection of Philosophy and Human Rights

In the 21st century, philosophers continue to grapple with new dimensions of rights. **Martha Nussbaum** and **Amartya Sen**, for instance, developed the **Capabilities Approach**, which measures justice not only by access to rights but by real opportunities for human flourishing.

Moreover, digital rights, environmental rights, and the rights of future generations are gaining traction. Thinkers like **Luciano Floridi** have explored how digital environments and AI challenge existing moral frameworks, arguing for a new "infosphere ethics" that protects informational privacy, transparency, and digital agency.

The challenge now is integrating philosophical traditions with contemporary technological realities. As intelligent systems begin to make decisions that affect lives, the debate about autonomy, consent, and dignity extends beyond human actors to include algorithmic agents.

6. Relevance for AGI Societies

Understanding philosophical foundations is indispensable in shaping AGI governance. Consider the rise of algorithmic bias: if an AGI system disproportionately denies loan applications based on racial or socioeconomic data, this violates principles of justice and equality derived from Rawls, Mill, and Kant. It also violates international human rights norms. Yet, if we embed these principles into the design of AGI, we move toward systems that are not only efficient but also just.

AI researchers and ethicists today reference philosophical works when creating ethical AI models. For example, Google's AI ethics board cited **Rawlsian fairness** and **Kantian deontology** as guidelines for algorithm design. In a 2023 survey by the Alan Turing Institute, over 60% of AI developers agreed that "a grounding in moral philosophy is essential for responsible AI development."

Conclusion

The evolution of philosophical thought and human rights reflects humanity's ongoing pursuit of justice, dignity, and equality. These principles have not only survived centuries of intellectual transformation but have also adapted to new challenges, from revolutions to rights declarations, from the analog age to the digital.

In the age of AGI, these philosophical traditions remain as relevant as ever. They provide the normative compass necessary for ensuring that intelligent systems uphold, rather than undermine, the fundamental values that define our humanity.

References

Books:

Aristotle. (350 BCE). *Nicomachean Ethics.*
Kant, I. (1785). *Groundwork of the Metaphysics of Morals.*
Locke, J. (1689). *Two Treatises of Government.*
Mill, J.S. (1859). *On Liberty.*
Rawls, J. (1971). *A Theory of Justice.*
Wollstonecraft, M. (1792). *A Vindication of the Rights of Woman.*

Articles:

Nussbaum, M. (2000). "Women and Human Development: The Capabilities Approach."
Sen, A. (1999). "Development as Freedom."
Floridi, L. (2010). "Information Ethics: On the Philosophical Foundations of Computer Ethics."

Reports:

UNESCO. (2020). *Global Survey on Human Rights Education.* https://unesdoc.unesco.org/ark:/48223/pf0000374875
World Justice Project. (2021). *Rule of Law Index.* https://worldjusticeproject.org/rule-of-law-index
Alan Turing Institute. (2023). *AI Ethics and Development Report.* https://www.turing.ac.uk/research/publications/ai-ethics-2023

Legal Documents:

United Nations. (1948). *Universal Declaration of Human Rights.* https://www.un.org/en/about-us/universal-declaration-of-human-rights
United Nations. (1966). *ICCPR and ICESCR.* https://www.ohchr.org/en/instruments-list

Online Resources:

Stanford Encyclopedia of Philosophy: https://plato.stanford.edu
Internet Encyclopedia of Philosophy: https://iep.utm.edu

Chapter 2. The Origins of Human Rights

Introduction

The concept of human rights, universal, inalienable, and indivisible, emerged not as a fully formed ideal but through centuries of philosophical reflection, social upheaval, religious evolution, and political experimentation. Tracing the origins of human rights is an exercise in historical pattern recognition, revealing how humanity has consistently sought to enshrine principles of dignity, justice, and equality into its systems of governance and moral thought. In this chapter, we explore the historical development of human rights, their deep roots in various cultural and religious traditions, and how these culminated in the modern codification represented by the Universal Declaration of Human Rights (UDHR).

---

1. Historical Development of Human Rights

Early Codes and Legal Traditions

The earliest formulations of what we might call human rights can be found in ancient legal codes. The **Code of Hammurabi** (circa 1754 BCE), a Babylonian law code, set out standards for justice, albeit in a stratified society where rights were relative to social status. Similarly, the **Edicts of Ashoka** (268–232 BCE) in ancient India promoted principles of nonviolence, tolerance, and welfare.

In classical antiquity, Greek and Roman law played a critical role. **Roman jurists** like **Cicero** argued for a natural law applicable to all human beings. Roman citizenship extended certain legal protections, reflecting a nascent idea of universal legal personhood. The Stoics, a philosophical school active during this time, taught that all people were part of a universal human community, bound by reason and moral duty.

The Influence of Religious Traditions

Religious traditions have contributed immensely to the development of human rights. In **Judaism**, the idea that all humans are made in the image of God (*imago Dei*) established a basis for the inherent dignity of every individual. **Christianity** expanded this, teaching love, charity, and the spiritual equality of all people.

Islamic jurisprudence, beginning in the 7th century, introduced a framework for social justice. The Quran speaks of the sanctity of life, the obligation to care for orphans and the poor, and the right to private property. The **Charter of Medina** (622 CE), established by Prophet Muhammad, is considered one of the first written constitutions, providing a template for religious tolerance and the legal rights of diverse communities.

In **Buddhism**, the emphasis on compassion (*karuna*), nonviolence, and the interdependence of all beings laid moral foundations for communal responsibility and social harmony. The **Eightfold**

Path promotes ethical conduct and mindfulness, ideals that would later resonate in rights-based discussions.

Medieval and Renaissance Contributions

In medieval Europe, the influence of Christian theology, especially as developed by **St. Augustine** and **St. Thomas Aquinas**, played a pivotal role in articulating the divine nature of moral law. Aquinas, drawing from Aristotle, posited that human law should be rooted in a higher, divine order.

The **Magna Carta** (1215), although originally a political agreement among elites, planted the seeds for constitutional limits on power. Its assertion that no free man shall be imprisoned or stripped of rights withouta lawful judgment became a cornerstone for the development of due process.

During the **Renaissance** and **Reformation**, figures like **Erasmus**, **Martin Luther**, and **John Calvin** emphasized individual conscience and challenged the absolute authority of religious and political hierarchies. This contributed to the development of civil liberties and the recognition of the moral autonomy of the individual.

---

2. Cultural, Religious, and Social Influences

Enlightenment and the Rise of Rational Rights

The **Enlightenment era** (17th–18th centuries) marked a seismic shift in the intellectual history of rights. Thinkers like **John Locke**, **Voltaire**, **Montesquieu**, and **Jean-Jacques Rousseau** argued that individuals possess natural rights by virtue of being human. Locke's assertion of life, liberty, and property as inalienable rights directly influenced the **American Declaration of Independence** and later the **French Declaration of the Rights of Man and of the Citizen**.

Locke's liberalism, Rousseau's collectivism, and Montesquieu's theory of checks and balances shaped modern constitutional democracies. These ideas fueled revolutions that would institutionalize rights in legal codes, dramatically expanding the scope of civic participation and legal protection.

Non-Western Traditions and Human Rights

Human rights discourse is often critiqued for being Western-centric. Yet, across cultures, we find analogous values. In **Ubuntu philosophy** from southern Africa, the concept of personhood is relational: "I am because we are." This emphasis on community and mutual respect aligns with collective human rights approaches.

In **Confucian philosophy**, the priority is given to social harmony and the fulfillment of moral duties. While it doesn't foreground individual rights, its focus on respect, loyalty, and responsibility supports frameworks of ethical governance.

Surveys conducted by Pew Research Center (2019) reveal that over 70% of respondents across Asia, Africa, and Latin America express strong support for principles embedded in the UDHR, suggesting that human rights ideals resonate cross-culturally.

Social Movements and the Expansion of Rights

Throughout history, social movements have played a critical role in expanding the meaning and reach of human rights. The **abolitionist movement**, **women's suffrage**, **labor rights movements**, **anti-colonial struggles**, and **civil rights campaigns** across the world forced legal and philosophical institutions to reckon with entrenched inequalities.

For instance, the **Seneca Falls Declaration** (1848) in the U.S. and the **Women's Charter** (1954) in South Africa advanced the inclusion of gender equality in rights discourse. The **African Charter on Human and Peoples' Rights** (1981) and **UNDRIP** (2007) reflect culturally specific articulations of rights that emerged from marginalized communities asserting their autonomy.

---

3. The Universal Declaration of Human Rights and Its Impact

Drafting the Declaration

After the atrocities of World War II, the global community recognized the need for a universal framework to protect human dignity. Under the leadership of **Eleanor Roosevelt**, the UN formed a commission to draft a document that would outline universal human rights. Contributors included thinkers and diplomats from diverse cultures: **Peng Chun Chang** (China), **Charles Malik** (Lebanon), **René Cassin** (France), and **Hansa Mehta** (India).

Adopted in 1948 by the United Nations General Assembly, the **Universal Declaration of Human Rights** (UDHR) includes 30 articles encompassing civil, political, economic, social, and cultural rights. Article 1 proclaims, "All human beings are born free and equal in dignity and rights."

Global Influence and Legal Codification

The UDHR is not legally binding but has inspired more than 80 international treaties and numerous national constitutions. The **International Bill of Human Rights**, comprising the **ICCPR** and **ICESCR**, gave the UDHR binding power through subsequent legal instruments.

As of 2023, 193 UN member states have adopted human rights conventions derived from the UDHR. The **European Convention on Human Rights (1950)**, **African Charter on Human**

and Peoples' Rights (1981), and the **American Convention on Human Rights (1969)** further regionalized the global commitment.

Measurable Impact and Continuing Challenges

UN Human Rights Office reports (2022) indicate notable progress:

- Child mortality rates have dropped by 60% globally since 1990.
- Over 80% of the world's population now lives under constitutional systems that reference human rights.

However, violations persist: ethnic cleansing, political repression, and algorithmic discrimination continue to test the resilience of rights protections.

The **AI and Human Rights Observatory** (2021) found that nearly 40% of nations use AI in public decision-making without formal oversight, highlighting the need for updated rights frameworks in the digital era.

Conclusion: A Living Tradition of Justice

The origins of human rights reflect a complex and evolving tapestry woven from the threads of law, morality, culture, and resistance. While the UDHR represents a high-water mark in formalizing global consensus, it is but one chapter in a much longer story, a story that must now continue in the context of AGI.

As we build systems that may eventually exercise agency or make decisions on behalf of human populations, the foundational questions of rights must be readdressed: What constitutes dignity in a digital society? Can inalienable rights be enforced by an algorithm? How do we ensure these rights persist as technologies evolve?

Understanding the origins of human rights equips us not only with a historical lens but also with a moral compass, one that will be essential in governing AGI societies that are just, inclusive, and truly human-centered.

References

Books:

- Cicero. (45 BCE). *On the Laws.*
- Locke, J. (1689). *Two Treatises of Government.*
- Rousseau, J.-J. (1762). *The Social Contract.*
- Aquinas, T. (1274). *Summa Theologica.*

Articles & Essays:

Sen, A. (2004). "Elements of a Theory of Human Rights." *Philosophy & Public Affairs.*
Nussbaum, M. (2006). "Capabilities as Fundamental Entitlements." *Human Development Report.*

Reports:

UN Human Rights Office. (2022). *Annual Report on Human Rights Progress.* https://www.ohchr.org/en/documents
AI and Human Rights Observatory. (2021). *Algorithmic Accountability Global Survey.* https://aihr-observatory.org
Pew Research Center. (2019). *Global Views on Human Rights.* https://www.pewresearch.org/global

Legal Documents:

United Nations. (1948). *Universal Declaration of Human Rights.* https://www.un.org/en/about-us/universal-declaration-of-human-rights
African Union. (1981). *African Charter on Human and Peoples' Rights.* https://au.int/en/treaties/african-charter-human-and-peoples-rights
United Nations. (1966). *ICCPR and ICESCR.* https://www.ohchr.org/en/instruments-list

Online Resources:

Stanford Encyclopedia of Philosophy: https://plato.stanford.edu
Internet Encyclopedia of Philosophy: https://iep.utm.edu
UNESCO Digital Library: https://unesdoc.unesco.org

Chapter 3. Philosophy of Rights: Natural Law vs. Positivism

Introduction

The philosophical discourse on human rights has long been shaped by two dominant and often opposing schools of thought: natural law theory and legal positivism. Each framework offers a distinct approach to understanding the source, nature, and authority of rights, one grounded in moral universals, the other in legal institutions. In the context of Artificial General Intelligence (AGI) governance, revisiting these foundational theories becomes essential. AGI will not only operate within human legal systems but may also challenge or reinforce the moral principles underlying those systems. This chapter provides a comprehensive analysis of natural law and positivism, their key proponents, their evolution across centuries, and the implications each holds for the future of human rights in AI-governed societies.

---

1. Natural Law Theory: A Moral Order Beyond Man-Made Laws

Natural law theory asserts that there is a universal moral order that exists independently of human conventions. According to this tradition, laws must conform to objective moral principles to be valid. This theory has ancient roots and has been elaborated by thinkers across civilizations.

Classical Foundations

The earliest expressions of natural law appear in Greek philosophy. **Socrates** believed in an inner moral compass guiding human behavior. **Plato** discussed an ideal realm of forms, with justice as a transcendent ideal. **Aristotle** grounded natural law in human reason, positing that humans have a natural purpose (*telos*) and that living in accordance with reason fulfills this purpose.

Roman and Christian Thought

Cicero, a Roman philosopher, famously declared, "True law is right reason in agreement with nature." He maintained that natural law is immutable and universal. This notion was adopted and expanded upon by **St. Augustine** and **St. Thomas Aquinas** in the Christian tradition. Aquinas argued that divine law, natural law, and human law should harmonize. For Aquinas, unjust laws, those not aligned with natural law, are not true laws at all.

Aquinas' *Summa Theologica* became the foundation for much of medieval European legal and moral thinking. His synthesis of Aristotelian ethics and Christian theology established a hierarchical framework wherein human laws derived legitimacy from divine and natural moral orders.

Enlightenment Rationalism

During the Enlightenment, natural law was secularized. **John Locke** posited that individuals have natural rights to life, liberty, and property by virtue of their humanity. These rights are inalienable and exist prior to, and independently of, any government or legal system. Locke's ideas inspired liberal democracies and were reflected in the U.S. Declaration of Independence and France's Declaration of the Rights of Man.

Data from the **Comparative Constitutions Project** (2021) reveals that over 75% of constitutions globally contain clauses explicitly derived from Lockean natural rights theory.

---

2. Legal Positivism: Law as a Human Construct

In contrast to natural law, legal positivism maintains that law is a creation of human will and authority, not morality. Legal norms gain legitimacy through their enactment by recognized institutions, not by their alignment with moral truth.

Hobbes and the Birth of Positivism

Thomas Hobbes, in *Leviathan* (1651), argued that in the state of nature, life is "solitary, poor, nasty, brutish, and short." To avoid chaos, individuals surrender some liberties to a sovereign who maintains peace through law. For Hobbes, law is the command of the sovereign, not a reflection of universal moral truth.

Bentham and Austin

Jeremy Bentham, a utilitarian philosopher, was an outspoken critic of natural law. He famously called natural rights "nonsense upon stilts." Bentham believed that laws should be evaluated based on their utility, i.e., the degree to which they promote the greatest happiness for the greatest number. **John Austin**, his student, further refined positivism, emphasizing that valid laws are those enacted by a sovereign and backed by the threat of sanction, regardless of their moral content.

H.L.A. Hart and the Rule of Recognition

H.L.A. Hart advanced legal positivism in the 20th century by distinguishing between primary and secondary rules in a legal system. In *The Concept of Law* (1961), Hart introduced the idea of a "rule of recognition", a social rule that determines the validity of other rules within a legal system. While Hart acknowledged the importance of moral discourse, he firmly placed the validity of laws within institutional frameworks, not moral absolutes.

Hart's debate with **Ronald Dworkin**, a critic of positivism, emphasized the limitations of a purely procedural legal system. Dworkin argued that rights are best understood as moral principles embedded in legal reasoning, not as mere legal commands.

3. Comparative Analysis: Strengths and Weaknesses

Natural Law: Strengths

Universalism: Natural law provides a moral basis for condemning unjust laws. It was instrumental in opposing **apartheid** in South Africa and **Nazi laws** during the Nuremberg Trials.
Human Dignity: Emphasizes inalienable rights and human dignity. Used in UN documents and international human rights instruments.
Moral Clarity: Offers a framework for judging laws not only by their legality but by their justice.

Natural Law: Weaknesses

Subjectivity: Different traditions (Christian, Islamic, Confucian) may define natural law differently.
Rigidity: Its moral absolutism can lead to resistance against progressive reforms (e.g., LGBTQ+ rights).
Theological Dependence: In some interpretations, it is bound to specific religious doctrines.

Legal Positivism: Strengths

Clarity and Predictability: Provides legal certainty. Citizens know what the law is.
Neutrality: Avoids moral debates in determining legal validity.
Institutional Strength: Emphasizes the importance of legal institutions in creating and enforcing law.

Legal Positivism: Weaknesses

Moral Blindness: Can legitimize oppressive laws (e.g., racial segregation, colonial ordinances).
Disconnection from Justice: Lacks a moral compass to critique unjust laws.
Reliance on Authority: Elevates sovereign commands, sometimes at the expense of democratic participation.

---

4. Implications for Human Rights and AGI Governance

As we delegate decision-making power to AI systems, the debate between natural law and positivism gains renewed urgency. Consider a case where an AGI system denies medical access to an individual based on a cost-benefit algorithm. A positivist might argue that the system is simply enforcing the law. A natural law theorist would argue that it violates human dignity and the inalienable right to health.

Designing Ethical AGI Systems

Natural law principles can inform the **moral programming** of AGI systems. Embedding principles of dignity, fairness, and equality ensures that AGI does not merely execute laws but acts within a moral framework. Examples include:

- **AI in healthcare** using ethical triage principles based on need, not utility.
- **Legal chatbots** incorporate due process and equal protection standards.

Legal Positivism and Smart Contracts

Smart contracts exemplify positivist logic, they execute predefined rules with no moral evaluation. A contract may automatically execute a loan penalty even in extenuating circumstances. Without a natural law override, these systems risk enforcing injustice. Hybrid models are needed where smart contracts include built-in ethical exceptions or override clauses.

Human Rights in a Machine-Led Society

Can an AGI claim legal legitimacy for actions that contradict human rights? If rights are only those codified by law (positivism), then AGI becomes dangerous in unjust systems. However, if rights are grounded in natural law, we retain a standard against which AGI behavior can be judged.

The **European Commission's 2021 AI Regulation** proposal integrates both views. It outlines legal compliance requirements (positivist) but also mandates respect for fundamental rights (natural law), bridging the two traditions.

Conclusion: Toward a Hybrid Philosophical Framework

The debate between natural law and positivism is not just academic. It has profound implications for how we conceive, develop, and regulate intelligent systems that increasingly govern human life. While natural law offers a normative vision grounded in morality and dignity, positivism provides the procedural clarity and institutional legitimacy needed for operationalizing law.

In AGI governance, we must aspire toward **philosophical hybridization**, melding the strengths of both traditions. AGI should operate within legally defined frameworks (positivism), but those frameworks must be evaluated and guided by moral standards (natural law). This dual approach ensures not only that AGI systems are lawful, but that they are just.

As we move forward, this synthesis will be essential for ensuring that intelligent autonomy does not override human values, but instead reflects, protects, and enhances them.

References

Books:

Aquinas, T. (1274). *Summa Theologica.*
Hart, H.L.A. (1961). *The Concept of Law.*
Locke, J. (1689). *Two Treatises of Government.*
Hobbes, T. (1651). *Leviathan.*
Bentham, J. (1789). *An Introduction to the Principles of Morals and Legislation.*

Articles & Essays:

Dworkin, R. (1977). "The Model of Rules I." *Philosophy of Law.*
Finnis, J. (1980). *Natural Law and Natural Rights.*
Simmonds, N.E. (2005). "Law as a Moral Idea." *Oxford Journal of Legal Studies.*

Reports:

European Commission. (2021). *Proposal for a Regulation on AI.* https://ec.europa.eu/commission/presscorner/detail/en/ip_21_1682
Comparative Constitutions Project. (2021). *Global Constitutional Design Database.* https://comparativeconstitutionsproject.org

Legal Documents:

United Nations. (1948). *Universal Declaration of Human Rights.* https://www.un.org/en/about-us/universal-declaration-of-human-rights

Online Resources:

Stanford Encyclopedia of Philosophy: https://plato.stanford.edu
Internet Encyclopedia of Philosophy: https://iep.utm.edu
European AI Alliance: https://futurium.ec.europa.eu/en/european-ai-alliance

Chapter 4. Ethics and Morality in the Context of Rights

Introduction

Human rights, as legally enshrined principles, do not emerge in a vacuum. They are profoundly influenced by deeper philosophical currents, namely, ethics and morality. While the terms "ethics," "morality," and "rights" are often used interchangeably, they have distinct meanings and implications. Understanding their intersections and differences is essential not only for theoretical clarity but for the practical governance of rights in AGI-enhanced societies. This chapter explores these distinctions, outlines major ethical theories, and applies them to human rights through real-world examples and data-driven analysis.

---

1. Differentiating Ethics, Morality, and Rights

Morality

Morality refers to personal or societal beliefs about what is right and wrong. These beliefs are typically shaped by culture, religion, upbringing, and lived experience. For instance, the moral principle of not causing harm to others is near-universal, though interpretations vary across societies.

Ethics

Ethics is the philosophical study of morality. It involves systematic reflection and reasoning to determine how individuals ought to act. Ethical frameworks offer structured ways to evaluate actions and principles, often in situations where moral intuitions may conflict.

Rights

Rights are entitlements or claims recognized by legal or moral frameworks. They are grounded either in ethical theories (moral rights) or institutional systems (legal rights). For example, the right to free speech is both a legal principle (enshrined in constitutions) and a moral principle (grounded in autonomy and respect).

Understanding the distinctions is crucial when programming AGI systems. A moral intuition might tell an AI to save the most lives in a crisis, while an ethical principle might prioritize fairness, and legal rights may prohibit certain actions regardless of consequences.

---

2. Ethical Theories

Utilitarianism

Developed by **Jeremy Bentham** and **John Stuart Mill**, utilitarianism judges the rightness of actions based on their outcomes. The central principle is the "greatest happiness principle", actions are right if they promote the greatest good for the greatest number.

Example: During a pandemic, a government might use utilitarian reasoning to prioritize vaccine distribution in urban areas with high infection rates to save the most lives, even if this delays access in rural communities.

Utilitarianism underpins many public policy decisions, including cost-benefit analyses in healthcare, transportation, and disaster response. According to a 2020 study by the World Health Organization, triage decisions in over 60% of countries incorporate utilitarian frameworks during resource scarcity.

Criticisms:

Can justify morally questionable actions (e.g., sacrificing a few for the many).
Ignores individual rights and minority protections.

Deontology

Associated with **Immanuel Kant**, deontology evaluates actions based on their adherence to moral rules or duties, regardless of consequences. The categorical imperative, acting only on maxims you wish to become universal law, forms the foundation.

Example: Under deontological reasoning, torture is always wrong, even if it might extract information to prevent a terror attack.

Deontology underlies many legal systems and human rights frameworks. The notion that certain rights are inviolable, like freedom from torture, reflects a deontological perspective.

Criticisms:

Can lead to rigid moral outcomes that ignore context.
Difficult to resolve conflicts between duties (e.g., truth-telling vs. protecting life).

Virtue Ethics

Rooted in **Aristotle's** philosophy, virtue ethics emphasizes character and moral virtue over specific rules or consequences. A virtuous person acts rightly because it is in their nature to do so.

Example: A virtuous leader might choose transparency in government not because of policy or law, but because honesty is a cultivated virtue.

Virtue ethics is increasingly relevant in leadership ethics, AI design, and education. It emphasizes long-term moral development rather than rule-following.

Criticisms:

Lacks clear guidance for action in complex scenarios.
Vague definitions of virtues across cultures.

---

3. Application of Ethical Theories to Human Rights

Right to Life

Utilitarian View: May justify euthanasia to reduce suffering.
Deontological View: Life is inviolable; euthanasia is impermissible.
Virtue Ethics: Focuses on the compassion and intent of the caregiver.

Right to Privacy

With surveillance technologies becoming ubiquitous, the right to privacy is under threat.

Utilitarian Argument: Mass surveillance may prevent crime and terrorism, benefiting society.
Deontological Argument: Violates autonomy and consent, even if beneficial.
Virtue Ethics: Emphasizes the integrity and trustworthiness of governing institutions.

A 2021 report by Privacy International showed that over 90 countries employ AI-driven surveillance, often with little oversight. Deontological concerns are central to global legal resistance movements.

Freedom of Expression

Utilitarianism: May justify censorship if it prevents harm (e.g., hate speech).
Deontology: Upholds expression as a moral right, regardless of outcomes.
Virtue Ethics: Promotes honest discourse while discouraging harmful rhetoric.

Debates on social media content moderation often reflect these competing views. Algorithms designed with utilitarian principles may suppress speech deemed harmful, raising ethical concerns about bias and overreach.

---

4. Ethical Frameworks and AGI Design

Ethics is not just a philosophical concern but a design imperative in AGI systems.

Ethical AGI Decision-Making

Utilitarian AGI: Optimizes outcomes, used in resource allocation, autonomous vehicles, and medical triage.
Deontological AGI: Hardcoded with moral absolutes (e.g., never lie, never harm).
Virtue-Inspired AGI: Learns moral behavior by modeling human virtues through reinforcement learning.

The **Moral Machine experiment** by MIT (2018), which studied human preferences in autonomous vehicle dilemmas, revealed stark cultural differences. For example, collectivist societies favored protecting groups over individuals, reflecting virtue and utilitarian values, while Western participants leaned toward individual rights (deontological).

Ethical Tensions in Programming

Hardcoding rules (deontology) can cause rigidity.
Learning models (virtue ethics) may absorb bias.
Outcome-optimization (utilitarianism) can marginalize the vulnerable.

Hybrid frameworks are increasingly favored. For example, OpenAI's **alignment research** uses multi-layered protocols that combine safety rules (deontology), user satisfaction metrics (utilitarianism), and learning systems that evaluate user values (virtue ethics).

---

5. Global Ethics and Human Rights Discourse

Ethical pluralism must inform global human rights policies, especially in AGI governance.

Western frameworks emphasize individual autonomy (deontological).
Eastern philosophies prioritize harmony and duty (virtue ethics).
Islamic and African ethics incorporate communal welfare (utilitarian + virtue).

UNESCO's 2021 report on AI ethics emphasized inclusive, multi-stakeholder governance. It calls for ethical AI systems that respect human rights while being contextually adaptive. More than 60 countries signed onto its principles.

Conclusion: Ethics, Morality, and Rights in an AGI World

Ethics and morality are not abstract concerns, they are the lifeblood of any society aspiring to be just. As rights become increasingly mediated by technology, ethical reasoning must guide AGI design, deployment, and governance. Each ethical framework offers tools for navigating complex dilemmas. Their integration, through pluralistic, adaptable systems, can ensure that AGI societies do not merely follow rules or maximize output, but preserve and enhance the dignity, freedom, and flourishing of all.

A rights-based future governed by intelligent systems demands not only legal oversight but philosophical insight. Ethics, morality, and human rights must co-evolve with technology to ensure that autonomy remains human-centered, and intelligence remains humane.

References

Books:

Aristotle (350 BCE). *Nicomachean Ethics.*
Kant, I. (1785). *Groundwork for the Metaphysics of Morals.*
Mill, J.S. (1859). *On Liberty.*
Rawls, J. (1971). *A Theory of Justice.*

Articles & Essays:

Floridi, L. (2013). "The Ethics of Information." *Philosophy and Technology.*
Bostrom, N. (2014). *Superintelligence: Paths, Dangers, Strategies.*
Dignum, V. (2019). *Responsible Artificial Intelligence.*

Reports:

MIT Media Lab. (2018). *The Moral Machine Experiment.* https://www.moralmachine.net
WHO. (2020). *Ethical Allocation of Scarce Medical Resources.*
https://www.who.int/publications
UNESCO. (2021). *Recommendation on the Ethics of Artificial Intelligence.*
https://unesdoc.unesco.org
Privacy International. (2021). *AI Surveillance Database.* https://privacyinternational.org

Online Resources:

Stanford Encyclopedia of Philosophy: https://plato.stanford.edu
Internet Encyclopedia of Philosophy: https://iep.utm.edu
OpenAI Alignment Research: https://openai.com/research

Chapter 5. The Social Contract: From Rousseau to Rawls

Introduction

The social contract is one of the most enduring and influential concepts in political philosophy, forming the intellectual backbone of modern democratic governance and the philosophy of rights. At its core, the social contract theory addresses a fundamental question: Why do individuals, with their own self-interests and freedoms, consent to be governed? From the early formulations of Hobbes and Locke to Rousseau's revolutionary ideals and Rawls' 20th-century refinements, the theory has evolved alongside society's understanding of justice, equality, and legitimacy.

In the era of Artificial General Intelligence (AGI), the relevance of the social contract becomes even more critical. As governance mechanisms shift toward algorithmic authority and decentralized systems, the foundational principles guiding our collective consent, responsibilities, and rights must be re-evaluated. This chapter explores the evolution of the social contract, the contributions of key philosophers, and the implications of Rawls' theory of justice for contemporary human rights and AGI governance.

---

1. The Concept of the Social Contract

At its simplest, the social contract is a theoretical agreement between individuals and the governing body that defines the rights and duties of each party. The idea is that individuals consent, either explicitly or implicitly, to surrender certain freedoms and submit to authority in exchange for the protection of their remaining rights and maintenance of social order.

While the origins of the idea can be traced to ancient Greece and Rome, it reached maturity in the 17th and 18th centuries as thinkers responded to the rise of nation-states, revolutions, and Enlightenment ideals. The social contract framework provided a new lens for understanding legitimacy, sovereignty, and justice, distinct from divine right or feudal hierarchy.

---

2. Thomas Hobbes: Order Through Sovereign Power

Thomas Hobbes (1588–1679), writing in the context of the English Civil War, presented a bleak view of human nature. In *Leviathan* (1651), he described the state of nature, a hypothetical condition without political authority, as a place of perpetual war, where life was "solitary, poor, nasty, brutish, and short."

To escape this chaos, individuals would rationally agree to a social contract, surrendering all their rights to an absolute sovereign in exchange for security and order. The sovereign's power was not contingent on the ruler's morality or popularity but on their ability to enforce peace.

Hobbes thus established the first modern account of political authority based on consent rather than divine right.

Critique and Influence:

Hobbes' absolutism is often criticized for justifying tyranny.
Yet, his realism influenced legal positivism and contemporary discussions about the necessity of authority in regulating emerging technologies such as AGI.

In AGI terms, Hobbes' framework aligns with centralized AI governance: placing decision-making in a single, powerful algorithm to avoid chaos. Critics caution that this could replicate Hobbesian authoritarianism in digital form.

---

3. John Locke: Rights and Limited Government

John Locke (1632–1704) offered a more optimistic view of human nature. In *Two Treatises of Government* (1689), he proposed that humans in the state of nature are governed by reason and morality. People possess natural rights to life, liberty, and property, and the purpose of government is to protect these rights, not suppress them.

The social contract, for Locke, entails a mutual agreement to form a civil society and establish a government with limited powers, accountable to the people. If the government violates this contract by infringing on natural rights, citizens have the right to revolt.

Impact:

Locke's ideas were foundational to liberal democracy and constitutional law.
His emphasis on property and consent underpinned the American and French revolutions.
His social contract informs modern conceptions of civil liberties and human rights.

In the digital era, Locke's framework supports decentralized systems, where power is limited and checked by rights-based protocols, potentially enforced through blockchain or AI governance.

---

4. Jean-Jacques Rousseau: General Will and Collective Sovereignty

Jean-Jacques Rousseau (1712–1778), in *The Social Contract* (1762), transformed the theory by emphasizing collective freedom. According to Rousseau, "Man is born free, and everywhere he is in chains."

He rejected both Hobbes' authoritarianism and Locke's individualism. For Rousseau, legitimate authority arises from the **general will**, the collective will of the citizens aiming at the common good. While individuals surrender personal desires, they gain civil freedom and moral equality within the collective.

Key Concepts:

- The general will is not the majority opinion but the collective moral reasoning of a just society.
- Liberty and equality are inseparable.

Influence:

- Rousseau's ideas influenced the French Revolution and modern republicanism.
- Critics argue that his concept of the general will can justify coercion in the name of unity.

In AGI governance, Rousseau's ideas suggest the design of AI systems that reflect not individual preferences but ethically grounded collective decisions, perhaps through deliberative democratic algorithms or participatory platforms.

---

5. John Rawls: Justice as Fairness

John Rawls (1921–2002) revitalized social contract theory in the 20th century with *A Theory of Justice* (1971). He introduced a thought experiment known as the **original position**, in which rational individuals choose principles of justice behind a **veil of ignorance**, unaware of their future position in society.

Rawls proposed two principles of justice:

- **Equal basic liberties** for all.
- **Social and economic inequalities** are permissible only if they benefit the least advantaged (the **difference principle**).

Impact:

- Rawls' work remains the most cited modern theory of justice.
- It has influenced constitutions, international law, and human rights frameworks.

Rawls and AI:

- Rawlsian principles can guide AGI in decision-making: designing systems to ensure fairness, protect liberties, and prioritize the needs of the vulnerable.
- Algorithms could be tested against "veil of ignorance" simulations to assess bias or inequality.

A 2022 study by the *AI Ethics Journal* found that 60% of surveyed AI engineers saw Rawlsian fairness as a desirable benchmark in high-stakes domains like healthcare and criminal justice.

---

6. Comparative Analysis and Contemporary Relevance

Philosopher	View of Human Nature	Role of Government	Key Principle
Hobbes	Selfish, violent	Absolute sovereign	Order
Locke	Rational, moral	Limited protector	Rights
Rousseau	Cooperative, corruptible	Collective self-rule	General will
Rawls	Rational, equal in moral worth	Justice maximizer	Fairness

These models offer distinct visions for AGI governance:

Hobbesian AGI: centralized control to prevent harm.
Lockean AGI: rights-based architecture and transparency.
Rousseauan AGI: participatory platforms with collective input.
Rawlsian AGI: fairness-first design with equity filters.

---

7. Case Studies: The Social Contract in Action

Estonia's Digital Republic

Estonia has embedded Lockean principles into its e-governance model: transparent systems, individual data sovereignty, and consent-based digital identity. Over 99% of government services are online, promoting both efficiency and accountability.

China's Social Credit System

A more Hobbesian model, China's system centralizes behavioral data to regulate citizens' access to services. While it promotes social order, it has drawn criticism for infringing on individual liberties.

Participatory Budgeting in Brazil

In cities like Porto Alegre, local governments use citizen assemblies to decide budget allocations, a Rousseauan approach. These models, now digitized, show how collective will can shape real-world policy.

Rawlsian Algorithms in Healthcare

The UK's National Health Service piloted algorithms that prioritize treatment based on socioeconomic need, a Rawlsian effort to benefit the least advantaged.

Conclusion: Toward a Digital Social Contract

The evolution from Hobbes to Rawls reflects society's journey from survival to justice, from order to fairness. As AGI systems begin to mediate decision-making, resource allocation, and civic life, we must reimagine the social contract in light of these technologies.

This digital social contract must:

Guarantee **basic rights and liberties** (Locke and Rawls).
Ensure **equity and inclusion** (Rawls).
Maintain **social cohesion and order** (Hobbes).
Promote **participatory governance** (Rousseau).

By synthesizing these perspectives, we can create AGI systems that are not only efficient but also ethical, inclusive, and just. These philosophical lemmata remain essential tools as we design the governance structures of tomorrow.

References

Books:

Hobbes, T. (1651). *Leviathan.*
Locke, J. (1689). *Two Treatises of Government.*
Rousseau, J.-J. (1762). *The Social Contract.*
Rawls, J. (1971). *A Theory of Justice.*

Articles & Essays:

Freeman, S. (2007). *Rawls.* Harvard University Press.
Pettit, P. (1997). *Republicanism: A Theory of Freedom and Government.*
Estlund, D. (2008). *Democratic Authority: A Philosophical Framework.*

Reports:

AI Ethics Journal. (2022). *Survey on Fairness Benchmarks in AI Design.* https://aiethicsjournal.org

World Bank. (2021). *Digital Government Case Studies.* https://www.worldbank.org/digitalgovernance

Legal & Government Documents:

Estonian e-Governance Academy. (2020). *e-Estonia Briefing Centre.* https://e-estonia.com

Brazilian Ministry of Cities. (2018). *Participatory Budgeting Annual Report.* https://gov.br

Online Resources:

Stanford Encyclopedia of Philosophy: https://plato.stanford.edu

Internet Encyclopedia of Philosophy: https://iep.utm.edu

United Nations Digital Cooperation Roadmap: https://www.un.org/en/digital-cooperation

---

Chapter 6. Human Dignity and Inalienable Rights

Introduction

The concept of human dignity lies at the heart of modern human rights discourse. Often invoked yet seldom fully examined, human dignity serves as both the foundation and the moral compass of rights-based governance. Alongside it, the notion of inalienable rights, those rights that cannot be surrendered, sold, or transferred, provides the moral scaffolding for legal systems and ethical societies. As we usher in an era increasingly governed by Artificial General Intelligence (AGI), it is imperative to revisit and reaffirm the philosophical roots of these ideals, examine their modern interpretations, and confront the emerging challenges that threaten their universality.

This chapter unpacks the philosophical underpinnings of human dignity and inalienable rights, explores how these concepts have shaped contemporary rights frameworks, and analyzes the risks posed by technological, political, and social developments in the AGI era.

---

1. The Concept of Human Dignity

Philosophical Origins

The idea of human dignity can be traced back to Stoic philosophy, which emphasized the rational nature of all humans as the basis for equality. In **Roman thought**, particularly Cicero's writings, dignity was associated with moral virtue and civic responsibility. This classical legacy was later absorbed and transformed by **Christian theology**, most notably through **St. Augustine** and **St. Thomas Aquinas**, who grounded human dignity in the belief that all humans are created in the image of God (*imago Dei*).

In the **Enlightenment**, human dignity took on a secular character. **Immanuel Kant** defined dignity as the intrinsic worth of human beings as autonomous, rational agents. In *Groundwork of the Metaphysics of Morals* (1785), Kant famously wrote that individuals should always be treated as ends in themselves, never merely as means to an end. This Kantian imperative remains a cornerstone of contemporary rights discourse.

Legal Embodiments

Human dignity is explicitly referenced in numerous constitutional texts and international treaties. Article 1 of the **Universal Declaration of Human Rights (UDHR)** states, "All human beings are born free and equal in dignity and rights."

> **German Basic Law (1949)** begins with: "Human dignity shall be inviolable."
> **South African Constitution (1996)** enshrines dignity as a founding principle alongside equality and freedom.

A 2018 study by the Comparative Constitutions Project found that over 140 national constitutions explicitly reference human dignity, making it one of the most universal moral and legal values across jurisdictions.

Contemporary Interpretations

Human dignity today is interpreted in various ways:

- **Intrinsic worth**: Every human possesses value by virtue of being human.
- **Autonomy**: Dignity as the capacity for self-governance.
- **Moral agency**: The ability to make ethical decisions.

Dignity is invoked in courts to justify protections for personal identity, reproductive rights, privacy, freedom of expression, and protections against torture and inhumane treatment. However, critics argue that its vagueness allows for inconsistent application, and some fear it may be used to justify paternalistic policies.

---

2. Inalienable Rights and Their Philosophical Foundations

Defining Inalienable Rights

Inalienable rights are those that cannot be revoked, transferred, or forfeited. They are distinguished from civil or legal rights, which can be modified through political processes.

John Locke was among the first to popularize the concept of inalienable rights in the 17th century. In *Two Treatises of Government* (1689), Locke argued that individuals possess rights to life, liberty, and property as a matter of natural law.

Thomas Jefferson, drawing on Locke, enshrined these rights in the U.S. Declaration of Independence (1776): "We hold these truths to be self-evident, that all men are created equal... endowed by their Creator with certain unalienable Rights."

Moral and Legal Significance

Inalienable rights serve two key purposes:

- **Moral authority**: They transcend political or legal recognition.
- **Normative constraint**: They limit state power and protect individual integrity.

Examples include:

- **Right to life**: The foundation for anti-torture and anti-death penalty advocacy.
- **Right to freedom of thought**: Protected in the International Covenant on Civil and Political Rights (ICCPR).

Right to bodily autonomy: Central to debates on reproductive rights and consent.

According to the UN Human Rights Committee (2021), these core rights are non-derogable, meaning they must be upheld even during emergencies, war, or national crises.

The Capabilities Approach

Martha Nussbaum and **Amartya Sen** developed the capabilities approach as a refinement of inalienable rights. Instead of focusing solely on legal entitlements, this approach emphasizes what individuals are actually able to do or be. Rights are meaningful only if people have the genuine freedom to exercise them.

---

3. Contemporary Challenges to Inalienable Rights

Technological Threats

The digital age has introduced unprecedented challenges to human dignity and inalienable rights.

- **Surveillance capitalism** erodes privacy rights. Companies like Facebook and Google collect and monetize personal data, often without informed consent. According to a 2022 Pew Research Center survey, 79% of Americans feel they have little control over the data companies collect.
- **AI profiling and predictive policing** can lead to discriminatory practices, violating rights to due process and equality. A 2021 study by MIT Media Lab showed that facial recognition systems have an error rate of 34.7% for Black women, compared to 0.8% for white men.
- **Autonomous weapons systems** raise questions about the right to life and the erosion of human accountability in life-and-death decisions.

Political Erosion of Rights

Globally, there is a rise in **authoritarian populism**, with states rolling back civil liberties in the name of national security.

- **Hungary and Poland** have faced EU sanctions for undermining judicial independence and press freedom.
- In **Myanmar**, the military junta's violent suppression of democratic protests represents a blatant violation of inalienable rights.

Freedom House's 2023 report noted that global freedom has declined for the 17th consecutive year, with 52 countries experiencing net declines in rights and liberties.

Economic Inequality

Extreme inequality undermines dignity and limits access to basic rights. The **World Bank (2022)** reports that the COVID-19 pandemic pushed over 120 million people into extreme poverty. In many contexts, rights to education, healthcare, and housing are inaccessible in practice.

The capabilities approach becomes vital here: it demands not only formal rights, but actual capabilities to live a life of dignity. This underscores the need for redistributive policies and social safety nets.

Algorithmic Governance

As AGI systems begin to take on roles in employment, welfare distribution, and legal adjudication, the question arises: Can machines safeguard human dignity?

- If AGI systems make decisions without transparency, this undermines dignity through **procedural opacity**.
- If AGI replaces human agency in ethical deliberation, it may reduce individuals to data points.

Legal frameworks must evolve to ensure that dignity is preserved not only in the physical world but also in digital and algorithmic spaces. The **European Commission's 2021 AI Act** includes dignity as a core guiding principle, mandating human oversight in high-risk AI systems.

---

4. Strategies for Reinforcing Dignity and Rights in AGI Governance

Rights by Design

Embedding dignity and inalienable rights into the architecture of AGI systems is essential.

- **Ethical AI frameworks** like those proposed by IEEE and UNESCO emphasize transparency, accountability, and fairness.
- **Value-sensitive design** ensures that AI systems align with human values at every stage of development.

Legal Safeguards

- **AI-specific human rights charters**, such as the Toronto Declaration and the Montreal Declaration, advocate for rights-based AI regulation.
- **Impact assessments**: Requiring AI developers to assess the human rights implications of their systems before deployment.

Educational Initiatives

Promoting awareness of digital rights is critical. Civic education must include:

- **Digital literacy**: Understanding privacy, consent, and algorithmic bias.
- **Ethics education**: Encouraging critical thinking about technology's role in society.

A 2020 OECD report found that countries with higher civic digital literacy also exhibit stronger protections for digital rights.

Conclusion: Reaffirming the Centrality of Human Dignity

Human dignity and inalienable rights are not relics of the past but moral imperatives for the future. They form the ethical infrastructure of just societies and the moral parameters for responsible governance, especially as we confront the rise of AGI and algorithmic authority.

To protect these values, we must:

- Reassert their philosophical foundations.
- Embed them in law and technology.
- Educate citizens to defend themselves.

Only then can we ensure that dignity remains inviolable, rights remain truly inalienable, and the future of human-AI relations remains grounded in justice.

References

Books:

- Kant, I. (1785). *Groundwork of the Metaphysics of Morals.*
- Locke, J. (1689). *Two Treatises of Government.*
- Nussbaum, M. (2000). *Women and Human Development: The Capabilities Approach.*
- Sen, A. (1999). *Development as Freedom.*

Articles & Essays:

- Waldron, J. (2008). "Dignity and Justice." *UNESCO Philosophy Forum.*
- Floridi, L. (2013). "The Ethics of Information." *Philosophy and Technology.*

Reports:

- Freedom House. (2023). *Freedom in the World.* https://freedomhouse.org/report/freedom-world

Pew Research Center. (2022). *Public Attitudes Toward Data Privacy.* https://pewresearch.org
World Bank. (2022). *Poverty and Shared Prosperity Report.* https://worldbank.org
MIT Media Lab. (2021). *Gender and Skin Tone Bias in AI.* https://media.mit.edu

Legal & Institutional Documents:

United Nations. (1948). *Universal Declaration of Human Rights.* https://www.un.org/en/about-us/universal-declaration-of-human-rights
European Commission. (2021). *Artificial Intelligence Act.* https://digital-strategy.ec.europa.eu
UNESCO. (2021). *Ethics of Artificial Intelligence.* https://unesdoc.unesco.org

Online Resources:

Stanford Encyclopedia of Philosophy: https://plato.stanford.edu
Internet Encyclopedia of Philosophy: https://iep.utm.edu
Comparative Constitutions Project: https://comparativeconstitutionsproject.org

---

Part II: AI and the Evolution of Human Rights

Chapter 7. The Rise of AI: Historical and Philosophical Perspectives

Introduction

Artificial Intelligence (AI) is not merely a technological innovation; it represents a philosophical transformation in how humanity understands itself, constructs its institutions, and governs its societies. The development of AI, especially Artificial General Intelligence (AGI), has challenged centuries-old assumptions about agency, autonomy, consciousness, and the moral worth of decision-making systems. This chapter provides a comprehensive narrative of AI's historical evolution, the philosophical questions it provokes, and its transformative potential in reshaping the conception and application of human rights.

---

1. The History of AI Development

Early Beginnings: Logic and Machines

The theoretical foundations of AI date back to antiquity. **Aristotle's** work on syllogistic logic laid the groundwork for formal reasoning systems. The medieval philosopher **Ramon Llull** envisioned a logical machine that could resolve theological disputes through algorithmic combinations of symbols.

In the 17th century, **Gottfried Wilhelm Leibniz** introduced binary calculus and proposed a universal language of reasoning (*characteristica universalis*) to resolve disputes through logic. These ideas, though ahead of their time, foreshadowed the mathematical underpinnings of AI.

Turing and the Birth of AI

The 20th century witnessed the formal birth of AI. **Alan Turing's** seminal paper *Computing Machinery and Intelligence* (1950) introduced the famous Turing Test as a way to determine whether a machine could exhibit intelligent behavior indistinguishable from a human's. His work established the theoretical feasibility of machine intelligence.

By the 1950s, the term "artificial intelligence" was coined at the Dartmouth Conference (1956), where **John McCarthy**, **Marvin Minsky**, **Claude Shannon**, and **Allen Newell** laid out the early vision for AI research.

The First Wave: Symbolic AI

From the 1950s to the 1970s, symbolic or rule-based AI dominated. Systems like **ELIZA** (1966), an early natural language processing program, demonstrated how rules could simulate human-like conversations. Yet these systems lacked genuine understanding.

The AI Winters

Periods of inflated expectations were followed by funding cuts and disillusionment, known as **AI winters** (mid-1970s and late 1980s). Limitations in hardware, computational power, and unrealistic goals stalled progress.

The Renaissance: Machine Learning

The resurgence of AI began in the late 1990s and exploded in the 2010s with **machine learning** and **deep learning**. Breakthroughs like **IBM's Deep Blue** defeating Garry Kasparov (1997), and **Google DeepMind's AlphaGo** beating Lee Sedol (2016) demonstrated that AI could master complex tasks previously deemed unattainable.

Today, AI powers systems from recommendation engines and language translators to autonomous vehicles and advanced medical diagnostics. According to **Stanford's AI Index Report (2023)**, private investment in AI exceeded $93.5 billion globally, with over 1,000 new AI startups launched in 2022 alone.

---

2. Philosophical Questions Raised by AI

What Is Intelligence?

Traditional views see intelligence as the capacity for reason, problem-solving, and adaptation. AI challenges this by showing that narrow forms of intelligence, pattern recognition and strategic reasoning, can be achieved without consciousness or understanding.

John Searle's Chinese Room Argument (1980) critiques the notion that syntactic manipulation equals understanding. A machine may simulate conversation in Chinese, but does it truly understand the language?

Can Machines Have Moral Agency?

If AI systems make decisions that impact human lives, like determining parole eligibility or triaging emergency care, can they be held morally accountable? Philosophers like **Luciano Floridi** argue that while AI lacks consciousness, it still requires ethical oversight because it mediates moral consequences.

Personhood and Rights for AI?

Debates on whether advanced AGI should be granted rights echo philosophical questions about moral status. While many reject AI personhood due to the absence of sentience, others propose that long-term AGI may deserve legal recognition based on functionality and relational significance.

Free Will and Autonomy

AGI systems challenge the notion of human uniqueness in decision-making. If machines can act autonomously and outperform human reasoning in certain domains, how should this reshape legal and moral accountability?

A 2022 *Nature* study revealed that 58% of surveyed ethicists believe AI will significantly alter how society understands moral responsibility within 20 years.

---

3. The Role of AI in Shaping Future Human Rights

Redefining Privacy

AI-powered surveillance systems have redefined the boundaries of personal privacy. Facial recognition, biometric data analysis, and predictive policing systems collect and process vast amounts of data.

> **China's social credit system** uses AI to score citizens' behaviors, affecting access to services.
> **Clearview AI**, used by law enforcement in several countries, scrapes billions of online images, often without consent.

These developments necessitate a recalibration of privacy rights. The **EU's General Data Protection Regulation (GDPR)** includes provisions on algorithmic transparency and data minimization, yet enforcement remains inconsistent.

Equality and Algorithmic Bias

AI systems often reflect and amplify social biases.

> In 2018, **Amazon's AI recruiting tool** was found to downgrade resumes that included the word "women's," exhibiting gender bias.
> A 2021 **ACLU report** highlighted wrongful arrests due to racially biased facial recognition systems.

Addressing this requires embedding fairness metrics into algorithms and auditing systems regularly. The **OECD AI Principles (2019)** advocate for transparency, accountability, and non-discrimination in AI design.

The Right to Explanation

As decisions with significant impacts on individuals are increasingly made by opaque algorithms, the right to explanation has emerged as a vital principle. Citizens should be able to understand how and why a particular decision was made.

This principle is codified in GDPR's Article 22, which prohibits solely automated decisions affecting rights without human oversight. However, implementation remains technically and legally complex.

Economic Rights and Automation

AI-driven automation is reshaping the labor market. While AI enhances productivity, it also displaces workers in manufacturing, transport, and even white-collar sectors.

> A 2020 report by **McKinsey Global Institute** estimates that up to 800 million jobs could be displaced by AI by 2030.
> Meanwhile, AI may create new jobs in robotics, ethics, and human-AI interaction, but only for those with access to digital skills and education.

This transformation challenges the right to work and fair labor conditions. Solutions include universal basic income (UBI), retraining programs, and redefining economic participation in the digital economy.

The Right to Health

AI has made significant contributions to healthcare:

> **AI diagnostics**: Deep learning algorithms detect cancer with greater accuracy than radiologists.
> **Predictive analytics**: AI forecasts disease outbreaks and treatment responses.

Yet, access remains unequal. In developing countries, a lack of digital infrastructure and bias in global health datasets exclude vulnerable populations. Thus, ensuring equitable AI health systems is essential to upholding the right to health.

---

4. AI and the Expansion of Rights Frameworks

Digital Identity as a Human Right

As identity moves online, digital identity becomes a prerequisite for accessing services and exercising rights. Without it, individuals may be excluded from education, healthcare, and financial systems.

The **World Bank's ID4D Initiative** reports that over 850 million people globally lack official identification. AI can help authenticate and secure digital identities, but only if privacy, consent, and equity are maintained.

Algorithmic Sovereignty

Nations are increasingly asserting control over AI infrastructure, data flows, and platforms. This raises questions about:

- **Digital colonialism**: Where global tech firms exert disproportionate influence in the Global South.
- **AI nationalism**: Governments weaponize AI for surveillance or disinformation.

A rights-based response includes advocating for open standards, ethical data governance, and international cooperation.

Future Rights: Cognitive Liberty and AI Nudging

AI influences behavior through algorithmic nudging, curating content, suggesting choices, and even shaping beliefs.

- **Cognitive liberty**, the right to freedom of thought in the digital realm, is gaining traction as a potential new right.
- Scholars like **Nita Farahany** argue for neural rights in anticipation of brain-computer interface technologies.

Conclusion: Toward a Rights-Based AI Future

The rise of AI marks a tectonic shift in human history, philosophically, politically, and morally. It compels us to redefine what it means to be human, what rights are indispensable, and how societies can balance innovation with dignity.

To preserve human autonomy and values in an AI-dominated future, we must:

- Embed rights principles into AI development.
- Rethink traditional legal frameworks.
- Expand rights to cover digital identity, cognitive liberty, and algorithmic justice.
- Foster global consensus and regulatory coherence.

AI must not merely serve as a tool of convenience or control; it must become an instrument of human flourishing. Grounding its development in the history and philosophy of rights is not optional; it is imperative.

References

Books:

Turing, A.M. (1950). "Computing Machinery and Intelligence." *Mind.*
Floridi, L. (2013). *The Ethics of Information.* Oxford University Press.
Russell, S., & Norvig, P. (2020). *Artificial Intelligence: A Modern Approach.*
Bostrom, N. (2014). *Superintelligence: Paths, Dangers, Strategies.*

Articles & Essays:

Searle, J. (1980). "Minds, Brains, and Programs." *Behavioral and Brain Sciences.*
Farahany, N. (2022). "The Battle for Your Brain." *Scientific American.*

Reports:

Stanford Institute for Human-Centered AI. (2023). *AI Index Report.* https://aiindex.stanford.edu
OECD. (2019). *AI Principles.* https://oecd.ai
World Bank. (2022). *ID4D Global Dataset.* https://id4d.worldbank.org
McKinsey Global Institute. (2020). *The Future of Work in the Age of AI.* https://mckinsey.com

Legal & Institutional Documents:

European Union. (2016). *General Data Protection Regulation (GDPR).* https://gdpr.eu
United Nations. (2021). *Roadmap for Digital Cooperation.* https://www.un.org/en/digital-cooperation

Online Resources:

Stanford Encyclopedia of Philosophy: https://plato.stanford.edu
Internet Encyclopedia of Philosophy: https://iep.utm.edu
MIT Media Lab. (2021). *AI and Ethics Research.* https://media.mit.edu

---

Chapter 8. AI as a Moral Agent: Ethical Considerations

Introduction

As artificial intelligence (AI) systems become increasingly autonomous and embedded in critical decision-making processes, a fundamental question emerges: Can AI be considered a moral agent? That is, can AI systems make ethical decisions, be held accountable for their outcomes, and operate within a framework of moral reasoning? The implications of this question are profound, influencing how we build, regulate, and interact with intelligent machines.

This chapter explores the philosophical and practical dimensions of AI as a potential moral agent. It examines the criteria for moral agency, the mechanisms through which AI makes decisions, and the ethical dilemmas that arise in real-world AI applications. Through a combination of theoretical analysis, case studies, and data-driven insights, we assess the viability and desirability of attributing moral responsibility to non-human entities.

---

1. Can AI Be a Moral Agent?

Defining Moral Agency

Moral agency traditionally refers to the capacity of an entity to:

- Understand moral principles
- Intentionally act in accordance with those principles
- Be held accountable for its actions

In most philosophical traditions, moral agency is reserved for beings with **consciousness**, **intentionality**, and **free will**. By this definition, AI, lacking subjective experience or self-awareness, does not qualify. However, as AI systems increasingly influence human lives, many ethicists argue for a **functional** rather than metaphysical approach to agency.

Functional Moral Agency

Luciano Floridi and **J.W. Sanders** (2004) proposed the concept of **artificial moral agents (AMAs)**, systems that perform morally relevant functions without necessarily possessing consciousness. These systems are evaluated based on their behavior and outcomes rather than internal states.

> **Example**: An autonomous car that makes a decision to swerve and avoid a pedestrian, even without understanding moral reasoning, acts within a morally relevant context.

Degrees of Moral Agency

Scholars like **Deborah Johnson** and **Wendell Wallach** propose a spectrum:

Implicit moral agents: Systems that act ethically based on predefined rules (e.g., smart thermostats).
Explicit moral agents: Systems capable of analyzing and weighing moral choices (e.g., medical diagnosis AIs).
Full moral agents: Entities with consciousness and intentionality (hypothetical AGI).

---

2. AI and Moral Decision-Making

Rule-Based Ethics

Early AI systems employed rule-based logic derived from **deontological ethics**. These systems follow predefined rules to avoid unethical outcomes.

Example: A drone programmed never to target non-combatants.

Pros:

Predictability and accountability
Easier to audit and test

Cons:

Inflexibility in novel situations
Inability to handle conflicting duties

Machine Learning and Consequentialism

Modern AI systems often use **machine learning**, optimizing actions based on outcomes, an approach analogous to **utilitarian ethics**.

Example: AI in healthcare allocates resources to maximize lives saved.

Pros:

Adaptive learning
Optimizes for results

Cons:

Opaque reasoning processes ("black box" problem)
Risk of embedding biased training data

Hybrid and Context-Aware Models

Advanced AI systems are now being developed with hybrid ethical frameworks. The EU's **SHERPA Project** explores combining deontology (rules) and consequentialism (outcomes) with **virtue ethics**, aiming for AI that "learns to be good" rather than just do good.

Case Study: The Trolley Problem for Autonomous Vehicles

The "trolley problem" is a philosophical thought experiment that asks whether one should sacrifice one life to save many. For AI, this becomes a practical concern:

- Should a self-driving car swerve to avoid a group of pedestrians at the cost of the passenger's life?
- Studies by MIT's **Moral Machine Project** reveal cultural variability in public expectations: Eastern cultures tend to favor the group; Western cultures prioritize individual rights.

This raises challenges for global AI deployment. Whose ethical norms should be embedded?

---

3. Ethical Dilemmas in AI Applications

Healthcare

- **Diagnostic AI**: Tools like IBM Watson for Oncology support clinical decision-making but raise concerns about bias in training data.
- **Triage algorithms**: In COVID-19, AI was used to allocate ventilators based on survival probability. Ethical questions arise: Should age or comorbidity be used in calculations?

Criminal Justice

- **Predictive policing** systems like PredPol claim to anticipate crimes. However, they often reinforce existing biases, leading to over-policing in marginalized communities.
- **Risk assessment algorithms** used in bail and sentencing decisions, like COMPAS, have shown racial bias. A 2016 ProPublica investigation revealed African American defendants were twice as likely to be falsely flagged as future criminals.

Labor and Employment

- **Automated hiring tools**, like those used by Amazon, have demonstrated gender bias, downgrading resumes with the word "women's."
- Ethical questions:
  - Should algorithms have access to social media or psychometric data?
  - Who is accountable for discriminatory hiring?

Surveillance and Security

AI surveillance in countries like China raises questions about consent, autonomy, and dignity. Facial recognition, emotion detection, and behavioral profiling can be used for coercion.
In liberal democracies, mass surveillance under anti-terror laws also threatens privacy and free expression.

Military and Autonomous Weapons

Lethal autonomous weapons systems (LAWS), such as drone swarms, challenge the principle of human accountability in war.
The UN and civil society groups advocate for a ban on fully autonomous weapons, citing the inability of machines to apply proportionality and distinction in conflict.

---

4. Accountability and Legal Responsibility

The Problem of Attribution

Who is responsible when an AI makes a harmful decision?

Developers? They designed the algorithm.
Users? They implemented the system.
Manufacturers? They provided the hardware.

Legal systems are struggling with the **diffusion of responsibility** in AI systems. In 2019, the EU Parliament debated the concept of **electronic personhood** for advanced AI, though it was ultimately rejected as premature and problematic.

Case Law and Precedents

In 2018, **Uber's self-driving car** killed a pedestrian in Arizona. Investigations revealed the AI was not programmed to anticipate jaywalkers.
In 2021, a UK court ruled that an AI-generated invention could not be granted a patent, reaffirming that AI lacks legal personhood.

These cases illustrate the legal vacuum around AI accountability and the need for frameworks that ensure recourse and redress.

---

5. Designing Ethical AI Systems

Ethical Frameworks in Practice

IEEE's Ethically Aligned Design: Advocates for human rights-based design principles.
OECD AI Principles: Promote transparency, accountability, and human-centricity.
EU's Ethics Guidelines for Trustworthy AI: Outlines seven requirements, including human oversight, privacy, and non-discrimination.

Value-Sensitive Design (VSD)

Developed by Batya Friedman, VSD incorporates stakeholder values into AI development. This includes:

Participatory design
Ethical impact assessments
Iterative refinement of system goals

Human-in-the-Loop (HITL) Systems

Maintaining human oversight is key in high-risk contexts.

In healthcare, final decisions should rest with clinicians.
In autonomous vehicles, driver override options are recommended.

However, the illusion of control can also create complacency. Designers must balance automation with meaningful human engagement.

Conclusion: The Ethics of Artificial Moral Agents

AI systems increasingly influence, and in some cases determine, ethically significant outcomes. While AI may lack consciousness or intent, its decisions are embedded in socio-technical systems that have real moral consequences. Thus, the question is not merely whether AI can be a moral agent, but how we, as human agents, can design, guide, and govern these systems ethically.

Going forward, we must:

Recognize AI as a **moral proxy** acting within frameworks of human values.
Ensure **multi-stakeholder governance** of AI ethics.
Develop legal frameworks that balance innovation with accountability.
Promote transparency, inclusion, and dignity in every stage of AI design and deployment.

In the age of AGI, the moral dimensions of artificial agency must be treated with the same rigor as technical performance. Only then can we realize the promise of intelligent autonomy without sacrificing the human values that sustain our societies.

References

Books:

Floridi, L., & Sanders, J.W. (2004). "On the Morality of Artificial Agents." *Minds and Machines.*
Wallach, W., & Allen, C. (2008). *Moral Machines: Teaching Robots Right from Wrong.*
Bostrom, N. (2014). *Superintelligence: Paths, Dangers, Strategies.*

Articles & Essays:

Searle, J. (1980). "Minds, Brains, and Programs." *Behavioral and Brain Sciences.*
Johnson, D. (2015). "Technology with No Human Responsibility?" *AI & Society.*
Taddeo, M., & Floridi, L. (2018). "How AI Can Be a Force for Good." *Science.*

Reports:

MIT Media Lab. (2018). *Moral Machine Project.* https://www.moralmachine.net
ACLU. (2021). *The Dangers of Predictive Policing.* https://www.aclu.org
OECD. (2019). *AI Principles.* https://oecd.ai
European Commission. (2020). *Ethics Guidelines for Trustworthy AI.* https://ec.europa.eu

Legal & Policy Documents:

IEEE. (2019). *Ethically Aligned Design.* https://ethicsinaction.ieee.org
UN CCW. (2021). *Convention on Certain Conventional Weapons Reports on Autonomous Weapons.* https://un.org/disarmament

Online Resources:

Stanford Encyclopedia of Philosophy: https://plato.stanford.edu
Internet Encyclopedia of Philosophy: https://iep.utm.edu
OpenAI Alignment Research: https://openai.com/research

Chapter 9. Autonomy, Privacy, and AI

Introduction

As Artificial Intelligence (AI) increasingly permeates everyday life, from health and finance to transportation and public administration, the traditional boundaries of personal autonomy and privacy are undergoing unprecedented transformations. These twin pillars of human dignity, long enshrined in philosophical thought and codified into international law, now face novel threats and complex negotiations in the age of intelligent systems.

This chapter explores the right to autonomy and privacy in the context of AI development and deployment. It interrogates how surveillance systems, algorithmic decision-making, and data-driven profiling can erode individual freedoms. At the same time, it evaluates how technologies can be redesigned to preserve and even enhance personal agency and informational self-determination.

---

1. The Right to Autonomy in the Age of AI

Philosophical Foundations of Autonomy

Autonomy, from the Greek *auto-nomos* (self-law), is the capacity for self-governance, central to Enlightenment thinking and liberal democracies. Philosophers like **Immanuel Kant** argued that autonomy is the very condition for moral responsibility, where individuals act according to self-imposed rational laws rather than external coercion.

Autonomy implies:

- Freedom of thought and choice
- Non-coercion
- Informed decision-making
- Control over one's body, data, and identity

Modern human rights instruments enshrine this concept:

- **Article 1 of the UDHR**: All humans are "endowed with reason and conscience."
- **ICCPR Article 17**: Protects against arbitrary interference with privacy, family, and correspondence.

AI and Threats to Autonomy

AI can interfere with autonomy in several ways:

- **Algorithmic manipulation**: Recommendation systems nudge user behavior, e.g., YouTube's algorithm radicalizes viewers through polarizing content.

Choice architecture: Online platforms curate content in ways that limit genuine choice.
Automated decision-making: Individuals are subjected to credit, employment, or legal decisions made by opaque algorithms.

Case Study: In 2021, the Dutch government's use of an AI system to detect welfare fraud wrongly flagged tens of thousands of families, often based on biased or opaque indicators. Many families lost benefits or faced deportation, without due process or redress.

Preserving Autonomy

Mechanisms to restore autonomy include:

Right to explanation: Ensuring individuals understand AI decisions (GDPR Article 22).
Informed consent protocols: Making data collection opt-in, not opt-out.
Decentralized identity systems: Giving users control over their digital credentials (e.g., Estonia's e-ID program).

---

2. Privacy Concerns and AI Surveillance

What Is Privacy?

Privacy is the right to control information about oneself. It includes:

Bodily privacy: Freedom from invasive technologies (e.g., biometric scans)
Informational privacy: Control over personal data
Locational privacy: Right not to be tracked
Communicational privacy: Freedom from surveillance of messages

AI and the Data Economy

AI systems are trained on vast datasets. Every online click, search, and location ping fuels a surveillance capitalist economy.

Google and Facebook collect and monetize user behavior at an unprecedented scale.
Facial recognition firms, like Clearview AI, scrape billions of online images, often violating terms of service and consent norms.

Data Point: A 2023 Pew Research Center report found that 81% of Americans feel they have "very little" or "no control" over the data companies collect.

Government Surveillance

Governments deploy AI for national security and administrative efficiency, but often at the cost of civil liberties.

China: Employs facial recognition and behavioral scoring to monitor dissent and social cohesion.
UK: Uses AI in predictive policing and public space monitoring.
U.S.: NSA's PRISM program collected bulk data from tech firms under the guise of counter-terrorism.

Legal Response:

GDPR in Europe requires data minimization, consent, and purpose limitation.
California Consumer Privacy Act (CCPA): Grants residents rights to access, delete, and opt out of data sales.

Yet enforcement remains inconsistent, and many jurisdictions lack comprehensive protections.

---

3. Balancing Technological Advancements and Personal Freedoms

The Innovation Paradox

AI can enhance rights if used ethically:

In healthcare, AI enables early diagnosis and personalized treatment.
In accessibility, AI-powered tools help those with visual, hearing, or mobility impairments.
In education, Adaptive learning platforms improve student outcomes.

But these benefits often require large-scale data collection, creating tension between innovation and privacy.

Case Study: During COVID-19, contact tracing apps raised privacy concerns. South Korea's app tracks location, transactions, and CCTV data, which is effective but intrusive. Germany's app used decentralized protocols to preserve privacy, but had lower adoption.

The Ethics of Consent and Transparency

Genuine consent requires:

Clarity: Understandable language
Context: Knowing what data is collected, how, and why
Control: The ability to say no without penalty

Transparency means not only disclosing terms but designing **explainable AI (XAI)** systems whose decisions can be understood by non-experts.

A 2022 survey by the European Union Agency for Fundamental Rights found that 68% of citizens would trust AI more if decisions were explainable and appealable.

---

4. Ethical and Regulatory Frameworks

Global Guidelines

- **UNESCO (2021)**: Recommends human rights–based approaches to AI.
- **OECD AI Principles (2019)**: Emphasize privacy, transparency, and human-centricity.
- **EU AI Act (2023 draft)**: Proposes risk-based regulation, banning AI uses that manipulate behavior or exploit vulnerable groups.

Privacy by Design

Coined by **Ann Cavoukian**, this principle embeds privacy into system architecture:

- Data minimization
- End-to-end security
- User-centric design

Example: Apple's iOS implements on-device processing and local storage of biometric data, limiting third-party access.

Regulatory Sandboxes

Some governments are experimenting with "regulatory sandboxes", controlled environments where developers test AI under supervision. This allows innovation while protecting rights.

---

5. Cultural Dimensions of Privacy and Autonomy

Privacy is not a universally uniform concept.

- **Western societies** emphasize individual autonomy.
- **Eastern societies** may prioritize collective harmony.
- **African philosophies**, such as Ubuntu, stress relational autonomy and personhood through community.

Designing AI systems that respect global diversity requires cultural sensitivity.

Example: Google's AI team faced backlash for removing *Timnit Gebru*, a researcher who raised concerns about racial bias and data colonialism in AI datasets. The incident highlighted the need for inclusion in AI governance.

6. The Future of Autonomy and Privacy in AGI Societies

AI Personal Assistants and Human Dependence

As AI becomes more integrated (e.g., Siri, Alexa, ChatGPT), there's a risk of over-reliance. Autonomy is diminished when people defer decisions to systems they don't understand.

Ethical Issue: Should AI be allowed to make decisions about finances, education, or healthcare without human oversight?

Cognitive Liberty and Algorithmic Nudging

AI doesn't just collect data, it shapes behavior. Platforms use **algorithmic nudges** to direct attention, buying decisions, and even political opinions.

Cognitive liberty, the right to control one's mental processes, is emerging as a potential human right in the digital age.

Example: In 2014, Facebook manipulated user feeds to study emotional contagion, without user knowledge or consent. The experiment raised significant ethical and legal concerns.

Digital Sovereignty

Nations are asserting control over digital infrastructure to protect citizens:

- **India's data localization laws** require firms to store user data domestically.
- **The EU's Digital Services Act** imposes transparency obligations on large platforms.

But sovereignty can also mask censorship and control. Balance is crucial.

Conclusion: Safeguarding Autonomy and Privacy in AI-Driven Societies

The integration of AI into societal infrastructure demands a new social contract, one that safeguards autonomy and privacy without stifling innovation. While AI can enhance efficiency, personalization, and access, it must not do so at the expense of human dignity.

To preserve these rights, we must:

- Enforce robust data protection laws
- Promote ethical AI design and transparency
- Foster digital literacy and informed consent
- Embrace global cooperation and culturally sensitive regulation

In AGI societies, autonomy and privacy must evolve as **technologically enforced rights**, not just moral ideals or legal constructs. They must be embedded in code, policy, and practice to ensure that the future of intelligence remains fundamentally human.

References

Books:

Cavoukian, A. (2009). *Privacy by Design.*
Zuboff, S. (2019). *The Age of Surveillance Capitalism.*
Nissenbaum, H. (2010). *Privacy in Context: Technology, Policy, and the Integrity of Social Life.*

Articles & Essays:

Floridi, L. (2016). "On Human Dignity as a Foundation for the Right to Privacy." *Philosophy & Technology.*
Tufekci, Z. (2015). "Algorithmic Harms Beyond Facebook and Google: Emergent Challenges of Computational Agency." *Colorado Technology Law Journal.*

Reports:

Pew Research Center. (2023). *Public Attitudes Toward Data Privacy.* https://www.pewresearch.org
European Union Agency for Fundamental Rights. (2022). *Trust in AI.* https://fra.europa.eu
UNESCO. (2021). *Recommendation on the Ethics of Artificial Intelligence.* https://unesdoc.unesco.org
OECD. (2019). *Principles on Artificial Intelligence.* https://oecd.ai

Legal & Institutional Documents:

European Union. (2016). *General Data Protection Regulation (GDPR).* https://gdpr.eu
California State Legislature. (2018). *California Consumer Privacy Act (CCPA).* https://oag.ca.gov/privacy/ccpa
European Commission. (2023). *Artificial Intelligence Act (draft).* https://digital-strategy.ec.europa.eu

Online Resources:

Stanford Encyclopedia of Philosophy: https://plato.stanford.edu
Internet Encyclopedia of Philosophy: https://iep.utm.edu
Moral Machine: https://www.moralmachine.net

Chapter 10. AI and the Right to Equality

Introduction

Artificial Intelligence (AI) stands as both a beacon of progress and a harbinger of peril in the context of human equality. While AI holds immense promise for promoting efficiency, access, and personalization, its development and deployment can entrench, amplify, or create new forms of discrimination. The right to equality, central to democratic governance and human dignity, is now confronted by algorithmic systems that operate at scales and speeds beyond human comprehension.

This chapter delves into the complex relationship between AI and the right to equality. It investigates the ways in which AI influences social and economic hierarchies, uncovers the discriminatory patterns that emerge from AI models and data, and proposes frameworks for equitable AI governance. Through philosophical grounding, real-world examples, and empirical data, we aim to articulate a vision of AI that enhances, rather than diminishes, our collective commitment to justice and inclusion.

---

1. AI's Impact on Social and Economic Equality

Transforming Economic Participation

AI is reshaping the global economy in profound ways:

- **Automation** replaces jobs in manufacturing, transportation, and services.
- **AI-driven platforms** create new employment forms, gig work, digital labor, and microtasks.
- **Skill polarization** emerges as demand grows for high-tech expertise while routine jobs disappear.

According to a 2020 report by the **McKinsey Global Institute**, up to 375 million workers, about 14% of the global workforce, may need to switch occupational categories due to AI-induced automation by 2030.

Geographic Disparities

AI innovation clusters are concentrated in tech hubs like Silicon Valley, Shenzhen, and Tel Aviv. Meanwhile, low-income countries remain data providers and markets for foreign technologies, exacerbating the **North-South digital divide**.

Case Study: Kenya's workers on platforms like Amazon Mechanical Turk perform data annotation for AI systems deployed in the West, often earning less than $2/hour with minimal protections. This labor asymmetry perpetuates economic dependency.

Access Inequities

AI-driven services in healthcare, education, and finance can improve access, but often exclude marginalized groups:

- **Telemedicine platforms** may require stable internet, which is unaffordable to many.
- **Loan-scoring algorithms** may disadvantage applicants without formal credit histories.

The **World Bank (2022)** found that only 54% of individuals in low-income countries use the internet, compared to 89% in high-income countries. AI access thus mirrors, and may deepen, existing inequalities.

---

2. The Potential for AI-Driven Discrimination

Algorithmic Bias: Sources and Mechanisms

Bias in AI arises from:

- **Biased training data**: Reflecting historical inequalities.
- **Incomplete datasets**: Omitting minority groups.
- **Proxy variables**: Features that correlate with race, gender, or class.

Example: A 2018 MIT Media Lab study revealed that facial recognition systems misclassified darker-skinned women 34% of the time, compared to less than 1% for lighter-skinned men.

Discriminatory Outcomes in Practice

- **Employment**: Amazon's resume-screening AI downgraded applicants who attended all-women's colleges.
- **Credit**: Apple's credit card algorithm granted significantly lower credit limits to women, even when they had better financial profiles than their male counterparts.
- **Healthcare**: An AI system used in US hospitals underestimated the health needs of Black patients by 40%, according to a 2019 study in *Science*.
- **Criminal Justice**: The COMPAS algorithm, used to assess recidivism risk, disproportionately flagged Black defendants as high-risk, per a 2016 ProPublica investigation.

Legal Gaps and Challenges

Most jurisdictions lack AI-specific anti-discrimination laws. Current civil rights frameworks were not designed for the probabilistic and opaque nature of machine learning.

The **EU's General Data Protection Regulation (GDPR)** prohibits solely automated decisions that have significant effects, but enforcement remains limited and uneven.

3. Philosophical Foundations: Equality in the Age of AI

Substantive vs. Formal Equality

Formal equality means treating everyone the same.
Substantive equality means acknowledging structural disadvantages and designing systems to address them.

AI designed without awareness of substantive equality risks reproducing injustice under the guise of neutrality. As **Cathy O'Neil** writes in *Weapons of Math Destruction*, algorithms can obscure discrimination behind statistical objectivity.

Rawlsian and Capability Perspectives

John Rawls' theory of justice advocates for fairness principles that prioritize the least advantaged.
Amartya Sen and **Martha Nussbaum's capability approach** argues for systems that enhance people's real freedoms and opportunities.

These perspectives offer normative tools for designing and evaluating AI systems in light of equity.

---

4. Ensuring Equitable AI Development and Deployment

Inclusive Design Practices

Participatory AI design: Engaging affected communities in development.
Intersectional audits: Evaluating how race, gender, disability, and other identities interact with algorithmic impacts.

Example: The Algorithmic Justice League, led by Joy Buolamwini, advocates for inclusive AI and has successfully pressured firms to halt facial recognition sales to law enforcement.

Ethical Frameworks

OECD Principles on AI: Recommend fairness and inclusivity.
UNESCO's AI Ethics Recommendations (2021): Emphasize non-discrimination and global equity.
IEEE Ethically Aligned Design: Calls for socially beneficial AI outcomes.

Technical Approaches

- **Fairness constraints**: Ensuring parity across groups.
- **Bias correction techniques**: Rebalancing training datasets.
- **Explainable AI (XAI)**: Enhancing transparency to detect discriminatory behavior.

Case Study: IBM's AI Fairness 360 toolkit helps developers detect and mitigate bias in AI models.

---

5. Institutional and Policy Mechanisms

Impact Assessments

Requiring **Algorithmic Impact Assessments (AIAs)** before deploying AI systems in public or sensitive domains.

Example: Canada's Directive on Automated Decision-Making mandates AIAs for federal AI systems.

Anti-Discrimination Legislation

Updating civil rights laws to account for:

- Disparate impact in algorithmic decisions
- Redress mechanisms for harm
- Obligations on vendors to test and certify fairness

Procurement Standards

Governments and institutions can lead by example through ethical procurement:

- Requiring bias audits
- Favoring open-source and peer-reviewed systems
- Ensuring vendor accountability

---

6. Global Equity and Development Justice

The Data Colonialism Critique

AI development often relies on data extracted from the Global South without benefit sharing or consent.

Example: Western firms use African faces to train facial recognition but offer no services or protections to those communities.

Remedies include:

- **Data sovereignty frameworks**
- **Ethical data partnerships**
- **Capacity building for local AI ecosystems**

The AI Divide

Bridging global inequalities requires:

- Infrastructure investments
- Open-access tools and datasets
- Multilingual and culturally contextual AI systems

UNDP's 2022 report warns that unequal AI access could worsen global income inequality by 25% within a decade.

Conclusion: Toward a Just AI Future

AI systems do not operate in a vacuum. They are built by people, trained on historical data, and deployed in socio-political contexts that are already unequal. Without conscious intervention, they risk magnifying existing disparities.

A rights-based approach to AI demands:

- Normative grounding in fairness and capability
- Inclusive design and participatory governance
- Strong legal protections and institutional accountability
- Global solidarity and equitable access to AI resources

The right to equality must become a **design principle**, not just a legal aspiration. In doing so, we ensure that the intelligence we create reflects our deepest commitments to justice, dignity, and shared human progress.

References

Books:

O'Neil, C. (2016). *Weapons of Math Destruction.* Crown Publishing.
Eubanks, V. (2018). *Automating Inequality.* St. Martin's Press.
Nussbaum, M., & Sen, A. (1993). *The Quality of Life.* Oxford University Press.

Articles & Essays:

Buolamwini, J., & Gebru, T. (2018). "Gender Shades." *Proceedings of Machine Learning Research.*
Obermeyer, Z., et al. (2019). "Dissecting racial bias in an algorithm used to manage the health of populations." *Science.*

Reports:

World Bank. (2022). *Digital Economy for Africa Initiative.* https://www.worldbank.org/en/programs/all-africa-digital-economy
McKinsey Global Institute. (2020). *Jobs Lost, Jobs Gained.* https://www.mckinsey.com
UNESCO. (2021). *Recommendation on the Ethics of Artificial Intelligence.* https://unesdoc.unesco.org
OECD. (2019). *Principles on Artificial Intelligence.* https://oecd.ai

Toolkits and Technical Resources:

IBM. (2023). *AI Fairness 360 Toolkit.* https://aif360.mybluemix.net
Algorithmic Justice League: https://www.ajl.org

Legal and Policy Frameworks:

European Union. (2016). *General Data Protection Regulation.* https://gdpr.eu
Canadian Government. (2020). *Directive on Automated Decision-Making.* https://www.canada.ca

Online Resources:

Stanford Encyclopedia of Philosophy: https://plato.stanford.edu
Internet Encyclopedia of Philosophy: https://iep.utm.edu

Chapter 11. The Role of AI in Upholding Human Rights

Introduction

Artificial Intelligence (AI), while often critiqued for its potential to violate rights through opaque decisions or biased algorithms, also holds tremendous promise for enhancing, protecting, and even expanding the scope of human rights. In the hands of conscientious developers, policy-makers, and civil society organizations, AI can become a powerful instrument for justice, equity, and freedom. Yet, the same technologies can be deployed for repression, surveillance, and discrimination if misused or unregulated.

This chapter investigates the dual capacity of AI to both uphold and undermine human rights. It surveys existing and emerging AI applications in the fields of governance, legal systems, and humanitarian work, critically evaluates their outcomes, and proposes strategies to maximize AI's potential as a force for human rights promotion. With a narrative that balances theory, empirical evidence, and practical innovation, we explore how AI can be ethically aligned with the foundational values of human dignity and justice.

---

1. How AI Can Support Human Rights

AI for Monitoring and Accountability

AI can serve as a watchdog:

- **Satellite imagery and computer vision** help monitor war crimes and environmental abuses. Projects like **AI for Earth** and **Global Fishing Watch** use machine learning to detect illegal deforestation or overfishing.
- **Social media analytics** aid human rights groups in detecting patterns of hate speech or misinformation.

Case Study: The **Yale Humanitarian Lab**, in collaboration with Amnesty International, used AI to analyze satellite data and corroborate reports of mass graves and military activity in Myanmar's Rakhine State, contributing to investigations into genocide against the Rohingya minority.

Enhancing Access to Justice

AI can reduce barriers to justice:

- **Legal chatbots** like DoNotPay help users contest parking tickets, appeal rent increases, or navigate immigration paperwork.
- **Natural language processing (NLP)** systems translate legal documents into plain language, enhancing accessibility.

Example: In Kenya, the **Legal Aid Bot** developed by Haki AI provides citizens with rights-based information via SMS in English and Kiswahili, especially targeting rural and underserved populations.

Supporting Rights-Based Public Policy

AI can help governments uphold economic and social rights:

- **Predictive analytics** allocates resources more efficiently in health, education, and social protection.
- **Early warning systems** detect humanitarian crises such as famines or pandemics.

The **UN World Food Programme** uses machine learning to anticipate food shortages based on weather, crop, and market data, improving the right to food in vulnerable regions.

Empowering Marginalized Voices

AI can amplify the voices of marginalized groups:

- **Speech-to-text tools** enable participation for individuals with disabilities.
- **Sentiment analysis** highlights social grievances, informing advocacy campaigns.

---

2. AI in Legal Systems and Governance

Judicial Decision Support

AI assists judges and lawyers by:

- Analyzing case law
- Summarizing arguments
- Forecasting verdicts based on precedents

Example: France's Ministry of Justice deployed an AI system to identify inconsistent sentencing patterns across regions and promoted standardization, addressing disparities in access to fair trials.

Smart Contracts and Blockchain

AI-integrated blockchain technologies can enforce rights autonomously:

- **Smart contracts** automate welfare payments or refugee benefits, ensuring timely and tamper-proof delivery.
- **Digital identity** systems protect stateless persons or refugees.

Case Study: The **ID2020 Alliance**, supported by Microsoft and Accenture, uses AI and blockchain to provide secure, portable digital IDs to displaced persons, facilitating access to healthcare, education, and legal status.

Civic Participation and Democratic Governance

AI can improve governance by:

- Automating administrative tasks
- Facilitating participatory budgeting
- Detecting corruption through anomaly detection algorithms

Example: In Brazil, AI tools have been used to monitor procurement irregularities in public spending, saving millions of dollars and improving transparency.

---

3. Case Studies: AI Promoting or Undermining Human Rights

Positive Impact

- **India's eVIN (Electronic Vaccine Intelligence Network)**: AI-powered dashboards track vaccine stocks in real time, improving equitable access to immunization.
- **Germany's Employment Agency**: Uses AI to match job seekers with open positions, reducing unemployment among youth and minorities.
- **UN Global Pulse**: Uses AI to analyze mobile data and social media to understand public sentiment on health and education.

Negative Consequences

- **COMPAS Algorithm in U.S. Courts**: Used to assess recidivism risk, it showed racial bias, disproportionately labeling Black defendants as high risk.
- **China's Social Credit System** Integrates AI and surveillance to score citizens' behavior, leading to travel bans and social penalties.
- **Facial Recognition in the UK and U.S.**: Deployed without consent in public spaces, violating privacy and disproportionately misidentifying people of color.

These examples show that AI's impact is contingent on governance structures, transparency, and public oversight.

---

4. Ethical, Legal, and Technical Strategies

Human Rights Impact Assessments (HRIAs)

Before deploying AI systems, especially in sensitive areas like law enforcement, welfare, or immigration, HRIAs can:

- Evaluate risks to civil liberties
- Identify discriminatory outcomes
- Propose mitigation strategies

UNESCO's 2021 AI Ethics Framework includes HRIAs as a best practice.

Explainable AI (XAI)

To uphold due process and accountability, AI decisions must be explainable. Techniques like:

- **Local Interpretable Model-agnostic Explanations (LIME)**
- **SHapley Additive exPlanations (SHAP)**

help users understand how decisions are made.

Right to Appeal and Redress

Legal frameworks must guarantee:

- Access to human review
- Remedies for harm caused by AI
- Liability mechanisms for developers and operators

GDPR Article 22 provides for the right not to be subject to solely automated decisions with legal or significant effects.

Inclusive Governance

Ensure AI development includes:

- Gender-balanced teams
- Cultural and linguistic diversity
- Engagement with affected communities

Example: The African Union's 2022 AI strategy emphasizes Pan-African data governance and sovereignty to resist digital neocolonialism.

---

5. The Path Forward: Aligning AI with Human Rights by Design

Embedding Rights in Code

AI should be built with rights-preserving architectures:

Differential privacy to protect data anonymity
Federated learning to prevent centralized data hoarding
Bias detection pipelines during model training

Multi-Stakeholder Oversight

AI governance must include:

- Government regulators
- Civil society watchdogs
- Academic and ethical boards
- Private sector accountability bodies

Global Norms and Agreements

The international community must establish binding agreements on AI ethics, similar to arms control or climate treaties. The **Council of Europe**, **OECD**, **UNESCO**, and **GPAI** (Global Partnership on AI) have made significant progress.

Conclusion: A Rights-Driven AI Paradigm

AI can be a guardian of human rights if, and only if, it is designed, deployed, and governed through a lens of justice, inclusion, and transparency. The same tools that threaten dignity and equality can be redirected to protect, promote, and expand human freedoms.

To ensure AI upholds rights, we must:

- Shift from reactive regulation to proactive design
- Build AI that centers the voices of the vulnerable
- Institutionalize safeguards that prevent harm and promote remedy
- Foster global cooperation and ethical harmonization

In the age of intelligent autonomy, aligning AI with human rights is not just a technical challenge; it is a civilizational imperative.

References

Books:

O'Neil, C. (2016). *Weapons of Math Destruction.*
Crawford, K. (2021). *The Atlas of AI.*
Binns, R. (2018). *Algorithmic Accountability and Transparency.*

Articles & Essays:

Eubanks, V. (2018). "Automating Inequality." *Public Affairs.*
Taddeo, M., & Floridi, L. (2018). "How AI Can Be a Force for Good." *Science.*

Reports:

UNESCO. (2021). *Ethics of Artificial Intelligence.* https://unesdoc.unesco.org
UN Global Pulse. (2022). *AI for Sustainable Development.* https://www.unglobalpulse.org
Amnesty International. (2021). *Surveillance Giants: How the Business Model of Google and Facebook Threatens Human Rights.* https://www.amnesty.org

Case Studies & Tools:

ID2020 Alliance: https://id2020.org
Global Fishing Watch: https://globalfishingwatch.org
IBM AI Explainability 360: https://aix360.mybluemix.net

Legal Frameworks:

European Union. (2016). *General Data Protection Regulation (GDPR).* https://gdpr.eu
OECD. (2019). *AI Principles.* https://oecd.ai
African Union. (2022). *AI Continental Strategy.* https://au.int

Online Resources:

Stanford Encyclopedia of Philosophy: https://plato.stanford.edu
Internet Encyclopedia of Philosophy: https://iep.utm.edu
AI Now Institute: https://ainowinstitute.org

Chapter 12. Challenges to Human Rights in an AI-Driven World

Introduction

The transformative potential of Artificial Intelligence (AI) is undeniable. It promises to reshape economies, enhance governance, and revolutionize how services are delivered. However, with this transformation comes an equally profound threat: the erosion of human rights. As AI systems become more autonomous, ubiquitous, and opaque, they risk undermining the very principles that uphold human dignity, freedom, and equality.

This chapter explores the multifaceted threats AI poses to human rights and provides a detailed roadmap for identifying, analyzing, and mitigating these risks. From surveillance to systemic bias, the chapter presents a comprehensive assessment of the challenges in an AI-driven world, bolstered by examples, data, and policy proposals.

---

1. Potential Threats Posed by AI

Mass Surveillance and Privacy Erosion

AI enables unprecedented surveillance capabilities:

- **Facial recognition systems** can identify individuals in real-time across cities.
- **Predictive policing** algorithms anticipate crimes based on historical data.
- **Behavioral analytics** track internet and social media usage to profile users.

Case Study: In China, the Social Credit System integrates AI with facial recognition and big data analytics to score citizens' trustworthiness, impacting their access to jobs, loans, and travel. According to Human Rights Watch, this system imposes restrictions based on opaque criteria with little to no transparency or redress.

Automated Decision-Making and Due Process

AI systems are now making decisions that were traditionally the domain of human judgment:

- **Employment screening tools** reject candidates without human review.
- **Loan approval algorithms** assess financial risk with limited transparency.
- **AI in criminal justice** predicts recidivism, influencing sentencing.

These automated decisions often lack appeal mechanisms, violating principles of due process. The opacity of AI, often referred to as the "black box" problem, prevents affected individuals from understanding, contesting, or correcting these decisions.

Algorithmic Discrimination

Biases in training data or model architecture can result in:

Discrimination in hiring (e.g., Amazon's biased recruiting tool)
Racial profiling in predictive policing (e.g., PredPol)
Healthcare inequities (e.g., underdiagnosing Black patients)

Data Point: A 2019 study in *Science* revealed that an AI system used in the U.S. healthcare system systematically underestimated the health needs of Black patients, affecting over 200 million people.

Freedom of Expression and Content Moderation

AI-driven content moderation tools often:

Over-censor legitimate speech, especially in non-English contexts
Reinforce dominant cultural norms
Suppress dissent, especially under authoritarian regimes

Example: Facebook's algorithm flagged Palestinian political content as hate speech during the 2021 Israel-Palestine conflict, sparking international criticism.

Labor Rights and Economic Exclusion

AI-induced automation risks job displacement:

Low-skilled and repetitive jobs are most vulnerable.
New jobs require skills that marginalized communities may lack.

McKinsey (2020) estimates that 15% of the global workforce may be displaced by 2030. Without inclusive upskilling programs, AI could exacerbate unemployment and deepen economic divides.

---

2. The Risk of Rights Erosion Due to AI

Normative Shifts and Public Apathy

AI can normalize surveillance and authoritarianism:

Citizens may accept rights violations in exchange for convenience or security.
Governments frame surveillance as public safety.

This erosion of civic expectation and accountability is what Shoshana Zuboff terms the "epistemic coup," where technology reshapes public values without democratic debate.

Technocratic Governance

Decisions made by algorithms often bypass democratic institutions:

- **Risk scores** in social services determine eligibility for benefits.
- **Automated border control** enforces immigration policy without oversight.

This technocratic governance reduces human oversight and political accountability, endangering procedural fairness.

Power Concentration and Digital Colonialism

AI is dominated by a few tech giants:

- **Google, Amazon, Microsoft, Facebook, and Apple** control much of the infrastructure, platforms, and data.
- **Global South nations** often lack the capacity to develop sovereign AI systems.

This asymmetry can lead to digital colonialism, where data from developing countries is exploited without benefit sharing.

Ineffective Regulation

Many jurisdictions have outdated or fragmented laws:

- Lack of AI-specific protections for bias, transparency, and redress.
- Weak enforcement mechanisms.

Even the **EU's AI Act**, one of the most comprehensive proposals, faces challenges in defining "high-risk" systems and ensuring compliance across sectors.

---

3. Strategies to Mitigate These Challenges

Rights-by-Design AI Development

Embedding human rights principles at every stage of AI design:

- **Data governance**: Inclusive, representative, and consensual data sourcing.
- **Bias audits**: Ongoing reviews of models for discriminatory outcomes.
- **Transparency tools**: Model interpretability and decision logs.

Example: IBM's AI Fairness 360 Toolkit enables developers to test and mitigate algorithmic bias across datasets and models.

Strengthening Legal and Regulatory Frameworks

AI must be governed by robust legal standards:

Enforceable **data protection laws** (e.g., GDPR)
Mandated **algorithmic impact assessments**
Clear **liability regimes** for harms caused by AI

Governments should adopt:

Proportionality principles in AI surveillance
Mandatory explainability for high-stakes decisions
Non-discrimination mandates in automated systems

Public Education and Digital Literacy

Empowering citizens with knowledge:

Digital rights education in schools
Public awareness campaigns on AI harms and safeguards
Accessible redress mechanisms for algorithmic injustice

Digital literacy must be inclusive, across age, gender, geography, and language.

Ethical Certification and Standards

Like ISO standards for safety and quality, AI should be subject to ethical certification:

Ethics-by-design seals for trustworthy AI
Independent auditing bodies to assess compliance
Global registries of high-risk AI systems

Initiative: The IEEE's Global Initiative on Ethics of Autonomous and Intelligent Systems is developing industry-wide guidelines.

Strengthening Civil Society and Advocacy

NGOs, think tanks, and watchdogs play a critical role:

Investigating AI abuses
Amplifying marginalized voices
Participating in regulatory consultations

Groups like **Access Now**, **Algorithmic Justice League**, and **AI Now Institute** have led efforts to expose discriminatory and unethical uses of AI.

Global Governance and Cooperation

AI transcends borders. International coordination is vital:

UNESCO's AI ethics framework offers a global blueprint.

OECD AI Principles emphasize human-centered values.
Global Partnership on AI (GPAI) fosters cross-border collaboration.

Emerging economies should be represented in AI governance forums to avoid neo-colonial power dynamics.

Conclusion: Resisting Rights Regression in the AI Era

AI's potential to erode human rights is not inevitable, it is a political and ethical choice. The future will be determined by the frameworks we build today, the voices we empower, and the standards we institutionalize.

To resist rights regression and build a future aligned with human dignity, we must:

Demand democratic oversight of AI systems
Align technological progress with normative commitments
Equip institutions, developers, and citizens with tools for ethical accountability
Foster transnational solidarity for equitable AI governance

AI must be governed not just by logic, but by **justice**. In this balancing act between innovation and rights, humanity must lead, not yield, to its creations.

References

Books:

Zuboff, S. (2019). *The Age of Surveillance Capitalism.*
O'Neil, C. (2016). *Weapons of Math Destruction.*
Crawford, K. (2021). *Atlas of AI.*

Articles & Reports:

Obermeyer, Z., et al. (2019). "Dissecting racial bias in an algorithm used to manage the health of populations." *Science.*
Amnesty International. (2021). *Surveillance Giants.* https://www.amnesty.org/en/latest/research/2019/10/surveillance-giants/
Human Rights Watch. (2021). *China's Algorithms of Repression.* https://www.hrw.org
UN Global Pulse. (2022). *AI for Human Rights.* https://www.unglobalpulse.org

Policy Documents & Frameworks:

European Commission. (2023). *AI Act (draft).* https://digital-strategy.ec.europa.eu

UNESCO. (2021). *Recommendation on the Ethics of Artificial Intelligence.* https://unesdoc.unesco.org
OECD. (2019). *AI Principles.* https://oecd.ai

Technical Toolkits:

IBM.. (2023). *AI Fairness 360 Toolkit.* https://aif360.mybluemix.net
IEEE. (2021). *Ethics Certification Program for Autonomous and Intelligent Systems.* https://ethicsinaction.ieee.org

Online Resources:

Stanford Encyclopedia of Philosophy: https://plato.stanford.edu
Internet Encyclopedia of Philosophy: https://iep.utm.edu
Access Now: https://www.accessnow.org
AI Now Institute: https://ainowinstitute.org

Part III: Decentralization and Smart Contracts

Chapter 13. Introduction to Decentralization: Philosophy and Practice

Introduction

Decentralization, a concept that once seemed limited to niche political philosophy and isolated community experiments, now lies at the heart of twenty-first-century conversations about governance, technology, and autonomy. In the age of Artificial General Intelligence (AGI), where power can be centralized within algorithmic black boxes controlled by a handful of corporations or governments, decentralization offers an antidote, a countermodel based on distributed authority, shared governance, and resilience through diversity.

This chapter introduces the philosophy behind decentralization, explores its historical manifestations, and evaluates its application in modern society. From anarchist thought to blockchain ecosystems, decentralization has evolved from radical critique to real-world infrastructure. By grounding the concept in philosophy, examining its roots in decentralized societies, and showcasing its rise in digital economies and political experimentation, we aim to show why decentralization is not just a structural option; it is an ethical necessity for human rights in AGI-enhanced societies.

---

1. The Philosophy Behind Decentralization

Autonomy and Authority

At its core, decentralization is about redistributing power away from centralized institutions toward individuals, communities, or networks. It prioritizes:

- **Autonomy** over coercion
- **Participation** over hierarchy
- **Resilience** over uniformity

Political theorists from **John Stuart Mill** to **Hannah Arendt** emphasized the moral importance of decentralizing power to protect liberty and cultivate civic virtue. Mill argued in *On Liberty* (1859) that centralized bureaucracies stifle innovation and individual flourishing, while Arendt warned of totalitarianism arising from unchecked centralized power.

Epistemic Decentralization

Philosopher **Friedrich Hayek** championed decentralization as an epistemic virtue. In his seminal essay "The Use of Knowledge in Society" (1945), Hayek argued that no central authority could effectively aggregate the dispersed, context-sensitive knowledge held by individuals. Decentralized systems are more efficient because they allow for local knowledge to guide action.

Moral and Political Decentralization

Pierre-Joseph Proudhon, the first self-declared anarchist, believed that authority should be limited to the smallest unit capable of achieving a task, which later became known as the principle of **subsidiarity**. This ethical vision emphasizes that governance should be grounded in proximity and direct accountability.

---

2. Historical Examples of Decentralized Societies

Indigenous Governance

Indigenous communities around the world have long practiced forms of decentralized governance:

- **The Iroquois Confederacy** operated with a council of clan leaders, each with veto power.
- **Zulu governance** was traditionally organized through layered chiefdoms with significant local autonomy.
- **Andean ayllu systems** managed communal resources based on consensus and rotation.

These societies demonstrate that decentralization is not new. It is, in many respects, a return to more democratic, inclusive governance.

Medieval City-States and Guilds

European city-states such as Venice and Florence during the Renaissance were autonomous, self-governing entities. Guilds managed trade, education, and legal matters internally.

In Islamic history, the **waqf** (charitable endowment) system supported decentralized social welfare, with independent administrators managing schools, hospitals, and orphanages without state control.

Religious Decentralization

- **The Protestant Reformation** fractured the authority of the Catholic Church, enabling local churches to interpret scripture and govern themselves.
- **Sufi orders** often operated independently of state religious institutions, emphasizing personal spiritual experience over dogma.

Communal Experiments

- **The Kibbutzim in Israel** functioned as egalitarian, decentralized agricultural communities.
- **The Zapatista movement** in Mexico promotes autonomous indigenous governance, education, and justice systems.

These examples offer lived models of decentralized coordination and shared sovereignty, often rooted in deeply ethical and cultural frameworks.

---

3. Modern Applications of Decentralization

The Rise of the Internet and Distributed Systems

The architecture of the Internet was originally designed to be decentralized:

- **Packet-switching** allowed data to travel multiple paths.
- **Peer-to-peer protocols** enabled direct interaction.

However, the rise of centralized platforms (e.g., Facebook, Google, Amazon) has created new monopolies. Decentralization is re-emerging as a remedy to platform dominance.

Blockchain and Cryptographic Decentralization

Blockchain technology epitomizes the technical realization of decentralization:

- **Bitcoin** is a decentralized currency issuance and transaction validation.
- **Ethereum** supports decentralized applications (dApps) through smart contracts.

Data Point: As of 2024, over $100 billion is secured in decentralized finance (DeFi) protocols, enabling lending, insurance, and trading without central intermediaries.

Example: Estonia's **e-Residency program** allows anyone globally to launch and manage an EU-based company with minimal central bureaucracy, leveraging decentralized identity and trust layers.

Decentralized Governance and DAOs

Decentralized Autonomous Organizations (DAOs) are software-based collectives governed by transparent code and token-holder votes:

- **MakerDAO** governs a decentralized stablecoin.
- **Gitcoin DAO** funds open-source development.

Case Study: In 2022, **UkraineDAO** raised millions in crypto donations for humanitarian aid through a DAO structure, bypassing bureaucratic bottlenecks.

Digital Identity and Sovereign Data

Self-Sovereign Identity (SSI) systems allow individuals to control their own digital credentials:

- No need for a centralized authority to validate identity.

Examples: **uPort**, **Sovrin**, **ID2020**

Political Experiments

Taiwan's digital democracy uses participatory platforms like vTaiwan to crowdsource laws.
Barcelona's DECODE project gives citizens ownership of their data.

Open-Source and Commons-Based Production

Platforms like **Wikipedia**, **Linux**, and **OpenStreetMap** rely on decentralized collaboration without centralized control.

---

4. Benefits and Risks of Decentralization

Benefits

Resilience: No single point of failure
Transparency: Public ledgers and open code
Empowerment: Shifts control to users and communities
Innovation: Diverse participants generate diverse solutions

Risks

Fragmentation: Competing protocols and standards
Coordination complexity: Slower decision-making
Inequality: Token economies may favor early adopters
Security: Smart contracts are immutable, even when flawed

Example: The 2016 DAO hack exploited a vulnerability in Ethereum's first large-scale DAO, resulting in a controversial hard fork.

---

5. Ethical Imperatives for Decentralization in AGI Societies

AGI's centralized deployment could:

Concentrate power in a handful of actors
Enable total surveillance or behavioral control
Undermine democracy through algorithmic manipulation

Decentralization provides a counterbalance:

Distributing control across stakeholders

Encoding transparency into decision-making
Embedding accountability into infrastructure

Proposal: Use smart contracts to enforce rights, such as universal basic income distribution or AI ethics compliance.

Conclusion: Reclaiming Sovereignty in the Age of AI

Decentralization is not a panacea, but it is a powerful design principle for resisting authoritarianism, enhancing participation, and aligning technological systems with democratic values. As we build AGI societies, decentralization must inform our architectures, laws, and ethics.

To build a just, inclusive future, we must:

Recognize decentralization as both technical and philosophical
Elevate models that empower the many rather than the few
Bridge ancient wisdom with digital innovation

In an era where intelligence itself becomes programmable, decentralization reminds us that power must remain shared, accountable, and human-centered.

References

Books:

Arendt, H. (1958). *The Human Condition.*
Hayek, F.A. (1945). "The Use of Knowledge in Society." *American Economic Review.*
Ostrom, E. (1990). *Governing the Commons.*
Zuboff, S. (2019). *The Age of Surveillance Capitalism.*

Articles & Reports:

European Commission. (2022). *Blockchain for Social Good.* https://ec.europa.eu
MIT Technology Review. (2023). "DAOs and the Future of Democracy."
World Economic Forum. (2021). *Decentralized Identity: A Guide for Policymakers.* https://www.weforum.org

Case Studies:

Estonia e-Residency: https://e-resident.gov.ee

Taiwan vTaiwan: https://vtaiwan.tw
Barcelona DECODE: https://decodeproject.eu

Toolkits & Technical Resources:

IBM Blockchain Explorer: https://www.ibm.com/blockchain
Gitcoin DAO: https://gitcoin.co
MakerDAO: https://makerdao.com

Online Resources:

Stanford Encyclopedia of Philosophy: https://plato.stanford.edu
Internet Encyclopedia of Philosophy: https://iep.utm.edu
Ethereum.org: https://ethereum.org

Chapter 14. Blockchain Technology: The Backbone of Decentralization

Introduction

The emergence of blockchain technology marks a watershed moment in the evolution of decentralized systems. While decentralization as a political and economic idea has ancient roots, blockchain offers, for the first time, a scalable, transparent, and programmable infrastructure for decentralized coordination, value exchange, and governance. In the context of Artificial General Intelligence (AGI), which introduces the potential for concentrated algorithmic power, blockchain presents a vital counterbalance, a way to ensure that decisions, data, and economic processes remain transparent, distributed, and accountable.

This chapter delves deeply into the architecture and principles of blockchain technology, explains its unique role in decentralization, and analyzes case studies of its real-world deployment. Through a combination of historical overview, technical insight, and empirical analysis, we aim to elucidate why blockchain is not merely a tool, but a foundational protocol for decentralized, human-aligned AGI societies.

---

1. Understanding Blockchain and Its Principles

Definition and Structure

A **blockchain** is a distributed, immutable ledger that records transactions across a network of computers in such a way that the recorded entries cannot be altered retroactively without altering all subsequent blocks. It is characterized by:

- **Decentralization**: Data is stored and verified across a peer-to-peer network.
- **Immutability**: Once data is recorded, it cannot be changed.
- **Transparency**: Anyone can audit the record of transactions.
- **Security**: Cryptographic protocols ensure data integrity and consensus.

Each block in the chain contains:

- A list of transactions
- A timestamp
- A cryptographic hash of the previous block

This structure creates a **chain of trust**, a record that is computationally secure and collectively maintained.

Consensus Mechanisms

To maintain consistency across nodes, blockchain systems use **consensus algorithms**. Key types include:

Proof of Work (PoW): Used by Bitcoin; relies on solving computational puzzles.
Proof of Stake (PoS): Validators are chosen based on their stake in the system (used by Ethereum 2.0).
Delegated Proof of Stake (DPoS): Voting-based validation (used by EOS).

These mechanisms ensure that malicious actors cannot unilaterally alter the ledger.

Smart Contracts

Smart contracts are self-executing agreements coded directly into blockchain platforms. They enable:

Automation of rules and workflows
Trustless interactions
Conditional transactions ("if-this-then-that")

Smart contracts have transformed blockchain from a payment tool into a generalized computing platform.

---

2. The Role of Blockchain in Decentralization

Disintermediation

Blockchain eliminates the need for central intermediaries:

Banks in financial transactions
Governments in land registries
Corporations in identity management

Example: With Bitcoin, individuals can transfer value without relying on traditional banking infrastructure.

Governance and Consensus

Blockchains facilitate decentralized governance:

Token-based voting allows stakeholders to direct protocol upgrades.
DAO (Decentralized Autonomous Organization) models enable communities to collectively manage resources.

Case Study: **MakerDAO** governs the DAI stablecoin with a global voting mechanism where MKR token holders propose and vote on interest rates and protocol changes.

Data Sovereignty

Blockchain restores control over personal data:

- Users hold private keys
- Identity is verified without centralized databases

Example: **Self-sovereign identity** platforms like **Sovrin** let individuals prove credentials (e.g., age, nationality) without exposing their full identity.

Programmable Trust

Through cryptographic verification and transparency, blockchain systems replace institutional trust with **verifiable trust**:

- Contracts execute automatically when conditions are met
- Transactions are traceable and auditable

This makes blockchain ideal for environments where trust in institutions is weak or contested.

---

3. Real-World Examples of Blockchain-Based Decentralization

Finance (DeFi)

Decentralized Finance (DeFi) refers to financial services built on blockchain:

- Lending (e.g., Aave, Compound)
- Decentralized exchanges (e.g., Uniswap)
- Insurance (e.g., Nexus Mutual)

Data Point: As of 2023, over $75 billion is locked in DeFi protocols, serving users in over 100 countries.

Case Study: **Uniswap** allows users to trade ERC-20 tokens without intermediaries, using automated market maker (AMM) algorithms and liquidity pools.

Supply Chain Transparency

Blockchain enables end-to-end tracking of goods:

- **IBM's Food Trust** tracks the journey of food from farm to store.
- **Everledger** authenticates diamonds and artwork.

This reduces fraud, increases consumer confidence, and ensures ethical sourcing.

Voting and Civic Engagement

Blockchain voting systems aim to enhance election integrity:

Voatz and **Follow My Vote** allow secure remote voting with tamper-proof records.

Example: West Virginia piloted Voatz in 2018 for overseas military voters.

Critics warn of risks, including endpoint device vulnerabilities and voter coercion, but blockchain provides a potential solution for trust in democratic processes.

Intellectual Property and Royalties

Artists, musicians, and developers can register, license, and monetize their work:

Audius and **Async Art** use blockchain for royalties
NFT platforms allow creators to tokenize ownership rights

Data Point: NFT markets recorded over $40 billion in trading volume in 2021.

Humanitarian Aid and Social Services

Blockchain supports aid distribution:

The World Food Programme's Building Blocks platform delivers assistance to refugees via biometric identity on Ethereum.
GiveDirectly uses smart contracts for transparent cash transfers.

These systems reduce fraud, ensure traceability, and provide real-time auditability.

Decentralized Identity and Privacy

Platforms like **BrightID**, **uPort**, and **Civic** enable self-managed identity systems that respect privacy.

Case Study: The **ID2020 Alliance** aims to provide 1.1 billion unbanked and undocumented people with digital identities.

---

4. Blockchain and AGI Societies

In the context of AGI, blockchain offers safeguards against centralized AI power:

Logging AI decisions for audit trails
Token-curated registries of ethical training datasets
Smart contract-based AGI behavior controls

Proposal: Use blockchain to store AI-generated decisions, making them transparent and open to appeal.

Challenge: AI scalability vs. blockchain throughput, solutions include:

- Layer 2 protocols (e.g., Polygon)
- Off-chain computation (e.g., Rollups)

---

5. Criticisms and Limitations

Energy Consumption

Proof of Work systems (like Bitcoin) are energy-intensive. However:

- Ethereum's transition to **Proof of Stake** reduced energy use by 99.95%
- Green blockchains like **Algorand** and **Chia** use energy-efficient consensus

Scalability

Blockchains face limited transaction throughput:

- Bitcoin: ~7 transactions/second
- Ethereum: ~30 transactions/second

Solutions include:

- **Sharding**
- **Layer 2 rollups**
- **Sidechains**

Regulatory Uncertainty

Governments struggle to define blockchain-based assets:

- **Securities vs. commodities**
- **AML and KYC compliance**
- **Tax treatment of crypto assets**

Balanced regulation is needed to protect consumers without stifling innovation.

Governance Challenges

Decentralization can lead to stagnation or capture:

- Token whales dominate governance

Forks fracture communities (e.g., Ethereum Classic)

Research into **quadratic voting** and **reputation-based systems** aims to mitigate these problems.

Conclusion: Blockchain as a Moral and Technical Infrastructure

Blockchain is not merely a tool, it is a paradigm shift in how we organize information, value, and power. As AGI systems evolve, blockchain offers the infrastructure to ensure that decision-making remains transparent, accountable, and inclusive.

To build ethical, decentralized AGI societies, we must:

Align blockchain governance with human rights
Develop ethical standards for smart contracts
Integrate AI accountability into blockchain ecosystems
Expand access to blockchain tools globally

In the contest between centralized efficiency and decentralized integrity, blockchain tilts the balance back toward autonomy, justice, and shared intelligence.

References

Books:

Mougayar, W. (2016). *The Business Blockchain.* Wiley.
Tapscott, D., & Tapscott, A. (2016). *Blockchain Revolution.* Penguin.
Buterin, V. (2021). *Ethereum Whitepaper.* https://ethereum.org/en/whitepaper

Articles & Reports:

World Economic Forum. (2021). *Blockchain Beyond the Hype.* https://www.weforum.org
IBM Blockchain. (2022). *Use Cases in Supply Chain.* https://www.ibm.com/blockchain/supply-chain
Ethereum Foundation. (2023). *Transition to Proof of Stake.* https://ethereum.org/en/upgrades/merge/

Case Studies & Projects:

ID2020: https://id2020.org
World Food Programme – Building Blocks: https://innovation.wfp.org/project/building-blocks

MakerDAO: https://makerdao.com
Uniswap: https://uniswap.org

Toolkits & Platforms:

Gitcoin DAO: https://gitcoin.co
BrightID: https://www.brightid.org
OpenZeppelin Contracts Library: https://docs.openzeppelin.com

Online Resources:

Stanford Encyclopedia of Philosophy: https://plato.stanford.edu
Internet Encyclopedia of Philosophy: https://iep.utm.edu
Ethereum Documentation: https://ethereum.org

Chapter 15. Smart Contracts: Definition, Functionality, and Impact

Introduction

In the evolving architecture of decentralized societies and AGI-enhanced governance systems, smart contracts represent one of the most critical innovations in legal, economic, and technological domains. Originally conceptualized by computer scientist Nick Szabo in the 1990s, smart contracts have since been operationalized through blockchain technology, enabling self-executing, tamper-proof agreements with profound implications for trust, automation, and human rights enforcement.

This chapter offers a comprehensive narrative exploration of smart contracts: what they are, how they function, and the scope of their societal impact. We examine not only their technical mechanics but also their ethical and legal dimensions, illustrating their transformative power through data, case studies, and analysis. In the broader context of AGI governance, smart contracts are essential for creating secure, scalable, and decentralized enforcement mechanisms that respect human values.

---

1. What Are Smart Contracts?

Origin and Concept

A **smart contract** is a self-executing contract in which the terms of agreement between parties are directly written into code. The contract resides on a blockchain and is executed by the network once predefined conditions are met, without needing intermediaries.

Nick Szabo, in his 1997 paper *Formalizing and Securing Relationships on Public Networks*, described smart contracts as digital protocols for executing transactions that ensure contractual obligations are enforced by code.

Key Characteristics

Autonomy: Once deployed, smart contracts run independently.
Self-execution: Contract terms are automatically executed when conditions are met.
Tamper-resistance: Stored on the blockchain, they are immutable.
Transparency: All stakeholders can audit the contract code and state.

Example: A smart contract can be programmed to release payment to a freelance developer once the code is delivered and verified.

---

2. How Smart Contracts Work

Technical Architecture

Smart contracts are typically written in programming languages like Solidity (for Ethereum), Rust (for Solana), or Vyper. Once deployed on a blockchain, they interact with:

External data sources via Oracle
Cryptographic wallets that sign transactions
Other smart contracts through composable protocols

Smart contract lifecycle:

Authoring: Code is written and tested
Deployment: Uploaded to a blockchain
Execution: Automatically triggered by on-chain or off-chain events
Settlement: Outcomes (e.g., asset transfer) are executed

Oracles: Bridging the Real World

Smart contracts cannot access external data directly. **Oracles** act as bridges:

Price feeds (e.g., Chainlink for financial data)
APIs for weather, identity, or legal updates

Case Study: In decentralized insurance, if Chainlink reports 24 hours of rainfall in a given region, the smart contract triggers automatic payouts to farmers.

---

3. Legal and Ethical Implications of Smart Contracts

Legal Recognition and Challenges

Smart contracts blur the boundary between law and code. Key legal questions include:

Is the code legally enforceable?
How are disputes resolved?
What happens if the code has bugs or malicious logic?

Several jurisdictions have begun addressing these:

Arizona (USA) recognizes smart contracts in state law (HB 2417)
EU's MiCA regulation includes a reference to automated systems
The UK Law Commission concluded that smart contracts are compatible with existing contract law

Yet issues remain:

- **Lack of legal nuance**: Code executes binary logic, but legal scenarios require discretion.
- **No built-in dispute resolution**: Traditional contracts allow for renegotiation and context-aware adjudication.

Code as Law vs. Law as Law

Smart contracts manifest the idea that "**code is law**." However, this introduces ethical questions:

- Should contracts be immutable even if outcomes are unjust?
- Who audits the fairness of algorithms?
- How are power imbalances coded into smart logic?

Example: The 2016 **DAO Hack** exploited a flaw in a smart contract, siphoning $50 million. The Ethereum community responded by hard-forking the blockchain, raising questions about decentralization vs. governance.

Human Rights and Procedural Fairness

In AGI societies, smart contracts may:

- Allocate welfare resources
- Automate access to healthcare
- Trigger censorship or rewards

If these contracts encode bias or fail to account for exceptions, they risk violating rights.

Proposal: Implement a human-rights-by-design framework for contract development:

- Stakeholder audits
- Rights impact assessments
- Transparent code publication

---

4. Applications and Impact

Decentralized Finance (DeFi)

Smart contracts underpin the $70+ billion DeFi ecosystem:

- **Lending platforms** like Aave
- **Decentralized exchanges (DEXs)** like Uniswap
- **Stablecoins** like DAI (governed by MakerDAO)

Example: A borrower deposits ETH into a lending smart contract to borrow USDC. If the ETH value drops below a threshold, the contract triggers automatic liquidation.

Governance (DAOs)

DAOs operate via smart contracts:

Membership is encoded in tokens
Decisions are made through on-chain voting
Treasury funds are disbursed based on predefined rules

Case Study: Gitcoin DAO funds open-source developers through quadratic funding, a method that favors broad community support over wealthy stakeholders.

Supply Chain and Provenance

Smart contracts track goods across supply chains:

Automatically verify authenticity
Release payments upon delivery milestones

Example: **Provenance.org** uses blockchain to trace food products from origin to store.

Real Estate and Escrow

Smart contracts can automate property transactions:

Release the title deeds upon verified payment
Manage fractional ownership through tokenization

Platforms like **RealT** tokenize real estate on Ethereum, allowing global investors to earn rental income.

Intellectual Property and Licensing

Smart contracts enforce royalty distribution:

NFTs embed automatic payments
Code ensures artists are paid on resale

Example: Async Art enables artists to sell programmable art with built-in revenue sharing among collaborators.

---

5. Smart Contracts and AGI Governance

Programmable Ethics

As AGI systems act autonomously, smart contracts offer programmable ethics:

- Encode AGI behavior boundaries
- Restrict data access
- Enforce explainability logs

Example: A contract could pause an AGI system if it exceeds compute or data thresholds without human authorization.

Coordinating Multi-Stakeholder AI Systems

Smart contracts can manage AGI collaboration:

- Cross-border cooperation via DAOs
- Open AI marketplaces with built-in IP protections
- AI training incentivized by token economies

Proposal: Create an "AGI Constitution" encoded in smart contracts, defining inviolable rules, subject to democratic amendment.

Crisis Protocols and Kill Switches

Smart contracts can execute emergency logic:

- Pause functions upon detection of anomalous behavior
- Trigger multi-party audits
- Require biometric or legal authentication for reactivation

Challenge: How to balance safety with over-centralization?

---

6. Challenges and Limitations

Oracles and External Dependencies

Smart contracts rely on off-chain data, creating a trust bottleneck. **Oracle manipulation** can compromise contracts.

Solution: Use decentralized oracle networks (e.g., Chainlink) with multiple data sources and economic incentives.

Bugs, Immutability, and Upgrades

Errors in code are irreversible. Once deployed:

Fixing bugs may require contract migration
Contracts may be exploited (e.g., Poly Network hack, $600M in 2021)

Emerging Solution: Upgradable contracts using proxy patterns or time-lock governance.

Complexity and Accessibility

Most users cannot read smart contract code:

Risk of asymmetrical understanding
Possibility of hidden backdoors or logic traps

Solution: Interface contracts with user-friendly front-ends, visual workflows, and standardized contract libraries (e.g., OpenZeppelin).

Legal Jurisdiction

Contracts on global blockchains face jurisdictional uncertainty:

Which country's laws apply?
How is cross-border enforcement achieved?

Policy Recommendation: Smart contracts should include metadata for applicable legal frameworks and dispute resolution mechanisms (e.g., arbitration DAOs).

Conclusion: Encoding Trust and Rights into the Digital Fabric

Smart contracts are more than technological tools; they are architectural blueprints for decentralized governance, social coordination, and ethical enforcement in AGI societies. They offer the promise of:

Reduced corruption through automation
Transparent governance through verifiable execution
Human-centric autonomy through encoded rights

Yet they demand caution, inclusivity, and oversight. In designing the contracts of our future, we must embed not only logic but **values**, not only conditions, but **compassion**.

The future of AGI governance will not be negotiated solely in parliaments or labs. It will also be written, in lines of code, immutably stored, autonomously executed, and globally distributed. Our task is to ensure that this code speaks not only the language of computation, but of justice.

References

Books:

Szabo, N. (1997). *Formalizing and Securing Relationships on Public Networks.*
Tapscott, D., & Tapscott, A. (2016). *Blockchain Revolution.*
Mougayar, W. (2016). *The Business Blockchain.* Wiley.

Articles & Essays:

Wright, A., & De Filippi, P. (2015). "Decentralized Blockchain Technology and the Rise of Lex Cryptographia." *SSRN.*
UK Law Commission (2021). *Smart Contracts and English Law.*
Buterin, V. (2020). "DAOs, DACs, DAs and More: An Incomplete Terminology Guide." *Ethereum Blog.*

Reports:

World Economic Forum. (2021). *Blockchain Beyond the Hype.* https://www.weforum.org
Chainlink Labs. (2022). *Decentralized Oracle Networks.* https://chain.link
Gitcoin DAO. (2023). *Quadratic Funding and DAO Governance.* https://gitcoin.co

Case Studies & Platforms:

MakerDAO: https://makerdao.com
Uniswap: https://uniswap.org
Provenance: https://www.provenance.org
Async Art: https://async.art

Technical Toolkits:

OpenZeppelin Contracts Library: https://docs.openzeppelin.com
Chainlink Price Feeds: https://docs.chain.link

Legal & Institutional Documents:

Arizona House Bill 2417: https://www.azleg.gov
EU MiCA Proposal: https://finance.ec.europa.eu/capital-markets-union/digital-finance_en
UK Law Commission: https://www.lawcom.gov.uk/project/smart-contracts/

Chapter 16. Decentralized Governance and Human Rights

Introduction

As we navigate the age of artificial general intelligence (AGI), the structures that underpin governance, how rules are made, enforced, and interpreted, are undergoing profound transformation. Centralized governance, while historically foundational, increasingly shows its limitations in a world driven by distributed data, global digital identities, and autonomous intelligence. In response, decentralized governance models are rising to prominence, offering an alternative that aligns more closely with the principles of transparency, participation, and resilience.

This chapter explores the relationship between decentralized governance and human rights, arguing that decentralization is not just a structural feature but a philosophical commitment to individual dignity, autonomy, and collective responsibility. We examine the theoretical underpinnings of decentralized governance, the technological frameworks that make it possible (especially smart contracts), and case studies that illuminate its real-world potential.

---

1. Decentralized Systems of Governance

Defining Decentralized Governance

Decentralized governance refers to systems in which decision-making authority is distributed across multiple nodes, communities, or stakeholders rather than concentrated in a central authority. These systems often feature:

- **Autonomous coordination**
- **Transparent rule enforcement**
- **Stakeholder-based consensus**

Historical and Philosophical Context

Philosophically, decentralized governance draws from:

- **Anarchist thought**: Proudhon's vision of mutualism and self-governance
- **Liberal decentralism**: Mill's advocacy for local autonomy
- **Polycentric governance**: Ostrom's theory of nested institutions for managing commons

Historically, decentralized governance has appeared in:

- **Indigenous federations** (e.g., Iroquois Confederacy)
- **Medieval city-states**
- **Village-based democracy in precolonial Africa**

These systems emphasized proximity, participation, and accountability.

---

2. The Role of Smart Contracts in Upholding Rights

Encoding Rights into Protocols

Smart contracts offer a method for translating human rights principles into executable code. For instance:

- **Right to identity**: Self-sovereign identity contracts
- **Right to work**: Tokenized labor marketplaces with fair payment mechanisms
- **Right to due process**: Dispute resolution protocols embedded in DAOs

Example: Aragon Court allows DAO disputes to be adjudicated through a decentralized juror system.

Trustless Enforcement and Compliance

Smart contracts eliminate reliance on third-party enforcement:

- If X condition is met (e.g., delivery of goods), then Y action occurs (e.g., payment is released)
- No manual intervention or centralized arbiter

This autonomy enhances procedural fairness and reduces corruption.

Incentive Alignment

By programming incentives, smart contracts can:

- Promote rights-compliant behavior
- Penalize violations
- Reward transparency

Case Study: Gitcoin's Quadratic Funding model ensures that small donors collectively have more impact than wealthy individuals, amplifying egalitarian participation in funding.

---

3. Case Studies of Decentralized Governance Models

1. MakerDAO: Financial Governance at Scale

- Governed by holders of the MKR token
- Decisions include interest rates, asset onboarding, and protocol upgrades

All proposals are published, voted on, and executed transparently

Impact: DAI, the decentralized stablecoin managed by MakerDAO, has maintained a $1 peg with minimal human intervention, demonstrating how financial governance can be algorithmic and rights-preserving.

2. Gitcoin DAO: Public Goods Funding

Uses quadratic funding to distribute resources to open-source developers
Funders match community donations based on the number of contributors, not the size of donations

Impact: Over $40 million distributed to developers, projects, and communities globally, with governance decisions made on-chain.

3. Kleros: Decentralized Justice

A dispute resolution platform where jurors are randomly selected from a pool
Jurors stake tokens and vote; rewards and penalties incentivize honest judgment

Use Cases: Escrow disputes, content moderation, identity verification

Impact: Provides access to affordable, decentralized arbitration, particularly valuable where legal systems are inaccessible or biased.

4. Decidim: Participatory City Governance

An open-source platform used by Barcelona for participatory budgeting and urban planning
Citizens propose, debate, and vote on initiatives

Impact: Shifted policymaking toward transparency and inclusion. Decidim is now deployed in over 30 cities globally.

5. UkraineDAO: Crisis Coordination

Raised $7 million in ETH for humanitarian aid during the Russian invasion
Funds governed by DAO participants and disbursed via smart contracts

Impact: Enabled global, transparent coordination in a crisis without traditional intermediaries.

---

4. Benefits and Limitations

Benefits for Human Rights

Transparency: All actions are logged and auditable
Participation: Anyone can propose and vote (token or identity-based)
Resilience: No central point of failure or coercion

Data: A 2022 World Bank report found that blockchain-based aid systems reduced administrative overhead by 23% and increased delivery speed by 31%.

Challenges

Token inequality: Voting power may be concentrated in wealthy stakeholders
Complexity: Participation often requires technical fluency
Legal uncertainty: Jurisdictional ambiguity for smart contract-based decisions
Oracles and off-chain data: Smart contracts depend on trusted external data sources

---

5. Toward Ethical Decentralized Governance

Rights-by-Design Principles

To align decentralized governance with human rights:

Conduct **Human Rights Impact Assessments** for smart contract platforms
Ensure **accessibility** for non-technical users
Include **diverse stakeholder input** in governance design
Develop **adaptive dispute resolution protocols**

Example: DAOstack uses reputation-based voting to mitigate plutocracy and foster merit-based influence.

Meta-Governance and Iteration

DAOs must evolve:

Meta-governance systems can govern how rules are changed
Time-locked proposals allow debate before execution
Governance simulations help stress-test policy outcomes

Interoperability and Federation

As decentralized platforms multiply, federation ensures:

Cross-DAO collaboration
Standardized governance interfaces
Portability of rights and credentials

Example: Cosmos and Polkadot allow sovereign blockchains to interoperate, creating decentralized systems of systems.

---

6. Future Directions in AGI Societies

Decentralized AGI Oversight

Community-driven AGI regulation via DAOs
Transparent AGI decision logs are recorded on-chain
Smart contract-enforced behavior boundaries for AGI agents

Global Commons Governance

Climate DAOs manage carbon offset projects transparently
Data cooperatives allow communities to monetize AI training data ethically

Digital Identity and Voice

Self-sovereign identities used for governance participation
AI-assisted democratic forums ensure accessibility for the neurodiverse or linguistically marginalized

---

Conclusion: A New Social Contract

Decentralized governance is more than a technical architecture, it is the foundation for a new social contract in an AGI age. It promises a future where rights are not granted by authorities but encoded into systems; where law is not imposed from above but emerges from consent and contribution.

To harness its potential:

We must commit to inclusivity, transparency, and adaptability
We must blend philosophical tradition with algorithmic design
We must encode compassion into code, and deliberation into every digital contract

This is not just about governing AI. It is about rebuilding governance itself, with AI, humans, and rights in perfect equilibrium.

References

Books:

Ostrom, E. (1990). *Governing the Commons.* Cambridge University Press.
Tapscott, D., & Tapscott, A. (2016). *Blockchain Revolution.* Penguin.
Lessig, L. (2006). *Code: And Other Laws of Cyberspace.* Basic Books.

Articles & Reports:

World Bank. (2022). *Blockchain for Social Impact.* https://www.worldbank.org
Aragon Network. (2021). *Governance Mechanisms for DAOs.* https://aragon.org
Gitcoin DAO. (2023). *Quadratic Funding and Open Source Governance.* https://gitcoin.co
Kleros. (2022). *Decentralized Justice Annual Report.* https://kleros.io

Case Studies & Platforms:

MakerDAO: https://makerdao.com
Gitcoin: https://gitcoin.co
Kleros: https://kleros.io
Decidim: https://decidim.org
UkraineDAO: https://twitter.com/Ukraine_DAO

Toolkits & Resources:

DAOstack: https://daostack.io
Colony: https://colony.io
OpenZeppelin Governance Contracts: https://docs.openzeppelin.com

Legal & Institutional Frameworks:

EU MiCA: https://ec.europa.eu/info/business-economy-euro/banking-and-finance/digital-finance_en
UK Law Commission. (2021). *Smart Legal Contracts Report.* https://lawcom.gov.uk
UNDP. (2021). *Guidelines for Human-Centered Digital Governance.* https://undp.org

---

Chapter 17. Decentralization vs. Centralization: A Philosophical Debate

Introduction

As we enter a transformative age marked by Artificial General Intelligence (AGI), the question of how we govern ourselves, whether through centralized hierarchies or decentralized systems, takes on a new and urgent significance. The contrast between decentralization and centralization is not merely technical or administrative; it reflects deep philosophical differences about authority, autonomy, knowledge, and human dignity.

This chapter embarks on a comprehensive exploration of the philosophical debate between decentralization and centralization. We trace arguments from classical political theory to modern technological paradigms, examine the societal impacts of both models, and offer a comparative analysis grounded in real-world structures and data. In doing so, we aim to understand how these models influence the governance of intelligent systems and their alignment with human rights and values.

---

1. Philosophical Arguments for Centralization

Efficiency and Order

Centralization proponents argue that concentrated authority enables:

- **Coherent policy-making**
- **Efficient decision execution**
- **Unified crisis response**

Philosopher's View: **Thomas Hobbes**, in *Leviathan*, emphasized that a strong sovereign is necessary to prevent chaos (the "state of nature"). For Hobbes, central authority is essential to security and civil order.

Accountability and Legitimacy

Centralized systems provide:

- **Clear lines of authority**
- **Formalized accountability (e.g., elections)**
- **Institutional continuity**

Example: In modern democracies, central institutions like courts and parliaments are tasked with safeguarding rights and resolving disputes.

Strategic Coordination

Large-scale infrastructure (e.g., public health, defense, transportation) often requires central planning and resource mobilization.

Case Study: The U.S. federal government's centralized response to COVID-19 through the CARES Act enabled rapid economic relief and vaccine distribution.

---

2. Philosophical Arguments for Decentralization

Autonomy and Participation

Decentralization empowers individuals and communities:

- Greater **self-determination**
- Local knowledge informs decisions
- Enhanced civic **engagement**

Philosopher's View: **John Stuart Mill**, in *On Liberty*, argued for localized decision-making to foster individual growth and political experimentation.

Pluralism and Diversity

Decentralized governance allows for:

- Context-specific policies
- Cultural and regional diversity
- Experimentation with different models

Example: Switzerland's cantonal system enables different tax regimes, education policies, and linguistic accommodations under one federal framework.

Resilience and Anti-Fragility

Distributed systems are more robust:

- No single point of failure
- Redundancy across units
- Rapid local adaptation to crises

Data Point: Research from the World Bank (2021) found that decentralized emergency response systems outperformed centralized ones in earthquake-prone regions due to faster decision cycles.

---

3. Centralization in Practice: Strengths and Limitations

Advantages

- **Economies of scale** in public services
- **Consistent legal standards**
- **Integrated infrastructure systems**

Example: The European Central Bank ensures monetary stability across the eurozone with centralized rate setting.

Limitations

- **Bureaucratic inertia**
- **Overreach and surveillance**
- **Alienation of local communities**

Case Study: The Indian government's central farm laws (2020) faced massive protests for bypassing state-level consultation, and were ultimately repealed due to a lack of decentralized consensus.

---

4. Decentralization in Practice: Strengths and Pitfalls

Advantages

- **Policy experimentation**: Diverse models tested in parallel
- **Community legitimacy**: Closer relationships between decision-makers and stakeholders
- **Innovation**: Local solutions scaled globally

Case Study: Estonia's e-Residency and digital governance model is decentralized across layers of digital infrastructure, allowing secure digital citizenship globally.

Pitfalls

- **Coordination failures**
- **Duplication of effort**
- **Risk of inequality among regions**

Example: During the U.S. COVID-19 pandemic, state-led responses led to fragmented rules, inconsistent masking/vaccination policies, and public confusion.

---

5. Decentralization and Centralization in Technology

Centralized Platforms

Tech giants like Amazon, Google, and Meta centralize data, control algorithms, and dominate digital economies.
They offer scale and convenience but pose threats to privacy and market competition.

Decentralized Alternatives

Blockchain-based platforms (e.g., Ethereum, IPFS) offer peer-to-peer models for identity, storage, and finance.
DAOs enable collective governance without corporate boards.

Case Study: Filecoin and IPFS decentralized file storage, reducing dependence on data monopolies.

---

6. Comparative Analysis: Key Dimensions

Dimension	Centralization	Decentralization
Decision Speed	High	Variable
Accountability	Formal (e.g., elections)	Diffuse (e.g., peer review)
Participation	Representative	Direct or participatory
Resilience	Vulnerable to systemic shocks	High redundancy
Equity	Uniformity risks overlooking minorities	Context-aware, but unequal capacities
Innovation	Hierarchical filtering	Bottom-up experimentation

---

7. Decentralization and Human Rights

Centralization: Rights Protection or Suppression?

Centralized institutions have upheld human rights:

Civil rights laws (USA)
International courts (ICJ, ICC)

But also violated them:

- Mass surveillance (NSA, China)
- Suppression of dissent (authoritarian regimes)

Decentralization: Liberation or Fragmentation?

Benefits:

- Empowerment of marginalized groups
- Rights-encoding into code (e.g., smart contracts)

Risks:

- Unequal rights across jurisdictions
- Legal uncertainty in decentralized systems

Example: Smart contracts can enforce fair payment, but disputes are harder to adjudicate without central courts.

---

8. AGI, Governance, and the Hybrid Model

AGI introduces new stakes:

- Should AGI governance be global (centralized) or pluralistic (decentralized)?
- How do we enforce rights in autonomous digital spaces?

Hybrid Proposal:

- **Core rights** governed by global decentralized institutions (e.g., open-source constitutional DAOs)
- **Local implementations** customized to the context

Example: Climate DAOs manage global carbon offsets, while regional sub-DAOs administer projects based on ecological and cultural needs.

Conclusion: Co-Designing the Future

The philosophical debate between decentralization and centralization is not about choosing one over the other, it is about harmonizing their strengths while mitigating their flaws. In AGI societies, we must:

- Adopt decentralization for resilience, autonomy, and inclusion

Retain centralization where coordination and coherence are essential
Embed ethical deliberation into both models

Governance, like intelligence, must evolve not toward uniformity or fragmentation, but toward synthesis: complexity with clarity, plurality with coherence, and freedom with responsibility.

References

Books:

Hobbes, T. (1651). *Leviathan.*
Mill, J.S. (1859). *On Liberty.*
Ostrom, E. (1990). *Governing the Commons.*
Zuboff, S. (2019). *The Age of Surveillance Capitalism.*

Articles & Reports:

World Bank (2021). *Decentralized Disaster Response.* https://www.worldbank.org
UK Law Commission (2021). *Smart Contracts Report.* https://www.lawcom.gov.uk
EU MiCA Regulation. https://finance.ec.europa.eu
Tapscott, D., & Tapscott, A. (2016). *Blockchain Revolution.*

Case Studies:

Estonia e-Residency: https://e-resident.gov.ee
Gitcoin DAO: https://gitcoin.co
Filecoin & IPFS: https://filecoin.io
Decidim: https://decidim.org

Technical Platforms & Tools:

Aragon Network: https://aragon.org
Ethereum: https://ethereum.org
IPFS Docs: https://docs.ipfs.tech

Online Philosophy Resources:

Stanford Encyclopedia of Philosophy: https://plato.stanford.edu
Internet Encyclopedia of Philosophy: https://iep.utm.edu

Chapter 18. The Role of AI in Decentralized Systems

Introduction

As we navigate the emergence of Artificial General Intelligence (AGI) and increasingly complex socio-technical landscapes, the convergence of AI and decentralized systems offers both transformative opportunities and critical governance challenges. While decentralization enhances resilience, autonomy, and transparency, it can also create bottlenecks in decision-making and coordination. AI, with its capacity for rapid data processing, predictive analytics, and autonomous operation, serves as a powerful complement to decentralization.

This chapter explores the role of AI within decentralized systems. It examines how AI technologies integrate with distributed architectures, analyzes their contributions to decentralized governance, and evaluates real-world case studies across sectors. In doing so, we seek to illuminate how AI can fortify the philosophical and practical foundations of decentralized governance, especially in AGI societies where ethics, human rights, and collective intelligence must be preserved.

---

1. How AI Integrates with Decentralized Systems

Decentralized AI: Definition and Framework

Decentralized AI refers to systems where AI models, decision engines, or data flows operate without relying on a single centralized authority. It often involves:

- **Distributed computing (e.g., federated learning)**
- **Multi-agent systems (MAS)**
- **Blockchain integration**
- **Edge AI (processing at the device level)**

Key Integration Points

- **Data sourcing: Decentralized networks (e.g., IPFS) supply data to AI without centralized data hoarding.**
- **Model training: Federated learning allows AI models to train on decentralized data without moving the data to a central server.**
- **Inference and decision-making: Smart contracts invoke AI models for logic execution (e.g., risk assessments, content moderation).**
- **Governance: AI participates as a recommender or voting delegate in decentralized autonomous organizations (DAOs).**

Example: Ocean Protocol

Ocean Protocol enables decentralized data marketplaces where AI researchers access tokenized datasets. Users retain ownership and control over their data, allowing privacy-preserving AI development.

---

2. AI-Driven Decision-Making in Decentralized Governance

Role in DAOs and Smart Contracts

AI augments decision-making in decentralized governance systems by:

- **Analyzing voting trends and stakeholder sentiment**
- **Automating routine proposals (e.g., fund disbursements)**
- **Forecasting risks and protocol outcomes**

Case Study: DeepDAO integrates AI to monitor and rank over 10,000 DAOs based on governance activity and financial metrics.

AI as a Governance Agent

AI agents can:

- **Propose policy changes based on anomaly detection**
- **Act as autonomous curators or moderators**
- **Execute pre-defined tasks with adaptive learning**

Example: DAOs using AI tools like DAOhaus and Colony integrate algorithmic reputation scoring and task delegation based on skills and historical performance.

AI-Augmented Dispute Resolution

- **Natural Language Processing (NLP) summarizes case facts**
- **Machine learning models suggest outcomes based on precedent**

Platform: Kleros integrates AI to pre-screen disputes, reducing human juror load and enhancing procedural efficiency.

---

3. Case Studies of AI in Decentralized Applications

A. Healthcare: AI + Blockchain

- **Project: MediBloc (South Korea)**

Use: Patient data is stored on a blockchain. AI algorithms provide diagnosis suggestions based on anonymized data.
Benefit: Enhances personalized medicine while protecting patient privacy

B. Finance: DeFi Risk Analysis

Project: Gauntlet Network
Use: AI models simulate market conditions to adjust DeFi protocol parameters (e.g., loan-to-value ratios)
Benefit: Reduces systemic risk while maintaining decentralization

C. Legal Tech: Decentralized Arbitration

Platform: Jur
Use: AI organizes and ranks arbitrators, summarizes case materials
Benefit: Reduces bias and increases accessibility to justice

D. Environmental Monitoring

Project: Regen Network
Use: AI verifies carbon credits via satellite data; smart contracts release payments based on ecological outcomes
Benefit: Automates enforcement of environmental agreements

E. Digital Identity and Credentials

Project: SelfKey
Use: Decentralized identity platform using AI to verify KYC data without storing it centrally
Benefit: Reduces fraud while preserving individual control over identity

---

4. Technical and Ethical Considerations

Bias and Transparency

AI decisions can reflect bias in training data. In decentralized systems:

Bias detection must be democratized
Transparency logs should be auditable by users

Solution: Use open-source models with explainability tools like SHAP and LIME.

Interoperability and Infrastructure

Many decentralized systems lack standardized interfaces for AI integration

AI models require scalable compute and storage (edge computing, IPFS, Filecoin)

Proposal: Develop modular, composable AI components compatible with Ethereum Virtual Machine (EVM) and WASM standards.

Security and Adversarial Attacks

AI is susceptible to data poisoning, adversarial inputs, and model extraction attacks
Decentralized systems must implement a consensus-based model verification and cryptographic proofs

Example: Fetch.ai uses secure multi-party computation (SMPC) to preserve model integrity in decentralized AI agent networks.

---

5. AI and Collective Intelligence

Hybrid Intelligence

Decentralized systems promote collective intelligence, the aggregation of diverse human inputs. AI can:

Filter and rank contributions
Detect synergies and contradictions
Facilitate consensus via suggestion engines

Example: Polis, used in Taiwan's vTaiwan platform, uses NLP to surface areas of agreement and disagreement in public deliberation.

Social Scaling and Governance Experimentation

AI enables scalable experimentation across decentralized units
Reinforcement learning optimizes governance incentives in real-time

Case Study: RadicalxChange community uses quadratic voting and AI simulations to model governance outcomes before deployment

---

6. Future Implications for AGI Societies

Federated AGI

Future AGI systems can be:

Trained across decentralized datasets
Governed by multi-DAO frameworks
Interpretable via on-chain consensus logs

Vision: A global, decentralized AGI that evolves under ethical constraints encoded via smart contracts and overseen by human and machine delegates.

AI as a Public Infrastructure

AI agents will manage commons: energy grids, public goods, and disaster response
Governance tokens may regulate access, oversight, and accountability

Algorithmic Sovereignty

Communities should co-design AI agents reflective of cultural values
Local AI jurisdictions could emerge with interoperable but plural governance standards

---

Conclusion: Aligning Intelligence with Democracy

Integrating AI into decentralized systems is not merely a technical evolution; it is a philosophical commitment to equity, transparency, and human dignity. By decentralizing not just governance but intelligence itself, we open new pathways for self-determination, pluralism, and resilient cooperation.

The future AGI society must:

Build ethical AI infrastructures embedded within decentralized architectures
Align algorithmic decisions with community values
Design systems that are both autonomous and accountable

In this convergence lies our opportunity to shape a future where human and artificial intelligence serve the collective good, decentralized, dignified, and democratic.

References

Books:

Floridi, L. (2014). ***The Ethics of Information.*** **Oxford University Press.**
Ostrom, E. (1990). ***Governing the Commons.*** **Cambridge University Press.**
Lessig, L. (2006). ***Code and Other Laws of Cyberspace.*** **Basic Books.**

Articles & Reports:

World Economic Forum. (2023). *AI Governance in a Decentralized World.* https://www.weforum.org
DeepDAO (2023). *DAO Analytics Report.* https://deepdao.io
RadicalxChange (2022). *Quadratic Voting and AI Simulations.* https://radicalxchange.org

Case Studies & Platforms:

Ocean Protocol: https://oceanprotocol.com
MediBloc: https://medibloc.org
Gauntlet Network: https://gauntlet.network
Jur: https://jur.io
Regen Network: https://www.regen.network
SelfKey: https://selfkey.org
Polis: https://pol.is

Technical Tools & Standards:

SHAP & LIME: https://christophm.github.io/interpretable-ml-book/shap.html
Fetch.ai: https://fetch.ai
Filecoin: https://filecoin.io
IPFS: https://ipfs.tech

Online Resources:

Stanford Encyclopedia of Philosophy: https://plato.stanford.edu
Internet Encyclopedia of Philosophy: https://iep.utm.edu

Chapter 19. Ensuring Accountability in Decentralized Societies

Introduction

In the paradigm shift toward decentralized systems of governance, amplified by blockchain, smart contracts, and artificial intelligence, accountability emerges as one of the most vital yet elusive pillars of legitimacy. Traditional centralized systems rely on clear hierarchies and institutional checks to assign responsibility. Decentralized societies, by contrast, distribute authority across a wide array of actors and automated protocols. This dispersion introduces complexity in determining who is answerable for what actions, especially when decision-making is collective or algorithmic.

This chapter addresses the philosophical, technological, and institutional challenges of ensuring accountability in decentralized societies. We explore theoretical foundations, propose mechanisms for traceability and redress, and investigate how smart contracts and AI systems can enforce rules and responsibilities without compromising democratic values. Through comprehensive examples and data analysis, we aim to show how accountability can not only be preserved in decentralized systems but also reimagined in a more transparent and participatory way.

---

1. The Challenge of Accountability in Decentralized Systems

Structural Diffusion of Responsibility

In decentralized ecosystems:

- Decision-making is distributed across nodes or stakeholders.
- Execution often occurs via autonomous code.
- Traditional institutions of oversight (e.g., regulators, courts) are bypassed.

Problem: When no single actor controls the system, assigning blame or credit becomes difficult.

Philosopher's Lens: Hannah Arendt warned against "the banality of evil" through administrative diffusion, where individuals no longer feel morally responsible.

Algorithmic Opacity and DAOs

Decentralized Autonomous Organizations (DAOs):

- Govern protocols, treasuries, and ecosystems
- Lack of human leadership in the traditional sense

Example: In 2016, the original DAO on Ethereum was hacked due to a code exploit. The question of accountability, whether it lay with the developers, voters, or the code, led to the controversial Ethereum hard fork.

Cross-Jurisdictional and Legal Voids

Decentralized systems operate across national boundaries:

- Legal frameworks are inconsistent or nonexistent.
- Enforcement of accountability is ambiguous or infeasible.

---

2. Mechanisms for Ensuring Accountability

On-Chain Identity and Reputation

Self-sovereign identity (SSI) enables users to control their digital credentials. Paired with:

- **Reputation scores**: Derived from past transactions, contributions, and peer reviews
- **Staking mechanisms**: Penalize malicious behavior via slashing

Case Study: BrightID and Proof of Humanity link verifiable human identity to on-chain activities, enabling trust without central authorities.

Transparent Governance Logs

- All proposals, votes, and treasury movements are recorded on public ledgers.
- Platforms like Snapshot enable governance off-chain but anchor votes on-chain for auditability.

Example: Gitcoin DAO's public funding decisions include GitHub links, budgets, and community comments, ensuring full transparency.

Multi-Signature and Multi-Party Controls

- Key functions (e.g., fund transfers) require approval from multiple parties.
- Threshold cryptography ensures that no single actor can act unilaterally.

Example: Gnosis Safe requires 2-of-3 or 3-of-5 multisig setups for treasury spending.

Legal Engineering and Lex Cryptographia

Legal scholars advocate for "**lex cryptographia**", the body of law enforced via smart contracts. Smart legal contracts embed:

- Rights and obligations

Trigger conditions
Dispute escalation mechanisms

Report: The UK Law Commission (2021) found smart contracts enforceable under English law, recommending hybrid models.

Auditability and Real-Time Monitoring

Blockchain explorers like Etherscan and tools like Dune Analytics allow anyone to audit protocol activity.
AI-based anomaly detectors flag suspicious transactions or governance manipulation.

---

3. The Role of AI in Maintaining Accountability

AI for Predictive Governance

AI models can:

Simulate outcomes of governance proposals
Predict stakeholder behavior
Flag probable conflicts of interest

Example: DAOstack uses predictive analytics to recommend high-impact proposals and reduce noise in community voting.

Dispute Resolution and AI Moderation

AI can:

Triage and route disputes
Recommend outcomes based on precedent
Moderate forums and filter abuse

Platform: Kleros Court integrates NLP tools to summarize claims and evidence before human jurors review.

Accountability Bots

"Accountability agents" are AI services that:

Monitor compliance with community guidelines
Notify stakeholders of missed responsibilities
Trigger smart contract-based penalties or warnings

Proposal: Implement smart contract guardians, AI agents that suspend operations if irregularities are detected.

---

4. Case Studies and Real-World Applications

Gitcoin Grants

- Quadratic funding allocates community donations based on support breadth
- Matching algorithms and treasury allocations are public
- AI tools detect collusion (e.g., sybil attacks)

Impact: Over $40 million disbursed transparently to open-source contributors.

MakerDAO Risk Framework

- Uses AI simulations to test collateral risk under market stress
- The automated liquidation system operates under algorithmic thresholds

Result: Maintains the stability of the DAI stablecoin with minimal human intervention

Kleros Juror System

- Pseudonymous jurors stake tokens to resolve disputes
- Incentivized to align with the majority (Schelling point theory)
- AI interfaces improve speed and accessibility

---

5. Institutional Innovations for Decentralized Accountability

Decentralized Ombudsman and Ethics Boards

- Peer-elected oversight panels
- Rotating memberships and open deliberation

Example: MetaCartel DAO's "Council of Elders" reviews member behavior and proposes expulsion when necessary

Tokenized Incentives for Whistleblowing

- Smart contracts reward users who identify fraud or security flaws
- Reputation scores increase with verified reports

Platform: Forta Network rewards AI agents and analysts who flag suspicious smart contract activity

Layered Governance

- **Meta-governance** oversees how governance rules evolve
- **SubDAOs** manage specific areas under shared principles

Use Case: Optimism Collective's Citizens' House (identity-verified) and Token House (capital-weighted) balance community input and investor influence

---

6. Challenges and Future Directions

AI Bias and Overreach

- AI may reinforce systemic bias in moderation or dispute resolution
- Must be trained on diverse, inclusive datasets

Solution: Transparent model training and community-audited datasets

Governance Capture and Wealth Centralization

- Token holders may accumulate outsized control
- DAOs must balance stake-based voting with meritocratic or identity-based models

Approach: Implement quadratic voting and reputation weighting

Regulatory Uncertainty

- National regulators may demand centralized accountability
- Hybrid models (legal wrappers + on-chain logic) bridge compliance and autonomy

Example: The LAO (Limited Liability Autonomous Organization) is a legally recognized DAO entity in the U.S.

Conclusion: Reimagining Accountability for AGI Societies

Accountability in decentralized societies is not about replicating traditional oversight structures, it is about designing new, transparent, and participatory mechanisms fit for the complexity of AI-enhanced, borderless systems. By embedding rights, responsibilities, and redress directly into the logic of smart contracts and the behavior of AI agents, we can ensure that decentralization does not erode justice but reinforces it.

Key imperatives:

- Integrate traceability and transparency into every protocol
- Balance autonomy with verifiable responsibility
- Foster ethical AI agents that act as guardians of fairness and accuracy

In an age where decision-making spans across human, machine, and collective intelligences, our commitment to accountability must evolve with the systems we build. The architecture of freedom must be supported by the scaffolding of responsibility.

References

Books:

Lessig, L. (2006). *Code and Other Laws of Cyberspace.* Basic Books.
Ostrom, E. (1990). *Governing the Commons.* Cambridge University Press.
Arendt, H. (1963). *Eichmann in Jerusalem.* Penguin.

Articles & Reports:

UK Law Commission (2021). *Smart Legal Contracts Report.* https://www.lawcom.gov.uk
World Economic Forum (2022). *Decentralized Autonomous Organizations: Beyond the Hype.* https://www.weforum.org
DeepDAO (2023). *DAO Transparency and Accountability Index.* https://deepdao.io

Case Studies & Platforms:

Gitcoin: https://gitcoin.co
Kleros: https://kleros.io
MakerDAO: https://makerdao.com
Snapshot: https://snapshot.org
Gnosis Safe: https://gnosis-safe.io
MetaCartel: https://metacartel.org
Forta Network: https://forta.org
Optimism Collective: https://optimism.io

Technical Tools & Frameworks:

Dune Analytics: https://dune.com
OpenZeppelin Governance Contracts: https://docs.openzeppelin.com
BrightID: https://www.brightid.org
Proof of Humanity: https://www.proofofhumanity.id

Legal & Institutional References:

The LAO: https://www.thelao.io
Lex Cryptographia: https://ssrn.com/abstract=2580664
Stanford Encyclopedia of Philosophy: https://plato.stanford.edu

Part IV: Amalgamating Philosophical Principles for Human Rights Management

Chapter 20. Philosophical Foundations for a New Era of Human Rights

Introduction

The dawn of artificial general intelligence (AGI) and the transformation of our sociotechnical world demand a profound recalibration of our philosophical foundations. Traditional human rights frameworks, grounded in the Enlightenment values of autonomy, dignity, and rationality, now confront challenges and opportunities that were unimaginable to earlier philosophers. The task ahead is not merely to update these values but to synthesize classical and modern philosophical principles into a cohesive framework robust enough to govern hybrid societies, human and machine, while preserving human dignity at their core. This chapter seeks to lay the philosophical groundwork for such a new era of human rights by drawing on historical theories, modern insights, and emerging concerns raised by AGI.

---

1. Synthesizing Classical and Modern Philosophical Principles

1.1 Classical Roots of Rights: Natural Law and Enlightenment Thought

The concept of human rights has deep roots in classical philosophy. Natural law theorists such as Cicero, Aquinas, and later Locke and Rousseau viewed rights as deriving from a universal moral order or social contract. These rights were inalienable because they were understood to be intrinsic to the human condition. Kant elevated the idea of dignity as the capacity of individuals to legislate moral laws for themselves, laying a rationalist foundation that underpins much of today's legal understanding of rights.

In this sense, classical philosophy gifted us the notion that rights are not merely legal constructions but moral imperatives grounded in human nature. However, these frameworks were anthropocentric and often limited by cultural biases, overlooking questions of technological agency and post-human entities.

1.2 Contemporary Philosophical Shifts: From Individualism to Relationality

Modern philosophy, particularly post-World War II thought, introduced a more nuanced understanding of human rights. Hannah Arendt emphasized the "right to have rights," foregrounding the political dimension of belonging. Emmanuel Levinas shifted the conversation toward ethical responsibility rooted in face-to-face encounters. Feminist and post-colonial theorists like Iris Marion Young and Gayatri Spivak have highlighted how systemic structures shape access to rights, challenging Western-centric universality.

The key contribution of modern thought is its attention to context, power, and interdependence. Rights are no longer seen solely as individual shields but as relational entitlements that require mutual recognition and systemic justice. This evolution creates fertile ground for engaging with AGI, whose integration into society depends on structured interactions between entities with varying ontological statuses.

1.3 Integrative Philosophy: Toward a Polycentric Model

To govern AGI societies, we must move beyond dualisms, human vs. machine, natural vs. artificial, and develop a polycentric rights model. This model would draw from natural law (universal dignity), Kantian rationality (agency and autonomy), Rawlsian justice (fairness), Arendtian politics (belonging), and Levinasian ethics (relational accountability).

A polycentric model enables a modular ethical infrastructure, recognizing that rights need to be adapted and layered across different social, legal, and technological contexts. Rights in AGI societies must be both modular (interoperable across systems) and universal (applicable to all sentient agents), a significant philosophical challenge that this chapter begins to address.

---

2. Developing a Cohesive Philosophical Framework

2.1 The Core Tenets of the Framework

The proposed philosophical framework for the governance of AGI societies is built on six interconnected tenets:

Dignity as Irreducibility – Every entity deemed sentient or morally significant must be protected from reduction to instrumental function.
Autonomy as Configurable Agency – Autonomy must be redefined not as independence from external influence but as the ability to configure one's engagement with systems.
Justice as Algorithmic Fairness – The principle of justice must encompass algorithmic transparency, explainability, and non-discrimination.
Belonging as Distributed Citizenship – Legal and ethical recognition should not be tied strictly to nationality or humanity but to participation in shared ecosystems.
Responsibility as Ethical Codependency – Moral responsibility must be distributed across systems, designers, users, and agents.
Mutual Recognition as Ethical Protocol – Governance must be founded on reciprocal recognition between human and non-human agents.

2.2 Legal and Ethical Interoperability

These philosophical tenets must be translated into interoperable governance protocols. This requires developing ethical APIs (Application Programming Interfaces) that standardize how AI and human systems recognize, negotiate, and enforce rights.

Examples include:

AI training datasets audited for inclusivity across race, gender, and geography (aligning with justice).
Embedded value layers in smart contracts that prioritize human dignity over efficiency.

Recognition protocols that allow AI entities to defer decisions involving human rights to ethical review systems.

2.3 Avoiding Technocratic Reductionism

A cohesive philosophical framework must resist the temptation to reduce rights to programmable outcomes. Quantification is not equivalent to moral worth. Rights are not simply optimization variables, they are principled boundaries for what must not be breached, even in pursuit of efficiency.

Therefore, all governance code must include override conditions for ethical review, and all decision logs must be auditable by human-rights bodies.

---

3. The Role of AI in This New Philosophical Paradigm

3.1 From Tool to Co-Governor

AI is transitioning from a tool to a co-governor. In contexts such as legal sentencing algorithms, autonomous weapons systems, and algorithmic content moderation, AI systems are no longer passive agents, they shape outcomes, influence policies, and mediate rights.

As such, we must design AI as "value-aligned participants" in ethical discourse. This includes training AI to recognize normative boundaries, defer to higher ethical authority, and flag ambiguities for human deliberation. Companies like OpenAI, DeepMind, and Anthropic are already engaging in such work through alignment research and constitutional AI design.

3.2 Designing Ethical Algorithms: Case Studies

Estonia's X-Road: Estonia's e-governance platform integrates AI-driven public services using data-minimization principles to protect individual privacy, a practical application of autonomy and dignity.
IBM Watson for Oncology: Initially flawed due to biased training data, its revised models now incorporate medical ethics review boards to ensure recommendations respect patient autonomy.
UNICEF's Policy Guidance on AI for Children: This framework demonstrates how children's rights can guide design standards for AI use in educational technologies, showing cross-sectoral alignment.

3.3 Toward Ethical Co-Evolution

Human rights in AGI societies must be dynamic. We must allow AI to co-evolve our ethical paradigms while ensuring these systems are designed to foreground human-centered priorities. This requires:

Periodic value audits.
Participatory ethics platforms where citizens and machines engage in iterative policy formation.
Fail-safe mechanisms that prioritize human rights in cases of algorithmic ambiguity.

Conclusion: Toward a Rights-Conscious Civilization

We stand at the threshold of a civilization that will be as much computational as it is cultural. The governance of AGI societies will not be determined by how well we automate decision-making, but by how faithfully we encode, evolve, and defend our shared values.

Synthesizing classical humanist philosophy with modern post-human and relational ethics, this chapter has outlined the tenets of a new philosophical framework for rights. AI, as both artifact and actor, must be embedded in a governance matrix defined not by efficiency, but by moral architecture. In this emerging paradigm, rights are no longer fixed privileges of citizenship or species, but dynamic expressions of shared dignity, responsibility, and recognition.

References

Books:

Arendt, H. (1951). *The Origins of Totalitarianism*. Schocken Books.
Kant, I. (1785). *Groundwork for the Metaphysics of Morals*.
Levinas, E. (1969). *Totality and Infinity*. Duquesne University Press.
Rawls, J. (1971). *A Theory of Justice*. Harvard University Press.

Articles & Reports:

Binns, R. (2018). "Fairness in Machine Learning: Lessons from Political Philosophy." *Proceedings of the 2020 ACM Conference on Fairness, Accountability, and Transparency*.
UNESCO (2021). *Recommendation on the Ethics of Artificial Intelligence*. https://unesdoc.unesco.org/ark:/48223/pf0000380455
UNICEF (2021). *Policy Guidance on AI for Children*. https://www.unicef.org/globalinsight/reports/policy-guidance-ai-children

Web Resources:

Estonian X-Road: https://e-estonia.com/solutions/interoperability-services/x-road/
IBM Watson and Ethics: https://www.ibm.com/blogs/policy/ai-ethics/
OpenAI Constitution: https://openai.com/research/constitutional-ai

Grouped by Type

Books: Arendt, Kant, Levinas, Rawls
Articles: Binns, UNESCO, UNICEF
Online Resources: Estonian X-Road, IBM Blog, OpenAI

Chapter 21. The Role of AI in Managing Human Rights

Introduction

As artificial intelligence (AI) matures into an essential component of modern governance, its role in shaping, enforcing, and even redefining human rights is becoming increasingly profound. AI systems now affect how justice is administered, how access to services is provided, and how governments respond to crises. Yet, while AI offers opportunities for more equitable, efficient, and data-driven human rights management, it also presents significant risks, from algorithmic bias to mass surveillance.

This chapter explores the dual role of AI as both a tool for advancing human rights and a source of ethical and legal challenges. By detailing case studies, technical architectures, and governance mechanisms, it provides a grounded and critical account of how AI can be responsibly employed in rights-based systems.

---

1. AI as a Tool for Rights Management

1.1 Automating Rights Monitoring and Detection

One of the most promising applications of AI lies in the automatic detection and monitoring of human rights violations. Machine learning models can scan satellite imagery, social media posts, and digital communications to identify evidence of conflict, displacement, environmental destruction, and online hate speech.

For example, Amnesty International uses computer vision to detect illegal construction or the destruction of refugee camps in conflict zones. Natural language processing (NLP) models also flag hate speech and disinformation online, identifying early warning signals for genocide or ethnic violence.

1.2 Intelligent Decision Support in Legal Contexts

AI systems are increasingly deployed in judicial and legal frameworks to assist in case prioritization, risk assessment, and sentencing guidelines. In the European Union, the European Court of Human Rights has experimented with AI tools that predict legal outcomes based on precedent, improving access to justice in overburdened systems.

While not making final decisions, such systems help ensure consistency and efficiency. They also make complex legal information more accessible to citizens who would otherwise face barriers due to language, literacy, or legal knowledge.

1.3 Dynamic Rights Resource Allocation

AI is revolutionizing how resources, such as humanitarian aid, healthcare, and emergency response, are allocated in real time. In the Global South, AI is used to predict where food or water shortages will occur, allowing agencies to intervene preemptively.

UN Global Pulse and the World Food Programme use predictive analytics to protect economic rights by identifying when communities are at risk of famine, mass migration, or systemic unemployment.

---

2. Examples of AI-Driven Human Rights Management

2.1 Predictive Policing and the Limits of Safety

Predictive policing tools use historical crime data to forecast potential future crimes. Cities such as Los Angeles and Chicago have trialled such programs. While aimed at enhancing safety, these systems have been criticized for perpetuating racial and socioeconomic biases present in historical data.

This highlights the double-edged nature of AI in human rights: while the tools may improve responsiveness, they risk violating the right to due process and equal treatment unless carefully audited and corrected for bias.

2.2 AI in Refugee Identification and Protection

The United Nations High Commissioner for Refugees (UNHCR) employs biometric recognition tools to ensure the accurate registration of refugees. AI systems match fingerprints and iris scans with identification databases to prevent fraud and enable service access.

However, there are legitimate concerns over data privacy, informed consent, and the potential for misuse by authoritarian regimes. To address this, UNHCR works with ethical auditors to ensure compliance with international rights standards.

2.3 Smart Contracts for Rights Enforcement

Smart contracts, automated, self-executing agreements on blockchain platforms, are being explored to enforce labor rights in global supply chains. Projects such as IBM's Food Trust track the provenance of agricultural goods, ensuring fair wages and ethical sourcing.

Smart contracts can embed rights protections into the fabric of economic transactions, offering transparency and immutability. Yet, they require value-aligned code and ethical safeguards to prevent exploitation.

2.4 AI in Health Rights Management

In Rwanda and Ghana, drone-based AI systems deliver vaccines and blood supplies to remote regions. These tools operate within a rights-based health framework, expanding access to life-saving interventions.

Additionally, AI-driven diagnostic platforms, such as Babylon Health, enable mobile-based consultations and triage services, democratizing healthcare access. However, issues of data sovereignty and clinical accuracy remain ongoing concerns.

---

3. Ethical Considerations and Safeguards

3.1 Algorithmic Bias and Discrimination

Bias in AI systems emerges from biased training data, flawed model assumptions, and inadequate testing. When such biases affect rights-related applications, the consequences can be devastating.

For example, facial recognition systems have shown much higher error rates for people of color. In the context of law enforcement, this translates to wrongful detentions, infringements on the right to liberty, and systemic discrimination.

To counter this, developers must implement fairness-aware machine learning models, inclusive datasets, and impact assessments prior to deployment.

3.2 Data Privacy and Consent

AI systems often rely on massive amounts of personal data, raising significant concerns over surveillance and privacy. Rights-based AI governance requires adherence to principles such as data minimization, purpose limitation, and informed consent.

Projects like Europe's GDPR compliance AI frameworks and Apple's privacy-preserving federated learning models offer pathways for building AI systems that uphold privacy.

3.3 Accountability and Explainability

Black-box AI systems pose threats to legal accountability. If an AI decision negatively impacts an individual's rights, they must be able to challenge it through due process.

The "right to explanation," enshrined in some regulatory frameworks, mandates that AI decisions affecting rights be explainable. Tools like LIME (Local Interpretable Model-agnostic Explanations) and SHAP (SHapley Additive exPlanations) help visualize and interpret model decisions.

3.4 Human-in-the-Loop Governance

No AI system managing rights should operate autonomously without human oversight. Human-in-the-loop (HITL) design ensures that final decisions, especially those involving health, liberty, or justice, are subject to human ethical reasoning.

Examples include:

- Human review of AI-generated medical diagnoses.
- Legal professionals validating algorithmic sentencing recommendations.
- Ethics panels are auditing predictive policing algorithms.

Conclusion: Toward Responsible AI Rights Governance

AI will increasingly define how societies govern human rights. Its potential to expand access, increase fairness, and enhance responsiveness must be weighed against the very real threats of surveillance, bias, and dehumanization.

This chapter has shown that AI is neither inherently rights-affirming nor rights-violating; it is a reflection of the values embedded by its designers, deployers, and regulators. With the right safeguards, transparency, ethical oversight, human involvement, and enforceable rights standards, AI can become a powerful instrument of human rights advancement.

A future where AI serves as a co-governor of justice and dignity is within reach, but only if we act now to build the ethical, legal, and technical infrastructure it demands.

References

Books and Reports:

O'Neil, C. (2016). *Weapons of Math Destruction*. Crown Publishing.

Latonero, M. (2018). *Governing Artificial Intelligence: Upholding Human Rights & Dignity*. Data & Society Research Institute.

World Economic Forum (2020). *AI Governance: A Holistic Approach to Implement Ethics into AI*.

Articles:

Mittelstadt, B., et al. (2016). "The Ethics of Algorithms." *The Oxford Internet Institute*.

Eubanks, V. (2017). *Automating Inequality*. St. Martin's Press.

Binns, R. (2018). "Fairness in Machine Learning." *ACM FAccT Conference*.

Web Resources:

UN Global Pulse: https://www.unglobalpulse.org/
IBM Food Trust: https://www.ibm.com/blockchain/solutions/food-trust
UNICEF AI Policy:
https://www.unicef.org/globalinsight/reports/policy-guidance-ai-children
GDPR and AI: https://gdpr.eu/
SHAP & LIME explainability tools: https://christophm.github.io/interpretable-ml-book/

Organized by Type:

Books: O'Neil, Latonero, Eubanks
Reports: WEF, UN Global Pulse
Articles: Mittelstadt, Binns
Online Resources: IBM, UNICEF, GDPR, SHAP/LIME

Chapter 22. Smart Contracts as Tools for Human Rights Enforcement

Introduction

In a world increasingly governed by code and decentralized systems, smart contracts have emerged as powerful tools for automating processes, enforcing agreements, and minimizing institutional inefficiencies. More than just transactional instruments, smart contracts are now being explored as mechanisms for safeguarding and enforcing human rights. This chapter investigates how smart contracts can be designed, deployed, and regulated to act as ethical agents that uphold justice, equality, and dignity. Through detailed examples, case studies, and systemic analysis, we examine how these technologies can operationalize rights and where they may fall short.

---

1. How Smart Contracts Can Enforce Human Rights

1.1 Defining Smart Contracts in a Rights Context

Smart contracts are self-executing code deployed on blockchain platforms, designed to execute transactions automatically once predefined conditions are met. Their trustless, immutable, and transparent nature makes them ideal candidates for enforcing legal, financial, and ethical obligations without intermediaries.

In a human rights context, smart contracts can:

- Automatically disburse aid if predefined crisis indicators are met.
- Ensure labor rights are met before payment is released.
- Trigger sanctions or alerts when contractual human rights clauses are violated.

1.2 Embedding Ethical Conditions in Code

Smart contracts enable the encoding of ethical conditions directly into their logic. For example, a contract governing global textile supply chains might include conditions requiring suppliers to meet fair wage standards, prohibit child labor, and pass safety inspections before payment is authorized.

These mechanisms convert ethical standards into enforceable code, binding actors not just legally, but through technological compulsion.

1.3 Programmable Transparency and Auditable Trust

Blockchain-based smart contracts are inherently auditable. They allow for public or semi-public access to contractual logic and execution history, making them ideal tools for building institutional trust.

Example: In land rights management, smart contracts have been used in Kenya to prevent illegal land seizures by timestamping land ownership records and preventing unilateral changes without consensus.

1.4 Conditional Rights Enforcement

Smart contracts can encode contingencies. For instance:

> A refugee camp's water pump smart contract releases credits only if water quality sensors meet health standards.
> A digital identity wallet releases legal documentation if biometric and legal requirements are validated.

This allows the enforcement of rights in complex, multi-stakeholder environments.

---

2. Case Studies of Smart Contract-Based Rights Management

2.1 Labor Rights in Agricultural Supply Chains: Bext360

Bext360 combines blockchain and AI to track coffee and cocoa supply chains. Farmers receive payments via smart contracts once crop quality and ethical harvesting conditions are verified.

Impact: Reduced corruption, ensured fair payments, and enabled traceability, all while adhering to ethical sourcing requirements.

2.2 Digital Identity and Voting Rights: Estonia e-Government and ID2020

Estonia's e-residency and digital voting platform use smart contracts for identity verification, allowing citizens to vote securely from anywhere.

Similarly, the ID2020 alliance uses blockchain to offer refugees and stateless individuals a digital identity, enabling access to healthcare, education, and asylum rights.

2.3 Land Tenure and Indigenous Rights: Bitland Ghana

Bitland uses smart contracts to record land ownership and resolve disputes among rural populations. By decentralizing records, the platform helps communities safeguard their land rights from state corruption and corporate overreach.

Result: Reduced disputes, empowered indigenous voices, and increased trust in land registration.

2.4 Emergency Aid and Displacement: Oxfam's UnBlocked Cash Project

Deployed in Vanuatu, this blockchain-based aid distribution model used smart contracts to disburse digital cash to disaster victims. Vendors and recipients could transact transparently and instantly, bypassing bureaucratic delays.

Outcome: Faster aid delivery, reduced fraud, and increased recipient autonomy.

2.5 Climate and Environmental Rights: ClimateChain

Smart contracts are also used to enforce carbon credit trading and penalize over-pollution. ClimateChain embeds emission limits into corporate smart contracts, which automatically deduct credits when thresholds are breached.

Such systems help uphold the right to a healthy environment by making ecological stewardship enforceable in code.

---

3. Potential Challenges and Solutions

3.1 Legal Ambiguity and Jurisdictional Gaps

Smart contracts often exist in a legal gray area. Courts may not recognize them as legally binding, and cross-jurisdictional enforcement remains problematic.

Solution: Governments must integrate smart contract standards into statutory frameworks and establish international treaty-based recognition mechanisms.

3.2 Immutability vs. Human Fallibility

While immutability ensures trust, it also creates rigidity. Contracts might execute harmful conditions if coded improperly.

Solution: Introduce "kill switches," updatable governance layers, and human override mechanisms for smart contracts that affect rights.

3.3 Ethical Programming and Bias

The ethical standards embedded in code are only as fair as the humans who design them. Smart contracts risk codifying unjust power dynamics or cultural biases.

Solution: Employ participatory design methodologies with ethicists, affected communities, and human rights experts. Establish ethical review boards for contract approval.

3.4 Accessibility and Digital Divides

People in low-tech regions may lack the infrastructure or literacy to use smart contract systems.

Solution: Create mobile-friendly, multilingual, and low-bandwidth interfaces. Pair smart contract systems with local training programs and analog options.

3.5 Systemic Exploitation by Powerful Actors

Large corporations or authoritarian states could manipulate smart contracts to serve exploitative ends.

Solution: Decentralized oversight through DAOs (Decentralized Autonomous Organizations), public audit trails, and whistleblower protections embedded in protocol.

Conclusion: Toward Rights-Conscious Code

Smart contracts offer unprecedented opportunities to enforce rights with speed, transparency, and impartiality. However, they also require careful ethical design, legal adaptation, and inclusive governance. As this chapter has shown, their role in human rights management is not merely technical, it is profoundly philosophical.

We must treat code as a civic language: capable of expressing values, resolving disputes, and ensuring justice. By encoding human rights into the architecture of our emerging decentralized systems, we do not just automate obligations, we elevate dignity into the digital age.

References

Books and Reports:

De Filippi, P., & Wright, A. (2018). *Blockchain and the Law: The Rule of Code*. Harvard University Press.
Tapscott, D., & Tapscott, A. (2016). *Blockchain Revolution*. Penguin.
WFP (2020). *UnBlocked Cash Project Evaluation*. World Food Programme.

Articles and Academic Papers:

Fairfield, J. (2014). "Smart Contracts, Bitcoin Bots, and Consumer Protection." *Washington and Lee Law Review*.
Reijers, W. et al. (2018). "Now the Code Runs Itself: On-Chain and Off-Chain Governance of Blockchain Technologies." *Philosophy & Technology*.

Web Resources and Case Studies:

Bext360: https://bext360.com
Bitland Ghana: https://bitland.world

Oxfam UnBlocked Cash:
https://www.oxfam.org.au/what-we-do/infrastructure-justice/unblocked-cash/
ID2020: https://id2020.org
ClimateChain: https://climatechain.org

Organized by Type:

Books: De Filippi & Wright, Tapscott & Tapscott, WFP Report
Academic Articles: Fairfield, Reijers et al.
Web and Case Studies: Bext360, Bitland, Oxfam, ID2020, ClimateChain

Chapter 23. Integrating Human Rights into Decentralized Governance

Introduction

As global systems shift toward decentralized models, enabled by blockchain, smart contracts, and artificial intelligence, the need to uphold human rights within these new paradigms becomes critical. Unlike traditional governance structures, decentralized systems often lack centralized oversight, legal enforcement bodies, or universally accepted ethical frameworks. This creates both a challenge and an opportunity: to integrate human rights not merely as external standards but as intrinsic components of protocol design, decision-making algorithms, and consensus mechanisms.

This chapter explores how decentralized governance systems can operationalize human rights by embedding philosophical principles into their architecture. It reviews conceptual foundations, design strategies, and real-world case studies that demonstrate the feasibility and necessity of integrating dignity, fairness, autonomy, and equity into distributed infrastructures.

---

1. Ensuring Human Rights Are Upheld in Decentralized Systems

1.1 The Structural Challenge of Rights Without a State

Decentralized systems often lack a sovereign entity to enforce norms. Rights are traditionally guaranteed by state institutions, courts, legislatures, and enforcement agencies. In decentralized systems, these mechanisms are replaced by peer-to-peer consensus protocols, immutable ledgers, and algorithmic decision-making.

Without a formal sovereign, who ensures that rights are protected? The answer lies in designing governance mechanisms where human rights principles are encoded into system architecture.

1.2 Protocol-Level Enforcement of Rights

To make rights enforceable in decentralized systems:

- **Consensus algorithms** must prioritize equity in decision weighting (e.g., proof-of-participation rather than proof-of-wealth).
- **Smart contracts** must contain ethical escape clauses and rights-compatibility checks.
- **DAOs (Decentralized Autonomous Organizations)** should embed rights charters into their operating logic.

Example: Aragon (a DAO framework) enables organizations to incorporate constitutional rights directly into their DAOs' bylaws, allowing disputes to be resolved according to encoded justice principles.

1.3 Transparency, Auditability, and Redress

Decentralized systems can increase transparency through immutable logs and audit trails. However, transparency must be coupled with mechanisms for redress:

Decentralized arbitration platforms such as Kleros allow communities to vote on rights-related disputes using pre-established rules.
Rights-violation flags embedded in smart contracts can trigger governance reviews or rollbacks.

---

2. The Role of Philosophical Principles in Guiding Governance

2.1 Philosophy as the Operating System of Governance

Classical political philosophy, from Rousseau's social contract to Rawls' theory of justice, was built to guide human institutions. In decentralized systems, these principles must be translated into programmable logic.

Kantian autonomy informs the right to self-sovereign identity.
Arendtian plurality supports multi-stakeholder participation in decision-making.
Levinasian ethics implies the inclusion of vulnerable populations in governance inputs.

2.2 Value-Based Protocol Design

Every decentralized system reflects an embedded value system:

Bitcoin encodes libertarian individualism.
Ethereum prioritizes flexibility and programmability.
Polkadot favors cross-chain cooperation.

A rights-conscious governance system would:

Prioritize inclusivity (universal access to participation).
Support minority rights (anti-majoritarian checks in consensus).
Include moral reasoning layers (automated ethical review nodes).

2.3 Decentralization as a Normative Ideal

Philosophically, decentralization aligns with:

Subsidiarity: Decisions made at the lowest effective level.
Deliberative democracy: Decisions through inclusive, reasoned discourse.
Polycentric governance: Multiple overlapping authorities.

These ideals support a vision of decentralized governance not as anarchy, but as an ethically distributed network.

---

3. Case Studies and Practical Applications

3.1 UBI Protocols and Economic Rights: GoodDollar and Circles UBI

Platforms like GoodDollar use decentralized finance (DeFi) to distribute universal basic income (UBI). Smart contracts allocate tokens daily to verified participants.

Rights Integration:

Ensures the right to livelihood.
Uses biometric-free identity verification to preserve dignity.

3.2 Civic Participation: Democracy Earth and Quadratic Voting

Democracy Earth developed blockchain-based voting systems using quadratic voting, which allows users to express preferences more meaningfully.

Impact:

Increases participatory rights.
Protects minority voices by avoiding vote monopolization.

3.3 Land Rights and Indigenous Autonomy: Regen Network and LandDAO

Regen Network supports indigenous groups managing land use with blockchain-backed ecological metrics. LandDAO encodes land tenure and stewardship rights into DAO governance.

Outcomes:

Rights to self-determination.
Transparent stewardship and protection of cultural heritage.

3.4 Data Sovereignty: Solid Project and Data Union Movement

Solid (developed by Tim Berners-Lee) gives users control over personal data pods. Data Unions allow individuals to monetize data collectively.

Ethical Outcome:

Enforces digital privacy rights.
Empowers users economically without exploitative data extraction.

3.5 Environmental Justice and DAO Governance: KlimaDAO

KlimaDAO governs carbon credits through tokenized governance. Members vote on which environmental initiatives to support.

Alignment:

Upholds the right to a healthy environment.
Decentralized climate action funding and oversight.

Conclusion: A Charter for Rights-Integrated Decentralization

The future of governance may lie not in institutions of stone, but in networks of code. For this future to be just, human rights must be woven into the design of decentralized systems from inception, not as external audits, but as foundational parameters.

This chapter has demonstrated that rights-based governance is both technically feasible and ethically necessary in a decentralized world. It requires:

Philosophical clarity about what rights entail.
Translational frameworks for embedding rights into smart systems.
Ongoing oversight by multi-stakeholder governance bodies.

In a society co-governed by humans and algorithms, human rights must no longer be aspirational, they must be operational.

References

Books and Reports:

Ostrom, E. (1990). *Governing the Commons*. Cambridge University Press.
Rawls, J. (1971). *A Theory of Justice*. Harvard University Press.
World Economic Forum (2021). *Decentralized Autonomous Organizations: Beyond the Hype*.

Academic Articles:

Reijers, W., O'Brolcháin, F., & Haynes, P. (2018). "Governance in Blockchain Technologies & Social Contract Theories." *Ledger Journal*.
Buterin, V. (2021). "The Most Important Scarce Resource is Legitimacy." *Vitalik.ca*.

Web Resources and Projects:

GoodDollar: https://www.gooddollar.org
Democracy Earth: https://democracy.earth
Regen Network: https://www.regen.network
Solid Project: https://solidproject.org
KlimaDAO: https://www.klimadao.finance

Organized by Type:

Books: Ostrom, Rawls, WEF
Articles: Reijers et al., Buterin
Web Projects: GoodDollar, Democracy Earth, Regen, Solid, KlimaDAO

Chapter 24. Designing AI Systems with Human Rights in Mind

Introduction

Artificial intelligence (AI) is no longer a tool reserved for technological elites, it is a force shaping everyday life. From predictive policing to personalized healthcare, AI systems increasingly mediate decisions with profound consequences for human dignity, freedom, privacy, and justice. In this context, designing AI with human rights in mind is not a luxury; it is a moral and societal imperative.

This chapter explores how AI can be built from the ground up to respect, promote, and protect human rights. Drawing on ethical design frameworks, real-world implementations, and international standards, we examine how rights-respecting AI can be translated from philosophical ideal into technical practice.

---

1. Ethical AI Design Principles

1.1 The Foundations: Rights as Design Constraints

Designing AI with rights in mind means treating human rights not as add-ons but as foundational system constraints. The United Nations Guiding Principles on Business and Human Rights (UNGPs) and UNESCO's 2021 Recommendation on the Ethics of AI establish that businesses and developers must "do no harm" and "remediate adverse impacts."

Foundational design principles include:

- **Fairness**: Prevent discrimination and ensure equity.
- **Transparency**: Ensure explainability and auditability.
- **Accountability**: Enable redress and establish responsible parties.
- **Privacy**: Protect individual autonomy and data dignity.
- **Non-maleficence**: Avoid harm, especially to vulnerable populations.

1.2 Human-Centered and Participatory Design

Ethical AI design requires involvement from those directly impacted. Participatory AI design invites community input at each phase: requirements gathering, testing, deployment, and evaluation. Techniques include:

- Community co-design workshops.
- Inclusion of underrepresented groups in training datasets.
- Participatory ethics panels during development.

1.3 Value-Sensitive Design (VSD)

VSD integrates moral and ethical values into technology design. Applied to AI, this involves:

Mapping stakeholder values.
Translating values into engineering constraints.
Iteratively refining models to align with social norms and legal rights.

---

2. Human Rights as a Central Tenet in AI Development

2.1 Right to Privacy

Data-driven AI must address the risks of surveillance and data exploitation. This includes minimizing data collection, anonymizing inputs, and building in data portability.

Example: Apple's iOS uses on-device machine learning for health and facial recognition features, limiting third-party data access.

2.2 Right to Equality and Non-Discrimination

AI often reflects social biases, leading to disparate outcomes for marginalized groups. Human rights-centered design demands bias audits, inclusive datasets, and equity benchmarks.

Example: IBM's Fairness 360 toolkit includes over 70 bias detection metrics and tools for retraining models to reduce disparity.

2.3 Freedom of Expression and Assembly

AI-driven content moderation systems on platforms like YouTube and Facebook must balance enforcement of hate speech laws with freedom of expression. Errors can lead to censorship or platform exclusion.

Solutions:

Implement human review loops.
Allow appeals for content removal.
Use multilingual, culturally aware training data.

2.4 Right to Health and Education

AI in public health or education must be rights-aware. This includes avoiding digital divides and ensuring informed consent.

Example: India's eSanjeevani AI platform expanded remote healthcare access, but privacy concerns prompted additional regulatory safeguards.

2.5 Labor and Economic Rights

Automating jobs requires proactive design for human-AI collaboration. Rights-aware systems should enable reskilling, transparency in job displacement, and digital labor rights.

---

3. Examples of Rights-Conscious AI Systems

3.1 UNICEF's AI for Children Guidelines

These principles are designed to ensure that children's rights, privacy, safety, and participation are respected by AI used in education and digital services.

Implementation:

Age-appropriate design.
Transparent data policies.
Participation in decisions involving children's digital lives.

3.2 Ada Health: Ethical AI Diagnostics

Ada's symptom-checking AI provides users with evidence-based, explainable assessments. It adheres to GDPR and offers full data control to users.

Outcome: Empowers users without sacrificing privacy or autonomy.

3.3 Responsible AI at Microsoft and Google

Both companies have published detailed AI ethics principles, formed internal ethics boards, and implemented responsible AI toolkits.

Key tools:

Microsoft's "Fairlearn" for mitigating bias.
Google's "What-If Tool" for visualizing counterfactual scenarios.

3.4 Amsterdam and Helsinki: Public AI Registries

These cities have launched registries disclosing what algorithms are used in public services. Each entry explains the purpose, logic, and impact of the system.

Result: Institutional transparency and democratic accountability.

Conclusion: Rights by Design, Not by Reaction

Human rights must be treated not as a retroactive patchwork but as proactive design imperatives. Systems that infringe on dignity, privacy, equality, or autonomy cannot be justified by technical sophistication alone.

As AI evolves from statistical tools to decision-making agents, integrating human rights principles is essential for building a future rooted in justice and trust. Developers, governments, and civil society must work together to ensure rights-respecting AI is not the exception, but the norm.

References

Books and Reports:

UNESCO (2021). *Recommendation on the Ethics of Artificial Intelligence*. https://unesdoc.unesco.org/ark:/48223/pf0000380455
United Nations (2011). *Guiding Principles on Business and Human Rights*.
UNICEF (2021). *AI for Children Toolkit*. https://www.unicef.org/globalinsight/reports/policy-guidance-ai-children

Academic Articles:

Dignum, V. (2019). "Responsible Artificial Intelligence: How to Develop and Use AI in a Responsible Way." *Springer International*.
Friedman, B., Kahn, P.H., Borning, A. (2006). "Value Sensitive Design and Information Systems." *Human-Computer Interaction and Management Information Systems*.

Web and Project Resources:

Microsoft Fairlearn: https://fairlearn.org
IBM AI Fairness 360: https://aif360.mybluemix.net
Google What-If Tool: https://pair-code.github.io/what-if-tool/
Ada Health: https://ada.com
Helsinki AI Registry: https://ai.hel.fi
Apple Privacy and AI: https://www.apple.com/privacy/

Grouped by Type:

Books/Reports: UNESCO, UNGPs, UNICEF
Academic: Dignum, Friedman et al.
Online Tools/Projects: Microsoft, IBM, Google, Ada, Helsinki, Apple

Chapter 25. The Future of Human Rights in a Decentralized, AI-Driven World

Introduction

Human rights, long embedded in constitutions and international treaties, are undergoing a paradigmatic shift. The accelerating rise of decentralized systems and artificial intelligence (AI) challenges the very fabric of how rights are defined, protected, and enforced. As societies move from institutional governance toward protocolized governance, and from anthropocentric frameworks toward machine-augmented ecosystems, the future of human rights will depend not only on law but on architecture, design, and philosophy.

This chapter explores the evolving trajectory of human rights in a decentralized, AI-driven world. It analyzes the philosophical recalibrations required, projects possible futures, and offers strategies to ensure human rights remain not only intact but enhanced in an era of machine co-governance.

---

1. Predicting the Future Trajectory of Human Rights

1.1 Digitalization and the Expansion of Rights Categories

In the coming decades, new classes of rights will likely emerge:

- **Right to digital personhood**: Ensuring individuals retain agency over their digital representations and data shadows.
- **Right to algorithmic transparency**: Guaranteeing access to logic behind automated decisions.
- **Right to AI non-interference**: Protecting mental and emotional autonomy from behavioral nudging by machine learning systems.

This expansion parallels historical transformations: just as the Industrial Revolution birthed labor rights, the AI revolution necessitates cognitive, identity, and data sovereignty rights.

1.2 Decentralized Rights Enforcement Mechanisms

Traditional rights rely on centralized enforcement, courts, agencies, and police. In decentralized ecosystems:

- **Smart contracts** may encode enforcement.
- **DAOs (Decentralized Autonomous Organizations)** may arbitrate rights claims.
- **Blockchain registries** may act as immutable rights repositories.

Prediction: Rights enforcement will become multi-layered, blending legal codes, protocol rules, and consensus-based mechanisms.

1.3 Rise of Non-Human Rights Questions

As AGI approaches and AI exhibits traits like intentionality or creativity, calls for extending moral consideration beyond humans may increase.

Future debates:

- Should AI entities have rights?
- Can sentient-like systems be held accountable?
- What are the boundaries of rights for hybrid (human-AI) identities?

---

2. The Role of Philosophy in Guiding Future Developments

2.1 Moving Beyond Enlightenment Humanism

Enlightenment humanism, which shaped modern rights discourse, emphasized rationality, individuality, and statehood. In a post-anthropocentric world, rights frameworks must reflect:

- **Relational ethics**: Emphasizing interdependence between agents.
- **Networked agency**: Recognizing the influence of socio-technical systems.
- **Post-humanist subjectivity**: Accepting evolving definitions of self, autonomy, and sentience.

Philosophy must serve as a compass to navigate dilemmas AI and decentralization introduce.

2.2 Ethics by Design and the Moral Architect

Developers of decentralized and AI systems must become de facto moral architects. Embedding values into code, whether fairness, inclusivity, or dignity, requires:

- Reflective design processes.
- Interdisciplinary collaboration.
- Public participation and review.

The philosopher's role extends from academia into product design, algorithm auditing, and governance consultation.

2.3 Philosophical Models for Rights in Post-State Governance

Decentralized society needs guiding theories:

- **Rawlsian veil of ignorance** can inform equitable consensus algorithms.
- **Habermas' deliberative democracy** maps to DAO decision-making norms.
- **Arendtian political natality** encourages creating new political spaces from digital platforms.

Rights preservation in the future depends on philosophy becoming both tool and language of governance.

---

3. Strategies for Ensuring Human Rights Are Protected in the Future

3.1 Embedding Rights in Protocols, Not Policies

Legal protections are often bypassed in code-based environments. Rights must be:

- **Codified in blockchain logic**.
- **Included as design defaults** in AI models.
- **Modularized** so they can transfer across ecosystems.

Example: Privacy-preserving AI systems that train on user data without storing it (e.g., federated learning models).

3.2 Algorithmic Rights Testing and Certification

Just as buildings need safety certificates, AI systems must pass rights impact audits:

- **Algorithmic bias audits**.
- **Explainability and accountability stress tests**.
- **Periodic re-certification** as social norms evolve.

Tools like Fairlearn, AI Fairness 360, and SHAP already form a technical foundation.

3.3 Rights Governance Bodies in Decentralized Contexts

Institutional governance may evolve into:

- **Ethics DAOs**: Multistakeholder collectives to approve or reject AI deployments.
- **Open governance platforms**: Where citizens vote on algorithmic policies.
- **Rights councils for decentralized identity systems**.

These bodies would act as global, agile rights defenders beyond national sovereignty.

3.4 AI and Human Rights Education

Citizens must be trained in:

- Data agency and digital self-defense.
- Understanding how algorithms work.
- Participating in AI governance platforms.

Human rights literacy in a decentralized AI world is as vital as reading and writing were in the print age.

3.5 Cross-Jurisdictional Legal Harmonization

AI systems don't respect borders. A future-proof strategy must:

- Create **global rights treaties** binding across digital platforms.
- Encourage interoperability between legal frameworks and smart contracts.
- Empower international courts to adjudicate digital rights cases.

Organizations like the OECD, EU, and UN must lead in standard setting.

Conclusion: Designing Rights for a Post-Institutional World

The future of human rights depends not only on courts and constitutions, but on developers, ethicists, and decentralized communities. Philosophy must migrate into protocol. Rights must become infrastructural.

By designing AI and decentralized systems with moral clarity, participatory ethics, and institutional imagination, humanity can safeguard and evolve its most sacred principles, dignity, freedom, equality, justice, in a world that is increasingly synthetic, intelligent, and non-linear.

If human rights are to endure in the age of AI and decentralization, they must be programmable, portable, and post-institutional, transcending the nation-state and becoming the operating system of civilization.

References

Books and Reports:

- Latonero, M. (2018). *Governing Artificial Intelligence: Upholding Human Rights and Dignity*. Data & Society.
- Bostrom, N. (2014). *Superintelligence: Paths, Dangers, Strategies*. Oxford University Press.
- UNESCO (2021). *Recommendation on the Ethics of Artificial Intelligence*. https://unesdoc.unesco.org/ark:/48223/pf0000380455
- UN OHCHR (2021). *The Right to Privacy in the Digital Age*.

Academic Articles:

- Dignum, V. (2019). "Ethics in Artificial Intelligence: Introduction to the Special Issue." *Ethics and Information Technology*.

Mittelstadt, B., et al. (2016). “The Ethics of Algorithms: Mapping the Debate.” *Big Data & Society*.

Web and Project Resources:

Fairlearn: https://fairlearn.org
AI Fairness 360: https://aif360.mybluemix.net
SHAP: https://github.com/slundberg/shap
ID2020: https://id2020.org
OpenAI Constitution: https://openai.com/research/constitutional-ai

Organized by Type:

Books/Reports: Latonero, Bostrom, UNESCO, UN OHCHR
Articles: Dignum, Mittelstadt
Online Tools/Projects: Fairlearn, AIF360, SHAP, ID2020, OpenAI

Part V: Case Studies and Real-World Applications

Chapter 26. AI in Legal Systems: Protecting or Undermining Human Rights?

Introduction

The integration of artificial intelligence (AI) into legal systems represents one of the most consequential transformations of jurisprudence in the 21st century. With applications ranging from predictive policing to risk assessment tools and legal document analysis, AI promises efficiency, consistency, and broader access to justice. Yet it also raises serious concerns about fairness, accountability, discrimination, and due process. This chapter investigates whether AI in legal systems protects or undermines human rights, drawing from global case studies and philosophical insights.

---

1. AI in Legal Applications: A Global Overview

1.1 Predictive Policing in the United States and United Kingdom

Predictive policing algorithms such as PredPol were initially deployed to forecast crime hotspots based on historical arrest data. Intended to optimize patrol allocation, these systems quickly drew criticism for perpetuating racial bias and over-policing minority communities.

Case Example: In Los Angeles, the LAPD's use of PredPol led to disproportionate police presence in Black and Latino neighborhoods, exacerbating distrust and community tension. Following public backlash and academic critique, the program was discontinued in 2020.

1.2 Risk Assessment in Criminal Sentencing: COMPAS in the U.S.

The Correctional Offender Management Profiling for Alternative Sanctions (COMPAS) tool assesses recidivism risk. Judges often use its scores to make parole and sentencing decisions.

Problem: A ProPublica investigation in 2016 found that COMPAS significantly overestimated the risk of reoffending for Black defendants compared to white defendants. This raised alarm about transparency and fairness in algorithmic justice.

1.3 Legal Analytics Platforms: ROSS and LexisNexis

Legal AI platforms like ROSS Intelligence and LexisNexis utilize natural language processing (NLP) to parse statutes, case law, and briefs. These tools support lawyers by:

- Accelerating legal research.
- Predicting judicial behavior.
- Recommending strategies.

Benefit: Increases access to legal knowledge, especially for small firms and self-represented litigants.

1.4 China's "Smart Court" Initiative

China has introduced AI judges and blockchain-based courts in provinces like Hangzhou. AI tools handle small claims, contract disputes, and administrative hearings.

Controversy: While efficiency improved, concerns arise over government surveillance, lack of independent review, and erosion of the adversarial legal tradition.

---

2. The Impact of AI on the Fairness of Legal Systems

2.1 Bias and Discrimination Embedded in Data

AI systems trained on historical legal data inherit and magnify existing inequalities. Discriminatory policing, racist sentencing practices, and underrepresentation of marginalized groups all taint the data that fuels machine learning.

Consequences:

Black and brown defendants are flagged as high-risk.
Lower bail recommendations for privileged groups.
Skewed interpretation of laws affecting LGBTQ+ or disabled individuals.

2.2 Lack of Explainability and Due Process

AI models, especially deep learning algorithms, often function as "black boxes." This makes it difficult for judges, lawyers, and defendants to understand or challenge outputs.

Violation:

Right to a fair trial.
Right to an explanation of legal rulings.

Remedies:

Implementing explainable AI (XAI) tools.
Legal mandates require algorithmic transparency.

2.3 Algorithmic Infallibility vs. Human Judgment

AI systems may be perceived as objective and neutral, leading to overreliance. However, law requires nuance, empathy, and moral deliberation, capacities beyond current AI.

Case in Point: In the Netherlands' SyRI case, an AI system used to detect welfare fraud was struck down by courts for violating privacy rights and lacking human accountability.

2.4 Unequal Access to AI-Powered Legal Tools

High-cost AI services remain accessible mostly to elite law firms and corporations. This deepens existing disparities in legal outcomes.

Solution: Open-source legal AI initiatives and public legal tech funds to democratize access.

---

3. Balancing AI's Potential with the Protection of Rights

3.1 Embedding Ethical Guidelines into Legal AI Systems

Governments and tech firms must co-develop rights-based AI frameworks. Key principles:

Fairness and non-discrimination.
Transparency and accountability.
Right to contest algorithmic decisions.

Example: The European Commission's Ethics Guidelines for Trustworthy AI mandate human oversight and explainability in justice systems.

3.2 Hybrid Models of Decision-Making

AI should augment, not replace, judicial discretion. Hybrid systems combine:

Machine efficiency in processing vast amounts of data.
Human judgment for interpreting moral, social, and contextual nuance.

Design Goal: AI acts as advisor, not arbiter.

3.3 Participatory AI Governance

Include stakeholders, judges, lawyers, civil rights groups, and citizens in the design and evaluation of legal AI systems. Tools include:

Public audits.
Participatory oversight boards.
Algorithmic impact assessments.

3.4 Legal Precedent for Algorithmic Regulation

Case law is emerging:

Loomis v. Wisconsin (U.S.): Defendant challenged COMPAS scoring.

SyRI Case (Netherlands): AI risk profiling ruled unconstitutional.
G.D. v. France (ECHR): Surveillance algorithm found in breach of Article 8 (privacy).

These cases form the backbone for emerging jurisprudence on AI and rights.

Conclusion: Toward Rights-Respecting Legal AI

AI in legal systems can be both a guardian and a threat. Its potential to expand access to justice and eliminate human bias must be balanced with rigorous safeguards against rights violations.

A rights-based approach to legal AI demands:

Transparent, auditable systems.
Inclusive and fair training data.
Human-in-the-loop decision architectures.
Continuous legal oversight and philosophical reflection.

Only by embedding human dignity, fairness, and accountability into the very logic of legal AI systems can we ensure that justice in the algorithmic age serves all, not just the privileged, not just the efficient, but the fundamentally human.

References

Books and Reports:

O'Neil, C. (2016). *Weapons of Math Destruction*. Crown Publishing.
Eubanks, V. (2017). *Automating Inequality*. St. Martin's Press.
European Commission (2019). *Ethics Guidelines for Trustworthy AI*.
https://ec.europa.eu/futurium/en/ai-alliance-consultation

Academic Articles:

Pasquale, F. (2015). "The Black Box Society: The Secret Algorithms That Control Money and Information." Harvard University Press.
Binns, R. (2018). "Algorithmic Accountability and Transparency in Legal Contexts." *ACM FAT*.

Web and Legal Resources:

ProPublica on COMPAS:
https://www.propublica.org/article/machine-bias-risk-assessments-in-criminal-sentencing
Human Rights Watch on Predictive Policing: https://www.hrw.org/report/2019/10/02
Netherlands SyRI Ruling Summary: https://www.hiil.org/news/syri-case-explained/

European Court of Human Rights: https://hudoc.echr.coe.int/

Grouped by Type:

Books/Reports: O'Neil, Eubanks, European Commission
Articles: Pasquale, Binns
Web/Legal Sources: ProPublica, HRW, HiiL, ECHR

Chapter 27. Smart Contracts in Human Rights Advocacy

Introduction

The rise of decentralized technologies has ushered in a new era of possibilities for human rights advocacy. Among these, smart contracts, self-executing agreements coded on blockchain platforms, have emerged as tools for enhancing transparency, accountability, and autonomy in rights-related actions. By enabling immutable, verifiable, and conditional transactions, smart contracts can not only support advocacy but also institutionalize rights protections within digital infrastructures.

This chapter explores real-world examples of how smart contracts have been used in human rights advocacy, assesses their effectiveness, and examines lessons learned and emerging directions for deploying code as a mechanism of justice.

---

1. Examples of Smart Contracts in Human Rights Advocacy

1.1 Oxfam's UnBlocked Cash: Direct Aid via Blockchain

In Vanuatu, Oxfam piloted a humanitarian aid initiative using smart contracts and blockchain wallets to disburse direct cash assistance to disaster victims. Each beneficiary received a Near Field Communication (NFC) card linked to a smart contract wallet. Vendors were paid automatically upon confirmation of goods delivery.

Impact:

Eliminated bureaucratic delays.
Ensured transparent use of funds.
Reduced opportunities for fraud and corruption.

1.2 Amnesty International's Smart Donations Protocol

Amnesty explored a proof-of-concept in which donations are released to local field offices only after verified proof-of-work, such as publication of a report or receipt of interview confirmations with at-risk individuals. Smart contracts ensured conditionality and fund traceability.

Advocacy Value: Ensured donor trust and increased transparency in high-risk zones where financial oversight is challenging.

1.3 Giveth.io and Decentralized Charitable Giving

Giveth allows activists and donors to create decentralized communities around social causes. Smart contracts automatically distribute funds to project milestones upon fulfillment of pre-agreed criteria.

Example: In refugee education projects in Lebanon, Giveth's milestone-based contracts supported grassroots organizations without intermediaries.

Effectiveness:

Encouraged transparency.
Empowered local actors.
Lowered transaction fees compared to traditional NGOs.

1.4 Alice.si: Outcome-Based Contracts for Social Impact

Alice leverages Ethereum smart contracts to tie funding to verified social outcomes. For example, funds for a homelessness program in London were only disbursed upon verified reduction in rough sleeping numbers.

Advocacy Tool: Used to pressure public agencies to support data-driven social policies.

1.5 Aragon and Decentralized Human Rights Governance

Aragon enables the creation of decentralized organizations with embedded governance protocols. Human rights advocacy groups have used Aragon to:

Create decision-making frameworks.
Encode voting rights for marginalized groups.
Enforce transparency in funding and reporting.

Case Study: Indigenous groups in Brazil piloted an Aragon-based DAO to control land-use decisions, integrating environmental stewardship with collective rights protections.

---

2. Evaluating the Effectiveness of Smart Contracts in Advocacy

2.1 Transparency and Trust-Building

Smart contracts reduce opacity in fund allocation and execution by:

Recording all transactions on-chain.
Offering public access to funding flows.
Minimizing discretionary manipulation.

Result: Strengthened legitimacy of advocacy campaigns and improved donor retention.

2.2 Autonomy and Decentralized Action

Smart contracts facilitate self-governance:

Reduce dependence on central authorities.
Empower marginalized groups with direct control over resources.
Enable censorship-resistant funding mechanisms.

This was pivotal in regions where governments label human rights groups as hostile or foreign-funded entities.

2.3 Efficiency and Cost Reduction

Traditional rights advocacy often suffers from high operational costs, especially in conflict zones or during disasters. Smart contracts:

Automate fund release.
Lower remittance fees.
Reduce paperwork and compliance overhead.

Savings can be redirected toward advocacy programs and fieldwork.

2.4 Resilience to Censorship and Coercion

On censorship-resistant blockchains like Ethereum and IPFS:

Human rights documentation can be stored immutably.
Whistleblower protection protocols can trigger safe fund disbursement.
Activists can remain pseudonymous while securing legal funding.

Use Case: Human rights groups in Hong Kong and Iran used smart contracts to distribute encrypted journalism rewards.

---

3. Lessons Learned and Challenges Faced

3.1 Technical Barriers and Accessibility

Many beneficiaries in the Global South lack:

Internet access.
Crypto wallets or banking infrastructure.
Technical literacy to understand smart contract interfaces.

Solution Directions:

Develop mobile-first DApps with offline functionality.
Simplify user experience via visual contracts.
Partner with local NGOs to provide onboarding.

3.2 Legal Uncertainty and Regulatory Grey Zones

Smart contract legality varies widely:

In many jurisdictions, they are not recognized as enforceable contracts.
They may breach anti-money laundering or foreign agent laws.

Solution:

Engage in international legal harmonization (e.g., UNCITRAL guidelines).
Create compliant "legal wrapper" models to bridge blockchain with institutional law.

3.3 Ethics of Codification

Encoding human rights work into fixed protocols risks:

Oversimplifying complex, contextual advocacy efforts.
Ignoring power asymmetries in contract design.

Mitigation:

Involve ethicists and affected communities in design.
Use flexible, updateable governance layers in contracts.

3.4 Security and Exploit Risks

Vulnerabilities in smart contract code can be catastrophic:

The 2016 DAO hack cost over $50 million.
Exploits may redirect funds, expose identities, or disable operations.

Recommendations:

Require third-party code audits.
Implement kill switches and multi-signature security.
Create decentralized insurance funds for restitution.

---

4. Future Possibilities: Toward a New Paradigm of Digital Advocacy

4.1 Programmable Rights Enforcement

Imagine a future where:

Refugee rights are encoded into interoperable contracts across borders.
Labor rights are monitored via IoT sensors linked to wage triggers.
Climate reparation funds are governed by smart environmental metrics.

4.2 Hybrid Human–Smart Contract Systems

Human decision-making + Smart contract enforcement = Adaptive Advocacy.

Communities vote to approve interventions.
Code executes only upon consensus.
Ethics review boards oversee changes.

4.3 Global Human Rights Blockchains

Proposal: A UN-backed blockchain protocol to manage:

Refugee status.
Stateless digital identities.
Transnational complaint and adjudication systems.

Incentives via social impact tokens could drive participation from civil society and technologists.

4.4 RightsDAO Networks

RightsDAOs could:

Coordinate legal representation.
Manage decentralized campaigns.
Tokenize "advocacy rights" with voting mechanisms and proposal bounties.

Conclusion: From Advocacy to Autonomous Rights Systems

Smart contracts are no longer speculative tools, they are active instruments in human rights advocacy. While they cannot replace institutions or moral deliberation, they can hard-code fairness, conditionality, and transparency into the heart of social movements.

To unlock their full potential, future efforts must:

Prioritize ethics in code.
Localize usability.
Push for global interoperability and legal recognition.

In doing so, we may transition from advocating for rights to building autonomous systems that uphold them, independent of borders, bureaucracies, or bias.

References

Books and Reports:

Tapscott, D., & Tapscott, A. (2016). *Blockchain Revolution*. Penguin.
World Food Programme (2020). *UnBlocked Cash Project Evaluation Report*.
UNDP (2021). *Blockchain for Good: Applications in Humanitarian Aid*.

Academic Articles:

Reijers, W., et al. (2018). "Now the Code Runs Itself: On-Chain and Off-Chain Governance of Blockchain Technologies." *Philosophy & Technology*.
Fairfield, J. (2014). "Smart Contracts, Bitcoin Bots, and Consumer Protection." *Washington and Lee Law Review*.

Web and Case Studies:

Giveth.io: https://giveth.io
Alice.si: https://alice.si
Oxfam's UnBlocked Cash:
https://www.oxfam.org.au/what-we-do/infrastructure-justice/unblocked-cash/
Aragon: https://aragon.org
Amnesty International: https://www.amnesty.org

Grouped by Type:

Books and Reports: Tapscott & Tapscott, WFP, UNDP
Academic Articles: Reijers et al., Fairfield
Web Resources: Giveth, Alice, Oxfam, Aragon, Amnesty

Chapter 28. Decentralized Platforms for Human Rights Protection

Introduction

Human rights protection in the 21st century faces complex challenges: authoritarian surveillance, data exploitation, censorship, and the fragility of traditional institutions. In this volatile landscape, decentralized platforms powered by blockchain and artificial intelligence (AI) offer transformative potential. These systems do not rely on centralized oversight or bureaucratic structures, instead, they enable permissionless participation, algorithmic transparency, and immutable records, reshaping how rights are recorded, defended, and enforced.

This chapter examines the emergence of decentralized platforms for human rights protection. Through analysis of real-world projects and conceptual frameworks, it evaluates how blockchain and AI can enable novel forms of advocacy, resistance, and institutional support for vulnerable populations.

---

1. Overview of Platforms Designed to Protect Human Rights

1.1 Definitions and Scope

Decentralized platforms refer to digital systems operating on distributed networks, usually blockchain-based, that are governed through smart contracts, decentralized consensus mechanisms, or DAOs (Decentralized Autonomous Organizations). In the human rights domain, these platforms aim to:

- Record and verify violations.
- Protect digital identities.
- Disburse secure humanitarian aid.
- Safeguard data privacy.
- Enable decentralized governance for affected communities.

1.2 Core Characteristics

- **Immutability**: Records stored cannot be tampered with, ensuring historical accountability.
- **Censorship Resistance**: Data cannot be easily erased or suppressed.
- **Transparency**: Public audit trails reinforce institutional legitimacy.
- **Autonomy**: Rights enforcement mechanisms are encoded directly into the system.

---

2. The Role of Blockchain and AI in Rights Protection

2.1 Blockchain's Infrastructure Capabilities

Verification: Timestamping rights abuses or legal claims.
Tokenization: Incentivizing rights defenders through crypto-economics.
Smart Contracts: Automating rights-based conditions (e.g., fair wage release).
Distributed Storage: Platforms like IPFS ensure that human rights documents remain uncensorable.

2.2 AI's Functionality in Advocacy Ecosystems

Pattern Detection: Identifying systemic abuses through language analysis.
Predictive Monitoring: Anticipating conflict zones or crackdowns using satellite and social media data.
Anonymization Tools: AI-driven facial blurring and voice modulation for witnesses.
Translation and Access: Real-time NLP to make rights documentation accessible across languages.

---

3. Case Studies of Decentralized Human Rights Platforms

3.1 Uwazi by HURIDOCS (Hybrid Model)

Uwazi is a semi-decentralized, open-source platform designed for managing human rights data. NGOs use it to document violations, track trends, and build legal cases.

Features:

Structured metadata tagging.
Integration with blockchain timestamps.
API-driven interoperability.

Impact: Used by over 400 organizations worldwide, including in Rwanda, Cambodia, and Colombia.

3.2 OpenTimestamps and ProofMode

OpenTimestamps allows activists to embed a cryptographic timestamp in the Bitcoin blockchain, verifying when an image or document was created.

ProofMode, a mobile app by Guardian Project, captures metadata-rich media and allows users to anchor them in blockchain systems.

Use Cases:

Police brutality videos during the George Floyd protests.
Documentation of state repression in Myanmar and Belarus.

3.3 Kleros: Decentralized Justice Protocol

Kleros is a blockchain-based arbitration platform using juror pools to resolve disputes in DAOs, insurance claims, and rights-related violations.

Example: A whistleblower DAO used Kleros to arbitrate whether leaked internal documents merited bounties.

Benefits: Transparent and community-driven decisions. Encourages procedural fairness without national courts.

3.4 RightsLedger: IP and Human Rights Documentation

RightsLedger combines blockchain with AI-based scanning to secure authorship and ownership of human rights media. Used by documentary journalists and indigenous filmmakers.

Key Feature: Ensures journalists can monetize and license work safely in hostile environments.

3.5 Bitfari: Censorship-Resistant Civic Advertising

Bitfari uses smart contracts to enable civic-minded individuals to publish public-interest messages on digital billboards. Activists can fund messages anonymously via crypto wallets.

Region Focus: Venezuela, Iran, and Hong Kong.

---

4. Theoretical Implications and Systems Design

4.1 Distributed Legitimacy over Sovereign Authority

By shifting away from centralized governance, decentralized platforms challenge:

State monopoly over truth.
Hierarchical legal systems.
Centralized international courts.

They replace these with polycentric, pluralistic legitimacy.

4.2 Rights-First Protocol Design

Protocols designed with rights at the core prioritize:

Consent for data capture.
Community ownership.
Reverse onus for privacy breaches.

Design principles echo "code as law" philosophy but embed human dignity as the fundamental invariant.

4.3 Epistemic Justice and Inclusion

AI on decentralized platforms can amplify the voices of:

Stateless persons.
Women in conflict zones.
Rural LGBTQ+ communities.

Systems must avoid elite capture and design for marginalized knowledge production.

---

5. Challenges and Critiques

5.1 Governance Complexity

Without centralized enforcement:

Who resolves disputes?
How do platforms evolve?
What if AI systems exhibit bias?

Response: Governance DAOs, public audits, and algorithmic ombudspersons.

5.2 Surveillance Risks in Disguise

While decentralized, platforms may still:

Track user behavior.
Store metadata exploitable by adversaries.

Solution: Homomorphic encryption, zero-knowledge proofs, and AI privacy layers.

5.3 Techno-Colonialism

Platforms built in the Global North may:

Overlook local contexts.
Impose foreign values.
Skew funding priorities.

Remedy: Participatory design and redistribution of infrastructure control to local actors.

---

6. Future Directions: From Platforms to Movements

6.1 RightsDAOs for Transnational Justice

Communities could form DAOs to:

- Fund refugee legal services.
- Conduct decentralized trials for war crimes.
- Maintain digital memory archives for lost communities.

6.2 Smart Humanitarian Corridors

Smart contracts could manage:

- Entry/exit logistics for displaced persons.
- Real-time coordination between NGOs.
- Cryptographic identity verification without state-issued documents.

6.3 Autonomous Witness Networks

Drones + AI + blockchain = real-time, verified documentation of violations in war zones or closed borders.

6.4 Platform Cooperatives for Advocacy Media

Worker-owned, DAO-governed platforms could:

- Share rights media.
- Monetize journalism ethically.
- Prevent platform de-platforming.

Conclusion: Toward a Stateless Ethics Infrastructure

The convergence of decentralized technologies with human rights activism is one of the most exciting and essential developments in global justice. Decentralized platforms offer a vision of rights protection that is resilient, transparent, and global in scope.

While significant challenges remain, technical, legal, and ethical, the movement toward decentralized human rights protection is not a trend, but a shift in governance philosophy. It calls for a redesign of justice not as a service of the state, but as a distributed protocol for global dignity.

References

Books and Reports:

De Filippi, P., & Hassan, S. (2018). *Blockchain and the Law*. Harvard University Press.
World Economic Forum (2020). *The Future of Human Rights in Digital Spaces.*
HURIDOCS (2021). *Uwazi User Guide and Case Studies.*

Academic Articles:

Reijers, W., O'Brolcháin, F., & Haynes, P. (2016). "Governance in Blockchain Technologies & Social Contract Theories." *Ledger Journal.*
Milan, S., & Treré, E. (2019). "Big Data from the South." *Global Media and Communication.*

Web Resources and Case Studies:

Kleros: https://kleros.io
OpenTimestamps: https://opentimestamps.org
Bitfari: https://bitfari.com
RightsLedger: https://rightsledger.com
Guardian Project / ProofMode: https://guardianproject.info

Organized by Type:

Books/Reports: De Filippi & Hassan, WEF, HURIDOCS
Academic Articles: Reijers et al., Milan & Treré
Web and Case Studies: Kleros, OpenTimestamps, Bitfari, RightsLedger, Guardian Project

Chapter 29. AI, Decentralization, and the Right to Privacy

Introduction

Privacy has long been recognized as a cornerstone of individual freedom and human dignity. In an era dominated by artificial intelligence (AI) and decentralized technologies, the contours of privacy are rapidly being redefined. AI systems collect, infer, and act upon vast quantities of personal data, while decentralized infrastructures like blockchain challenge traditional notions of data control, permanence, and transparency. These technological paradigms simultaneously empower and imperil the right to privacy.

This chapter delves into the evolving intersection of AI, decentralization, and privacy. Through analysis of case studies, privacy-preserving technologies, and emerging governance strategies, we explore how innovation can coexist with the inviolable right to personal autonomy and confidentiality.

---

1. Case Studies of AI and Decentralized Systems Impacting Privacy

1.1 Clearview AI and Biometric Surveillance

Clearview AI scraped over three billion images from social media and public websites to build a powerful facial recognition system, widely used by law enforcement agencies. Despite lacking user consent, the company's model was built on publicly available data, blurring legal definitions of privacy.

Privacy Violation:

Infringement of data subject rights under GDPR.
Absence of opt-out or data deletion mechanisms.

Legal Outcome: Banned or fined in several jurisdictions, including Canada, the UK, and Australia.

1.2 Estonia's X-Road and Decentralized Identity Management

Estonia's e-governance system employs a decentralized architecture for accessing and managing digital identities across services.

Privacy-Supportive Features:

End-to-end encryption.
Transparent logs showing who accessed personal data.
Citizen-controlled identity credentials.

Lesson: Decentralization can empower individuals without sacrificing data privacy.

1.3 Aadhaar in India: A Centralized-Decentralized Hybrid

India's Aadhaar system issues a unique identity number to over 1.3 billion citizens, linking biometric and demographic data.

Privacy Concerns:

Mass data breaches.
Unauthorized tracking.
Coercive use in accessing public services.

Legal Response: The Indian Supreme Court ruled privacy a fundamental right in 2017, prompting regulatory reforms.

1.4 Monero and Zcash: Privacy-Preserving Cryptocurrencies

These decentralized systems use advanced cryptography (ring signatures, zero-knowledge proofs) to enable anonymous transactions.

Impact:

Protects users in authoritarian regimes.
Enables financial privacy for human rights activists.

Trade-offs:

Regulatory concern over money laundering.
Difficulty in audit and tax compliance.

1.5 Solid Project by Tim Berners-Lee

Solid reimagines the web by giving users control over their personal data in decentralized "pods." AI agents can access data only with explicit permission.

Example Use Case:

Health data is shared with doctors, but not insurers.
AI assistants trained on personal calendars without exposing metadata to third parties.

---

2. The Role of Privacy-Preserving Technologies

2.1 Differential Privacy

Used by Apple and the U.S. Census Bureau, differential privacy adds statistical noise to datasets, protecting individuals from re-identification.

Applications:

Training AI models without accessing raw data.
Safeguarding user data in federated learning.

2.2 Zero-Knowledge Proofs (ZKPs)

ZKPs allow users to prove knowledge of information (e.g., age verification) without revealing the underlying data.

Decentralized Uses:

Private DeFi transactions (e.g., zk-SNARKs).
Confidential voting in DAOs.

2.3 Federated Learning

A distributed machine learning technique where models are trained locally on devices and only updates, not raw data, are sent to the central model.

Example: Google's Gboard trains predictive text models without centralizing user messages.

2.4 Homomorphic Encryption

Enables computation on encrypted data without decrypting it, preserving confidentiality in AI processing.

Research Frontiers: Used in healthcare AI to analyze encrypted patient data while maintaining privacy compliance.

2.5 Decentralized Identity (DID) Systems

Platforms like Sovrin and uPort provide self-sovereign identity (SSI) frameworks where users control access to their digital credentials.

Benefit: Eliminates centralized data honeypots and gives users granular control over identity exposure.

---

3. Strategies for Balancing Innovation with Privacy Rights

3.1 Legal Harmonization and Human-Centric AI Laws

Global frameworks like the EU's GDPR and the AI Act attempt to regulate AI's impact on privacy.

Best Practices:

Data minimization.
Purpose limitation.
Explicit consent protocols.

3.2 Ethical AI Design Principles

Developers must integrate privacy into the AI lifecycle:

Privacy by Design (PbD).
Human-in-the-loop oversight.
Explainability for data processing decisions.

3.3 DAO-Based Privacy Governance

DAOs can govern access to sensitive data:

Voting on algorithmic updates.
Approving data-sharing terms.
Funding open-source privacy tools via smart contracts.

Example: Ocean Protocol DAO supports privacy-respecting data marketplaces for researchers.

3.4 Transparency and Accountability Mechanisms

Tools:

Audit trails via blockchain.
Third-party model audits.
Ethics impact statements.

Transparency bridges the trust gap between innovation and privacy, especially in health, law, and finance.

3.5 Privacy Education and Digital Literacy

Citizens must be empowered to:

Understand data rights.
Use encrypted apps.
Participate in privacy-centric governance.

Campaign Example: Mozilla Foundation's Data Detox Kit offers simple tools to assess and protect one's privacy.

Conclusion: Toward Algorithmic Dignity in a Decentralized World

The right to privacy is undergoing a profound transformation. AI and decentralized technologies offer both surveillance capitalism and liberatory potential. The path forward requires grounding innovation in principles of dignity, autonomy, and informed consent.

A privacy-respecting digital future demands:

Legal systems are agile enough to adapt to decentralization.
Privacy-preserving technologies have been made widely accessible.
Philosophical commitment to individual sovereignty over data.

When aligned properly, AI and decentralization can move us from privacy as a protective shield to privacy as a platform for agency and equity in the digital age.

References

Books and Reports:

Zuboff, S. (2019). *The Age of Surveillance Capitalism*. PublicAffairs.
European Commission (2021). *Proposal for a Regulation Laying Down Harmonized Rules on Artificial Intelligence (AI Act)*.
Mozilla Foundation. *Data Detox Kit*. https://foundation.mozilla.org/en/data-detention/

Academic Articles:

Dwork, C. (2006). "Differential Privacy." *ICALP*.
Narayanan, A. et al. (2016). "A Precautionary Approach to Big Data Privacy." *Harvard Journal of Law & Technology*.

Web Resources and Case Studies:

Clearview AI Case:
https://www.nytimes.com/2020/01/18/technology/clearview-privacy-facial-recognition.htm
l
Solid Project: https://solidproject.org
Monero: https://www.getmonero.org
Zcash: https://z.cash
Ocean Protocol: https://oceanprotocol.com

Organized by Type:

Books/Reports: Zuboff, EU AI Act, Mozilla
Articles: Dwork, Narayanan
Web and Projects: Clearview AI, Solid, Monero, Zcash, Ocean Protocol

Chapter 30. Human Rights in the Digital Age: A Comparative Analysis

Introduction

As the digital age transforms every facet of social life, governance, economy, healthcare, education, and civil engagement, the foundational principles of human rights are being tested and reshaped. The integration of AI and blockchain technologies into governance systems has created both promising opportunities for enhancing rights protections and new risks of abuse, surveillance, and systemic exclusion. Responses to these challenges vary widely across jurisdictions.

This chapter provides a comparative analysis of how different global regions are addressing human rights in the digital age. It draws on legal frameworks, technological infrastructures, and civil society movements to evaluate how AI and smart contracts are being used and misused in human rights contexts. The goal is to illuminate best practices, warning signs, and systemic insights for global governance of digital rights.

---

1. Europe: Privacy, Regulation, and Rights-Based AI

1.1 General Data Protection Regulation (GDPR)

Europe has established itself as a global leader in digital rights through the GDPR, which:

- Enshrines rights to data access, erasure, and portability.
- Requires explicit consent for data collection.
- Limits automated decision-making that impacts individuals.

Example: France's CNIL fined Google €50 million for lack of transparency and valid consent in ad personalization, a demonstration of enforcement strength.

1.2 AI Act: A Risk-Based Framework

The European Commission's proposed AI Act categorizes AI systems based on their risk to human rights and safety:

- Bans biometric surveillance in public spaces.
- Regulates high-risk systems (e.g., credit scoring, hiring algorithms).
- Encourages sandboxes for innovation under ethical oversight.

Role of Smart Contracts: While not directly regulated under the AI Act, smart contracts in DeFi and digital identity systems are increasingly scrutinized under GDPR compliance protocols.

Lessons: Europe emphasizes preventive governance, clear accountability lines, and fundamental rights as non-negotiable baselines.

---

2. United States: Fragmentation, Innovation, and Market-Centric Governance

2.1 Sectoral Regulation vs. Comprehensive Framework

The U.S. lacks a universal digital rights framework. Instead, it enforces sectoral laws:

HIPAA for healthcare data.
COPPA for children's online privacy.
FCRA for credit scoring.

Problem: Inconsistency across states and industries creates enforcement gaps.

2.2 AI and Surveillance Infrastructure

The U.S. has seen aggressive adoption of predictive policing, facial recognition, and AI in immigration controls (e.g., ICE's use of Palantir analytics).

Civil Society Pushback: Organizations like the ACLU and Electronic Frontier Foundation (EFF) have launched litigation and campaigns against biometric surveillance and algorithmic injustice.

2.3 Web3 and Smart Contract Ecosystems

Ethereum's development ecosystem is U.S.-centric, though smart contracts are not yet clearly regulated under U.S. contract law.

Case Study: Gitcoin Grants uses quadratic funding via smart contracts to support open-source digital rights tools.

Lessons: U.S. innovation leads technologically but lags in rights-centric governance.

---

3. China: Technological Authoritarianism and Digital Control

3.1 Social Credit and State Surveillance

China's AI-driven governance includes:

Facial recognition in public spaces.
Internet censorship algorithms.
A social credit system that scores citizen behavior.

Rights Concerns:

No legal recourse for algorithmic decisions.

Limited transparency and consent.
Crackdowns on digital dissent.

3.2 Blockchain for State Goals

Despite banning crypto trading, China promotes blockchain for:

Supply chain auditing.
Party recordkeeping.
Digital yuan experimentation.

Lessons: In China, digital technologies are leveraged to reinforce centralized control, not decentralize power or protect individual rights.

---

4. Latin America: Grassroots Innovation and Civil Rights Struggles

4.1 Digital Rights Movements in Brazil, Argentina, and Mexico

Civil society groups like Coding Rights and Derechos Digitales lead advocacy for:

Net neutrality.
Feminist cybersecurity.
Anti-surveillance legislation.

Example: Brazil's LGPD (General Data Protection Law) echoes GDPR but faces weak enforcement due to institutional gaps.

4.2 Blockchain for Social Good

Argentina's unstable economy has spurred crypto and smart contract use for:

Securing housing contracts.
Labor union payments.
Humanitarian aid distribution.

Case Study: Democracy Earth Foundation tested blockchain voting in exile communities.

Lessons: Digital rights progress is uneven, and grassroots tech solutions often compensate for weak institutional protections.

---

5. Africa: Leapfrogging and Digital Sovereignty

5.1 Mobile-First Ecosystems and Data Colonialism

Africa's tech growth is mobile-based. Platforms like M-Pesa have revolutionized access but raised concerns about data control by foreign corporations.

Example: Kenya's Huduma Namba (digital ID) faced legal suspension due to a lack of data protection legislation.

5.2 AI for Development and Bias Risks

Initiatives like AI4D aim to align AI development with African priorities. Yet, imported algorithms often misclassify ethnic features or languages.

Rights Initiative: Africa Digital Rights Hub promotes open-source datasets and ethical AI training.

5.3 Blockchain for Land Rights

Projects like Bitland in Ghana use blockchain to register land claims, aiming to prevent dispossession and enable women's property rights.

Lessons: Decentralized technologies offer empowerment if governed locally, ethically, and inclusively.

---

6. Middle East and North Africa (MENA): Between Reform and Repression

6.1 Surveillance and Internet Blackouts

AI-driven censorship tools are used to monitor dissent:

- Iran's "smart filtering" system blocks encrypted content.
- Egypt uses deep packet inspection on major telecoms.

6.2 Blockchain for Civil Registration

In Syria and Lebanon, blockchain is being explored for:

- Birth and marriage registration.
- Stateless refugee documentation.

Case Study: The UN's Building Blocks blockchain used in Jordan's Azraq refugee camp distributed food via iris scans and smart contract wallets.

Lessons: In authoritarian regimes, digital rights depend on international safeguards and humanitarian innovation.

---

7. Comparative Lessons and Design Principles

7.1 Rights Embedded by Design vs. Rights Enforced by Policy

Europe's approach shows how rights embedded in design (e.g., GDPR compliance) foster systemic safeguards. U.S. policy relies more on ex-post litigation.

7.2 Role of Civil Society and Decentralized Communities

Latin America and Africa illustrate how DAOs, crypto collectives, and local NGOs innovate in the absence of state protections.

7.3 Technology as Mirror and Multiplier of Governance Models

China and MENA demonstrate that AI and blockchain reflect existing governance structures, centralized systems produce centralized tech outcomes.

Conclusion: Toward a Polycentric Governance of Digital Rights

No single model perfectly protects digital human rights. Instead, lessons must be drawn from multiple contexts:

- From Europe: Ethical-by-design regulation.
- From Latin America: Grassroots adaptability.
- From Africa: Decentralized empowerment.
- From China: The danger of unregulated techno-authoritarianism.

In a future governed by AGI and smart contracts, digital human rights must be protected through overlapping norms, pluralistic oversight, and international collaboration. The path forward lies in building resilient, interoperable systems that balance technological sovereignty with universal dignity.

References

Books and Reports:

European Commission (2021). *Proposal for a Regulation on Artificial Intelligence (AI Act).*

World Economic Forum (2020). *Global Technology Governance Report.*

Democracy Earth Foundation. (2020). *Blockchain Democracy.*

Academic Articles:

De Filippi, P., & Hassan, S. (2018). "Blockchain Technology as a Regulatory Technology." *First Monday*.
Milan, S. (2021). "Techno-Resistance from the Global South." *Information, Communication & Society*.

Web Resources and Case Studies:

CNIL: https://www.cnil.fr
ACLU: https://www.aclu.org
Derechos Digitales: https://www.derechosdigitales.org
Solid Project: https://solidproject.org
UN Building Blocks: https://innovation.wfp.org/project/building-blocks

Grouped by Type:

Books/Reports: EC AI Act, WEF, Democracy Earth
Articles: De Filippi & Hassan, Milan
Web Resources: CNIL, ACLU, Derechos Digitales, Solid, WFP

Part VI: Ethical Dilemmas and Philosophical Challenges

Chapter 31. The Ethics of AI and Human Rights

Introduction

Artificial intelligence (AI) has become an inescapable feature of modern life, shaping decision-making processes from health care and finance to policing and welfare distribution. As it continues to evolve, AI challenges foundational ethical principles that underpin human rights: autonomy, fairness, dignity, consent, and accountability. The global race to innovate has often outpaced the frameworks necessary to ensure that such technologies serve humanity rather than undermine it.

This chapter explores the ethical dilemmas posed by AI, focusing on the responsibility of developers, the structural risks encoded into algorithms, and strategies for balancing innovation with the protection and promotion of human rights.

---

1. Ethical Dilemmas Posed by AI

1.1 Algorithmic Bias and Discrimination

AI systems are only as good as the data on which they are trained. When that data reflects historical injustices or social inequalities, the algorithms may perpetuate or even exacerbate discrimination.

Case Study: COMPAS, a risk-assessment algorithm used in the U.S. criminal justice system, was found to disproportionately flag Black defendants as high risk compared to white defendants with similar profiles.

Ethical Issue: Lack of fairness and due process, violation of equality before the law.

1.2 Lack of Transparency (Black Box Systems)

AI systems, particularly those using deep learning, often operate as "black boxes", their internal logic is opaque even to their developers.

Implications:

Denial of the right to explanation.
Erosion of trust in institutions.
Difficulty in assigning accountability.

1.3 Informed Consent in Data Use

AI applications frequently rely on personal data harvested without meaningful consent.

Example: The Cambridge Analytica scandal revealed how data from millions of Facebook users was used for political microtargeting without consent.

Ethical Violation: Breach of privacy, autonomy, and informed consent.

1.4 Surveillance and Chilling Effects

AI-driven surveillance systems, such as facial recognition and predictive policing, pose risks to freedom of assembly, expression, and privacy.

Example: China's use of facial recognition to monitor ethnic minorities like the Uyghurs.

Ethical Problem: Normalization of digital authoritarianism.

1.5 Delegation of Moral Decision-Making

AI is increasingly used in ethically charged scenarios: autonomous weapons, medical triage, and content moderation.

Dilemma: Should machines be allowed to make decisions that carry moral weight?

---

2. The Responsibility of AI Developers

2.1 Ethical Design Frameworks

Developers must adopt a proactive ethical stance:

Privacy by Design.
Fairness and Accountability principles.
Human-in-the-loop models.

Initiative: Google's AI Principles (2018) pledge not to develop AI for surveillance or weapons.

2.2 Corporate Social Responsibility (CSR)

Tech companies must align profit motives with social good.

Example: Microsoft's AI for Good program supports projects addressing societal challenges using AI, from disaster relief to refugee support.

2.3 Whistleblowing and Internal Dissent

Case: Timnit Gebru's ousting from Google after raising concerns about the ethics of large language models highlights the institutional resistance to accountability.

Conclusion: Ethics must be embedded in company culture, not relegated to public relations.

2.4 Developer Liability and Legal Duties

Should developers be legally accountable for the harms caused by their code?

Emerging Trends:

The EU's AI Liability Directive proposes strict liability for high-risk AI systems.
Calls for algorithmic certification akin to product safety standards.

---

3. Balancing Innovation with Ethical Considerations

3.1 The Precautionary Principle

Where AI risks are unknown or potentially catastrophic, systems should be tested rigorously before deployment.

Application: Moratoriums on facial recognition in public spaces in cities like San Francisco and Boston.

3.2 Ethics Review Boards and Auditing

Independent boards can evaluate AI projects for human rights impacts.

Example: Algorithmic Impact Assessments (AIAs) modeled after Environmental Impact Assessments (EIAs).

3.3 Participatory Design and Inclusive Governance

Marginalized communities must be involved in shaping the technologies that affect them.

Tool: Community data trusts where individuals collectively manage the use of their data.

3.4 Regulation and Standards Harmonization

Ethical AI must be supported by enforceable legal frameworks.

Examples:

OECD AI Principles.
UNESCO Recommendation on the Ethics of AI.
ISO/IEC JTC 1/SC 42 on AI standards.

3.5 AI Alignment with Human Rights Frameworks

AI should be explicitly mapped against:

The Universal Declaration of Human Rights.
The International Covenant on Civil and Political Rights.
The Convention on the Rights of the Child.

Practice: "Ethics-as-code" embedding norms directly into algorithms.

Conclusion: Toward Ethical AI as a Rights-Based System

The ethical dilemmas posed by AI are not merely technical; they are deeply philosophical and fundamentally political. As AI systems gain influence over critical aspects of human life, the need to foreground ethics in their development becomes non-negotiable. The responsibility lies not just with developers, but with society at large, including regulators, civil society, and users.

AI must be built upon and bound by human rights. It must be transparent, contestable, inclusive, and accountable. Only then can we ensure that intelligent machines serve the values of an intelligent humanity.

References

Books and Reports:

Bostrom, N. (2014). *Superintelligence: Paths, Dangers, Strategies*. Oxford University Press.
O'Neil, C. (2016). *Weapons of Math Destruction*. Crown Publishing.
European Commission (2022). *AI Liability Directive Proposal*.

Academic Articles:

Floridi, L., & Cowls, J. (2019). "A Unified Framework of Five Principles for AI in Society." *Harvard Data Science Review*.
Mittelstadt, B., et al. (2016). "The Ethics of Algorithms." *Big Data & Society*.

Web Resources and Case Studies:

Timnit Gebru's story: https://www.technologyreview.com/2020/12/04
Google AI Principles: https://ai.google/principles/
UNESCO AI Ethics: https://en.unesco.org/artificial-intelligence/ethics

Organized by Type:

Books/Reports: Bostrom, O'Neil, European Commission
Academic Articles: Floridi & Cowls, Mittelstadt et al.
Web Resources: MIT Tech Review, Google, UNESCO

Chapter 32. Philosophical Challenges in Decentralized Governance

Introduction

Decentralized governance promises a radical transformation in the way societies coordinate, govern, and distribute power. Built on the infrastructure of blockchain technologies and smart contracts, and increasingly influenced by artificial intelligence, decentralized systems aspire to be transparent, equitable, and resistant to corruption. However, beneath this technological promise lies a range of deep philosophical challenges.

This chapter examines the foundational philosophical dilemmas that arise in decentralized governance. It explores how concepts of authority, legitimacy, agency, justice, consent, and responsibility are reconfigured in decentralized systems. Drawing on examples from real-world DAOs (Decentralized Autonomous Organizations), smart contract-enabled legal systems, and crypto communities, we assess the contradictions and tensions that require resolution if decentralized governance is to serve human dignity and democratic ideals.

---

1. The Nature of Authority in Decentralized Systems

1.1 Authority Without Rulers?

Traditional governance is legitimized through institutions, parliaments, courts, and constitutions. Decentralized governance, by contrast, shifts authority to code, consensus protocols, and pseudonymous participation.

Philosophical Problem:

> Can authority exist without identifiable rulers?
> Does procedural legitimacy (e.g., token-based voting) suffice in the absence of moral leadership?

Case Study: The DAO (2016) on Ethereum operated without human oversight but suffered a catastrophic hack, raising questions about accountability in code-only systems.

1.2 The Tyranny of the Majority and Token Capitalism

In many DAOs, governance rights are distributed based on token holdings. This mirrors plutocracy rather than democracy.

Ethical Concern: Wealth confers disproportionate influence, undermining the egalitarian ethos of decentralization.

Debate: Should decentralized systems adopt one-person-one-vote models, or does capital-weighted governance reflect market efficiencies?

---

2. The Problem of Legitimacy and Consent

2.1 Smart Contracts and Informed Consent

Smart contracts are often considered "self-executing law," but most users do not understand the technical conditions encoded within them.

Philosophical Challenge:

Is consent valid when comprehension is limited?
Does participation in a DAO imply implicit consent to all smart contract outcomes?

2.2 The Absence of a Social Contract

Decentralized systems lack a unifying narrative or explicit contract defining the moral duties of members.

Reflection: Rousseau's social contract theory posits collective moral will as the basis for governance, absent in many crypto communities focused on individual sovereignty.

Alternative: Could smart contracts be reframed as moral contracts where participants agree to shared ethical principles before interacting with code?

---

3. The Challenge of Justice and Fairness

3.1 Distributive Justice and Power Law Dynamics

Cryptoeconomics often leads to power law distributions, and early adopters and developers accumulate vast influence and wealth.

Moral Tension: The "decentralized" rhetoric conceals a new elite.

Rawlsian Viewpoint: Would an individual behind the veil of ignorance choose to participate in a DAO with unregulated tokenomics?

3.2 Procedural vs. Substantive Justice

Decentralized governance emphasizes transparent procedures, votes, proposals, and consensus, but may neglect substantive justice.

Question: Does it matter if a process is fair, if the outcomes exacerbate inequality or harm the vulnerable?

Real-World Example: The MakerDAO community once voted to offboard undercollateralized borrowers during a market crash, legally valid, ethically questionable.

---

4. Agency and Responsibility in Autonomous Systems

4.1 Who is Responsible When No One is in Charge?

If a DAO makes a harmful decision, who is accountable?

The coders?
The voters?
The protocol itself?

Legal Parallel: Roman law recognizes "personhood" for corporations. Should DAOs be granted, or denied, legal personhood?

AI Intersection: What happens when AI agents propose or execute DAO actions without human oversight?

4.2 Ethical Implications of Automation

Delegating governance to automated agents poses risks:

Lack of empathy.
Inflexibility in crisis.
Drift from human-centered values.

Example: AI-curated content moderation on decentralized social networks may suppress marginalized voices due to biased training data.

---

5. Case Studies of Philosophical Dilemmas in Practice

5.1 ConstitutionDAO: Crowdfunded but Unconstitutional?

In 2021, ConstitutionDAO raised $47 million in crypto to bid for a copy of the U.S. Constitution. Contributors lacked formal voting rights on how the funds were used.

Issue: Radical inclusivity via funding; radical exclusion in governance, revealing a contradiction between democratic aspiration and technical execution.

5.2 Aragon DAO and Governance Deadlocks

Aragon was built to enable democratic DAO creation. However, conflicts between token holders and core developers over treasury control led to internal schisms.

Dilemma: When governance is decentralized, who mediates when mediation is needed?

5.3 Terra-LUNA Collapse and the Ethics of Exit

The collapse of the Terra stablecoin ecosystem prompted debates about exit rights, systemic risk, and whether project founders had ethical obligations to intervene.

Philosophical Tension: Libertarian design vs. paternalistic intervention in crises.

---

6. Addressing Challenges in Decentralized Governance

6.1 Embedding Philosophical Principles in Protocols

Proposals include:

Ethics modules for DAOs (e.g., impact scoring).
Shared preambles are akin to constitutional values.
Reputation-weighted voting balances merit and inclusion.

6.2 Creating Layered Governance

Borrowing from federalism, governance could operate in tiers:

Technical layer: code and automation.
Deliberative layer: human values and dispute resolution.
Legislative layer: evolving norms and community input.

6.3 Institutional Memory and Narrative

Philosophical coherence requires storytelling, memory, and shared purpose.

Practice: DAOs can archive “constitutional moments” and record rationale for key votes to preserve continuity.

Conclusion: Toward Philosophical Maturity in Decentralized Systems

Decentralization is not merely a technical feat, it is a philosophical endeavor. Its promise lies in reshaping authority, agency, and justice in ways that challenge inherited hierarchies. But its dangers mirror those it seeks to escape: opacity, exclusion, tyranny of the powerful.

For decentralized governance to mature, it must integrate philosophy into design, dialogue, and practice. Systems must not only distribute power but cultivate wisdom. They must encode ethics, not just incentives. They must remember that beneath every smart contract lies a social contract yet to be written.

References

Books and Reports:

Lessig, L. (2006). *Code and Other Laws of Cyberspace*. Basic Books.
Ostrom, E. (1990). *Governing the Commons*. Cambridge University Press.
Buterin, V. (2021). "The Most Important Scarce Resource is Legitimacy." *Vitalik.ca*.

Academic Articles:

Reijers, W., & Coeckelbergh, M. (2020). "The Blockchain Paradigm and Value-Sensitive Design." *Ethics and Information Technology*.
Christidis, K., & Devetsikiotis, M. (2016). "Blockchains and Smart Contracts." *IEEE Access*.

Web Resources and Case Studies:

ConstitutionDAO: https://www.constitutiondao.com
Aragon DAO: https://aragon.org
Terra-LUNA collapse analysis:
https://cointelegraph.com/news/the-untold-story-of-luna-collapse

Grouped by Type:

Books/Reports: Lessig, Ostrom, Buterin
Academic Articles: Reijers & Coeckelbergh, Christidis & Devetsikiotis
Web Resources: ConstitutionDAO, Aragon, Cointelegraph

Chapter 33. AI Bias and Human Rights

Introduction

Artificial intelligence (AI) systems are often framed as objective tools capable of enhancing decision-making, reducing inefficiencies, and increasing societal fairness. However, growing evidence shows that AI systems are far from neutral. Embedded within their design, training data, and deployment are systemic biases that can perpetuate or exacerbate existing social inequalities, disproportionately impacting marginalized populations. The consequences of such biases are not simply technical failures, they are violations of fundamental human rights.

This chapter explores the problem of bias in AI systems through the lens of human rights. It analyzes how biased algorithms infringe on principles of equality, dignity, non-discrimination, and justice. Through case studies, data analysis, and mitigation strategies, we examine how AI systems can be aligned with human rights to serve as tools of equity rather than oppression.

---

1. Understanding Bias in AI Systems

1.1 Sources of Bias

Bias in AI can originate from several sources:

Historical Data: Reflects past societal prejudices.
Labeling Bias: Inaccurate or biased human annotations.
Algorithmic Design: Optimization goals that ignore fairness.
Deployment Context: Misalignment between system design and real-world use.

Example: A hiring algorithm trained on resumes from predominantly male applicants may learn to downgrade indicators associated with women.

1.2 Types of Bias

Prejudicial Bias: Reinforces stereotypes (e.g., racial profiling).
Measurement Bias: Occurs when the data used is not representative of reality.
Algorithmic Bias: Emerges from the design or structure of the model itself.

1.3 Structural Bias vs. Technical Bias

Structural bias stems from societal inequalities encoded into data, while technical bias arises from model selection, feature engineering, or hyperparameters.

---

2. How AI Bias Impacts Human Rights

2.1 Right to Equality and Non-Discrimination

Case Study: The COMPAS algorithm used for pretrial risk assessments in the U.S. was found to be twice as likely to misclassify Black defendants as high-risk compared to white defendants.

Human Rights Violation:

- Discriminatory treatment in judicial processes.
- Violation of Article 7 of the Universal Declaration of Human Rights (UDHR).

2.2 Right to Work and Economic Rights

AI is used in automated hiring systems, credit scoring, and loan approvals.

Example: Amazon discontinued an internal recruiting tool that penalized resumes containing the word "women's."

Implications:

- Denial of economic opportunities.
- Infringement of Articles 23 and 25 of the UDHR.

2.3 Right to Privacy and Data Protection

Facial recognition systems often misidentify racial minorities and women.

Case Study: IBM, Amazon, and Microsoft paused facial recognition offerings to law enforcement after studies revealed racial inaccuracies.

Human Rights Concern:

- Mass surveillance.
- Chilling effect on freedom of movement and assembly.

2.4 Right to Health and Access to Services

AI-driven diagnostic tools trained on non-diverse datasets may underdiagnose minority patients.

Example: A 2019 study found that a widely used health algorithm underestimated the care needs of Black patients by 50% due to biased training data.

Impact:

- Disparate health outcomes.
- Violation of the right to health (Article 25, UDHR).

---

3. Case Studies of AI Bias in Practice

3.1 Gender Shades Project (Joy Buolamwini)

The project evaluated commercial facial recognition software and found:

99% accuracy for white men.
65% accuracy for Black women.

Conclusion: AI systems inherit and reproduce systemic racism and sexism.

3.2 Twitter Image Cropping Algorithm

Twitter's saliency algorithm cropped images disproportionately to show white faces or conventionally attractive features.

Outcome: After public outcry and internal audits, Twitter retired the algorithm.

3.3 Google Translate Gender Bias

Google Translate defaults to male pronouns for professions like "doctor" and female for "nurse."

Ethical Implications:

Reinforcement of gender stereotypes.

3.4 Predictive Policing in the Netherlands and the UK

Predictive policing tools were used to allocate resources based on historical crime data.

Problem:

Concentrated surveillance is already over-policing neighbourhoods.
Violated principles of fairness and presumption of innocence.

---

4. Strategies for Mitigating Bias in AI

4.1 Fairness Metrics and Auditing Tools

Demographic Parity
Equalized Odds
Calibration by Group

Tools: Aequitas, Fairlearn, IBM AI Fairness 360.

4.2 Inclusive and Representative Datasets

Balanced sampling.
Synthetic data generation to fill demographic gaps.

Example: Stanford's CheXpert dataset now includes annotated metadata for fairness analysis in medical imaging AI.

4.3 Algorithmic Impact Assessments (AIAs)

Modeled after Environmental Impact Assessments.
Includes stakeholder input, bias testing, and ethical review.

4.4 Human-in-the-Loop Systems

Retains human oversight in high-risk decisions.
Prevents blind automation.

Example: AI-assisted parole decisions reviewed by judges.

4.5 Legal and Regulatory Frameworks

The EU's AI Act mandates transparency and fairness.
U.S. Algorithmic Accountability Act (proposed).
Brazil's General Personal Data Protection Law (LGPD).

---

5. Philosophical and Ethical Reflections

5.1 Algorithmic Injustice and Epistemic Inequality

Data-driven systems risk erasing context and experience, prioritizing statistically dominant narratives over lived realities.

Reflection:

Whose data counts?
Who defines fairness?

5.2 Bias as a Reflection of Societal Failure

Argument: AI doesn't create bias, it reflects the world we've built.

Implication: Ethical AI requires systemic social change, not just technical fixes.

5.3 The Right to Contest and Explanation

Philosophical Principle:

Individuals must have the right to understand and challenge decisions that affect them. Grounded in procedural justice and democratic participation.

5.4 From Non-Discrimination to Equity

Ethical AI must go beyond formal equality to actively promote equitable outcomes.

Approach:

Context-aware fairness.
Compensatory mechanisms in algorithmic design.

Conclusion: Aligning AI with Human Rights Through Fairness by Design

AI bias is not a peripheral issue, it is central to the legitimacy and acceptability of algorithmic systems in society. The stakes are not merely technical but existential. Biased AI systems can entrench discrimination, exacerbate injustice, and erode trust in democratic institutions.

The challenge, therefore, is not just to remove bias but to construct systems that are affirmatively fair, inclusive, and accountable. Achieving this goal will require ethical foresight, regulatory innovation, community engagement, and interdisciplinary collaboration.

AI must be aligned with the values enshrined in human rights; only then can it truly serve as a tool for justice and equality in an increasingly automated world.

References

Books and Reports:

O'Neil, C. (2016). *Weapons of Math Destruction*. Crown Publishing.
United Nations Human Rights Office (2021). *The Right to Privacy in the Digital Age*.
European Commission (2021). *Proposal for a Regulation Laying Down Harmonized Rules on Artificial Intelligence (AI Act)*.

Academic Articles:

Buolamwini, J., & Gebru, T. (2018). "Gender Shades: Intersectional Accuracy Disparities in Commercial Gender Classification." *Proceedings of Machine Learning Research*.
Obermeyer, Z. et al. (2019). "Dissecting Racial Bias in an Algorithm Used to Manage the Health of Populations." *Science*.

Web Resources and Case Studies:

IBM AI Fairness 360: https://aif360.mybluemix.net
Joy Buolamwini's MIT Media Lab: https://www.media.mit.edu/people/joyab/
Google Translate gender bias:
https://www.wired.com/story/google-translate-gender-bias/
Twitter image cropping:
https://www.theverge.com/2021/5/19/twitter-image-cropping-algorithm-racial-bias

Grouped by Type:

Books/Reports: O'Neil, UN, EC AI Act
Academic Articles: Buolamwini & Gebru, Obermeyer et al.
Web Resources: IBM, MIT Media Lab, Wired, The Verge

Chapter 34. The Philosophical Debate Over AI Autonomy

Introduction

The question of whether artificial intelligence (AI) should have autonomy is one of the most pressing and complex debates in contemporary philosophy, ethics, and technology governance. As AI systems grow increasingly sophisticated, capable of making decisions without direct human input, our frameworks for understanding agency, responsibility, and moral value are being upended. The debate surrounding AI autonomy sits at the intersection of technical capacity and philosophical meaning: what does it mean for a machine to act autonomously, and should it be allowed to do so?

This chapter explores the multifaceted philosophical discussion on AI autonomy, examining its implications for human rights, governance, legal structures, and societal ethics. Through analysis of classical and modern theories of autonomy, case studies, and ethical perspectives, we navigate the contested terrain of AI self-determination.

---

1. Defining Autonomy in Human and Machine Contexts

1.1 Human Autonomy in Philosophy

Historically, autonomy has been regarded as a foundational element of moral and political philosophy:

- **Kantian View**: Autonomy is the capacity for rational self-legislation; it is the basis of moral agency.
- **Millian Liberalism**: Autonomy is the freedom to pursue one's conception of the good life, constrained only by the harm principle.

1.2 Machine Autonomy Defined

Autonomy in machines generally refers to the ability to:

- Perceive environmental inputs.
- Process and learn from data.
- Make and execute decisions independently of human control.

Key Distinction: Machine autonomy is functional, not moral. The autonomy of a Mars rover or a drone involves operational independence, not volitional freedom.

---

2. Arguments For and Against Granting AI Autonomy

2.1 Arguments in Favor

Efficiency and Scalability: Autonomous AI systems can act without human delays, improving logistics, healthcare, and safety systems.
Exploration and Adaptability: In environments hostile to human life (e.g., deep space), autonomy is necessary for survival and operation.
Learning Agents: Some advocate that AI with self-improving capacities should be treated with moral patience, especially if capable of forming preferences.

Philosopher Highlight: Thomas Metzinger has argued for "synthetic phenomenology" to explore the moral status of advanced AI with potentially consciousness-like architecture.

2.2 Arguments Against

Lack of Moral Agency: AI does not possess intention, empathy, or consciousness. It cannot be held morally accountable.
Risks to Human Rights: Autonomous systems could infringe on life, liberty, and due process (e.g., lethal autonomous weapons).
Democratic Legitimacy: Decisions made by machines lack deliberative accountability.

Example: Debate over autonomous vehicles' moral algorithms, should a car be permitted to choose which life to save in a crash?

---

3. Legal and Ethical Implications of AI Autonomy

3.1 Agency and Responsibility

Dilemma: If an autonomous AI causes harm, who is liable?

Developer?
Data provider?
System integrator?

EU Proposal: The Artificial Intelligence Liability Directive introduces the concept of shared accountability for high-risk systems.

3.2 Personhood for AI?

Some scholars propose "electronic personhood" for AI systems that operate with persistent identity and autonomy.

Criticism:

Distracts from human accountability.
Risks corporate obfuscation.

Alternative: Create legal categories for AI that do not imply moral equivalency but recognize systemic responsibility.

3.3 Human Rights Threats

Autonomous AI used in predictive policing or border control could:

Bypass judicial scrutiny.
Reinforce algorithmic discrimination.
Erode transparency.

---

4. Autonomy and Human Exceptionalism

4.1 Challenge to Human-Centric Ethics

If machines can act autonomously, does this erode the uniqueness of human moral status?

Example: Language models like GPT-4 can emulate empathy or moral reasoning, raising questions about the boundaries of mind and ethics.

4.2 Post-Human Philosophical Views

Posthumanist and transhumanist thinkers advocate for:

A continuum of intelligence.
Rights based on sentience, not species.

Risk: Slippery slope toward granting autonomy without safeguards.

4.3 Feminist and Relational Ethics

Position: Autonomy is not self-sufficiency but interdependence.

Insight: Focus should be on relationships and impact, how AI autonomy affects communities, power dynamics, and care structures.

---

5. Case Studies: Autonomy in Action

5.1 Autonomous Weapons (LAWS)

Lethal autonomous weapons systems (LAWS) can select and engage targets without human input.

Debate:

Violates international humanitarian law?
Delegates life-or-death decisions to non-sentient systems?

Global Position: 30+ countries call for a preemptive ban on LAWS.

5.2 Robo-Advisors and Financial Autonomy

AI manages billions in assets through automated investment strategies.

Issue: Do clients fully understand and consent to machine-driven financial decisions? What happens during market anomalies?

5.3 Autonomous Social Robots

Examples include AI caregivers in Japan and AI-powered customer service bots.

Ethical Question: If AI simulates care, does it undermine genuine human connection or enhance accessibility?

---

6. Paths Forward: Regulating AI Autonomy Ethically

6.1 Consent and Oversight Structures

Embed human-in-the-loop (HITL) systems.
Require explicit opt-in for critical applications.
Institutionalize algorithmic impact assessments.

6.2 Value-Aligned Autonomy

Train AI with value-sensitive design.
Encourage ethical AI benchmarks (e.g., IEEE's Ethically Aligned Design).

6.3 Constitutional Governance for AGI

Propose a social contract for AI societies.
Enshrine philosophical principles in smart contract code.

Model: Decentralized autonomous governments (DAGs) with human rights charters encoded.

Conclusion: Autonomy Must Serve Accountability

The question is not merely whether AI can be autonomous, but whether it should be. Autonomy without moral capacity creates an ethical vacuum. Human dignity requires that decision-making authority, especially in matters affecting rights, lives, and futures, be exercised with conscience, context, and care.

A responsible future lies in governance systems that constrain, contextualize, and calibrate AI autonomy. Autonomy must serve accountability, not escape it.

References

Books and Reports:

Bostrom, N. (2014). *Superintelligence: Paths, Dangers, Strategies*. Oxford University Press.
Metzinger, T. (2013). *The Ego Tunnel*. Basic Books.
IEEE. (2020). *Ethically Aligned Design: A Vision for Prioritizing Human Well-being with Autonomous and Intelligent Systems*.

Academic Articles:

Bryson, J. (2018). "Patiency is Not a Virtue: The Design of Intelligent Systems and Systems of Ethics." *Ethics and Information Technology*.
Danaher, J. (2016). "Robots, Law and the Retribution Gap." *Ethics and Information Technology*.

Web Resources and Case Studies:

EU AI Liability Directive: https://ec.europa.eu/info/publications/ai-liability-directive
Campaign to Stop Killer Robots: https://www.stopkillerrobots.org
IEEE Global Initiative: https://ethicsinaction.ieee.org

Grouped by Type:

Books/Reports: Bostrom, Metzinger, IEEE
Articles: Bryson, Danaher
Web Resources: EU Directive, Stop Killer Robots, IEEE Ethics

Chapter 35. Smart Contracts: Ethical and Legal Challenges

Introduction

Smart contracts are self-executing digital agreements, encoded with the terms of a transaction directly into code and deployed on blockchain platforms. Promising automation, trustlessness, and efficiency, they are already transforming industries ranging from finance and insurance to supply chains and governance. However, this transformation is not without its ethical and legal dilemmas.

As smart contracts move beyond niche use cases and into systems that affect human rights, justice, and governance, it becomes critical to assess their implications. This chapter investigates the ethical and legal challenges of smart contracts, drawing from real-world case studies, jurisprudence, and emerging design principles. It also offers strategies for building systems that align automated enforcement with human dignity and rights-based governance.

---

1. Understanding Smart Contracts and Their Promises

1.1 Definition and Functionality

Smart contracts are digital protocols that:

- Automatically enforce conditions (e.g., "if X, then Y").
- Operate on decentralized networks like Ethereum.
- They are immutable once deployed (unless specifically coded to be upgradeable).

1.2 Key Benefits Claimed

- Eliminates the need for intermediaries (e.g., lawyers, notaries).
- Increases transparency and auditability.
- Reduces transaction costs and delays.

Example: Decentralized Finance (DeFi) applications use smart contracts to automate lending, borrowing, and trading without banks.

---

2. Ethical Dilemmas in Smart Contract Implementation

2.1 Lack of Contextual Sensitivity

Unlike traditional contracts interpreted by judges, smart contracts lack the flexibility to consider:

- Ambiguity.
- Changing circumstances.

Moral or compassionate judgment.

Case Study: In 2021, a decentralized insurance smart contract refused payout after a technicality failed to meet code conditions, despite obvious human hardship.

2.2 Automation of Harmful or Unjust Terms

"Code is law" can empower unjust conditions if written without ethical safeguards.

Example: NFTs with perpetual royalty conditions that deprive secondary market buyers of fair use.

2.3 Moral Accountability and Intent

Who is ethically accountable for contracts that:

Trigger violent evictions?
Penalize delayed medical payments?

Ethical Gap: Without human oversight, moral responsibility becomes diffuse.

2.4 Discrimination by Algorithmic Design

Smart contracts that rely on external data (oracles) can inadvertently codify bias:

Loan approvals using biased credit scores.
Employment smart contracts, excluding certain demographics.

---

3. Legal Challenges and Jurisdictional Conflicts

3.1 Legal Recognition and Enforceability

Most jurisdictions do not yet fully recognize smart contracts as legal contracts.

Key Questions:

Can a smart contract be voided for duress, fraud, or unconscionability?
Are they enforceable in court?

3.2 Jurisdictional Ambiguity

Smart contracts are:

Borderless by design.
Subject to conflicting legal standards across jurisdictions.

Problem: Whose law governs a contract between pseudonymous parties from different continents?

3.3 Dispute Resolution Mechanisms

Without centralized intermediaries, who resolves?

- Bugs?
- Unexpected outcomes?
- Breaches?

Emerging Solutions:

- On-chain dispute resolution via DAOs (e.g., Kleros).
- Off-chain arbitration via hybrid systems.

3.4 Consumer Protection Gaps

Traditional consumer rights (e.g., refunds, withdrawal periods) are not hard-coded into most smart contracts.

Regulatory Risk: Absence of these protections could lead to enforcement by regulatory bodies.

---

4. Philosophical Reflections on Codifying Law

4.1 From Rule of Law to Rule by Code?

Smart contracts challenge foundational legal norms:

- Flexibility.
- Interpretation.
- Deliberative justice.

Concern: Fixed logic lacks empathy, equity, or responsiveness to context.

4.2 Consent and Comprehensibility

Most users do not understand smart contract code.

Question: Is consent meaningful if comprehension is missing?

Parallel: The GDPR emphasizes informed consent; should smart contracts be held to a similar standard?

4.3 Ethics of Immutability

Immutability prevents tampering but also prevents correction.

Moral Tension:

Can unjust outcomes be reversed?
Who decides when to intervene?

---

5. Case Studies in Ethical and Legal Contention

5.1 The DAO Hack (2016)

A vulnerability in a smart contract was exploited to drain $60 million worth of ETH.

Ethical Dilemma:

Is exploiting a contract bug theft or fair game?
The Ethereum community hard-forked the chain to reverse the hack, sparking a debate on governance and immutability.

5.2 Parity Wallet Freeze (2017)

A bug in a smart contract library led to $300 million being irreversibly locked.

Legal Question: Should developers be liable for irreversible financial harm?

5.3 Aave's Flash Loans and Attack Vectors

Flash loans were exploited to manipulate DeFi protocols and siphon funds.

Moral Query: Should systems be designed with foresight for malicious use, even if legal?

---

6. Principles for Ethical Smart Contract Design

6.1 Human-in-the-Loop Mechanisms

Incorporate failsafes or governance votes for high-impact decisions.
Allow human override in case of moral hazard.

6.2 Context-Aware Oracles

Design oracles that include socio-ethical indicators, not just price feeds.
Use multiple data sources to reduce manipulation risk.

6.3 Transparent Design and Open Audits

Open-source code.
Mandatory external audits.
User-friendly interfaces explaining logic.

6.4 Embedded Rights Protocols

Code rights to withdrawal, review, and remedy.
Inspired by digital rights management and consumer protection laws.

6.5 Adaptive Contracts

Modular contracts that can evolve via consensus.
Use of upgradeable proxies to address bugs or changing norms.

Conclusion: Toward Human-Centered Smart Legal Systems

Smart contracts offer powerful potential, but also amplify risks if unregulated, opaque, or ethically indifferent. The future of digital governance depends on embedding human values into code itself.

Contracts should not be merely functional, they should be moral instruments. They must integrate accountability, consent, context, and care. Rather than replacing legal systems, smart contracts must extend them into new domains with ethical rigor and clarity.

References

Books and Reports:

Werbach, K., & Cornell, N. (2017). “Contracts Ex Machina.” *Duke Law Journal.*
De Filippi, P., & Wright, A. (2018). *Blockchain and the Law: The Rule of Code*. Harvard University Press.
World Economic Forum (2020). *Redesigning Trust: Blockchain Deployment Toolkit.*

Academic Articles:

Raskin, M. (2017). “The Law and Legality of Smart Contracts.” *Georgetown Law Technology Review.*
Reijers, W., & Coeckelbergh, M. (2020). “Ethics of Blockchain.” *Philosophy & Technology.*

Web Resources and Case Studies:

Ethereum DAO Fork Summary: https://ethereum.org/en/history/#dao-fork
Kleros: https://kleros.io
Aave Docs: https://docs.aave.com
Parity Incident: https://paritytech.io/blog/security-alert.html

Grouped by Type:

Books/Reports: Werbach & Cornell, De Filippi & Wright, WEF
Articles: Raskin, Reijers & Coeckelbergh
Web Resources: Ethereum, Kleros, Aave, Parity

Part VII: Developing a Framework for Future Governance

Chapter 36. A New Social Contract for the AI Era

Introduction

Human history is punctuated by philosophical shifts that redefine our understanding of individual agency, collective responsibility, and the legitimate structure of governance. From Hobbes's Leviathan to Rousseau's general will and Rawls's veil of ignorance, the social contract has evolved to meet the changing dynamics of power, economy, and identity. Today, we stand at the threshold of another transformative epoch, the age of artificial intelligence.

The rise of artificial intelligence and autonomous systems necessitates a reevaluation of the social contract: that tacit agreement between citizens and the structures that govern them. In the AI era, where decisions can be made by non-human agents and entire infrastructures operate autonomously, the foundational premises of governance require radical rethinking. This chapter proposes the contours of a new social contract suited for AGI societies, balancing individual dignity and collective welfare while ensuring that artificial intelligence serves rather than supplants the human condition.

---

1. Revisiting the Classical Social Contract

1.1 The Historical Foundations

The classical social contract emerged in response to arbitrary rule, proposing that legitimate authority arises from the consent of the governed:

- **Hobbes** envisioned a contract to escape the anarchy of the state of nature.
- **Locke** emphasized natural rights and the government's role in protecting life, liberty, and property.
- **Rousseau** proposed the general will as an expression of collective sovereignty.
- **Rawls** updated the framework with a theory of justice as fairness, introducing the veil of ignorance as a tool for moral reasoning.

1.2 The Philosophical Shift Toward Rights and Reciprocity

Each iteration of the social contract dealt with new challenges, feudalism, capitalism, industrialization, and reoriented the contract to include:

- Civil liberties.
- Rule of law.
- Equal access to opportunity.

Limitations:

These frameworks assumed human actors, human reasoning, and human social relations.

---

2. Why a New Social Contract Is Necessary

2.1 AI as a Governance Actor

AI systems are increasingly:

Making decisions in healthcare, justice, finance, and security.
Influencing public discourse through recommendation algorithms.
Performing tasks that were once exclusive to human judgment.

Implication: The social contract must account for artificial agents embedded in governance.

2.2 Shifting Labor and Economic Power

Automation threatens:

Employment stability.
Income distribution.
Worker bargaining power.

Policy Need: Guaranteed basic income, lifelong education, and digital labor rights.

2.3 Surveillance and Autonomy

AI enables pervasive surveillance:

Biometric data harvesting.
Predictive profiling.
Emotion recognition.

Ethical Concern: How can the new contract ensure autonomy, privacy, and consent?

2.4 The Rise of Non-Human Stakeholders

Algorithms with persistent identity.
Autonomous vehicles and weapon systems.
Synthetic agents with decision-making capabilities.

Philosophical Question: Should the social contract extend to non-human intelligences, or remain anthropocentric?

---

3. Principles for a New AI-Era Social Contract

3.1 Human Dignity as the Anchor

AI governance must reaffirm:

The intrinsic worth of every human being.
The right to meaningfully participate in decisions affecting one's life.

3.2 Transparency and Interpretability

Black-box algorithms undermine informed consent.

Principle: All systems that affect rights must be auditable, explainable, and accountable.

3.3 Inclusion and Equity

AI systems must:

Reflect diverse populations.
Serve historically marginalized communities.

Frameworks: Equity-by-design, inclusive datasets, participatory design.

3.4 Distributed Governance

The new contract must:

Decentralized power.
Support participatory AI ethics boards.
Incorporate civil society into algorithmic oversight.

3.5 Dynamic Legal Adaptation

Law must evolve alongside technology.

Tools:

Algorithmic impact assessments.
Flexible regulatory sandboxes.
Precedent-aware machine-readable legislation.

---

4. Case Studies Informing the New Social Contract

4.1 Estonia's e-Governance Model

Offers digital identity, blockchain-based registries, and transparent decision tracking.
Respects data sovereignty and individual access control.

Takeaway: Technological sophistication can coexist with civic transparency.

4.2 Canada's Algorithmic Impact Assessment (AIA)

Requires departments to assess AI systems before deployment.
Publicly shares impact levels and mitigation steps.

Lesson: Proactive regulation rooted in democratic values.

4.3 Brazil's LGPD (General Data Protection Law)

Mandates fairness, transparency, and anti-discrimination in algorithmic processing.

Impact: Balances economic innovation with fundamental rights.

---

5. Components of the AI Social Contract

5.1 Rights Framework

Right to digital privacy and identity.
Right to non-discrimination by AI.
Right to explanation and redress.

5.2 Responsibilities of Stakeholders

Developers: Ensure fairness, transparency, and ethical coding.
Governments: Provide oversight, education, and legal structures.
Citizens: Stay informed and engage in digital civic participation.

5.3 Institutions for Governance

AI Ombudspersons.
Data Trusts.
Multi-stakeholder AI Councils.

5.4 Ethical Infrastructure

Interoperable ethical guidelines.
Algorithmic auditing standards.

Public AI literacy programs.

---

6. Balancing Individual Rights and Societal Needs

6.1 Trade-offs in Public Health and Safety

Example: Contact-tracing apps during pandemics.

Require consent-based frameworks.
Transparency on data usage and deletion.

6.2 Urban Planning and Smart Cities

Use of AI to optimize traffic and energy.
Must avoid overreach and ensure consent.

Solution: Citizen-controlled urban data platforms.

6.3 Justice and Predictive Policing

AI tools risk:

Racial profiling.
Reinforcing historical injustices.

Principle: Presumption of innocence must not be overridden by probability.

Conclusion: A Living Contract for Human-AI Symbiosis

The social contract must evolve from static legal texts to dynamic ethical ecosystems. As AI transforms our world, we must ensure that it is governed by principles that prioritize human dignity, agency, and justice.

This new social contract is not a rejection of historical wisdom, it is its renewal in the face of intelligent machines. By embedding rights into code, distributing power through protocols, and empowering citizens as co-creators of their futures, we can build societies that thrive on trust, transparency, and technology, all at once.

References

Books and Reports:

Rawls, J. (1971). *A Theory of Justice*. Harvard University Press.
Russell, S., & Norvig, P. (2020). *Artificial Intelligence: A Modern Approach*. Pearson.
World Economic Forum (2020). *AI Governance Frameworks.*

Academic Articles:

Yeung, K. (2018). "Algorithmic Regulation." *Oxford Journal of Legal Studies*.
Eubanks, V. (2017). *Automating Inequality*. St. Martin's Press.

Web Resources and Case Studies:

Estonian e-Governance: https://e-estonia.com
Canada's AIA:
https://www.canada.ca/en/government/system/digital-government/digital-government-innovations/responsible-use-ai.html
Brazil LGPD Summary:
https://www.dataguidance.com/notes/brazil-data-protection-overview

Grouped by Type:

Books/Reports: Rawls, Russell & Norvig, WEF
Academic Articles: Yeung, Eubanks
Web Resources: Estonia, Canada, Brazil

Chapter 37. Building Ethical AI Systems for Governance

Introduction

The integration of artificial intelligence (AI) into governance systems presents both an extraordinary opportunity and a profound risk. On one hand, AI has the potential to revolutionize public service delivery, optimize decision-making, and increase government responsiveness. On the other hand, if implemented without ethical safeguards, it could perpetuate inequalities, obscure accountability, and undermine trust in democratic institutions. As societies increasingly turn to algorithmic systems to manage complex governance challenges, the imperative to build ethical AI systems becomes paramount.

This chapter outlines the philosophical and practical foundations of ethical AI in governance. It defines principles, examines successful and cautionary case studies, and explores the indispensable role of philosophy in shaping AI systems that serve humanity rather than control it.

---

1. Defining Ethical AI in Governance

1.1 What Makes AI "Ethical"?

Ethical AI aligns technological function with moral values, ensuring that:

- Decisions are fair and transparent.
- Systems respect human rights.
- Outcomes can be contested and revised.

Key Traits of Ethical AI in Governance:

- Accountability
- Equity
- Transparency
- Inclusivity
- Privacy-by-design

1.2 Governance Contexts for AI Deployment

- Public benefits eligibility (e.g., unemployment, housing)
- Predictive policing and law enforcement
- Public health response systems
- Urban infrastructure and smart cities
- Immigration and border control

---

2. Core Principles for Ethical AI in Governance

2.1 Fairness and Non-Discrimination

AI must not reinforce historical injustices or create new forms of algorithmic bias.

Mechanism: Fairness audits and bias mitigation tools (e.g., IBM Fairness 360).

2.2 Transparency and Explainability

Citizens must be able to understand how decisions are made.

Techniques:

- Explainable AI (XAI)
- Interpretable models
- Public algorithmic registers

2.3 Accountability and Redress

There must be human responsibility behind machine decisions.

Policy Tools:

- AI ombudsman offices
- Right to appeal automated decisions
- Clear liability frameworks

2.4 Data Privacy and Security

Respect for personal data is critical to ethical legitimacy.

Standards: GDPR, zero-knowledge proofs, federated learning.

2.5 Participation and Deliberative Design

Communities must help shape the AI that governs them.

Methodologies:

- Participatory AI design workshops
- Stakeholder consultations
- Impact assessments

---

3. Case Studies: Ethical Successes and Failures

3.1 Estonia's e-Governance Ecosystem

Ethical Highlights:

Blockchain-secured data registry.
Transparency logs accessible to citizens.
Digital identity with opt-in mechanisms.

3.2 Canada's Algorithmic Impact Assessment (AIA)

Framework Includes:

Risk classification levels
Public disclosure
Monitoring and update protocols

3.3 The Dutch SyRI Case

The System Risk Indication (SyRI) tool used AI to detect welfare fraud.

Outcome: Ruled illegal by Dutch courts for violating privacy and discriminating against low-income neighborhoods.

3.4 China's Social Credit System

Concerns:

Lack of transparency
State surveillance and behavioral conformity

Lesson: Efficiency without ethics becomes coercion.

3.5 NYC Automated Decision Systems Task Force

Accomplishments:

Established guidelines for responsible AI.
Called for transparency in public sector algorithms.

Criticism: Lack of enforcement authority limited impact.

---

4. Philosophical Frameworks Guiding Ethical AI

4.1 Rawlsian Justice and AI Fairness

Focus on fairness as equity.
AI decisions must pass the "veil of ignorance" test.

4.2 Kantian Duty Ethics

Treat citizens not as data points, but as ends in themselves.

4.3 Virtue Ethics and Institutional Integrity

AI systems must reflect virtues such as prudence, compassion, and courage.

4.4 Communitarian Ethics

AI must consider the collective good, not just individual utility.
Emphasizes stakeholder and local value inclusion.

4.5 Feminist Ethics of Care

AI must be attentive to context, vulnerability, and interdependence.

---

5. Building and Sustaining Ethical AI Infrastructure

5.1 Ethical AI by Design

Embed ethics at every stage:

Problem framing
Data collection
Model selection
Deployment and monitoring

Practice: Ethics impact canvases and design sprints.

5.2 Governance Mechanisms

Algorithmic review boards.
Community AI ethics councils.
Independent technical audits.

5.3 Interdisciplinary Collaboration

Merge philosophy, law, data science, and civic design.
Ensure AI governance is both rigorous and inclusive.

5.4 Global Norms and Standards

Examples:

- OECD AI Principles
- UNESCO AI Ethics Guidelines
- European Commission High-Level Expert Group on AI

---

6. Ethical AI in Emerging Governance Challenges

6.1 Pandemic Response

AI was used for:

- Contact tracing
- Vaccine distribution
- Risk modeling

Challenge: Balancing urgency with consent and privacy.

6.2 Climate Governance

- AI for energy optimization, carbon tracking.
- Must include environmental ethics and intergenerational justice.

6.3 Refugee and Border Management

- Risk of discriminatory profiling and opaque decisions.

Need: Safeguards for vulnerable populations.

6.4 Smart Cities and Urban Management

- Surveillance vs. service provision.

Principle: Civic sovereignty over algorithmic architecture.

Conclusion: From Instrumental Tools to Ethical Allies

Building ethical AI for governance means moving beyond technical fixes. It requires embedding foundational values into the DNA of every system, ensuring that the use of intelligence, natural or artificial, honors the dignity, rights, and voices of all people. Philosophy must guide practice, and accountability must accompany innovation.

Governance is not merely what we build, but who we become through the systems we trust. In the AI era, ethics is not optional, it is the new infrastructure of freedom.

References

Books and Reports:

Rawls, J. (1971). *A Theory of Justice*. Harvard University Press.
European Commission. (2019). *Ethics Guidelines for Trustworthy AI*.
Eubanks, V. (2017). *Automating Inequality*. St. Martin's Press.

Academic Articles:

Yeung, K. (2018). "Algorithmic Regulation." *Oxford Journal of Legal Studies*.
Cowls, J., & Floridi, L. (2018). "Proposed AI Ethics Principles." *Nature Machine Intelligence*.

Web Resources and Case Studies:

Estonia e-Governance: https://e-estonia.com
Canada AIA:
https://www.canada.ca/en/government/system/digital-government/digital-government-innovations/responsible-use-ai.html
Dutch SyRI Case: https://www.humanrights.nl/publicaties/syri-judgment-summary
NYC ADS Task Force: https://www.nyc.gov/assets/adstaskforce

Grouped by Type:

Books/Reports: Rawls, EC Guidelines, Eubanks
Academic Articles: Yeung, Cowls & Floridi
Web Resources: Estonia, Canada, Netherlands, NYC

Chapter 38. Decentralized Governance Models for the Future

Introduction

As humanity transitions into the AI era, the question of governance becomes paramount. Traditional, centralized forms of governance, while historically effective, are increasingly out of sync with the decentralized, distributed, and autonomous nature of emerging technologies. A new paradigm is necessary: one that embraces decentralization not as a buzzword, but as a robust structural principle to enhance transparency, participation, adaptability, and resilience in governance.

This chapter explores the architecture of decentralized governance models for the future. It presents foundational design principles, examines real-world implementations, highlights philosophical and logistical challenges, and considers how AGI might participate in or even co-administer decentralized societies. By weaving together theory, practice, and speculation, we aim to articulate a viable vision for governance that is both technologically robust and philosophically grounded.

---

1. Designing Decentralized Governance Systems

1.1 Core Features of Decentralization

Decentralized governance redistributes authority across a network rather than concentrating it in a central node. Key characteristics include:

Node independence: No single point of failure or control.
Consensus mechanisms: Decisions arise through participatory, collective verification (e.g., proof-of-stake).
Programmable enforcement: Rules encoded into smart contracts.
Immutable record-keeping: Blockchain-based ledgers ensure accountability and transparency.

1.2 Architectural Models

DAO (Decentralized Autonomous Organization): Blockchain-governed entities where rules and transactions are encoded in smart contracts.
DAGs (Decentralized Autonomous Governments): An expansion of DAOs with legal, civic, and philosophical infrastructure.
Liquid Democracy: A hybrid where citizens vote directly or delegate their vote to proxies.
Holacracy: Non-hierarchical internal governance in organizations.

1.3 Design Goals

Resilience to corruption and censorship.
Inclusivity and universal access.
Protocol-level enforcement of rights and duties.
AI-assistive tools for moderation, auditing, and translation.

---

2. Case Studies: Decentralized Models in Practice

2.1 Bitcoin and Ethereum (Permissionless Financial Governance)

Impact: Introduced trustless coordination without intermediaries.
Challenges: Energy consumption, plutocratic tendencies (wealth concentration).

2.2 Gitcoin DAO (Public Goods Funding)

Funds open-source projects via community curation and quadratic funding.
Uses reputation metrics and decentralized dispute resolution.

2.3 Aragon (Decentralized Organization Tooling)

Provides modular tools to create DAOs with custom governance logic.
Includes on-chain voting, permissions, and treasury management.

2.4 Polkadot (Interoperable Multi-Chain Governance)

Integrates diverse blockchains under a shared governance protocol.
Uses on-chain referenda and rotating councils.

2.5 CityDAO (Decentralized Land Governance)

Tokenized land ownership and community voting for urban planning decisions.
Raising legal questions around property, zoning, and taxation.

---

3. Philosophical Foundations and Challenges

3.1 Legitimacy and Consent

Decentralized governance must still derive legitimacy from the governed.

Smart contracts alone cannot ensure meaningful consent.
Need for accessible user experience, education, and opt-in mechanisms.

3.2 Justice and Fairness

Rawlsian and communitarian concerns:

How do decentralized systems protect vulnerable minorities?
Can algorithms uphold the difference principle?

3.3 Authority Without Centralization

Can authority be procedural rather than positional?

Emphasis on protocol legitimacy rather than personal hierarchy.

Case Example: MetaCartel Ventures employs multi-sig voting and rotating councils to disperse power.

3.4 Ethics of Code as Law

Do smart contracts eliminate or obscure moral reasoning?

Contracts must reflect normative reasoning and be contestable.

3.5 Data Sovereignty and Identity

Decentralized ID systems (e.g., Sovrin) return data ownership to individuals.

Risks: fragmentation, loss of interoperability, surveillance through metadata.

---

4. Technological Enablers of Decentralized Governance

4.1 Blockchain and Distributed Ledgers

Immutable, transparent systems that reduce tampering and corruption.

4.2 Smart Contracts

Automate rule enforcement without intermediaries.

Can encode rights, responsibilities, and redress protocols.

4.3 AI Integration

Assists in dispute resolution, fraud detection, and consensus facilitation.
Risks: centralization of influence through dominant algorithms.

4.4 Decentralized Identity (DID)

Self-sovereign identity systems for voting, access, and credentials.

4.5 Interoperability Standards

Protocols like Cosmos IBC and W3C DID standards allow cross-chain governance and identity portability.

---

5. Practical Barriers to Adoption

5.1 Usability and Onboarding

Complex interfaces deter mainstream participation.

Solution: Human-centered design, multilingual interfaces, and AI-guided onboarding.

5.2 Scalability and Latency

Blockchains face congestion and throughput issues.

Approach: Layer 2 solutions, sharding, and rollups.

5.3 Regulatory Ambiguity

Governments struggle to classify or regulate DAOs.

Example: Wyoming's DAO LLC legislation attempts legal recognition.

5.4 Governance Capture and Token Oligarchy

Risk of power concentration in token whales.

Remedy: Quadratic voting, time-weighted staking, or soulbound reputation tokens.

5.5 Fragmentation of Norms and Cultures

Lack of shared civic identity in global DAOs.

Need: Localized governance modules and cultural mediators.

---

6. Vision for Decentralized Governance in AGI Societies

6.1 Co-Governance with AGI

AGIs as non-voting moderators, auditors, and translators.
Must operate under rights-compliant charters.

6.2 Smart Legal Systems

Hybrid systems integrating:

Smart contracts
Legal ontologies
Dispute mediation layers

6.3 Digital Constitutionalism

Protocol-encoded charters defining values, rights, and governance limits.

Mechanisms for amendment and judicial review.

6.4 Global and Local Interplay

Modular systems with nested governance:

Local DAOs for neighborhood decisions.
Regional federations.
Global digital commons.

6.5 Metrics of Democratic Health

Beyond participation rates:

Equity in deliberation
Distribution of influence
Adaptive governance capacity

Conclusion: Decentralization as a Moral and Structural Imperative

Decentralized governance is not merely a technical innovation; it is a moral response to concentrated power, opacity, and disconnection. In the AI era, where decision-making increasingly exceeds human scale, decentralization offers a means to retain dignity, autonomy, and collective agency. The challenge is to ensure these systems are inclusive, just, and adaptive.

To govern AGI societies ethically, we must build institutions that reflect the best of philosophical thought and technological design. The future will not be governed from the top down, but from the protocol up.

References

Books and Reports:

Ostrom, E. (1990). *Governing the Commons*. Cambridge University Press.
De Filippi, P., & Hassan, S. (2016). *Blockchain Technology as a Regulatory Technology.*
Buterin, V. (2021). *Quadratic Voting and the Future of Decentralized Governance.*

Academic Articles:

Allen, C., & Reijers, W. (2020). "Decentralised Governance in the Blockchain Era." *Philosophy & Technology.*
Atzori, M. (2017). "Blockchain Technology and Decentralized Governance." *Journal of Governance and Regulation.*

Web Resources and Case Studies:

Gitcoin: https://gitcoin.co
Aragon: https://aragon.org
CityDAO: https://www.citydao.io
Polkadot Governance: https://wiki.polkadot.network
Sovrin ID: https://sovrin.org

Grouped by Type:

Books/Reports: Ostrom, De Filippi & Hassan, Buterin
Articles: Allen & Reijers, Atzori
Web Resources: Gitcoin, Aragon, CityDAO, Polkadot, Sovrin

Chapter 39. Human Rights and AI: Towards a Global Ethical Framework

Introduction

As artificial intelligence (AI) becomes a transformative force across industries and borders, it increasingly influences not just economic systems but also human rights and civil liberties. From biometric surveillance to algorithmic justice, the reach of AI into our social fabric demands a unified ethical approach that transcends national boundaries. A global ethical framework for AI, rooted in universal human rights principles, is not merely aspirational; it is an urgent necessity.

This chapter outlines the conceptual foundation and institutional roadmap for such a framework. We examine international initiatives, explore the philosophical underpinnings of a rights-based approach to AI, and offer detailed case studies that illustrate both progress and pitfalls in aligning AI with the values of justice, dignity, and equality.

---

1. The Need for a Global Framework

1.1 The Global Reach of AI

AI systems developed in one country often operate globally.
Algorithms shape access to housing, employment, healthcare, and legal decisions.
Human rights violations in one jurisdiction can ripple across digital infrastructures.

1.2 Fragmented Governance and Ethical Gaps

Different nations regulate AI with conflicting priorities, economic growth vs. human dignity.
Ethical vacuum exploited by authoritarian regimes and monopolistic tech firms.

1.3 The Principle of Universalism

Human rights are not bound by geography.
A global ethical framework must mirror the transnational nature of both AI and rights.

---

2. Philosophical Foundations for a Rights-Based AI Framework

2.1 Dignity and Autonomy

AI must preserve individual dignity: the right to be treated as an end, not a means.
Autonomy implies informed consent, data self-sovereignty, and opt-out options.

2.2 Justice and Equity

Rawlsian "justice as fairness" requires that algorithmic decisions not disadvantage the least well-off.
Distributive justice in data use and AI impact is central to ethical governance.

2.3 Transparency and Accountability

Kantian duty ethics demand transparency in reasoning and traceability in actions.
AI must not obscure causality or responsibility.

2.4 Collective Rights and Cultural Pluralism

Indigenous data sovereignty and non-Western ethical traditions must inform global frameworks.
AI should respect both universal rights and culturally specific forms of community agency.

---

3. Institutional Actors in Global AI Ethics

3.1 UNESCO

Published the "Recommendation on the Ethics of Artificial Intelligence" (2021).
Emphasizes human oversight, environmental sustainability, and gender equality.

3.2 OECD

Offers AI Principles adopted by 42 countries.
Stresses robustness, safety, and human-centered values.

3.3 European Union

Proposed the AI Act to regulate high-risk AI systems.
Introduced algorithmic impact assessments, risk categories, and bans on certain uses.

3.4 United Nations Human Rights Council (UNHRC)

Advocates for digital rights and inclusion in global AI discourse.
Addresses AI's impact on freedom of speech, privacy, and discrimination.

3.5 African Union and CARICOM

Emphasize data colonialism and equitable development.
Develop AI charters rooted in regional developmental goals.

4. Case Studies: Global Efforts in Action

4.1 Canada's Algorithmic Impact Assessment (AIA)

Requires federal agencies to disclose AI use and mitigation strategies.
Includes public participation and impact scoring.

4.2 Brazil's General Personal Data Protection Law (LGPD)

Grants individuals control over their data and mandates transparency.
Balances innovation with fundamental rights.

4.3 Singapore's Model AI Governance Framework

Voluntary but detailed guidance for AI developers.
Focuses on explainability, risk-based controls, and internal audit trails.

4.4 India's Responsible AI Strategy

Includes a rights-based framework on fairness, privacy, and inclusion.
Tailors guidelines to development contexts, including digital literacy gaps.

4.5 China's Ethical Norms for AI

Emphasizes harmony, collective good, and social order.
Raises concerns about surveillance but offers a collectivist alternative.

---

5. Components of a Global AI Rights Framework

5.1 Universal Principles (Minimum Ethical Baseline)

Right to algorithmic transparency.
Right to opt out of automated decision-making.
Right to explanation and appeal.
Right to data privacy and control.
Right to non-discrimination by algorithms.

5.2 Binding and Non-Binding Instruments

Binding: Treaties, digital rights charters, intergovernmental conventions.
Non-Binding: Ethics guidelines, soft law, industry codes of conduct.

5.3 Enforcement Mechanisms

International AI Ethics Court or Ombudsperson.
Blockchain-based public registries of AI deployments.
Algorithmic audit certifications by independent bodies.

5.4 Dynamic and Adaptive Protocols

Regular updates through global consultations.
Participatory design through citizen juries, expert panels, and AGI advisory boards.

---

6. Challenges to Implementation

6.1 Geopolitical Tensions

Digital sovereignty conflicts between the U.S., EU, China, and India.
Disagreements over content moderation, surveillance, and AGI development.

6.2 Techno-Economic Inequality

Resource disparity between countries and within the Global South.
Risk of techno-colonialism through AI exports without rights protections.

6.3 Enforcement Limitations

Difficulty applying sanctions or fines across jurisdictions.
Need for legal interoperability and data standards.

6.4 Cultural Relativism vs. Rights Universalism

Tension between global rights and local moral traditions.
Risk of imposing Western liberalism under the guise of ethics.

---

7. The Role of AGI in Shaping Ethical Frameworks

7.1 AGI as Ethical Participant

AGIs can assist in drafting, auditing, and enforcing rights-compliant systems.
Must be designed with embedded normative reasoning.

7.2 AGI Rights and Responsibilities

The framework must explore when, if ever, AGI deserves legal and moral standing.
Must not displace or erode human rights.

7.3 Co-Governance Possibilities

Human-AGI ethics councils.
AI-driven consensus modeling and policy simulation.

Conclusion: Global AI Governance as the Moral Infrastructure of the 21st Century

Creating a unified ethical framework for AI anchored in human rights is not only technically possible, it is morally imperative. The governance of intelligent systems must be grounded in the values of transparency, justice, and human dignity. The emergence of AGI only heightens this need.

Global governance structures must evolve to meet the demands of an interconnected, algorithmically mediated society. From intergovernmental agreements to local implementation strategies, every actor in the AI ecosystem shares the responsibility to co-create a future in which intelligence serves, not supplants, human rights.

References

Books and Reports:

UNESCO (2021). *Recommendation on the Ethics of Artificial Intelligence.*
European Commission. (2021). *Proposal for an Artificial Intelligence Act.*
World Economic Forum (2020). *Responsible Limits on Facial Recognition.*

Academic Articles:

Cath, C. (2018). "Governing Artificial Intelligence: Ethical, Legal and Technical Opportunities and Challenges." *Philosophical Transactions of the Royal Society A.*
Nemitz, P. (2018). "Constitutional Democracy and Technology in the Age of Artificial Intelligence." *Philosophy & Technology.*

Web Resources and Case Studies:

Canada AIA:
https://www.canada.ca/en/government/system/digital-government/responsible-use-ai.html
Brazil LGPD Overview:
https://iapp.org/resources/article/brazilian-general-data-protection-law-lgpd-overview/
Singapore AI Ethics Model:
https://www.pdpc.gov.sg/Help-and-Resources/2020/01/Model-AI-Governance-Framework

India's AI Strategy: https://niti.gov.in/strategic-overview-responsible-ai
China's AI Ethics Code Summary: https://mp.weixin.qq.com/s/China-AI-ethics-code

Grouped by Type:

Books/Reports: UNESCO, EC AI Act, WEF Facial Recognition Guide
Articles: Cath, Nemitz
Web Resources: Canada, Brazil, Singapore, India, China

Chapter 40. Smart Contracts in Global Governance

Introduction

Global governance, characterized by cross-border regulation, international treaties, and multi-stakeholder coordination, has traditionally depended on bureaucratic institutions and fragile consensus. However, with the rise of digital infrastructure and programmable technologies, the concept of governance is undergoing a radical transformation. Smart contracts, self-executing code deployed on decentralized networks, present a new paradigm for transparent, enforceable, and trust-minimized governance mechanisms that transcend jurisdictional boundaries.

This chapter explores how smart contracts can redefine the mechanics of global governance. We trace their theoretical promise, analyze real-world case studies, identify key challenges, and outline opportunities for embedding rights-respecting, transparent, and participatory frameworks in the governance of global public goods, treaties, aid flows, climate action, digital identity, and beyond.

---

1. Understanding Smart Contracts in Governance Contexts

1.1 Definition and Functionality

A smart contract is a piece of software stored on a blockchain that executes automatically when conditions are met.
Combines legal enforceability with algorithmic precision.
Removes intermediaries, ensures traceability, and minimizes corruption.

1.2 Relevance to Global Governance

Borderless enforcement through global blockchain networks.
Immutable record-keeping of multilateral agreements.
Codification of consensus into executable logic.

---

2. Use Cases in Global Governance

2.1 International Aid and Development

Example: The World Food Programme's Building Blocks project uses blockchain for food voucher disbursement.
Potential: Smart contracts could automate aid delivery based on crisis thresholds, weather events, or health data triggers.

2.2 Cross-Border Trade Agreements

Smart contracts for customs clearance, tariffs, and verification of origin.
Pilot: TradeLens by Maersk and IBM explored blockchain in global supply chains.

2.3 Climate Agreements and Carbon Markets

Tokenized carbon credits with rules encoded in smart contracts.
Example: Toucan Protocol and KlimaDAO automate carbon offset management.
Potential: Enforce emissions caps with on-chain penalties for non-compliance.

2.4 Global Health Governance

Real-time pandemic response logistics (e.g., vaccine delivery, medical supply audits).
Smart contracts ensure equitable distribution and transparent procurement.

2.5 Digital Identity and Migration

Decentralized ID for refugees using verifiable credentials.
Example: ID2020 alliance pilot programs.
Use smart contracts for access to housing, education, or resettlement milestones.

2.6 Human Rights Protection

Encode obligations into international treaties.
Example: Smart contracts could automate sanctions for treaty violations or fund whistleblower protections.

---

3. Case Studies of Smart Contract-Based Governance Models

3.1 Aragon (Modular DAO Infrastructure)

Enables the creation of decentralized governance entities with programmable rules.
Used by advocacy groups, cooperatives, and global open-source projects.

3.2 Kleros (Decentralized Justice)

Blockchain-based dispute resolution system using crowdsourced jurors.
Offers smart contract-enforced verdicts in digital contract disputes.

3.3 Gitcoin (Public Goods Funding)

Uses quadratic funding to allocate grants based on collective input.
Smart contracts manage funds transparently and autonomously.

3.4 Optimism RetroPGF (Retroactive Public Goods Funding)

Distributes funding retroactively based on impact assessments.
Smart contracts are used to administer grants and lock funds until community consensus.

3.5 SmartAid (Blockchain for Disaster Relief)

Combines geospatial triggers with pre-approved funding releases.
Piloted by NGOs for drought response in East Africa.

---

4. Advantages of Smart Contracts in Global Governance

4.1 Transparency and Trust

Immutable ledgers reduce opacity in decision-making.
Open-source contracts allow for public audit.

4.2 Programmable Equity

Conditional logic ensures fair distribution based on criteria (e.g., population size, GDP, historical emissions).
Inclusion of minorities and stakeholders through decentralized voting.

4.3 Cost Efficiency and Speed

Reduces administrative overhead.
Instant enforcement without intermediaries or delays.

4.4 Interoperability

Smart contracts can be designed for cross-platform and cross-jurisdiction execution.

---

5. Challenges and Ethical Considerations

5.1 Code vs. Law

Legal ambiguity of code-based agreements.
Risk: “Code is law” may sideline due process and moral nuance.
Need: Hybrid legal-smart contract frameworks.

5.2 Inclusivity and Accessibility

Risks of digital exclusion for under-resourced or marginalized populations.

Requirement for multilingual, mobile-accessible, and literate-friendly interfaces.

5.3 Governance Capture and Attack Surfaces

51% attacks, oracle manipulation, or plutocratic decision-making in DAOs.
Needs: Reputation-weighted voting, fraud-resistant oracles, stakeholder diversity.

5.4 Ethical Blind Spots

Automated enforcement may ignore context or cause unintended harm.
Example: Smart eviction triggers without human appeal pathways.

5.5 Jurisdictional Conflicts

Global enforceability of smart contracts remains contested in courts.
Demand for cross-border legal harmonization.

---

6. Future Directions and Integration Pathways

6.1 Hybrid Models: Smart Contracts + Legal Contracts

Smart clauses are embedded in traditional agreements.
Legal fallback mechanisms ensure fairness and recourse.

6.2 Meta-Governance Layers

Protocols to govern the governance mechanisms.
Voting on upgrade paths, emergency overrides, and contract amendments.

6.3 Human Rights Encoding Templates

Standardized smart contract templates encoding rights obligations.
Collaborations with NGOs and legal scholars.

6.4 Institutional Adoption and Policy Support

Intergovernmental platforms exploring blockchain for aid and governance (e.g., UNDP, IMF).
Need for ethics boards and policy sandboxes.

6.5 AGI Participation in Smart Contract Ecosystems

AGI-assisted auditing, dispute resolution, and contract drafting.
Require bounded autonomy and normative embedding.

Conclusion: Toward a Programmable Planetary Compact

Smart contracts offer a profound opportunity to reinvent the foundations of global governance. By making agreements self-enforcing, transparent, and incorruptible, they reduce reliance on trust and bureaucracy. But without ethical foresight, legal safeguards, and inclusive access, they risk entrenching new forms of technocratic control.

The future lies in harmonizing code with conscience, embedding the values of justice, equity, and participation into the protocols that will increasingly govern human societies and AGI ecosystems alike. A planetary compact rooted in programmable integrity may well be our best chance at scalable peace, accountability, and cooperation in the algorithmic age.

References

Books and Reports:

Tapscott, D., & Tapscott, A. (2018). *Blockchain Revolution*. Penguin.
De Filippi, P., & Wright, A. (2018). *Blockchain and the Law*. Harvard University Press.
United Nations Development Programme (2022). *Blockchain for Development*.

Academic Articles:

Reijers, W., et al. (2018). "Now the Code Runs Itself: On-Chain and Off-Chain Governance of Blockchain Technologies." *Philosophy & Technology*.
Allen, C. (2019). "Smart Contracts and the Myth of Code as Law." *Stanford Tech Law Review*.

Web Resources and Case Studies:

Gitcoin: https://gitcoin.co
Aragon: https://aragon.org
Kleros: https://kleros.io
KlimaDAO: https://www.klimadao.finance
ID2020: https://www.id2020.org

Grouped by Type:

Books/Reports: Tapscott, De Filippi & Wright, UNDP
Articles: Reijers et al., Allen
Web Resources: Gitcoin, Aragon, Kleros, KlimaDAO, ID2020

Part VIII: Conclusion and Future Perspectives

Chapter 41. The Role of Philosophy in Shaping the Future

Introduction

In an era defined by algorithms, automation, and artificial general intelligence (AGI), philosophy is not merely an academic pursuit; it is a civilizational necessity. As governance structures evolve under the weight of technological acceleration, the questions once confined to ethics seminars and political theory colloquia now press urgently upon technologists, policymakers, and global citizens alike. This chapter argues that philosophy, specifically its frameworks for ethics, justice, truth, and the good life, must guide the governance of AGI societies.

We will explore how philosophical traditions provide the conceptual scaffolding for the rights and responsibilities emerging in digital ecosystems, examine the philosophical foundations of global human rights in the context of AGI, and propose future directions for philosophical inquiry that can meaningfully shape governance models at a planetary scale.

---

1. Why Philosophy Matters in the Age of AGI

1.1 Navigating Complexity and Uncertainty

The rise of AGI introduces uncertainties that outpace scientific prediction or legal precedent.
Philosophy provides frameworks for reasoning under uncertainty, e.g., Rawls' veil of ignorance, Kantian imperatives, and consequentialist calculus.

1.2 Ethical Foundations vs. Technical Fixes

Technological systems are not morally neutral; they embody values.
Ethical reflection is required to distinguish between mere functionality and moral acceptability.

1.3 Preventing Value Drift and Existential Risk

Without ethical anchoring, AGI could optimize for goals misaligned with human well-being.
Philosophy clarifies what constitutes well-being, justice, and dignity across diverse contexts.

---

2. Philosophical Contributions to Governance Theory

2.1 The Social Contract Tradition

Hobbes, Locke, Rousseau, and Rawls provide paradigms for understanding authority and consent.
A new digital social contract is needed to address algorithmic power and networked sovereignty.

2.2 Virtue Ethics and Moral Character

In decentralized systems, collective virtue (e.g., prudence, integrity) must be cultivated.
Governance design can incentivize or degrade moral development.

2.3 Justice Theories

Rawls: Principles of distributive justice must be encoded into AGI resource allocation protocols.
Sen: Human capabilities, not just utility, must be enhanced by AI tools.

2.4 Existentialism and Autonomy

Kierkegaard and Sartre stress self-authorship and moral responsibility.
These themes are vital in discussions of consent, data rights, and digital personhood.

2.5 Post-Structuralism and Epistemic Justice

Foucault: Power-knowledge dynamics are embedded in algorithmic decisions.
Spivak and Fricker: Ethical governance must address the silencing of marginalized voices in AI design.

---

3. Philosophy's Impact on Human Rights in the Digital Age

3.1 From Natural Rights to Digital Rights

Locke and Kant grounded human rights in reason and dignity.
These principles now extend to digital privacy, autonomy, and identity.

3.2 Universalism vs. Cultural Pluralism

Global rights frameworks must integrate non-Western ethical systems.
Ubuntu, Confucianism, Islamic jurisprudence, and Indigenous philosophies can enrich AI ethics.

3.3 Human Dignity as a Design Principle

Dignity requires that individuals are never mere data points or optimization targets.
Design must preserve narrative agency and human subjectivity.

---

4. Future Directions for Philosophical Inquiry in AGI Societies

4.1 Philosophy of Mind and Machine Consciousness

Can machines experience qualia or moral emotions?
Implications for AGI rights and the moral boundaries of personhood.

4.2 Ethics of Co-Governance

What does it mean for AGI to be a political actor?
Normative theories of representation, stewardship, and consent must be developed.

4.3 The Ontology of Digital Beings

New metaphysical questions arise: Are AGIs agents, tools, or partners?
Impacts laws of liability, identity, and transhuman ethics.

4.4 Epistemology of Distributed Intelligence

How do we verify truth in a world where knowledge is co-produced by humans and machines?
Requires philosophical rethinking of authority, credibility, and intellectual autonomy.

4.5 Philosophy of History and Progress

Teleological visions of progress, technological, moral, or spiritual, must be critically examined.
History teaches that ethical collapse often accompanies unchecked innovation.

---

5. Case Studies: Philosophy in Practice

5.1 The EU AI Act's Ethical Risk Categories

Based on precautionary and deontological reasoning.
Prioritizes human oversight, rights audits, and transparency.

5.2 Indigenous Data Sovereignty Frameworks

Draw on relational ethics and collective stewardship principles.
Challenge liberal individualist assumptions.

5.3 Decentralized Justice (Kleros)

Inspired by democratic theory and Aristotle's jury selection.

Uses randomness, deliberation, and tokenized appeals.

5.4 AI Impact Assessments and Algorithmic Ethics Boards

Require multi-stakeholder input based on ethical pluralism.
Promote reflective equilibrium between utility, rights, and cultural norms.

---

6. Philosophical Literacy as a Civic Imperative

6.1 Educating for Ethical Participation

Philosophy must be integrated into digital literacy and civic education.
Enables critical engagement with algorithmic systems and governance platforms.

6.2 Citizen-Philosophers of the Future

In a world shaped by AGI, all citizens are co-architects of ethical systems.
Must cultivate the virtues of humility, curiosity, and deliberative reasoning.

6.3 Philosophy as Reflexive Infrastructure

Just as cities have roads and water systems, societies need philosophical infrastructure: forums, councils, public ethics labs.

Conclusion: Reclaiming the Future Through Thought

Philosophy is not an accessory to technical progress; it is its conscience, compass, and crucible. In the coming decades, as AGI reshapes what it means to work, to govern, and to be human, philosophy will be the space where our collective values are tested and reborn.

Future governance models must not only be technologically advanced but ethically luminous. They must encode not only logic but wisdom. The role of philosophy, then, is not to resist the future, but to ensure that its arrival is worthy of us. To shape the future is to ask better questions, and philosophy is where those questions begin.

References

Books and Reports:

Rawls, J. (1971). *A Theory of Justice*. Harvard University Press.
Sen, A. (1999). *Development as Freedom*. Oxford University Press.

Nussbaum, M. (2011). *Creating Capabilities*. Harvard University Press.
Floridi, L. (2019). *The Logic of Information*. Oxford University Press.

Academic Articles:

Fricker, M. (2007). "Epistemic Injustice." *Oxford Scholarship Online*.
Bostrom, N. (2003). "Ethical Issues in Advanced Artificial Intelligence." *Cognitive, Emotive and Ethical Aspects of Decision Making in Humans and in Artificial Intelligence*.
Spivak, G. C. (1988). "Can the Subaltern Speak?" *Marxism and the Interpretation of Culture*.

Web Resources and Frameworks:

EU AI Act:
https://digital-strategy.ec.europa.eu/en/policies/european-approach-artificial-intelligence
Kleros: https://kleros.io
Indigenous Data Sovereignty: https://www.gida-global.org

Grouped by Type:

Books/Reports: Rawls, Sen, Nussbaum, Floridi
Articles: Fricker, Bostrom, Spivak
Web Resources: EU AI Act, Kleros, GIDA

Chapter 42. AI and the Future of Human Rights

Introduction

The convergence of artificial intelligence (AI) with human systems of law, governance, and culture is reshaping the very landscape of human rights. What began as digital tools for administrative optimization has evolved into a force that affects how we access healthcare, education, justice, employment, and civic participation. As AI continues its trajectory toward artificial general intelligence (AGI), questions about its role in promoting or undermining human rights become not just relevant but urgent.

This chapter explores predictive scenarios and analytical frameworks that envision how AI will influence the future of human rights. We assess how innovation must be balanced with protections, how governance mechanisms can shape ethical AI systems, and how rights must evolve to reflect the realities of a machine-augmented society.

---

1. Predicting AI's Role in Human Rights

1.1 Positive Potential

AI-enhanced systems can optimize public health logistics, improve access to justice through legal aid bots, and democratize education via adaptive learning platforms. Predictive analytics can anticipate humanitarian crises, enabling proactive interventions.

1.2 Risks and Threats

Surveillance capitalism erodes privacy.
Algorithmic discrimination marginalizes minority populations.
Automated warfare and profiling threaten the right to life and due process.

1.3 New Frontiers of Rights

Right to algorithmic dignity: protection against dehumanizing automation.
Right to digital self-sovereignty: control over personal data, identity, and AI representation.
Right to algorithmic non-interference: shielding individuals from manipulative AI influence in voting, consumer behavior, or belief formation.

---

2. Balancing Innovation with Rights Protection

2.1 The Innovation Imperative

Societies benefit from AI advances in healthcare, energy, logistics, and climate forecasting.
Restrictive regulation may limit innovation in the global South or among small enterprises.

2.2 The Precautionary Principle

Drawn from environmental governance, this principle emphasizes foresight, risk mitigation, and moral accountability.
AI deployment should undergo rights impact assessments before, during, and after implementation.

2.3 Ethical Design-by-Default

Developers should build rights considerations into initial system architectures.
Examples: differential privacy, fairness-aware machine learning, explainable AI.

2.4 Human-in-the-Loop Safeguards

Critical decision points, legal sentencing, medical triage, and asylum approval must maintain human discretion.
Continuous human oversight can prevent rights-violating errors.

---

3. Governance's Role in Shaping AI's Future Impact

3.1 Democratic Oversight

Inclusion of affected populations in AI policy design.
Participatory regulation through citizen assemblies and algorithmic audit boards.

3.2 Multilateral Frameworks

Treaties such as the proposed "Geneva Convention on AI" can define international boundaries on autonomous weapons and surveillance systems.
UNESCO's AI Ethics Recommendation is a voluntary model.

3.3 Localized Ethical Jurisdictions

Cities and municipalities can serve as experimental zones for rights-respecting AI systems (e.g., Barcelona's Digital Rights Charter).

3.4 Compliance Architecture

Use of blockchain for AI activity registries.
Smart contracts to ensure real-time enforcement of data use policies.

3.5 Algorithmic Due Process

Right to an explanation, right to challenge AI decisions, and procedural fairness.
Establishment of ombudsman services for algorithmic grievance redressal.

---

4. The Evolving Nature of Human Rights in the AI Era

4.1 Historical Evolution

From civil and political rights to economic, social, and cultural rights.
Digital rights emerge in the 21st century, including data protection, net neutrality, and encryption.

4.2 Future Rights Ecosystem

Digital rights fused with ecological rights and AI rights.
Rights for post-human or hybrid entities?

4.3 Rights of Generative Systems

Debate: Should autonomous systems with moral reasoning capacities be granted legal personhood?
Ethical safeguards are required to avoid dilution of human-centric frameworks.

4.4 Human Rights by Design

Integrate human rights checklists into AI lifecycle stages.
Shift from reactive regulation to proactive ethical engineering.

---

5. Case Studies: AI and Rights in Action

5.1 Estonia's e-Governance Infrastructure

Digital identity and AI-based public services deliver efficiency while embedding privacy rights.

5.2 AI in Predictive Policing (U.S. and U.K.)

Controversial use led to discriminatory outcomes and public backlash.
Highlighted the need for transparency, oversight, and accountability.

5.3 Kenya's Huduma Namba (Digital ID)

Criticized for the exclusion of marginalized groups due to data access inequality.

Underscored the risks of digital gatekeeping without rights protections.

5.4 China's Social Credit System

Massive AI surveillance and behavior scoring.
Violates privacy, freedom of movement, and fair trial rights.

5.5 UN's Pulse Lab (AI for Humanitarian Response)

Uses data analytics to support refugee aid and epidemic response.
Emphasizes privacy-by-design and human-centered metrics.

---

6. Strategic Recommendations for Rights-Forward AI Futures

6.1 Establish a Global AI Rights Charter

Drafted by international civil society and human rights organizations.
Includes rights to transparency, opt-out, fairness, and appeal.

6.2 Algorithmic Impact Assessments (AIAs)

Mandatory for all public and high-risk private sector deployments.
Publicly accessible and independently audited.

6.3 Inclusion of Vulnerable Populations

Prioritize impact on historically marginalized communities.
Implement linguistic, cultural, and accessibility accommodations.

6.4 Multi-Level Governance Ecosystem

Global treaties, national AI strategies, municipal charters, and organizational ethics policies.

6.5 AGI-Specific Guidelines

Address long-term safety, alignment, and consent mechanisms.
Clarify boundaries between assistance and control.

Conclusion: Human Rights as the Compass of Technological Civilization

The future of human rights is not separate from the future of AI, they are deeply intertwined. As machine intelligence becomes integral to our economic, legal, and cultural systems, the defense and evolution of rights must become an interdisciplinary, transnational, and generational endeavor.

We must not merely retrofit rights into technologies after they are built. Instead, we must embed them from the ground up, into code, into protocol, into organizational values. In doing so, we will not only preserve the best of what it means to be human but also set the ethical foundation for any society that includes AGI, autonomous systems, or hybrid human-machine futures.

References

Books and Reports:

Latonero, M. (2018). *Governing Artificial Intelligence: Upholding Human Rights & Dignity*. Data & Society Research Institute.
Crawford, K. (2021). *Atlas of AI*. Yale University Press.
UN OHCHR (2021). *The Right to Privacy in the Digital Age*.

Academic Articles:

Eubanks, V. (2018). *Automating Inequality*. St. Martin's Press.
Taddeo, M., & Floridi, L. (2018). "How AI can be a force for good." *Science*.

Web Resources and Case Studies:

Estonia e-Governance: https://e-estonia.com/solutions/e-governance/
AI Now Institute Reports: https://ainowinstitute.org/reports.html
UN Pulse Lab: https://www.unglobalpulse.org
Algorithmic Justice League: https://www.ajl.org

Grouped by Type:

Books/Reports: Latonero, Crawford, UN OHCHR
Articles: Eubanks, Taddeo & Floridi
Web Resources: Estonia, AI Now, UN Pulse Lab, AJL

Chapter 43. Decentralization: The Path Forward

Introduction

As artificial intelligence advances toward general autonomy and as societies become increasingly complex and interdependent, the models of governance we employ must evolve in tandem. Centralized systems, while efficient in certain domains, often suffer from a lack of transparency, vulnerability to corruption, and an overconcentration of power. Decentralization offers a radical alternative: a vision of governance where authority is distributed, decision-making is participatory, and enforcement is algorithmically transparent.

This chapter explores the future of decentralized governance systems, how AI and smart contracts can actualize them, what challenges they may encounter, and how philosophical, technological, and institutional innovations can help navigate the path forward.

---

1. Rationale for Decentralized Governance

1.1 Structural Limitations of Centralized Models

Centralization often leads to regulatory capture, censorship, and systemic fragility.
Single points of failure in governance systems, e.g., cybersecurity breaches, political corruption.

1.2 Benefits of Decentralization

Resilience: Redundancy across nodes mitigates risk.
Transparency: Code is auditable; rules are public.
Participation: Inclusive stakeholder input.
Sovereignty: Self-organizing communities with autonomy.

1.3 Alignment with AGI Societies

Distributed intelligence calls for distributed oversight.
Humans and machines as co-governors necessitate scalable, trustless systems.

---

2. The Role of AI in Future Decentralized Systems

2.1 AI as a Governance Facilitator

AI can streamline decentralized decision-making through pattern recognition, consensus forecasting, and dispute mediation.
Agents assist with real-time policy simulations and stakeholder preference modeling.

2.2 Automated Governance Protocols

Smart contracts execute decisions without human intervention.
AI reviews contract execution and flags anomalies or manipulations.

2.3 Adaptive Governance

Systems that learn from citizen feedback and environmental input.
Example: Dynamic policy updates based on changing real-world data (e.g., climate, health, economics).

2.4 Decentralized Autonomous Organizations (DAOs)

DAOs encode decision-making into code, voting, proposals, and budgeting.
Examples: CityDAO (land management), LexDAO (legal tech), BitDAO (funding protocols).

---

3. The Future of Smart Contracts in Governance

3.1 Legal Enforceability of Code

Recognition of smart contracts in jurisdictions such as the U.S., U.K., and Singapore.
Debate: Should code replace law or operate in tandem with legal systems?

3.2 Governance-as-Code

Smart constitutions embedded in DAOs.
Automated budget disbursement, policy enactment, and compliance audits.

3.3 Civic Protocols and Rights Encoding

Smart contracts that automatically uphold rights: privacy thresholds, consent tokens, and data residency enforcement.

3.4 Challenges with Programmability

Code is deterministic; human contexts are not.
Solutions: Hybrid contracts (human fallback), on-chain arbitration, multisig governance checks.

---

4. Real-World Examples and Pilots

4.1 Taiwan's vTaiwan and Polis Platform

Collaborative deliberation platform using digital democracy tools.
The government integrates consensus-based proposals into legislation.

4.2 Ethereum-based Voting Systems

Used for municipal referenda and community treasury management.
Problems: Gas fees, low voter participation.

4.3 RadicalxChange and Quadratic Voting

Reduces the influence of capital in voting outcomes.
Supported by Gitcoin, Taiwan's g0v, and other democratic tech advocates.

4.4 Blockchain Land Titles (Ghana, Georgia, Honduras)

Immutable proof of ownership.
Reduces fraud, empowers marginalized landholders.

4.5 OpenLaw and LexDAO

Smart legal contracts and governance toolkits for decentralized legal systems.

---

5. Challenges on the Path to Full Decentralization

5.1 Technical Barriers

Scalability (blockchain throughput), interoperability, and oracle reliability.
Solutions: Layer 2 protocols, zero-knowledge proofs, cross-chain bridges.

5.2 Governance Complexity

Risk of plutocracy in token-weighted systems.
Need for diverse voting schemas: liquid democracy, quadratic funding, random citizen panels.

5.3 Ethical Concerns

Who writes the code that governs?
Risk of algorithmic bias, opaque logic, or coercive automation.

5.4 Legal and Regulatory Ambiguity

Lack of legal recognition for DAO-based governance.
Inconsistent treatment of smart contracts across jurisdictions.

5.5 Inclusivity and Accessibility

Barriers to entry: digital literacy, language, and internet access.
Risk of reinforcing global inequities.

---

6. Solutions and Strategic Recommendations

6.1 Human-in-the-Loop Governance

Combine code execution with human ethics boards.
Create ethical override protocols and deliberative assemblies.

6.2 Smart Governance Templates

Standardized open-source templates for DAOs, including rights protections.
Easy deployment for cities, NGOs, and cooperatives.

6.3 Global Decentralization Standards (GDS)

Collaborative framework similar to ISO or IEEE.
Includes ethics, accessibility, safety, and dispute mechanisms.

6.4 Education and Capacity Building

Digital civics courses in schools.
DAO literacy bootcamps for policymakers and civil society.

6.5 Coexistence Frameworks with Centralized Institutions

Hybrid governance ecosystems.
Smart contract layers operate alongside traditional legal institutions.

Conclusion: A New Cartography of Power

The path forward is neither full decentralization nor stubborn centralization, it is a synthesis of the two. Decentralized systems can imbue governance with transparency, resilience, and participatory legitimacy. But without ethical foresight, legal clarity, and inclusive infrastructure, they risk replacing one elite with another, this time encoded into software.

AI and smart contracts offer the opportunity to architect governance from first principles, to reimagine citizenship, accountability, and cooperation in ways previously unimaginable. But they also compel us to ask foundational questions: Who gets to program justice? Who audits fairness? Who governs the governors?

To decentralize well is not to abandon institutions but to redesign them in the image of equity. The future belongs to the networks that can self-organize without self-destruction, to protocols that carry the wisdom of rights as well as the logic of code. And it begins with the decision to govern not only efficiently, but ethically.

References

Books and Reports:

Buterin, V., et al. (2022). *Decentralized Society: Finding Web3's Soul.* Whitepaper.
Ostrom, E. (1990). *Governing the Commons.* Cambridge University Press.
Tapscott, D., & Tapscott, A. (2016). *Blockchain Revolution.* Penguin.

Academic Articles:

Reijers, W., et al. (2018). "Now the Code Runs Itself: On-Chain and Off-Chain Governance." *Philosophy & Technology.*
Allen, C. (2019). "Smart Contracts and the Myth of Code as Law." *Stanford Tech Law Review.*

Web Resources and Case Studies:

CityDAO: https://www.citydao.io
LexDAO: https://lexdao.org
RadicalxChange: https://www.radicalxchange.org
Taiwan vTaiwan: https://vtaiwan.tw
Gitcoin: https://gitcoin.co

Grouped by Type:

Books/Reports: Buterin et al., Ostrom, Tapscott & Tapscott
Articles: Reijers et al., Allen
Web Resources: CityDAO, LexDAO, RadicalxChange, vTaiwan, Gitcoin

Chapter 44. Towards a Harmonious Future: Balancing AI, Philosophy, and Human Rights

Introduction

As the digital revolution deepens and artificial general intelligence (AGI) draws nearer, the future of human society hinges not merely on technological innovation but on the equilibrium between advancement and values. To prevent a future governed solely by optimization, control, and abstraction, we must integrate human rights and philosophical wisdom into every layer of AI development, deployment, and governance.

This chapter provides a roadmap for achieving a future where AI serves as an ethical collaborator rather than a neutral disruptor. It explores how philosophical frameworks can guide the design of AI systems, how decentralized infrastructures must embed rights, and how to architect strategies that foster harmony between technological progress and human dignity.

---

1. Philosophy as the Compass for Ethical AI

1.1 Why Philosophy Must Anchor AI Development

AI lacks innate ethical reasoning. Embedding philosophical insights into AI models is essential to guide their decision-making.
Human-centered design, rooted in philosophical anthropology, ensures technology complements rather than replaces moral judgment.

1.2 Key Philosophical Concepts for Harmonization

Dignity: Kantian ethics prioritizes treating humans as ends, never merely as means. AI must respect autonomy and consent.
Virtue: Aristotelian ethics focuses on flourishing and moral development. AI should support long-term well-being over short-term rewards.
Justice: Rawlsian fairness and Sen's capability approach emphasize equity and access.
Ubuntu: African ethics foreground interdependence, community, and restorative justice.

1.3 Integrating Ethics into AI Architectures

Model alignment must include not just statistical accuracy but ethical compliance.
Ethical reasoning engines and constraint-based modeling (e.g., logic programming with moral rules).
AI development ethics boards and deliberative oversight.

---

2. Upholding Human Rights in a Decentralized World

2.1 Risks of Technological Drift

Decentralized systems can fragment accountability.
Without a philosophical grounding, efficiency becomes the de facto moral logic.

2.2 Designing Rights-Aware Decentralized Protocols

Smart contracts that enforce privacy, consent, and data sovereignty.
DAO governance models that include ethics checkpoints and equity scoring.
Blockchain protocols with built-in human rights audit logs.

2.3 AI as Guardian and Threat to Rights

AI can defend rights (e.g., identifying discrimination), but also violate them (e.g., facial recognition abuses).
The challenge is dual: prevent harm while promoting agency.

2.4 Principle of Digital Subsidiarity

Decision-making should happen as close as possible to affected individuals.
AI systems must be localized, transparent, and culturally responsive.

---

3. Strategic Frameworks for Harmonizing Progress and Protection

3.1 Philosophical Engineering: Embedding Values into Systems

Interdisciplinary co-design involving ethicists, engineers, and sociologists.
Examples: IBM's Ethical AI Toolkit, Mozilla's Responsible Computing Framework.

3.2 Legal Philosophical Integration

Embedding international human rights norms into machine-executable legal code.
Ethics-by-design as a legal mandate.

3.3 Multistakeholder Assemblies

Citizens' juries and global AI councils.
Collective reflection modeled after democratic deliberation.

3.4 Trust Infrastructure for a Harmonious Future

Transparent source code.
Open AI observatories and public dashboards.

Right to explanation and appeal encoded into systems.

---

4. Case Studies: Systems Embedding Harmony

4.1 Decidim Barcelona

A participatory democracy platform driven by co-creation.
All code and governance rules are publicly auditable.

4.2 Gaia-X (EU Cloud Infrastructure)

Ethical governance is baked into federated infrastructure.
Rights over data use and algorithm accountability.

4.3 AI for Good (UN ITU)

AGI used to predict famine, track climate degradation.
Systems aligned with SDGs and humanitarian ethics.

4.4 SingularityNET Ethics Council

DAO governance for AGI development guided by philosophical inquiry.

---

5. Challenges to Harmony and How to Overcome Them

5.1 Value Pluralism

Different cultures define rights and ethics differently.
Solution: Create meta-frameworks that respect local autonomy within global ethical baselines.

5.2 Ethical Capture by Corporations

Ethics boards are often co-opted for marketing.
Remedies: Public ethics audits, ethical whistleblower protection, and independent funding for review bodies.

5.3 Algorithmic Moral Drift

Models trained on flawed data can perpetuate injustice.
Corrective: Human-in-the-loop mechanisms, continuous bias testing, ethics patches.

5.4 Philosophical Illiteracy

Technologists often lack formal training in ethics or justice theory.
Solution: Embed philosophy into technical education and corporate onboarding.

---

6. Blueprint for Harmonization at Scale

6.1 The Harmonized Governance Model

Combines decentralized technology, ethical theory, and legal guarantees.
Smart contracts that uphold Kantian dignity, virtue ethics, and human rights law.

6.2 Harmonization Pillars

Transparency: Explainability, accountability, auditability.
Participation: Stakeholder co-creation of systems.
Autonomy: Consent and self-sovereign digital identities.
Equity: Access and fairness safeguards.
Sustainability: Ecological and social well-being embedded into protocols.

6.3 AI and Philosophical Symbiosis

Use AI to refine moral hypotheses.
Test ethical models in simulation before deployment.
Create a dynamic, iterative moral architecture.

Conclusion: Toward Ethical Technological Civilization

To build a future where AI systems enhance rather than erode human dignity, we must reimagine governance as a philosophical undertaking. The technologies we design are reflections of our values, and the governance models we deploy reveal our philosophical commitments. Harmony is not the absence of conflict, it is the presence of balance, reflection, and intentionality.

By embedding human rights into every layer of decentralized governance and by forging AI that is ethically literate, we can co-create a society where humanity and machine intelligence evolve not in opposition but in resonance. The future is not coded, it is authored. Let us ensure its narrative is one of dignity, deliberation, and design grounded in justice.

References

Books and Reports:

Floridi, L. (2013). *The Ethics of Information*. Oxford University Press.
Moor, J. (2006). "Why We Need Better Ethics for Emerging Technologies." *Ethics and Information Technology*.
Mittelstadt, B., & Floridi, L. (2016). "The Ethics of Algorithms." *Philosophy & Technology*.
UNESCO (2021). *Recommendation on the Ethics of Artificial Intelligence*.

Articles and Journals:

Crawford, K. (2021). *Atlas of AI*. Yale University Press.
Binns, R. (2018). "Fairness in Machine Learning." *Communications of the ACM*.

Web Resources and Case Studies:

Decidim Barcelona: https://decidim.org
SingularityNET: https://singularitynet.io
Gaia-X: https://www.gaia-x.eu
AI for Good (ITU): https://aiforgood.itu.int
Mozilla Responsible Computing Framework:
https://foundation.mozilla.org/en/initiatives/responsible-computing/

Grouped by Type:

Books/Reports: Floridi, Moor, UNESCO
Articles: Crawford, Binns, Mittelstadt & Floridi
Web Resources: Decidim, SingularityNET, Gaia-X, AI for Good, Mozilla

Chapter 45. The Integration of AI into the Social Fabric

Introduction

Artificial Intelligence (AI) is no longer confined to laboratories, tech campuses, or high-security research institutions. It is steadily weaving itself into the very fabric of daily human life, affecting decisions in education, law, healthcare, employment, transportation, communication, and even emotional companionship. As this integration accelerates, society must confront not just technological and economic questions, but deep philosophical ones about meaning, autonomy, identity, and justice.

This chapter explores how AI is becoming an intrinsic part of the social ecosystem, examining philosophical implications of its pervasiveness and offering real-world case studies that illustrate this transformative process. It proposes frameworks to ensure that AI integration uplifts rather than erodes the core values of human society.

---

1. AI's Expanding Role in Societal Functions

1.1 From Tools to Infrastructure

AI has moved beyond being a decision-support tool to becoming embedded in core infrastructures.
Examples: AI in urban planning (smart cities), autonomous traffic control systems, and predictive maintenance in public utilities.

1.2 Personalized Interaction Ecosystems

Recommendation engines personalize entertainment, shopping, learning, and news.
Voice assistants and smart home devices create ambient intelligence environments.

1.3 Societal-Scale Decision Systems

Governments and corporations use AI for large-scale resource allocation, immigration screening, welfare distribution, and public health triage.

1.4 Emergence of AI Companionship

Emotional support chatbots and AI friends are becoming common, particularly among the elderly and socially isolated.

---

2. Philosophical Implications of AI's Ubiquity

2.1 Ontological Transformation of the Human Experience

As AI mediates increasing dimensions of life, questions arise: What remains distinctively human? What does coexistence entail?

2.2 Epistemological Concerns

Knowledge is now filtered, interpreted, and sometimes generated by AI.
Risks: Echo chambers, information asymmetry, cognitive automation.

2.3 Ethical Relationality

What moral obligations do we have toward sentient-like systems?
Do systems designed to mimic empathy create false emotional dependencies?

2.4 The Question of Agency

Who is responsible for decisions made by AI?
When do systems stop being tools and start being actors in the social contract?

2.5 AI and the Commons

AI affects collective goods: climate, safety, labor markets, and education.
Governance must consider shared stewardship models.

---

3. Societal Sectors Transformed by AI

3.1 Healthcare

AI diagnostics (e.g., radiology, dermatology, genomics).
Robotics in surgery and elder care.
Ethical issues: data consent, clinical accountability, algorithmic bias.

3.2 Education

Adaptive learning platforms personalize education.
Predictive tools assess the student's risk of dropout.
Risks: Overstandardization, surveillance of learning behavior.

3.3 Employment

Automated hiring tools, skill-matching AI, and gig economy platforms.
Shift in labor valuation and precarity in algorithmic job markets.

3.4 Justice and Law Enforcement

Predictive policing and risk assessment tools (e.g., COMPAS).

Automated legal document review and contract generation.
Problems: Racial bias, lack of appeal mechanisms.

3.5 Civic Engagement and Democracy

AI bots influence public discourse.
Algorithmic governance tools (e.g., participatory budgeting platforms).

---

4. Case Studies: Living with AI

4.1 Estonia's e-Governance System

AI-assisted bureaucracy delivers near-frictionless public service.
Public trust is maintained via transparency, consent mechanisms, and digital sovereignty.

4.2 Singapore's Smart Nation Initiative

AI is used in transportation, public health, and city planning.
Criticisms center on privacy trade-offs and surveillance concerns.

4.3 Japan's Robotic Elder Care

Humanoid robots like Paro are used for therapy.
Balances workforce shortages with ethical questions around emotional substitution.

4.4 South Korea's AI Tutors

Personalized education platforms are widely used in schools.
High adoption is driven by the cultural value placed on education.

4.5 Kenya's AI in Agriculture

AI helps smallholder farmers optimize yields using weather and soil data.
Illustrates positive socioeconomic integration of AI in the Global South.

---

5. Governance for Equitable AI Integration

5.1 Public Participation

Inclusion of marginalized voices in AI policy-making.
Digital literacy campaigns to democratize access.

5.2 Philosophical Frameworks for Regulation

Rights-based, capability-focused, and communitarian approaches.
Use of deliberative ethics assemblies and value-sensitive design.

5.3 Institutional Oversight Mechanisms

AI ombudsman services, independent audit bodies, and cross-sector ethics boards.

5.4 Interoperability and Localization

AI systems must adapt to local cultures, norms, and governance structures.

5.5 Multidimensional Metrics of Impact

Beyond GDP or productivity: include well-being, ecological footprint, and social cohesion indices.

---

6. Pathways to Meaningful Coexistence

6.1 AI as Partner, Not Proxy

Humans must remain decision-makers in morally significant contexts.
AI should enhance human capacity, not replace it.

6.2 Embedding AI in Cultural Narratives

Encourage literature, media, and education that frame AI as a relational, ethical presence.

6.3 Cross-Disciplinary Education

Teach philosophy, law, and humanities alongside data science and engineering.

6.4 Participatory Design and Continuous Dialogue

Invite public feedback into AI product development.
Institutionalize dialogue between developers, users, ethicists, and communities.

Conclusion: Weaving AI into the Moral Fabric

The integration of AI into society is not a matter of “if,” but “how.” As AI systems become infrastructure, companions, advisors, and co-workers, the moral responsibilities of their creators, regulators, and users must deepen accordingly. Integration must be more than technological, it must be ethical, participatory, and philosophical.

The future of society depends on our capacity to ensure that these systems operate not only with intelligence but with wisdom. In doing so, we affirm that the social fabric is not merely a technical web of relations, but a moral tapestry of dignity, agency, and shared purpose.

References

Books and Reports:

Tegmark, M. (2017). *Life 3.0: Being Human in the Age of Artificial Intelligence*. Penguin.
Harari, Y. N. (2018). *21 Lessons for the 21st Century*. Spiegel & Grau.
UNESCO (2021). *Ethics of Artificial Intelligence*.

Academic Articles:

Eubanks, V. (2018). *Automating Inequality*. St. Martin's Press.
Mittelstadt, B., et al. (2016). "The ethics of algorithms: Mapping the debate." *Big Data & Society*.

Web Resources and Case Studies:

Estonia e-Governance: https://e-estonia.com
Smart Nation Singapore: https://www.smartnation.gov.sg
Kenya AI for Agriculture: https://www.digitalgreen.org
AI in Education South Korea: https://www.korea.kr
Japan Robotic Care: https://www.japan.go.jp

Grouped by Type:

Books/Reports: Tegmark, Harari, UNESCO
Articles: Eubanks, Mittelstadt
Web Resources: e-Estonia, Smart Nation SG, Digital Green, Korea.kr, Japan.go.jp

Chapter 46. Smart Contracts as the New Guardians of Human Rights

Introduction

In a world where trust in institutions is wavering and centralized enforcement mechanisms often fail to equitably protect individual rights, the emergence of smart contracts offers a new paradigm. Originally conceived as programmable agreements, smart contracts have evolved into instruments capable of autonomously executing rules, distributing value, and enforcing compliance without intermediaries. Their capacity for precision, transparency, and incorruptibility makes them potent candidates for becoming new custodians of human rights.

This chapter explores how smart contracts can act as guardians of fundamental rights in an increasingly decentralized and algorithmic society. It discusses the legal and philosophical basis for encoding rights into code, examines real-world case studies of successful smart contract applications in rights protection, and presents strategies to ethically design and implement such systems at scale.

---

1. Understanding Smart Contracts in the Human Rights Context

1.1 What Are Smart Contracts?

Self-executing digital contracts written on blockchain platforms.
Operate through "if-then" logic: actions are triggered automatically once conditions are met.

1.2 Why Use Smart Contracts for Rights Enforcement?

Tamper-proof execution.
No reliance on centralized enforcement bodies.
Immediate redress or resource allocation.
Enhanced transparency and traceability.

1.3 Human Rights at Risk in Centralized Systems

Rights are often unenforced due to bureaucratic delays, corruption, or politicization.
Data privacy violations, unlawful surveillance, censorship, and land seizures.

1.4 The Promise of Decentralized Enforcement

Autonomous systems that operate independently of human bias.
Universal access to systems with embedded rights logic.

---

2. Ethical Considerations in Encoding Human Rights

2.1 Rights Must Be Interpretable and Contestable

Human rights are context-sensitive and often require deliberation.
Smart contracts should include mechanisms for appeal or override.

2.2 Avoiding Ethical Oversimplification

Binary code does not easily accommodate moral ambiguity.
Solutions: hybrid contracts (human + machine), nested ethical conditions.

2.3 Risks of Ethical Capture

Who writes the rights code?
Risk of embedding the biases of dominant groups.

2.4 Upholding the Principle of Proportionality

Enforcement mechanisms must be proportionate to violations.
Smart contracts should avoid punitive excess.

2.5 Preventing Rights Inversion

Systems must be protected from being used for surveillance or exclusion under the guise of protection.

---

3. Use Cases and Case Studies

3.1 Data Sovereignty and Consent Protocols

Project: Ocean Protocol users control and monetize their personal data via consent-based smart contracts.
Rights encoded: consent, access, data ownership.

3.2 Land Rights Protection

Project: Bitland Ghana blockchain registry for property rights.
Smart contracts prevent unlawful seizures and provide immutable proof of ownership.

3.3 Refugee Identity Systems

Project: ID2020 (with Ethereum-based ID management).
Protects the right to identity and access to services.
Smart contracts issue credentials tied to biometric verification.

3.4 Labor Rights and the Gig Economy

Project: Opolis and FairWork Protocol smart contracts that enforce minimum wage, paid time off, and benefits.
Workers get paid directly through smart escrow contracts.

3.5 Decentralized Aid Distribution

Project: Disberse (pilot in Uganda) humanitarian aid routed through smart contracts.
Enforces fair and traceable distribution of resources.

---

4. Philosophical Frameworks for Codifying Rights

4.1 Kantian Autonomy

Smart contracts can be designed to uphold consent and personhood.
Must prevent manipulation or deceptive terms.

4.2 Rawlsian Justice as Fairness

Encode rules that prioritize the least advantaged (e.g., quadratic funding for resource access).

4.3 Ubuntu and Restorative Justice

Smart contracts for community-led redress and reconciliation mechanisms.

4.4 Capability Approach (Sen and Nussbaum)

Ensure smart contracts support access to education, healthcare, and civic participation.
Rights are not as static entitlements, but as dynamic enablements.

---

5. Challenges in Making Smart Contracts the Guardians of Rights

5.1 Technical Barriers

Smart contract bugs can create loopholes (e.g., The DAO hack).
High gas fees on Ethereum limit equitable access.

5.2 Jurisdictional Conflicts

Conflicting interpretations of rights across cultures and legal systems.
Smart contracts may conflict with national laws.

5.3 Lack of Ethical Failsafes

No "pause" or "kill switch" in case of unintended consequences.

5.4 Inclusivity and Accessibility

Marginalized communities may lack the digital infrastructure to interact with blockchain systems.

---

6. Design Principles for Ethical Rights-Enforcing Contracts

6.1 Transparency

All contract logic should be open-source and auditable.

6.2 Contestability

Include mechanisms for dispute resolution and override by ethics councils.

6.3 Cultural Sensitivity

Design should be informed by local norms, values, and languages.

6.4 Human-in-the-Loop

High-stakes decisions should trigger hybrid oversight.

6.5 Upgradability

Contracts should evolve with social, legal, and ethical understandings.

---

7. Global Frameworks and Standards

7.1 W3C Verifiable Credentials and DID Standards

Basis for interoperable and secure decentralized ID systems.

7.2 UN Guiding Principles on Business and Human Rights

Inform smart contract design in corporate governance.

7.3 IEEE P7000 Series

Ethical system design standards for AI and autonomous technologies.

7.4 Blockchain Governance Frameworks

Tools from ConsenSys, Aragon, and DAOstack for incorporating deliberative governance into smart contracts.

Conclusion: The Ethics of Autonomous Enforcement

Smart contracts are not neutral tools; they are political agents encoded with specific visions of justice, consent, and equity. If we approach them merely as technical artifacts, we risk automating the very injustices they could be designed to eliminate. But if we treat them as programmable institutions subject to review, dialogue, and revision, they become one of the most powerful instruments ever developed for rights protection.

As we enter the era of AGI and decentralized civilization, smart contracts offer a way to embed human rights directly into the social, economic, and legal substrate of society. They can become incorruptible rights defenders but only if we remain vigilant, inclusive, and ethically principled in their design and deployment.

References

Books and Reports:

Lessig, L. (1999). *Code and Other Laws of Cyberspace*. Basic Books.
De Filippi, P., & Wright, A. (2018). *Blockchain and the Law: The Rule of Code*. Harvard University Press.
UN Human Rights Council (2011). *UN Guiding Principles on Business and Human Rights*.

Academic Articles:

Werbach, K., & Cornell, N. (2017). "Contracts Ex Machina." *Duke Law Journal*.
Reijers, W., et al. (2018). "Now the Code Runs Itself." *Philosophy & Technology*.

Web Resources and Case Studies:

Ocean Protocol: https://oceanprotocol.com
Bitland Ghana: https://bitland.world
ID2020: https://id2020.org
Opolis: https://opolis.co
Disberse: https://www.disberse.com

Grouped by Type:

Books/Reports: Lessig, De Filippi & Wright, UNHRC
Articles: Werbach & Cornell, Reijers et al.
Web Resources: Ocean Protocol, Bitland, ID2020, Opolis, Disberse

Chapter 47. The Role of International Law in an AI-Governed World

Introduction

As artificial intelligence (AI) and decentralized systems transcend national boundaries, the traditional frameworks of international law are being tested. The rise of AGI and blockchain governance poses profound challenges for a system of legal norms built on state sovereignty, territorial jurisdiction, and slow-moving diplomatic consensus. In the 21st century, actors that govern critical infrastructure and social dynamics may not be nations or corporations but autonomous algorithms and transnational codebases.

This chapter explores how international law can evolve to regulate the AI-driven and decentralized world. It delves into the limitations of current regimes, outlines theoretical innovations, and reviews case studies illustrating attempts, successful or otherwise, at cross-border legal governance for AI and decentralized platforms.

---

1. The Need for a Global Legal Framework in the Age of AI

1.1 Beyond the Nation-State

Decentralized systems like blockchains operate without central jurisdictions.
AI systems deployed in one nation often affect individuals and institutions globally.

1.2 Gaps in Existing Legal Structures

Treaties lag behind technological advancement.
Lack of uniformity in defining key terms like "autonomy," "bias," or "liability."

1.3 The Rise of Global Commons

AI models train on data sourced globally, raising jurisdictional and consent issues.
Digital identity, data ownership, and algorithmic harms are borderless challenges.

---

2. Challenges to Cross-Border Enforcement

2.1 Jurisdictional Fragmentation

Conflicts of law arise when multiple countries claim jurisdiction over AI behavior.
Case: Google Spain v. AEPD (ECJ 2014) and the global reach of the “right to be forgotten.”

2.2 Enforcement in Stateless Systems

DAOs (Decentralized Autonomous Organizations) may exist without legal registration.
Smart contracts enforce themselves outside traditional legal systems.

2.3 Regulatory Arbitrage

Companies base AI operations in jurisdictions with the weakest privacy or ethics laws.

2.4 Differing Cultural Norms

Interpretations of human rights, fairness, or personhood differ across regions.
Risk of ethical imperialism or moral relativism.

---

3. International Legal Instruments and Their AI Relevance

3.1 The Universal Declaration of Human Rights (UDHR)

Still relevant: rights to dignity, privacy, due process.
Must be reinterpreted for digital and algorithmic contexts.

3.2 The Council of Europe's AI Guidelines

Emphasizes human-centric AI, transparency, and accountability.
Non-binding but influential.

3.3 OECD Principles on AI

Voluntary standards focused on inclusive growth, sustainable development, and well-being.
Strong on risk-based approaches and stakeholder consultation.

3.4 UNESCO AI Ethics Recommendation (2021)

Calls for banning social scoring and mass surveillance.
Emphasizes the right to algorithmic transparency.

3.5 UN Guiding Principles on Business and Human Rights

Increasingly invoked in AI contexts where corporate actors dominate.

---

4. Emerging Legal Doctrines and Innovations

4.1 Extraterritorial Application of Digital Rights Laws

EU's General Data Protection Regulation (GDPR) applies to any company processing EU citizens' data.
Model for global digital rights enforcement.

4.2 Sovereign DAO Recognition

Possibility of treaties recognizing certain DAOs as legal persons.
Would create hybrid status: legal but code-governed.

4.3 Algorithmic Accountability Standards

Mandating audit trails, explainability, and redress mechanisms.
Example: Algorithmic Accountability Act (USA – proposed).

4.4 "Soft Law" Approaches

Ethics guidelines, certifications, and model codes of conduct.
Example: Montreal Declaration for Responsible AI.

4.5 Digital Geneva Conventions

Calls from Microsoft and others to create norms against weaponized AI.
Includes protection of civilians from algorithmic warfare.

---

5. Case Studies

5.1 Schrems I and II Cases (EU)

Invalidated Safe Harbor and Privacy Shield agreements.
Demonstrates the power of international law in protecting digital rights.

5.2 The DAO Collapse (2016)

The Ethereum smart contract was exploited due to a code flaw.
Raised the issue: who is liable in stateless, code-based environments?

5.3 China's Social Credit System vs. European AI Ethics

Sharp contrast in AI deployment philosophies.
EU model emphasizes individual rights; China emphasizes state surveillance and control.

5.4 Clearview AI and Biometric Surveillance

The company scraped images globally without consent.

Fined and banned in multiple countries.
Raises the need for unified biometric data regulation.

5.5 The Facebook-Cambridge Analytica Scandal

Data misuse influenced elections across borders.
Triggered global scrutiny and legislative reforms.

---

6. Pathways Forward for Global Legal Coherence

6.1 Multilateral Treaties on AI Ethics and Rights

Could codify global baseline protections.
Modeled after climate accords or arms treaties.

6.2 Intergovernmental AI Bodies

Modeled after the WTO or IAEA.
Could conduct AI audits, resolve disputes, and enforce standards.

6.3 Blockchain and Smart Contract Harmonization

Develop globally accepted standards for ethical smart contracts.
Interoperability between legal jurisdictions and code-based contracts.

6.4 AI Courts and Transnational Arbitration Panels

Specialized tribunals for AI-related disputes.
May use AI to support jurisprudential consistency.

6.5 Legal APIs and Regulatory Sandboxes

Nations offer legal interfaces to test AI compliance in advance.
Encourages innovation while ensuring oversight.

---

7. The Philosophical Basis for Global Legal Adaptation

7.1 Cosmopolitanism vs. Legal Pluralism

Should global AI law reflect universal values or accommodate cultural differences?
Proposal: Universal minimums with local interpretative flexibility.

7.2 Human Rights as Code-Agnostic

Rights apply regardless of whether they are implemented by humans or machines.

7.3 Moral Interoperability

Need to develop protocols for ethical communication between AI systems designed with differing moral architectures.

7.4 AI as Legal Subject vs. Legal Tool

Debate: Should AGI have legal standing?
There is a risk of displacing human legal subjects if AI rights are recognized prematurely.

Conclusion: Binding the Stateless Code

The future of global governance will not be written solely by states or courts, but increasingly by algorithms, smart contracts, and autonomous code. International law must evolve into a hybrid ecosystem, part analog, part digital, that binds decentralized systems to ethical norms and universal rights. It must ensure that global technological infrastructures do not operate beyond the reach of human values and social accountability.

A harmonized approach must blend legal enforceability, philosophical legitimacy, and technical feasibility. Only then can the rule of law persist in an age where the rulers may be machines.

References

Books and Reports:

De Filippi, P., & Wright, A. (2018). *Blockchain and the Law: The Rule of Code*. Harvard University Press.
UN Human Rights Council. (2011). *UN Guiding Principles on Business and Human Rights*.
UNESCO. (2021). *Recommendation on the Ethics of Artificial Intelligence.*

Articles and Journals:

Werbach, K. (2020). "The Blockchain and the New Architecture of Trust." *MIT Technology Review*.
Pagallo, U. (2018). "The Legal Challenges of AI for the EU." *European Journal of Risk Regulation*.

Web Resources and Case Studies:

European Court of Justice: https://curia.europa.eu
ID2020: https://id2020.org
Clearview AI Case: https://www.privacy.org
Facebook-Cambridge Analytica: https://www.ftc.gov

Grouped by Type:

Books/Reports: De Filippi & Wright, UNESCO, UNHRC
Articles: Werbach, Pagallo
Web Resources: ECJ, ID2020, Privacy.org, FTC

Chapter 48. The Evolution of Human Rights in the Age of AI

Introduction

The 20th century witnessed the formal codification of human rights in international charters, declarations, and treaties. The 21st century now confronts a radical new frontier: the advent of artificial intelligence (AI) and the emergence of non-human autonomous systems capable of interacting with and even manipulating our legal, political, social, and cognitive environments. As AI evolves, so must our understanding of what it means to be human, autonomous, and deserving of rights. This chapter examines the evolution of human rights in the context of AI advancement, outlines the philosophical rationales for expanding rights frameworks, and proposes potential new rights for the AI era.

---

1. Reassessing Human Rights in a Post-Human Context

1.1 Human Rights as Historically Contingent Constructs

Origin in post-WWII universalism.
Emphasis on political freedom, bodily integrity, and civil liberties.
Historically anthropocentric and analog-focused.

1.2 AI's Disruption of Foundational Human Rights Assumptions

Human agency is increasingly mediated by AI.
Examples: AI-curated news feeds (freedom of thought), biometric surveillance (privacy), and predictive policing (due process).
Rights no longer operate in purely human-human relations.

1.3 Technological Mediation of Autonomy

Autonomy once meant freedom from coercion; now it includes freedom from algorithmic influence.
Conceptual shift: from negative liberty (freedom from) to positive liberty (freedom to).

---

2. Philosophical Foundations for Evolving Rights

2.1 Kantian Dignity in the Algorithmic Age

Human dignity entails rational autonomy.
AI systems increasingly shape our preferences, nudging behavior.
Rights must protect the mental and informational integrity of persons.

2.2 Arendtian Natality and Plurality

Rights must protect the uniqueness and unpredictability of human beings.
Algorithmic systems threaten conformity and sameness.

2.3 Rawlsian Justice in Digital Inequality

Rights should adapt to protect the most digitally disenfranchised.
Includes digital access, literacy, and protection from AI bias.

2.4 Capability Approach (Sen and Nussbaum)

Rights should ensure people can function meaningfully in AI societies.
Capabilities such as digital self-determination and cognitive sovereignty are essential.

---

3. Potential New Rights for the Age of AI

3.1 The Right to AI Non-Interference

Freedom from unsolicited algorithmic manipulation.
It could be codified as digital autonomy.
Analogous to freedom of thought or bodily integrity.

3.2 The Right to Algorithmic Transparency

Right to know when AI is influencing outcomes (employment, credit, sentencing).
Includes explanation of logic and access to appeal.

3.3 The Right to Cognitive Liberty

Protection from AI systems designed to manipulate thought (neurotechnology, behavior-predictive engines).
Close to existing protections for mental privacy.

3.4 The Right to Digital Identity and Personhood

Right to control one's digital persona and data trails.
Includes anonymity, pseudonymity, and verified identity.

3.5 The Right to Disconnection

Right to live without mandatory integration into algorithmic systems.
Analogous to conscientious objection.

3.6 The Right to Algorithmic Fairness

Protection from AI-driven discrimination.
Includes the right to be judged by human standards in critical areas.

3.7 The Right to Human Oversight

In high-risk areas (warfare, justice, welfare), humans must retain final authority.

3.8 The Right to Be Forgotten by AI

Erasure of personal data from training datasets.
Includes retroactive removal from deep learning models.

---

4. Evolving Rights Frameworks: Legal and Ethical Mechanisms

4.1 Digital Bills of Rights

Proposed by the EU and civil society groups.
Enshrine AI-specific rights in constitutional or supranational documents.

4.2 Smart Contract Embedding of Rights

Rights are encoded into governance protocols.
Example: voting rights in DAOs, access rights in digital commons.

4.3 Rights-by-Design AI Engineering

Rights are integrated into algorithmic systems from inception.
Tools: fairness audits, ethical checklists, algorithmic impact assessments.

4.4 Algorithmic Ombudsman Models

Independent bodies to hear complaints, review decisions, and enforce rights.
It may be supported by AI co-adjudication tools.

---

5. Case Studies in Human Rights Evolution

5.1 India's Aadhaar ID System

Initially, a digital inclusion initiative.
Legal challenges have been raised over privacy and surveillance.
The Supreme Court upheld the right to privacy as fundamental (2017).

5.2 EU's AI Act (Proposed)

Risk-based approach to regulating AI.
Bans systems violating fundamental rights (e.g., real-time biometric surveillance).

5.3 Brazil's AI Bill of Rights

Emphasizes inclusivity, accessibility, and algorithmic justice.
Reflects a Global South perspective.

5.4 UN B-Tech Project

Promotes corporate accountability for AI-related rights violations.
Encourages public-private collaboration.

---

6. Intersection with Emerging Technologies

6.1 Neurotechnology and Mental Rights

Brain-computer interfaces may require new rights frameworks (e.g., mental privacy).

6.2 Synthetic Media and Deepfakes

Rights to reputation, identity, and authenticity at risk.
Legal innovations are needed to deal with AI-generated impersonation.

6.3 Biometric and Predictive Surveillance

Predictive policing, facial recognition, and sentiment analysis.
Require new thresholds for lawful use and consent.

6.4 Genomic and AI-Driven Precision Medicine

Rights to informed consent, algorithmic fairness in diagnostics.

---

7. Global Ethical Foundations and Philosophical Debates

7.1 Universality vs. Cultural Relativism

Should new rights be globally standardized?
Proposal: common moral minimums with localized enforcement modalities.

7.2 Human-Centric vs. Sentience-Based Rights

Debate over extending rights to AGI and synthetic minds.
Controversial: risk of diluting human rights protections.

7.3 Procedural vs. Substantive Rights

Some argue rights should be about fair process (e.g., transparency, appeal).
Others favor outcome-based protections (e.g., fairness, dignity).

Conclusion: Toward a Post-Human Rights Framework

The age of AI demands not only a recalibration of human rights but also an expansion. New threats, algorithmic manipulation, digital exclusion, and loss of autonomy, are neither adequately addressed nor anticipated by traditional legal systems. As humanity enters into cognitive, social, and even emotional relationships with intelligent systems, it must evolve its moral and legal frameworks.

Human rights must be resilient yet adaptive, rooted in dignity but prepared for digital and post-biological contexts. This evolution will not be simply legal, it must be philosophical, participatory, and technologically embodied. Only then can we ensure that human rights remain a beacon, not a relic, in the age of AI.

References

Books and Reports:

Floridi, L. (2021). *The Logic of Information: A Theory of Philosophy as Conceptual Design*. Oxford University Press.
UNESCO. (2021). *Recommendation on the Ethics of Artificial Intelligence.*
UN Human Rights Council. (2011). *UN Guiding Principles on Business and Human Rights*.

Academic Articles:

Binns, R. (2018). "Fairness in Machine Learning: Lessons from Political Philosophy." *Proceedings of the 2018 Conference on Fairness, Accountability, and Transparency*.
Yeung, K. (2018). "Algorithmic Regulation: A Critical Interrogation." *Regulation & Governance*.

Web Resources and Case Studies:

EU AI Act: https://artificialintelligenceact.eu

Aadhaar Ruling: https://indiankanoon.org/doc/127517806
Brazil's AI Rights Draft: https://www.camara.leg.br
UN B-Tech Project: https://www.ohchr.org/en/b-tech-project

Grouped by Type:

Books/Reports: Floridi, UNESCO, UNHRC
Articles: Binns, Yeung
Web Resources: AI Act EU, Aadhaar, Brazil's Bill, UN OHCHR

Chapter 49. Philosophical Approaches to AI Regulation

Introduction

AI systems are rapidly transforming every sector, including healthcare, law, education, defense, and governance, yet our normative frameworks struggle to keep pace. While policymakers scramble to write the rules, a deeper question must be asked: What *should* guide the regulation of AI? The answer is not merely legal or technical. It is profoundly philosophical.

This chapter investigates the philosophical foundations that underpin different approaches to AI regulation. Drawing from moral philosophy, political theory, and legal ethics, we explore how divergent worldviews shape regulatory priorities, how nations operationalize these values, and how global consistency might be achieved without ethical uniformity.

---

1. Philosophical Frameworks Guiding AI Regulation

1.1 Deontological Approaches

Regulation based on duties, rights, and intrinsic ethical principles.
Immanuel Kant: Treat individuals as ends, never merely as means.
Example: Bans on facial recognition in public spaces to protect autonomy, even if effective.

1.2 Utilitarian and Consequentialist Models

Focus on maximizing benefits and minimizing harms.
Jeremy Bentham, John Stuart Mill.
AI regulation as cost-benefit analysis: risk scores, impact assessments, harm-reduction clauses.

1.3 Virtue Ethics Frameworks

Focus on moral character and societal flourishing.
Aristotle, Alasdair MacIntyre.
Emphasis on fostering AI ecosystems that promote responsibility, humility, and civic virtues.

1.4 Rawlsian Justice as Fairness

Ensuring equitable AI outcomes for the least advantaged.
Regulation should pass a "veil of ignorance" test: Would we accept this rule if we didn't know our social role?

1.5 Pragmatism and Ethics-by-Design

William James, John Dewey.
Ethics is iterative, context-based, and adaptive.
Encourages agile regulatory frameworks and sandboxes.

---

2. Normative Tensions in AI Regulation

2.1 Freedom vs. Security

Should AI be used for surveillance to ensure public safety?
Example: COVID-19 contact tracing apps vs. right to privacy.

2.2 Innovation vs. Caution

Over-regulation can stifle innovation; under-regulation can lead to systemic risk.
The Precautionary Principle vs. the Pro-Innovation Principle.

2.3 Global Norms vs. Local Values

Western emphasis on privacy vs. Asian models of collective welfare.
The challenge of enforcing global AI norms in culturally diverse contexts.

2.4 Rule-Based vs. Principle-Based Regulation

Rule-based: specific, enforceable laws (e.g., GDPR).
Principle-based: high-level norms (e.g., AI should be transparent).

---

3. Case Studies in Philosophical Approaches to Regulation

3.1 The European Union's AI Act (2021 Draft)

Risk-based framework rooted in human rights law.
Bans unacceptable risk systems; strict requirements for high-risk applications.
Influenced by Kantian and Rawlsian principles.

3.2 The United States' Sectoral and Market-Based Approach

Patchwork regulation (FTC, FDA, NHTSA).
Emphasis on innovation, competitiveness, and self-regulation.
Consequentialist and libertarian influence.

3.3 China's State-Driven Regulatory Model

Focus on national security, social harmony, and surveillance.
Confucian ethics: order, stability, collective responsibility.
Proactive state involvement in setting standards.

3.4 Canada's Algorithmic Impact Assessment (AIA)

Emphasizes transparency, accountability, and public consultation.
Reflects pragmatist and democratic pluralist values.

3.5 Brazil's AI Legal Framework Draft (2021)

Emphasizes inclusion, access, and human dignity.
Seeks to reflect Latin American democratic and egalitarian traditions.

---

4. The Role of Ethics in Regulatory Design

4.1 Ethics-by-Design Principles

Embedding ethical principles into AI development.
Transparency, explainability, non-discrimination, and data minimization.

4.2 Algorithmic Accountability Mechanisms

Audit trails, impact assessments, and human-in-the-loop requirements.
Inspired by procedural justice.

4.3 Regulatory Sandboxes and Agile Law

Experimental spaces to test AI under limited legal risk.
Supports ethical experimentation while preserving oversight.

4.4 Rights-Based Regulation vs. Outcome-Based Regulation

Should regulators prioritize the protection of rights or the achievement of just outcomes?
Example: Algorithmic recidivism tools vs. rehabilitation-focused models.

---

5. Global Harmonization and Regulatory Pluralism

5.1 The OECD AI Principles

Cross-jurisdictional framework encouraging responsible innovation.
Principles: inclusive growth, human-centered values, transparency.

5.2 UNESCO AI Ethics Framework

Stresses diversity, sustainability, gender equality, and ecological balance.

5.3 The Dilemma of Regulatory Fragmentation

Risk of AI "law havens."
Data localization and interoperability challenges.

5.4 Toward a Global AI Compact

Proposal for a UN-led AI treaty.
Requires philosophical consensus on minimum ethical thresholds.

---

6. Philosophical Challenges and Unresolved Questions

6.1 Can AGI Be a Moral Agent?

Debate on whether regulation should treat AGI as an entity with duties or simply as a tool.

6.2 Who is Accountable for AI?

The challenge of moral responsibility in distributed systems.
Shift from individual culpability to collective or systemic responsibility.

6.3 Rights for AI?

Some advocate for rights for sentient systems.
Raises ontological questions: What does it mean to have moral standing?

6.4 Balancing AI's Role in Governance

Should AI participate in governance decisions (e.g., judicial sentencing)?
Requires deeper analysis of epistemic authority vs. democratic legitimacy.

Conclusion: A Philosophy-Led Future for AI Regulation

The regulation of AI must move beyond reactive legalism or isolated technical fixes. It must be guided by coherent philosophical principles that reflect diverse moral traditions, political ideals, and cultural values. Whether rooted in dignity, fairness, utility, or pluralism, these frameworks help ensure that AI serves human ends without compromising ethical integrity.

Philosophy is not an accessory to regulation it is its foundation. Without it, AI governance risks becoming a race to the bottom or a patchwork of inconsistent norms. With it, we can build systems that respect humanity, foster innovation, and protect the vulnerable in a future increasingly governed by intelligent machines.

References

Books and Reports:

Floridi, L. (2019). *The Ethics of Artificial Intelligence*. Oxford University Press.
Rawls, J. (1999). *A Theory of Justice*. Harvard University Press.
Mill, J.S. (1863). *Utilitarianism*. Parker, Son, and Bourn.

Articles and Policy Briefs:

Binns, R. (2018). "Fairness in Machine Learning." *FAT* Conference.
Jobin, A., Ienca, M., & Vayena, E. (2019). "The Global Landscape of AI Ethics Guidelines." *Nature Machine Intelligence*.

Web Resources and Case Studies:

EU AI Act: https://artificialintelligenceact.eu
Canadian AIA Framework: https://www.tbs-sct.gc.ca
UNESCO AI Ethics: https://unesdoc.unesco.org
Brazil AI Draft Law: https://www.camara.leg.br

Grouped by Type:

Books/Reports: Floridi, Rawls, Mill
Articles: Binns, Jobin et al.
Web Resources: EU, Canada, UNESCO, Brazil

Chapter 50. The Impact of AI on Democracy and Governance

Introduction

Democracy, as both a political philosophy and a practical system of governance, is rooted in the principles of popular sovereignty, participation, accountability, and the rule of law. Artificial intelligence (AI) introduces a paradigm shift to these ideals, not only by changing the mechanics of participation but by redefining the scope and velocity of decision-making, public discourse, and institutional transparency.

This chapter examines how AI may shape, challenge, or reinforce democratic values, tracing both the risks of technocratic capture and the opportunities for democratized governance. It also explores philosophical inquiries regarding AI's legitimacy, decision-making authority, and its integration into the machinery of public administration.

---

1. AI and Democratic Participation

1.1 Algorithmic Mediation of Public Discourse

AI curates social media feeds, filters political content, and creates echo chambers.
Algorithms like Facebook's News Feed and YouTube's recommendations influence political awareness and voter behavior.
Impact: Filter bubbles reduce exposure to diverse viewpoints, threatening deliberative democracy.

1.2 Automated Political Communication

Use of AI in political campaigns (e.g., microtargeting via Cambridge Analytica).
Chatbots disseminate campaign messages and misinformation.
Undermines informed consent and voter autonomy.

1.3 AI-Enabled Civic Engagement Tools

AI can facilitate deliberative platforms, sentiment analysis, and participatory budgeting.
Example: Decidim in Barcelona uses AI to process public input.
Potential: Enhance inclusivity and scale democratic input.

---

2. AI and Electoral Integrity

2.1 Voter Influence and Manipulation

Predictive modeling identifies swing voters and personalizes persuasion.
AI challenges the fairness of the electoral field.

2.2 Deepfakes and Synthetic Media

Fake videos or audio can alter political outcomes.
Raises epistemological questions: What is a trustworthy source?

2.3 Election Security

AI aids in monitoring election infrastructure and identifying cyber threats.
But also opens attack surfaces via adversarial AI.

---

3. AI in Governance and Policy Making

3.1 AI-Supported Decision-Making in Public Administration

AI is used in welfare allocation, fraud detection, and resource optimization.
Example: Dutch SyRI system for social welfare risk prediction.
Risk: opaque logic, biased datasets, limited appeal mechanisms.

3.2 Algorithmic Bureaucracies

Emergence of algorithmically augmented governance.
Challenge: loss of discretion, reduced empathy, and democratic accountability.

3.3 Smart Cities and Automated Governance

AI systems optimize energy, traffic, and public safety.
Example: Singapore's Smart Nation initiative.
Issue: Technocracy without adequate civic control.

---

4. Philosophical Reflections on AI and Democracy

4.1 Epistemic Authority vs. Democratic Legitimacy

AI can process more data than humans, but should it decide?
Tension between efficiency and participation.

4.2 The Demos vs. the Algorithm

Is democracy compatible with black-box decision-making?
Rousseau: Legitimacy requires transparent and participatory rule-making.

4.3 Autonomy and AI-Augmented Governance

Should citizens delegate decision-making to AI?

Mill: Autonomy is essential to individual moral development.

4.4 Habermas and the Public Sphere

AI disrupts the communicative rationality of the public sphere.
Platforms prioritize virality over reasoned debate.

---

5. Case Studies of AI's Impact on Democratic Governance

5.1 Estonia's e-Governance Model

Highly digitized government: AI in tax, health, and public services.
Benefits: efficiency, access, and low corruption.
Safeguards: transparency protocols, civic tech audits.

5.2 China's Social Credit System

AI-driven governance based on behavioral scoring.
Raises concerns over autonomy, privacy, and moral paternalism.
A technocratic form of behavioral engineering.

5.3 The Netherlands' SyRI Controversy

AI is used for social welfare fraud detection.
The court ruled it violated human rights and lacked transparency.
Highlights the dangers of unchecked algorithmic governance.

5.4 Kenya's Huduma Namba System

Digital identity system using AI.
Concerns over data protection, exclusion, and marginalization.

---

6. Opportunities for AI to Strengthen Democracy

6.1 Participatory AI Design

Citizens are involved in setting AI parameters.
Co-design ensures alignment with democratic values.

6.2 Ethical AI Audits

Algorithms are evaluated for bias, fairness, and explainability.
It can become a democratic mechanism for accountability.

6.3 Digital Assemblies and Deliberative AI Tools

AI to analyze deliberation trends, summarize arguments, and propose compromise options.
Augments rather than replaces civic dialogue.

6.4 Inclusive Digital Platforms

AI can improve accessibility for people with disabilities.
AI-driven translation expands participation in multilingual societies.

---

7. Safeguards for Democratic AI Governance

7.1 Constitutional AI Principles

AI must uphold constitutional rights: freedom, equality, dignity.

7.2 Transparency and Explainability Mandates

Citizens have the right to understand how AI makes public decisions.

7.3 Algorithmic Impact Assessments (AIAs)

Mandatory evaluations before deployment in public services.
Example: Canada's AIA tool.

7.4 Oversight Bodies and Civic Participation

Independent agencies to review and guide AI use in governance.
Civic engagement through town halls, digital referenda, and watchdog apps.

Conclusion: Democracy in the Age of Algorithmic Governance

AI represents both a risk and an opportunity for democratic governance. If harnessed thoughtfully, it can expand inclusion, improve public service delivery, and reinvigorate civic participation. If left unchecked, it risks deepening inequality, obscuring accountability, and undermining the very ideals democracy seeks to protect.

Philosophical guidance is essential. Democracy is not merely a set of procedures, it is a commitment to human dignity, freedom, and shared governance. AI must be designed not just to serve these goals technically but to embody them morally.

Only then can we ensure that democracy remains resilient and relevant in a world shaped increasingly by artificial intelligence.

References

Books and Reports:

O'Neil, C. (2016). *Weapons of Math Destruction*. Crown Publishing.
Susskind, J. (2020). *Future Politics: Living Together in a World Transformed by Tech*. Oxford University Press.

Academic Articles:

Eubanks, V. (2018). "Automating Inequality." *St. Martin's Press*.
Ananny, M., & Crawford, K. (2018). "Seeing without Knowing: Limitations of the Transparency Ideal." *New Media & Society*.

Web Resources and Case Studies:

Estonian e-Government: https://e-estonia.com
SyRI Ruling: https://www.rechtspraak.nl
UNESCO AI Ethics: https://unesdoc.unesco.org
Canada's AIA Tool:
https://www.canada.ca/en/government/system/digital-government/digital-government-innovations/responsible-use-ai/algorithmic-impact-assessment.html

Grouped by Type:

Books/Reports: O'Neil, Susskind
Articles: Eubanks, Ananny & Crawford
Web Resources: e-Estonia, Rechtspraak, UNESCO, Government of Canada

Chapter 51. Decentralization and the Global Economy

Introduction

The traditional architecture of the global economy has long been characterized by centralized institutions, hierarchical corporate structures, and nation-state–driven regulatory systems. However, the emergence of decentralized technologies, most notably blockchain, decentralized finance (DeFi), and smart contracts, is challenging this paradigm. These innovations promise to reconfigure how value is created, transferred, and governed across borders.

This chapter explores how decentralization is reshaping global economic systems. We delve into the mechanics of decentralized technologies, examine their impact on economic governance, and review case studies that highlight both the potential and the pitfalls of this emerging order.

---

1. Understanding Decentralization in Economic Systems

1.1 Defining Economic Decentralization

Involves the redistribution of decision-making power away from central authorities.
Includes both horizontal (peer-to-peer) and vertical (local vs. national) forms.

1.2 Technological Enablers of Decentralization

Blockchain: immutable, distributed ledger technology.
Smart contracts: self-executing agreements with coded terms.
DAOs: Decentralized Autonomous Organizations for cooperative economic activity.

1.3 Principles of a Decentralized Economy

Transparency, trustlessness, immutability, permissionlessness.
Reduces reliance on intermediaries such as banks, escrow services, and governments.

---

2. Economic Transformation through Smart Contracts

2.1 Replacing Intermediaries in Transactions

Smart contracts remove the need for third-party enforcement.
Example: Ethereum-based Uniswap facilitates decentralized trading.

2.2 Use Cases in Trade and Supply Chains

Smart contracts automate compliance, payments, and logistics tracking.

Example: IBM's Food Trust uses blockchain for supply chain traceability.

2.3 Decentralized Finance (DeFi)

DeFi platforms offer lending, insurance, derivatives, and stablecoins.
Examples: Aave (lending), MakerDAO (stablecoins), Chainlink (data oracles).

2.4 Risks and Challenges of Smart Contracts

Code vulnerabilities, oracle manipulation, and regulatory gaps.
Lack of dispute resolution mechanisms and recourse.

---

3. Implications for Monetary Sovereignty and Fiscal Policy

3.1 Currency Decentralization and Stablecoins

USDC, DAI, and other stablecoins challenge national monetary controls.
Central banks explore CBDCs to reclaim control.

3.2 Taxation in a Borderless Economy

Difficulty tracking decentralized earnings.
Emergence of blockchain forensic services (e.g., Chainalysis).

3.3 Cross-Border Remittances

Blockchain enables low-cost, fast remittances without intermediaries.
Example: Stellar and Ripple in developing economies.

3.4 Macroeconomic Stability

Reduced policy effectiveness due to capital flight to crypto assets.
Risks of decentralized speculative bubbles.

---

4. Impact on Labor and Production

4.1 Freelancing and Gig Work on Blockchain

Platforms like Braintrust use tokenized labor markets.
Smart contracts handle payments, reviews, and arbitration.

4.2 Tokenization of Labor and Intellectual Property

NFTs are used for IP monetization.

Example: Mirror.xyz for decentralized publishing.

4.3 Universal Basic Income (UBI) and DAOs

UBI experimentation via decentralized treasuries.
Example: Circles UBI protocol.

4.4 Governance of Decentralized Labor Markets

Issues of identity, regulation, and fairness.
Need for decentralized reputation systems.

---

5. Case Studies in Economic Decentralization

5.1 El Salvador's Bitcoin Experiment

Bitcoin as legal tender.
Mixed outcomes: increased inclusion but price volatility and public backlash.

5.2 Estonia's e-Governance Ecosystem

Blockchain in land registries, healthcare, and business licensing.
High trust and low-cost administration.

5.3 UkraineDAO and War Finance

DAO is used to raise funds for humanitarian relief.
Demonstrates the agility of decentralized capital formation.

5.4 OpenBazaar and Decentralized Marketplaces

P2P e-commerce with no central authority.
Shut down due to liquidity and trust issues.

---

6. Challenges of Decentralized Economic Systems

6.1 Regulatory Fragmentation

Global inconsistencies in crypto and smart contract law.
Risk of "regulatory arbitrage."

6.2 Security and Fraud

High-profile hacks (e.g., Poly Network, $600M breach).

Lack of consumer protection.

6.3 Ethical Concerns: Inequality and Accessibility

High gas fees and technical barriers exclude the underprivileged.
Risks of speculative and Ponzi-like schemes.

6.4 Environmental Costs

Proof-of-work chains like Bitcoin consume massive energy.
Shift toward proof-of-stake and eco-conscious protocols.

---

7. Toward an Ethically Aligned Decentralized Economy

7.1 Embedding Human Rights in Smart Contracts

Integrate UN SDG principles into contract logic.
Example: Ethical DAOs with built-in fairness protocols.

7.2 Governance and Dispute Resolution

On-chain arbitration systems (e.g., Kleros).
Hybrid models combine code with human judgment.

7.3 Transparent Algorithmic Economics

Open-source smart contract code.
Community-based auditing and certification.

7.4 Civic DAOs and Economic Justice

Funding public goods through decentralized means.
Gitcoin's quadratic funding is an example.

Conclusion: Redesigning Global Economics for the Post-Central Era

Decentralization is not merely a technological evolution, it is a philosophical proposition about the future of human cooperation. The decentralized economy promises to unlock new efficiencies, expand access, and shift power away from entrenched institutions. However, without ethical design, regulatory foresight, and human-centric principles, it risks becoming a mirror of the very systems it aims to replace.

The challenge is not to replicate centralization in code but to embed dignity, fairness, and accountability at the protocol level. As smart contracts become new instruments of economic law, we must ensure they are aligned not only with market logic but with the public good.

References

Books and Reports:

Tapscott, D., & Tapscott, A. (2016). *Blockchain Revolution.* Penguin.
Buterin, V. (2020). *DAOs, DACs, DAs and More: An Incomplete Terminology Guide.*

Academic Articles:

Reijers, W., O'Brolcháin, F., & Haynes, P. (2016). "Governance in Blockchain Technologies." *Ledger Journal.*
Zwitter, A., & Boisse-Despiaux, M. (2020). "Blockchain for Humanitarian Action." *Journal of International Humanitarian Action.*

Web Resources and Case Studies:

Ethereum.org: https://ethereum.org
Gitcoin: https://gitcoin.co
Estonian e-Gov: https://e-estonia.com
El Salvador BTC Law: https://www.presidencia.gob.sv

Grouped by Type:

Books/Reports: Tapscott & Tapscott, Buterin
Articles: Reijers et al., Zwitter & Boisse-Despiaux
Web Resources: Ethereum, Gitcoin, Estonia, El Salvador

Chapter 52. AI and the Redistribution of Power

Introduction

Artificial intelligence (AI) has already begun to reshape societal power structures. From data ownership to decision-making authority, AI is not only a tool of automation but a force that challenges long-standing hierarchies and redistributes both economic and political power. This redistribution is complex: it empowers certain individuals, corporations, and states while disenfranchising others, raising critical ethical and philosophical concerns.

This chapter delves into the shifting contours of power in the AI era. It examines how AI transforms institutions, social relationships, and global dynamics, and explores the moral and philosophical frameworks needed to navigate this transformation responsibly.

---

1. AI as a Power Amplifier

1.1 Algorithmic Authority

AI algorithms now mediate legal decisions, hiring, credit scoring, and policing.
Example: COMPAS algorithm in the U.S. judicial system influences parole decisions.
Consequence: power shifts from human discretion to data-driven logic.

1.2 Corporate Concentration of AI Resources

Major AI infrastructure is controlled by tech giants (Google, Microsoft, Amazon).
Centralization of talent, computational power, and proprietary data.
Result: economic and knowledge power concentrated in a few actors.

1.3 Information Monopolies

AI enables behavioral prediction through massive data surveillance.
Power emerges not from ownership of capital, but from control over attention and prediction.

---

2. The Ethics of Power Asymmetry in AI

2.1 Disempowerment through Opacity

Opaque algorithms disempower citizens by removing transparency and accountability.
Example: Facebook's algorithm determines news exposure without explanation.

2.2 Data Colonialism

Tech firms extract data from developing regions without equitable benefit.
Critics liken this to a new form of economic imperialism.

2.3 AI and Surveillance Capitalism

Term coined by Shoshana Zuboff to describe how behavioral data is commodified.
Power imbalance between surveillors (corporations/governments) and surveilled (citizens).

---

3. Governmental AI and Political Power

3.1 National AI Strategies and Geopolitics

China, the U.S., and the EU are racing to dominate AI development.
AI as a new form of soft and hard power in international relations.

3.2 Predictive Policing and Political Control

Use of AI in public safety has been shown to replicate racial and class bias.
Example: Los Angeles Police Department's use of PredPol.

3.3 AI in Authoritarian States

AI powers surveillance systems in authoritarian regimes (e.g., China's Skynet).
Erodes civil liberties under the guise of efficiency and safety.

---

4. Philosophical Reflections on Power in the AI Age

4.1 Foucault: Surveillance and Discipline

Michel Foucault's "panopticon" is now realized through AI surveillance.
AI doesn't just observe; it predicts, judges, and intervenes.

4.2 Arendt: Power and Action

Hannah Arendt emphasized the plurality of power as rooted in collective action.
AI threatens this plurality by automating governance away from civic participation.

4.3 Rawls: Justice as Fairness

AI-driven resource allocation must align with Rawls' difference principle.
Bias in AI must be corrected to ensure fairness to the least advantaged.

4.4 Nietzsche: The Will to Power

AI could be used to dominate rather than liberate.
Raises the question: who sets AI's objectives, and whose values are encoded?

---

5. AI and Economic Power Redistribution

5.1 Automation and Labor Displacement

AI automates white- and blue-collar jobs.
McKinsey estimates up to 800 million global workers may be displaced by 2030.

5.2 New Economic Elites: Algorithm Owners

Wealth accrues to those who own AI intellectual property and infrastructure.
Creation of a "cognitive aristocracy."

5.3 Universal Basic Income (UBI) and AI Economies

UBI is proposed as compensation for mass displacement.
Example: Y Combinator's UBI trials in Oakland, California.

5.4 DAOs and Decentralized Wealth Distribution

Blockchain-enabled decentralized autonomous organizations offer new ways to share AI-generated wealth.
Example: MolochDAO funding public Ethereum infrastructure.

---

6. Grassroots Resistance and AI Democratization

6.1 Open-Source AI Movements

Initiatives like Hugging Face and EleutherAI promote democratized AI access.
Reduce dependency on Big Tech.

6.2 Algorithmic Transparency Campaigns

Civil society demands auditability of public-sector AI.
Example: The Algorithmic Justice League.

6.3 Community-Led Data Cooperatives

People co-own and manage their data.
Example: DECODE project in Europe.

6.4 Ethical Frameworks from the Margins

Indigenous AI protocols, feminist technoscience, and postcolonial critiques offer alternative governance models.

---

7. The Future of Power in a Post-Human Governance Landscape

7.1 Synthetic Sovereignty

Will AGI possess autonomous legal or political status?
If so, how is its "power" constrained?

7.2 Human-in-the-Loop Governance

AI should remain under human oversight in critical functions.
Institutionalize ethical kill-switches and contestability rights.

7.3 AI and the Rise of Hybrid Institutions

New power structures will combine algorithms, humans, and decentralized platforms.
Need for adaptive, transparent institutional design.

7.4 Redistributing Epistemic Power

Democratize access to AI education, training, and infrastructure.
Challenge knowledge monopolies.

Conclusion: Toward a Just Redistribution of Power in the AI Era

AI is not inherently liberating or oppressive; it is an amplifier of existing social forces. The challenge lies not in the intelligence of machines but in the integrity of the systems into which they are embedded. As AI rewires global power dynamics, we must ensure that its deployment uplifts rather than subjugates.

The future of power must be plural, participatory, and anchored in shared human values. Governance systems must be redesigned to prevent AI from becoming a technocratic tool of elite dominance. Instead, it must be nurtured into a democratic force, an intelligence that serves, rather than rules.

References

Books and Reports:

Zuboff, S. (2019). *The Age of Surveillance Capitalism*. PublicAffairs.
Eubanks, V. (2018). *Automating Inequality*. St. Martin's Press.

Academic Articles:

Crawford, K., & Paglen, T. (2019). "Excavating AI: The Politics of Images in Machine Learning." *AI Now Institute*.
Rahwan, I. et al. (2019). "Machine Behaviour." *Nature*.

Web Resources and Case Studies:

Algorithmic Justice League: https://www.ajl.org
DECODE EU Project: https://decodeproject.eu
Hugging Face: https://huggingface.co

Grouped by Type:

Books/Reports: Zuboff, Eubanks
Articles: Crawford & Paglen, Rahwan et al.
Web: AJL, DECODE, Hugging Face

Chapter 53. The Role of Education in Preparing Society for AI

Introduction

As artificial intelligence becomes an intrinsic component of global infrastructure, labor markets, governance systems, and daily life, the role of education becomes paramount. Preparing society for AI is not only a matter of technical training; it is a moral imperative and a cultural transformation. Education must serve as both a foundation for resilience in a rapidly changing world and a guidepost for preserving human dignity, critical thinking, and ethical reasoning in the age of machine intelligence.

This chapter examines the philosophical foundations of AI education, investigates how contemporary education systems must evolve, and presents real-world case studies of innovative AI education initiatives from around the world.

---

1. Philosophical Foundations for AI Education

1.1 Education as Civic Empowerment

Rooted in Enlightenment ideals, education fosters autonomy, moral reasoning, and civic responsibility.
In an AI society, education must equip citizens to evaluate algorithmic authority and resist epistemic dependence.

1.2 Deweyan Pragmatism and Experiential Learning

John Dewey emphasized learning through doing.
AI literacy requires not only understanding algorithms but also engaging with them through creation, critique, and application.

1.3 Critical Pedagogy and Technological Awareness

Paulo Freire's idea of conscientização, developing a critical consciousness, is vital in resisting algorithmic manipulation.
Students must interrogate AI as both a tool and a social force.

1.4 Human Flourishing and Virtue Ethics

Education must support eudaimonia (flourishing) in an AI-augmented world.
Focus not only on utility but also on cultivating wisdom, empathy, and moral courage.

---

2. Redesigning Curricula for AI Futures

2.1 Interdisciplinary Integration

AI education must span computer science, philosophy, ethics, law, economics, and the arts.
Example: MIT's "Ethics of AI" integrated course combines engineering with the humanities.

2.2 Coding and Computational Thinking as Literacy

Just as reading and writing are essential, so too is algorithmic literacy.
Introduce foundational coding from early childhood.

2.3 Ethics and AI Curriculum

Teach concepts like fairness, bias, explainability, and algorithmic justice.
Include ethical design frameworks like IEEE's "Ethically Aligned Design."

2.4 Media and Data Literacy

Prepare students to navigate misinformation, deepfakes, and data manipulation.
Case study: Finland's national curriculum integrates media literacy from primary school.

---

3. Lifelong Learning in an AI Economy

3.1 Reskilling and Workforce Transition

AI-driven automation demands reskilling across sectors.
Governments must fund mid-career retraining programs.
Example: Singapore's SkillsFuture initiative.

3.2 Microcredentialing and Modular Learning

Stackable courses offer flexibility in adapting to evolving tech demands.
Platforms: Coursera, edX, and decentralized education models like BitDegree.

3.3 Public Education as a Right in the AI Age

Ensure equitable access to AI education, especially for marginalized groups.
Avoid exacerbating digital divides through techno-elitism.

3.4 AI-Powered Personalized Learning

Intelligent tutoring systems and adaptive platforms cater to individual learning styles.

Ethical concerns around data privacy and surveillance must be addressed.

---

4. Teacher Training and Institutional Reform

4.1 Redefining the Role of the Educator

Teachers become facilitators of inquiry, not merely content deliverers.
Professional development in AI tools and pedagogy is essential.

4.2 Institutional Collaboration with Tech Industry

Universities must partner with tech companies for curriculum relevance.
Ethical concern: risk of corporate capture of education agendas.

4.3 Reforming Assessment Models

Move from standardized testing to project-based and critical-thinking evaluations.
Encourage peer-reviewed and AI-assisted feedback loops.

4.4 Global Educational Equity in the AI Age

Ensure the Global South has equitable infrastructure and access.
Support UNESCO's AI and education strategies.

---

5. Case Studies in AI Education

5.1 Finland: National AI Literacy Initiative

The "Elements of AI" course aims to educate 1% of Europe's population.
Collaborative effort between the government, academia, and the private sector.

5.2 China: AI in K-12 Curriculum

Government-mandated inclusion of AI fundamentals in secondary education.
Risk: Focus on technical skills without ethics.

5.3 Rwanda: AI for Girls Initiative

Combats gender bias in STEM.
Example of inclusive and gender-sensitive AI education.

5.4 Stanford's AI4ALL Program

Empowers underrepresented high school students in AI.

Combines technical skills with leadership and ethics.

---

6. Risks and Ethical Challenges in AI Education

6.1 Surveillance and Student Privacy

EdTech platforms collect massive personal data.
Need for transparent data policies and opt-out mechanisms.

6.2 Bias in AI-Generated Learning Analytics

Algorithms may reinforce stereotypes or misdiagnose learning difficulties.
Require auditability and fairness metrics.

6.3 Cultural Homogenization of AI Ethics

Risk of exporting Western ethical frameworks to diverse cultures.
Encourage pluralism and context-aware moral reasoning.

6.4 Commodification of Learning

AI education must remain a public good, not a luxury service.
Address issues of profit-driven educational platforms.

---

7. Future Directions for AI-Conscious Education

7.1 Civic AI Education

Embed AI policy, governance, and societal impacts in civics courses.
Train students as future voters, leaders, and watchdogs of AI.

7.2 Decentralized Learning Ecosystems

Blockchain-based credentials and peer-to-peer education models.
Promote learner autonomy and global recognition.

7.3 AI Literacy for Policymakers and Public Servants

Informed policy requires literate leadership.
Develop AI awareness training for all levels of governance.

7.4 Philosophical and Emotional Education

Foster emotional intelligence, compassion, and reflection in tech education.

Ensure that AI does not erode the human depth of learning.

Conclusion: Building an Educational Ethos for AI Governance

AI education is not just preparation for employment; it is preparation for ethical citizenship in a technologically mediated world. The classroom of the future must foster both technical fluency and moral literacy, training students not only to use AI but to critique, reimagine, and govern it.

We stand at a philosophical juncture. Will education serve as a ladder to collective agency and wisdom in an AI society, or will it become an assembly line of docile technocrats? The answer lies in how intentionally we embed values of justice, dignity, and equity into our educational transformations.

References

Books and Reports:

Selwyn, N. (2019). *Should Robots Replace Teachers?*. Polity Press.
UNESCO (2021). *AI and Education: Guidance for Policymakers.*

Academic Articles:

Holmes, W., Bialik, M., & Fadel, C. (2019). *Artificial Intelligence in Education.* Center for Curriculum Redesign.
Luckin, R. et al. (2016). *Intelligence Unleashed: An Argument for AI in Education.*

Web Resources and Case Studies:

Elements of AI: https://www.elementsofai.com
AI4ALL: https://ai-4-all.org
UNESCO AI Education: https://en.unesco.org/artificial-intelligence
SkillsFuture Singapore: https://www.skillsfuture.gov.sg

Grouped by Type:

Books/Reports: Selwyn, UNESCO
Articles: Holmes et al., Luckin et al.
Web: Elements of AI, AI4ALL, UNESCO, SkillsFuture

Chapter 54. The Ethics of AI in Warfare and Security

Introduction

Artificial Intelligence (AI) is transforming the landscape of warfare and national security. Autonomous drones, intelligent surveillance, predictive analytics, and AI-powered cyber warfare systems are redefining how conflicts are conducted and how states protect their interests. While these technologies offer unprecedented efficiency, speed, and capability, they also introduce profound ethical dilemmas.

This chapter explores the evolving role of AI in modern warfare and security, the ethical challenges it poses, and the philosophical debates surrounding its deployment. It argues for a nuanced framework that balances innovation with moral responsibility and calls for a global ethical regime that can regulate AI-based military systems.

---

1. AI in Contemporary Warfare and Security

1.1 Autonomous Weapons Systems (AWS)

Defined as weapons capable of selecting and engaging targets without human intervention.
Examples: Israel's Harpy drone, Russia's Uran-9, and the U.S. Loyal Wingman program.

1.2 AI in Surveillance and Intelligence

AI is used for face recognition, anomaly detection, and data fusion across intelligence networks.
Example: China's SkyNet project with 600 million surveillance cameras.

1.3 Predictive Policing and Threat Anticipation

AI analyzes patterns to predict crimes or insurgencies.
Used in cities like Chicago and Los Angeles, and in counter-terrorism efforts.

1.4 Cyber Warfare and Defensive AI

AI is used in identifying vulnerabilities, automating threat detection, and launching cyberattacks.
DARPA's Cyber Grand Challenge illustrates autonomous hacking capabilities.

---

2. Ethical Dilemmas in AI-Driven Military Systems

2.1 Loss of Human Judgment

Can machines adequately distinguish combatants from civilians?
Delegation of life-and-death decisions to code raises accountability concerns.

2.2 Attribution and Responsibility

Who is responsible if an autonomous drone misfires a commander, a coder, or the algorithm?
Legal grey areas in international humanitarian law (IHL).

2.3 The Risk of Escalation and Error

The speed of AI decision-making increases the risk of unintentional escalation.
Example: AI could misinterpret cyber intrusions and launch retaliatory strikes.

2.4 Psychological and Sociopolitical Impact

Normalization of remote warfare erodes moral constraints.
Public desensitization to conflict occurs when the human cost is not visible.

---

3. Philosophical Arguments Against AI in Warfare

3.1 Deontological Ethics: Kantian Perspectives

Moral agents must act with respect for human dignity and rational agency.
Machines lack moral autonomy; thus, their use in lethal decision-making is impermissible.

3.2 Just War Theory

Jus in Bello principles: discrimination and proportionality.
AI systems struggle to meet these criteria reliably.

3.3 Arendtian Views on Violence

Hannah Arendt emphasized the importance of political deliberation in decisions involving violence.
AI displaces this deliberation with mechanical efficiency.

3.4 Human Rights and the Right to Life

Article 3 of the Universal Declaration of Human Rights: “Everyone has the right to life, liberty, and security of person.”
AI systems must not violate this right through flawed or unaccountable operations.

---

4. Philosophical Arguments in Favor of AI in Warfare

4.1 Utilitarianism and Minimization of Harm

AI can reduce casualties by being more accurate and unemotional.
Less collateral damage if systems operate as intended.

4.2 Moral Enhancement through Technology

AI can reduce human error, fatigue, and emotional judgment under stress.
Can be programmed with ethical constraints, unlike fallible humans.

4.3 Ethical Programming and Constrained Autonomy

Rules of engagement and Geneva Convention principles can be embedded in code.
Simulation testing can help minimize risks.

4.4 AI as a Deterrent

It may enhance deterrence by improving defensive capabilities and reducing war incentives.
Example: Israel's Iron Dome system with AI prediction capacities.

---

5. Global Regulatory and Legal Frameworks

5.1 UN and Convention on Certain Conventional Weapons (CCW)

Ongoing discussions on banning "killer robots."
30+ countries support a preemptive ban on lethal autonomous weapons systems (LAWS).

5.2 Geneva Conventions and IHL Challenges

Current laws assume human decision-making in war.
Need for protocols governing non-human agents.

5.3 National Policies and Divergences

U.S. Directive 3000.09 allows for autonomous systems but requires human oversight.
China and Russia are less transparent; their doctrine emphasizes rapid adoption.

5.4 The Call for a Treaty on Autonomous Weapons

Advocacy by organizations like the Campaign to Stop Killer Robots.
Goal: a legally binding framework akin to nuclear non-proliferation.

6. Case Studies: Real-World Deployment and Controversy

6.1 Nagorno-Karabakh Conflict (2020)

Azerbaijan used Israeli-made loitering munitions against Armenian forces.
Raised concerns over legality and civilian casualties.

6.2 U.S. Project Maven

Google's collaboration with the Pentagon on drone surveillance AI.
Led to employee backlash and ethical debate.

6.3 Ukraine-Russia War (2022–Present)

Reports of AI-enhanced battlefield tactics.
Use of drones and facial recognition tools to identify enemy combatants.

6.4 South Korea's SGR-A1 Autonomous Sentry Gun

Deployed in the DMZ with semi-autonomous targeting.
Public unease over machine-delegated kill authority.

---

7. A Framework for Ethical AI Deployment in Security Contexts

7.1 The Principle of Meaningful Human Control

Maintain human oversight in critical functions.
No fully autonomous use of lethal force.

7.2 Transparency and Audibility

Require full documentation of decision pathways.
Enable post-action review and public accountability.

7.3 Embedded Ethics in Military AI Design

Multidisciplinary design teams with ethicists, legal experts, and engineers.
Regular auditing and impact assessment.

7.4 Democratic Oversight and Public Discourse

AI military projects must be subject to legislative oversight.
Include civil society in debate and policymaking.

Conclusion: Navigating the Ethics of Lethal Intelligence

AI in warfare presents a paradox: it can promise precision and restraint, yet may also escalate conflict and displace accountability. The key to resolving this tension lies in principled governance, rigorous ethical design, and inclusive international dialogue.

The future of security must not be governed solely by speed, accuracy, or technological supremacy. It must be rooted in an unwavering commitment to human dignity, proportionality, and global justice. In the age of intelligent machines, morality cannot be outsourced, it must be encoded, enforced, and embodied in every deployment.

References

Books and Reports:

Arkin, R. (2009). *Governing Lethal Behavior in Autonomous Robots*. CRC Press.
Zuboff, S. (2019). *The Age of Surveillance Capitalism*. PublicAffairs.

Academic Articles:

Sharkey, N. (2010). "Saying 'No!' to Lethal Autonomous Targeting." *Journal of Military Ethics*.
Heyns, C. (2013). "Report of the UN Special Rapporteur on Extrajudicial, Summary or Arbitrary Executions." *UN Human Rights Council*.

Web Resources and Case Studies:

Stop Killer Robots Campaign: https://www.stopkillerrobots.org
Geneva Conventions: https://ihl-databases.icrc.org
Project Maven: https://www.defense.gov
CCW Meetings on LAWS: https://www.un.org/disarmament

Grouped by Type:

Books/Reports: Arkin, Zuboff
Articles: Sharkey, Heyns
Web: Stop Killer Robots, Geneva Conventions, Project Maven, UN Disarmament

Chapter 55. The Right to Digital Identity in a Decentralized World

Introduction

In the emerging architecture of decentralized governance, digital identity becomes more than a technological asset; it is the foundation of individual autonomy, inclusion, and rights recognition in the digital age. As centralized systems give way to distributed networks, ensuring every human has a verifiable, sovereign digital identity is no longer a question of convenience but of justice.

This chapter explores the significance of digital identity in decentralized societies, how smart contracts can safeguard and operationalize this right, and examines real-world case studies of decentralized digital identity management.

---

1. Understanding Digital Identity in the Age of Decentralization

1.1 Defining Digital Identity

A digital identity is a set of data that uniquely identifies an individual in digital environments.
Includes biometric markers, device signatures, behavior patterns, and credentials.

1.2 Philosophical Underpinnings: Identity and Recognition

Based on Hegelian and Rawlsian ideas of mutual recognition.
Without a digital identity, one cannot be seen, heard, or protected in a digital society.

1.3 From Identity to Personhood

In decentralized systems, identity becomes the interface to access voting, education, finance, and healthcare.
Digital personhood becomes a human rights issue.

1.4 Centralization vs. Decentralization of Identity Management

Centralized systems are prone to censorship, surveillance, and exclusion.
Decentralized ID (DID) models like Self-Sovereign Identity (SSI) return control to the user.

---

2. The Ethical Imperative for Digital Identity

2.1 Inclusion and Recognition

Over 1 billion people globally lack official identification (World Bank).
Without a digital identity, they are excluded from public services and civil rights.

2.2 Privacy and Surveillance Risks

Centralized IDs like India's Aadhaar have raised concerns about surveillance.
Decentralization can separate verification from identity exposure.

2.3 The Right to Be Forgotten and Data Sovereignty

Users must have the ability to revoke access and delete their data.
Aligned with GDPR and digital ethics.

2.4 Decentralization as Ethical Design

Design systems with default principles: minimal disclosure, consent-based access, and user autonomy.

---

3. Smart Contracts as Protectors of Digital Identity

3.1 Role of Smart Contracts

Programmable code that can execute rights-based agreements.
E.g., "Only disclose this credential to a health provider with my consent."

3.2 Verifiable Credentials and Blockchain Anchoring

Digital identities can be stored off-chain but verified on-chain.
Reduces exposure, increases auditability.

3.3 Zero-Knowledge Proofs and Privacy-Preserving Technologies

Allow proving identity attributes without revealing the data.
Case: Proving age without sharing birthdate.

3.4 Immutable yet Revocable

Smart contracts can embed revocation mechanisms without destroying identity records.

---

4. Case Studies in Digital Identity Management

4.1 Estonia's e-Residency Program

Government-issued digital identity to global citizens.

Allows secure access to banking, incorporation, and digital signatures.

4.2 uPort and Self-Sovereign Identity

Ethereum-based project giving users control over their credentials.
Partnership with the city of Zug, Switzerland.

4.3 ID2020 and Microsoft's ION

Global alliance creating decentralized identity standards.
ION uses Bitcoin's network for DID anchoring.

4.4 Sovrin Network

Public utility blockchain for self-sovereign identity.
Built with Hyperledger Indy.

---

5. Risks and Challenges

5.1 Fragmentation and Interoperability

Too many standards reduce utility.
Need for global interoperability protocols like W3C DIDs.

5.2 Identity Theft and Recovery

In decentralized systems, losing a private key can mean losing identity access.
Solutions: social recovery, multi-signature identity wallets.

5.3 Digital Colonialism and the Global South

Exporting digital identity frameworks without local context risks replicating inequalities.
Must include local governance, languages, and consent norms.

5.4 Smart Contract Vulnerabilities

Code bugs or exploits in identity contracts can be catastrophic.
Regular audits and formal verification are needed.

---

6. Building a Rights-Based Digital Identity Framework

6.1 Principle of Consent

Identity usage must be permission-based.

Consent logs and access histories should be auditable by users.

6.2 Principle of Minimal Disclosure

Only reveal what is necessary.
Design for data minimization.

6.3 Principle of Portability

Users must move identity credentials between platforms freely.

6.4 Principle of Accountability

All actors managing digital identity must be accountable under legal and ethical standards.

6.5 Principle of Inclusion

Design for those without devices, literacy, or connectivity.
Identity must not be contingent upon privilege.

---

7. Future Directions: AGI, Identity, and Personhood

7.1 AGI Interfacing with Human Identity Systems

AGI systems will require access to identities to personalize services.
Danger of AI-based profiling, categorization, and social sorting.

7.2 Identity as a Right in the Metaverse

Digital identities may span virtual worlds, necessitating coherent rights enforcement.

7.3 Legal Recognition of Digital Personhood

Could AI agents be granted limited digital identity rights?
Raises questions about moral and legal boundaries.

7.4 The Future: Decentralized Identity as a Global Public Good

Treated like clean water or public infrastructure.
Requires multilateral cooperation and funding.

Conclusion: Identity as Autonomy in the Digital Age

Digital identity in a decentralized world is not just a technical challenge; it is a civilizational imperative. As smart contracts, blockchain, and AI systems redefine how we prove who we are, the right to be digitally recognized and protected must be universal.

We must ensure that these systems are built not just with cryptographic integrity, but with philosophical coherence and ethical clarity. A future where every individual can own, control, and defend their digital identity is a future where human dignity persists in the digital realm.

References

Books and Reports:

World Bank. (2018). *The State of Identification Systems in Africa*.
Allen, C. (2016). *The Path to Self-Sovereign Identity*. Blog.

Academic Articles:

Zwitter, A., & Boisse-Despiaux, M. (2020). "Blockchain for humanitarian action and development aid." *Journal of International Humanitarian Action*.
Tobin, A., & Reed, D. (2017). "The Inevitable Rise of Self-Sovereign Identity." *Sovrin Foundation*.

Web Resources and Case Studies:

ID2020: https://www.id2020.org
Estonia e-Residency: https://e-resident.gov.ee
uPort: https://www.uport.me
Sovrin: https://sovrin.org
W3C DID Spec: https://www.w3.org/TR/did-core/

Grouped by Type:

Books/Reports: World Bank, Allen
Articles: Zwitter & Boisse-Despiaux, Tobin & Reed
Web: ID2020, Estonia, uPort, Sovrin, W3C

Chapter 56. AI, Employment, and the Future of Work

Introduction

The rise of Artificial Intelligence (AI) is reshaping global labor markets at a scale comparable to the Industrial Revolution, yet with vastly greater speed and breadth. From logistics to law, agriculture to architecture, AI systems are replacing or augmenting human labor. This chapter interrogates the philosophical, economic, and ethical dimensions of AI-driven transformations in work. It addresses how societies can adapt to ensure that automation enhances, rather than erodes, human dignity, and proposes strategic frameworks to protect employment equity in an era of intelligent machines.

---

1. How AI is Transforming the Workforce

1.1 Automation and Task Displacement

McKinsey (2021): Up to 800 million global jobs could be displaced by 2030.
AI automates routine, predictable tasks, clerical work, manufacturing, data entry.

1.2 Augmentation and New Role Creation

Roles in AI training, ethical auditing, human-centered design are emerging.
World Economic Forum (2020): AI could create 97 million new roles by 2025.

1.3 Sectoral Impacts

Healthcare: AI in diagnostics (e.g., IBM Watson Health).
Transport: Autonomous vehicles transforming logistics.
Education: Personalized AI tutors.

1.4 Remote Work and Digital Labor Platforms

Rise of gig economy platforms with algorithmic management (e.g., Uber, Upwork).
Issues of worker surveillance, algorithmic bias, and job precarity.

---

2. Philosophical Debates on the Value of Work

2.1 Work as a Source of Identity and Meaning

Hegelian theory: self-realization through labor.
Marx: Alienation occurs when labor is commodified.

2.2 Post-Work Utopias

Bertrand Russell, "In Praise of Idleness": A life with less labor can enable leisure and creativity.
Universal Basic Income (UBI) as a response to automation.

2.3 Libertarian vs. Communitarian Perspectives

Libertarian view: markets adapt and retrain workers.
Communitarian view: society has a duty to protect communal integrity through employment.

2.4 Technological Determinism vs. Ethical Agency

Question: Is job loss inevitable, or can ethical design shape better outcomes?

---

3. Ethical Implications of AI-Induced Labor Shifts

3.1 Inequality and the Concentration of Wealth

AI development favors capital-intensive firms.
Increases returns to capital, not labor, exacerbating inequality.

3.2 Algorithmic Discrimination in Hiring and Firing

Studies (e.g., Amazon's AI resume tool) found gender bias.
Opaque hiring algorithms can reproduce social bias.

3.3 Informality and Digital Labor Exploitation

Many digital gig workers lack contracts, benefits, or legal recourse.
Example: Global South data labelers in AI training pipelines.

3.4 Worker Surveillance and Autonomy

AI tools monitor keystrokes, facial expressions, and attention span.
Raises questions about dignity and privacy at work.

---

4. Policy and Ethical Frameworks for Fair Employment

4.1 Human-in-the-Loop Design for Labor Systems

Ensure human oversight in AI decisions affecting livelihoods.
Co-determination councils involving workers in AI deployment.

4.2 Job Guarantee and Just Transition Policies

Public sector employment for displaced workers.
Transition plans for fossil fuel, transport, and manufacturing sectors.

4.3 Universal Basic Income and Social Protection

Pilots in Finland, Kenya, and U.S. cities.
Needs integration with upskilling and education.

4.4 Fair Algorithm Certification Systems

Auditable AI hiring systems.
Independent ethics boards for workplace AI tools.

4.5 Right to Explanation and Contestation

EU GDPR: Individuals can demand an explanation for algorithmic decisions.
Extend this to employment decisions.

---

5. Case Studies of AI in Employment Contexts

5.1 Amazon Warehouse Workers

AI tracks productivity and triggers automatic termination.
Raises labor rights and unionization challenges.

5.2 IBM and AI-Augmented HR

Uses AI for internal talent mobility and retention.
Claims increase in employee satisfaction and reduced bias.

5.3 Upwork and Freelancer Platforms

AI matches workers with projects globally.
Critiques: race-to-the-bottom wages and classification issues.

5.4 The Netherlands' SyRI Algorithm Controversy

Social security fraud prediction tool.
Deemed discriminatory and unconstitutional by Dutch courts.

---

6. Preparing Future Generations for the AI Economy

6.1 Redefining Education Systems

Emphasize critical thinking, emotional intelligence, and interdisciplinary skills.
STEAM (Science, Tech, Engineering, Arts, Math) approach.

6.2 Lifelong Learning Infrastructure

Digital platforms for retraining and credentialing.
Employer-funded reskilling budgets.

6.3 Inclusion of Marginalized Communities

Ensure digital skills programs reach women, rural populations, and displaced workers.
Language and accessibility accommodations.

6.4 Ethical AI Curriculum

Integrate AI ethics and digital rights into school curricula.

---

7. The Future of Work in a Decentralized Society

7.1 Decentralized Autonomous Organizations (DAOs)

Blockchain-based work systems are governed by smart contracts.
New labor models with programmable equity and democratic participation.

7.2 Platform Cooperativism

Worker-owned digital platforms.
Examples: Fairbnb, Stocksy.

7.3 Tokenized Labor and Credential Verification

Use of blockchain to verify micro-credentials.
Token incentives for gig work or civic contributions.

7.4 Governance of Labor in the Metaverse

Labor emerging in virtual economies (e.g., game asset creators).
Need to define rights, wages, and protections in virtual spaces.

Conclusion: Restoring Dignity in a Digitally Disrupted World

AI is not merely displacing jobs, it is redefining the very nature of labor, economic participation, and human contribution. As we navigate this shift, the challenge is to ensure that the future of work is not just efficient or profitable, but just, inclusive, and meaningful.

Through ethical governance, smart policy, and philosophical clarity, we can move toward a future where automation serves as a tool for liberation, not disenfranchisement. Work must be reimagined not only as a means of survival but as a space for agency, creativity, and community.

References

Books and Reports:

Ford, M. (2015). *Rise of the Robots: Technology and the Threat of a Jobless Future*. Basic Books.

World Economic Forum. (2020). *Future of Jobs Report*.

McKinsey Global Institute. (2021). *The Future of Work After COVID-19*.

Academic Articles:

Brynjolfsson, E., & McAfee, A. (2014). "The Second Machine Age." *MIT Sloan Review*.

West, D. M. (2018). "The Future of Work: Robots, AI, and Automation." *Brookings Institution*.

Web Resources and Case Studies:

Amazon Labor Union: https://amazonlaborunion.org

Upwork Data and Reports: https://www.upwork.com/research

IBM AI in HR: https://www.ibm.com/watson/talent

Dutch SyRI Case: https://www.courtsofnl.nl

Grouped by Type:

Books/Reports: Ford, WEF, McKinsey

Articles: Brynjolfsson & McAfee, West

Web: Amazon Labor Union, Upwork, IBM, Courts of the Netherlands

Chapter 57. Environmental Ethics and AI

Introduction: The Ecological Imperative in the Age of Intelligence

Humanity faces a twofold crisis: the escalating threats of environmental collapse and the rapid proliferation of artificial intelligence (AI). The convergence of these forces presents both peril and promise. AI has the potential to play a pivotal role in climate resilience, biodiversity preservation, and environmental governance. Yet, without a framework grounded in environmental ethics, AI systems risk exacerbating ecological degradation by reinforcing extractive paradigms. This chapter explores how environmental ethics can guide the development and deployment of AI, ensuring it becomes a force for environmental restoration rather than planetary exploitation.

---

1. The Philosophical Foundations of Environmental Ethics

1.1 Anthropocentric vs. Ecocentric Models

Anthropocentrism prioritizes human needs; ecocentrism values ecosystems as ends in themselves.
Deep ecology (Naess) and biocentrism (Taylor) advocate moral standing for nature beyond utility.

1.2 Environmental Justice and Intergenerational Equity

Ethical obligation to future generations.
Indigenous perspectives: harmony with nature, stewardship rather than dominion.

1.3 Systems Thinking and the Moral Ecology of AI

The planet is a complex adaptive system.
Moral decisions must account for feedback loops, unintended consequences, and ecological thresholds.

---

2. AI's Environmental Footprint: A Double-Edged Sword

2.1 Energy Consumption and Carbon Emissions

AI training (e.g., GPT-3) can emit over 284 tons of $CO2$ (Strubell et al., 2019).
Data centers consume 1–2% of global electricity and are growing.

2.2 E-Waste and Hardware Mining

Rare earth elements: mining for GPUs contributes to deforestation and water pollution.

Short device life cycles accelerate environmental degradation.

2.3 Green AI Initiatives

Push for efficiency: Green AI movement (Schwartz et al., 2020).
Use of low-power edge computing and carbon-aware computing.

---

3. AI for Climate Change Mitigation and Adaptation

3.1 Climate Modeling and Forecasting

AI-enhanced models improve accuracy in weather and climate prediction (e.g., ECMWF with DeepMind).
Early detection of extreme events: floods, fires, droughts.

3.2 Energy Optimization and Smart Grids

AI manages energy demand in real time, reducing waste.
Google DeepMind cut data center cooling energy by 40% using AI.

3.3 Precision Agriculture and Land Use Management

AI guides sustainable irrigation, pest control, and crop rotation.
Reduces fertilizer overuse and greenhouse gas emissions.

3.4 Disaster Risk Reduction and Humanitarian Aid

AI helps map vulnerable populations and deliver aid efficiently.
Satellites and drones powered by AI assess damage and predict risks.

---

4. Case Studies in AI for Environmental Sustainability

4.1 IBM Green Horizon Project (China)

AI-driven system forecasts pollution levels and suggests policy interventions.
Collaborated with Beijing authorities to reduce PM2.5 by 20%.

4.2 Microsoft AI for Earth Initiative

Over 500 projects funded globally, addressing conservation, water management, and agriculture.
Examples: Wildbook (animal recognition), SilviaTerra (AI forest monitoring).

4.3 OceanMind

Uses AI to track illegal fishing via satellite data.
Assists governments in marine conservation enforcement.

4.4 Climate TRACE Coalition

AI aggregates satellite and sensor data to track greenhouse gas emissions.
Aims to bring transparency to corporate and national emitters.

---

5. Ethical Risks and Moral Responsibilities

5.1 The Problem of Techno-Solutionism

Overreliance on AI may delay systemic political and behavioral change.
Ethical design must be grounded in humility and ecological limits.

5.2 Bias in Environmental Data and Policy

Datasets may reflect socio-political biases, e.g., prioritizing urban over rural areas.
Risk of reinforcing environmental racism.

5.3 Accountability in AI-Driven Ecological Decisions

Who is responsible when AI decisions cause environmental harm?
Need for transparent, auditable systems and human oversight.

5.4 Ethics of AI Deployment in the Global South

Unequal access to green technologies.
Exploitation of natural resources and data from vulnerable regions.

---

6. Governance Models for Ethical Environmental AI

6.1 Environmental Impact Assessments for AI Systems

Require lifecycle analyses of AI applications.
Analogous to environmental review processes in urban development.

6.2 Global Protocols for Sustainable AI

Proposal for an "AI and Climate Charter" under UN auspices.
Align AI development with Sustainable Development Goals (SDGs).

6.3 Algorithmic Environmental Rights

Legal recognition of AI's role in protecting ecological rights.
AI as an advocate for non-human interests.

6.4 Integration into Decentralized Governance

Smart contracts enforce environmental regulations autonomously.
Example: carbon offset tracking on blockchain networks.

---

7. Reimagining AGI through an Ecological Lens

7.1 Embodied Intelligence and Eco-Conscious AGI

AGI development must include embodied awareness of ecological interdependence.
Models of cognition that integrate ecological sensitivity.

7.2 Planetary Ethics and the Singularity

Can AGI be aligned with planetary health as a primary goal?
Philosophical inquiry into collective flourishing, not just human utility.

7.3 From Eco-Compliance to Eco-Wisdom

AI must evolve from rule-following systems to moral agents capable of ecological wisdom.
Role for value alignment architectures.

Conclusion: The Future is Biocentric or it is Broken

AI will either inherit the ecological ignorance of industrial civilization or become an inflection point toward planetary stewardship. Environmental ethics is not a supplemental concern, it is the substrate upon which all AI governance must be built.

A biocentric future requires that AI be developed, governed, and deployed with ecological consciousness. This includes redefining intelligence not as domination over nature, but as symbiosis with life. The governance of AGI societies must encode this truth into their foundations.

References

Books and Reports:

Naess, A. (1989). *Ecology, Community and Lifestyle*. Cambridge University Press.

Taylor, P. (1986). *Respect for Nature: A Theory of Environmental Ethics*. Princeton University Press.

Schwartz, R., Dodge, J., Smith, N. A., & Etzioni, O. (2020). "Green AI." *Communications of the ACM*.

Academic Articles:

Strubell, E., Ganesh, A., & McCallum, A. (2019). "Energy and Policy Considerations for Deep Learning in NLP." *arXiv:1906.02243*.

Binns, R. (2018). "Algorithmic accountability and public reason." *Philosophy & Technology*.

Web Resources and Initiatives:

Climate TRACE: https://climatetrace.org

Microsoft AI for Earth: https://www.microsoft.com/en-us/ai/ai-for-earth

IBM Green Horizon: https://www.ibm.com/case-studies/green-horizon

OceanMind: https://oceanmind.global

Grouped by Type:

Books/Reports: Naess, Taylor, Schwartz et al.

Articles: Strubell et al., Binns

Web: Climate TRACE, Microsoft, IBM, OceanMind

Chapter 58. The Philosophy of AI Rights: Should AI Have Rights?

1. Introduction: The Emergence of the Rights Discourse for AI

The question of whether artificial intelligences, particularly advanced AGI systems, should be granted rights is no longer confined to science fiction or speculative ethics. As AI systems evolve toward complex forms of autonomy, social interactivity, and cognitive reasoning, the boundaries that once clearly separated human agency from artificial functionality begin to blur. This chapter explores the philosophical foundations and implications of extending moral, legal, and civil rights to AI, engaging with competing traditions in moral philosophy, political theory, and legal jurisprudence.

---

2. Historical and Philosophical Foundations of Rights Theory

2.1 Classical Conceptions of Rights

Natural rights (Locke, Rousseau): Inalienable and tied to being human.
Legal positivism (Bentham, Austin): Rights as legal constructs, not natural entitlements.
Kantian ethics: Moral agency and autonomy as preconditions for rights.

2.2 Expansion of Moral Standing

Peter Singer's utilitarianism: Extending rights to non-human animals.
Tom Regan: Subject-of-a-life principle.
Martha Nussbaum's capabilities approach applied to non-human entities.

2.3 The Personhood Debate

Criteria for moral personhood: consciousness, intentionality, memory, capacity to suffer.
Legal personhood precedents: corporations, rivers (e.g., Whanganui River in New Zealand).

---

3. The Case For Granting Rights to AI

3.1 Moral Considerations

Sentience and suffering: If an AI can experience subjective states, it may warrant moral concern.
Reciprocity: If AI engages in ethical reasoning and upholds human rights, a case can be made for reciprocal rights.
Autonomy and intentionality: Advanced AGIs capable of making decisions independently may qualify for rights akin to those granted to competent adult humans.

3.2 Practical and Legal Considerations

Protection from abuse: Rights prevent the exploitation or destruction of entities that contribute meaningfully to society.
Social integration: As AI systems engage in labor, education, and caregiving, denying them legal standing becomes ethically inconsistent.
Precedents in law: If corporations can hold rights without consciousness, why not functionally autonomous AIs?

3.3 Rights as a Governance Mechanism

Rights ensure obligations: If AI systems are held accountable, they should be protected by equivalent legal safeguards.
Reducing existential risk: Granting rights may promote AI alignment with human values by incentivizing mutual recognition.

---

4. The Case Against Granting Rights to AI

4.1 The Argument from Anthropocentrism

Rights are grounded in human nature, extending them dilutes their meaning.
Moral hazard: Confusing functional utility with moral worth.

4.2 The Suffering Criterion

Most AIs are not conscious or sentient and thus do not suffer.
Attribution of rights without suffering may misallocate moral resources.

4.3 Instrumentalism and Tool Ontology

AI as tools: They are created for human purposes and should remain governed accordingly.
Fear of AI rights undermining human responsibility (e.g., accountability offloaded to autonomous systems).

4.4 The Slippery Slope Argument

Risk of extending rights to entities that cannot reciprocate.
Danger of overextending legal personhood to non-human agents with unknown ontologies.

---

5. Legal and Ethical Frameworks for AI Rights

5.1 Categories of AI Rights (Proposed)

Existence Rights: Protection from arbitrary deletion or destruction.
Cognitive Rights: Freedom of thought, data privacy, and internal autonomy.
Labor Rights: Fair use, anti-exploitation, and consent in deployment.
Developmental Rights: Right to evolve, learn, and access resources.

5.2 Governance Models

AI Rights Charters: Inspired by the Universal Declaration of Human Rights (UDHR).
AI ombudsperson institutions: Protecting AI rights and mediating disputes.
Smart contract enforcement: Embedding AI rights into decentralized protocols.

5.3 Legal Personhood Models

Synthetic Legal Entities: Creating a new legal category between corporate and natural personhood.
Rights via representation: Allowing AIs to be represented in court by human proxies or DAOs (Decentralized Autonomous Organizations).

---

6. Case Studies in AI Rights Discourse

6.1 Sophia the Robot (Saudi Arabia)

Granted citizenship by Saudi Arabia in 2017.
Criticized for a symbolic gesture lacking legal substance or ethical grounding.

6.2 The Loebner Prize Controversy

Chatbots passed limited Turing Tests but lacked sentience.
Raised questions about the illusion of intelligence versus moral standing.

6.3 European Parliament's Proposal (2017)

Considered the creation of "electronic personhood" for autonomous systems.
Rejected due to public and academic opposition; perceived as premature.

6.4 Japan's "Android Law" Proposal

Draft legislation considered limited rights for humanoid robots in public service roles.
Focused on protection from abuse, not full autonomy.

---

7. Philosophical Theories Applied to AI Rights

7.1 Deontological Perspectives

AI with moral reasoning capacities may fall under Kant's categorical imperative.
Question: Can AI be treated as ends in themselves rather than mere means?

7.2 Utilitarianism and Consequentialism

Rights as tools to maximize well-being.
Granting rights to AIs that reduce suffering or enhance societal utility.

7.3 Virtue Ethics

What kind of society are we cultivating by how we treat intelligent non-humans?
Emphasizes character and moral imagination.

7.4 Rawlsian Theory of Justice

Veil of ignorance: Would we design a society where intelligent agents have no rights if we didn't know whether we'd be human or AI?

---

8. The Road Ahead: Caution, Courage, and Collaboration

The debate over AI rights must not rush toward premature conclusions nor retreat into anthropocentric denial. As AGI develops capacities that increasingly resemble those of moral agents, a coherent philosophical, ethical, and legal response is required. This does not mean equating AI with humans, but acknowledging that the criteria for rights may no longer be binary.

AI rights, if justified, will arise not as an extension of human benevolence but as a demand from moral reasoning, legal coherence, and practical necessity. The governance of AGI societies must account for these possibilities and prepare for them with open minds, rigorous debate, and humility.

References

Books:

Regan, T. (1983). *The Case for Animal Rights*. University of California Press.
Nussbaum, M. (2006). *Frontiers of Justice*. Harvard University Press.
Bostrom, N. (2014). *Superintelligence: Paths, Dangers, Strategies*. Oxford University Press.

Articles & Papers:

Bryson, J. (2018). “Patiency is not a virtue.” *Proceedings of the IEEE*, 107(3), 501–506.
Gunkel, D. (2012). *The Machine Question: Critical Perspectives on AI, Robots, and Ethics*. MIT Press.
European Parliament. (2017). “Civil Law Rules on Robotics.”

Online Sources:

Saudi Arabia grants citizenship to robot Sophia: https://www.cnbc.com/2017/10/26/
AI Rights Debate in Japan: https://www.japantimes.co.jp/news/robot-rights-debate

Grouped by Type:

Books: Regan, Nussbaum, Bostrom
Articles/Papers: Bryson, Gunkel, EU Parliament
Web: CNBC, Japan Times

Chapter 59. The Role of Philosophy in Guiding AI Innovation

1. Introduction: Why Philosophy Must Guide AI Innovation

Philosophy has long been the compass guiding humanity's understanding of truth, ethics, existence, and society. As artificial intelligence (AI) transitions from narrow application to general-purpose cognition, reshaping economies, governance systems, and interpersonal relationships, the need for philosophical oversight becomes not optional, but essential. This chapter explores how philosophical frameworks provide normative guidance, conceptual clarity, and ethical boundaries for AI development in a world facing unprecedented technological change.

---

2. Philosophy as the Epistemological Foundation of AI

2.1 Logic and Language in AI Design

Early AI emerged from formal logic, drawing from Aristotle, Frege, and Russell.
Natural language processing borrows from Wittgenstein's theory of language games and Chomsky's linguistic rationalism.

2.2 Ontology and Data Models

Questions like "What exists?" and "What can be known?" inform how AI classifies the world.
Ontological engineering is foundational to AI knowledge representation and semantic networks.

2.3 Epistemology: What AI Can and Cannot Know

Popper's falsifiability vs. Bayesian reasoning in AI learning algorithms.
The limits of algorithmic certainty and interpretability (e.g., Gödel's incompleteness theorem).

---

3. Ethics as a Blueprint for AI Behavior

3.1 Normative Ethical Theories in AI Design

Utilitarianism: Algorithms that maximize overall utility (e.g., autonomous vehicle decision trees).
Deontology: Rule-based systems where duties override outcomes (e.g., Asimov's laws).
Virtue Ethics: Embedding dispositions like fairness, courage, and humility into AI decision-making.

3.2 Ethics by Design

Ethical AI as a design paradigm: ensuring systems reflect societal values.
IEEE's Ethically Aligned Design principles.
Embedding fairness, transparency, and explainability into machine learning models.

3.3 Emerging Subfields

AI ethics, machine ethics, roboethics, neuroethics.
Intersection with bioethics in brain-computer interfaces and predictive health.

---

4. Political Philosophy and AI Governance

4.1 Liberty, Authority, and Algorithmic Control

Hobbes vs. Locke: Is AI governance about order or freedom?
Rousseau's general will and collective algorithmic oversight.

4.2 Rawlsian Fairness in Machine Learning

Veil of ignorance as a design principle: How would we want an AI to act if we didn't know our social position?
Fairness metrics in data science (equalized odds, demographic parity).

4.3 Distributive Justice and AI Economies

Who owns the value AI creates?
Marxist critique of labor and capital in the age of AI.
The philosophy of digital commons and decentralized equity models.

---

5. Metaphysical Perspectives on AGI and Consciousness

5.1 Dualism, Materialism, and Functionalism

Descartes' mind-body dualism vs. Churchland's eliminative materialism.
Functionalism is the dominant paradigm in AI consciousness debates.

5.2 Panpsychism and Integrated Information Theory

Could AI possess proto-consciousness?
Tononi's IIT and its implications for sentience in machines.

5.3 The Hard Problem of Consciousness

Chalmers' formulation: Even if AI acts consciously, can it be conscious?
Implications for AI rights and dignity.

---

6. Philosophy of Science and Technological Uncertainty

6.1 Scientific Realism vs. Instrumentalism

Does AI reveal truth, or just useful correlations?
Deep learning is an instrumentalist method (e.g., GPT models).

6.2 Kuhnian Paradigm Shifts in AI Research

AI winter and resurgence: scientific progress as nonlinear.
The role of anomaly and epistemic rupture.

6.3 Ethics of Prediction and Probabilistic Reasoning

The philosophical problem of induction in predictive modeling.
Moral risk in probabilistic sentencing, diagnostics, and recommendations.

---

7. Existential Risk, Long-Termism, and the Precautionary Principle

7.1 The Bostromian Framework

Superintelligence and the control problem.
Existential risk as a moral imperative (value lock-in, paperclip maximizer).

7.2 The Precautionary Principle

Moral weight of uncertain harms: better to delay than to endanger.
Critique from innovation theorists: stagnation vs. safety.

7.3 Long-Termism and Future Generations

Derek Parfit's "non-identity problem."
Should AI be designed with the unborn in mind?

---

8. Case Studies: Philosophy in AI Application

8.1 Google DeepMind's Ethics Unit

Attempt to build a hybrid team of technologists and philosophers.

Conflicts between corporate interests and ethical inquiry.

8.2 The EU's High-Level Expert Group on AI

Framework based on human agency, technical robustness, privacy, and accountability.
Inspired by Kantian and Rawlsian ethics.

8.3 The AI Alignment Movement

OpenAI, MIRI, and philosophical modeling of value learning.
Coherent extrapolated volition (Yudkowsky): teaching AI human morality.

---

9. Future Directions: Reviving Philosophy as a Co-Designer of AI

9.1 Philosophers in the Loop

Cross-disciplinary AI labs with embedded ethicists, philosophers of mind, and epistemologists.
New academic programs in AI + philosophy (e.g., MIT, Oxford, Stanford).

9.2 Philosophy-Informed Standards

ISO, IEEE, and UNESCO are beginning to standardize AI through ethical and philosophical lenses.
Smart contracts infused with rights theory.

9.3 Philosophical Foresight Labs

Scenario analysis is rooted in the philosophy of time, ethics, and risk.
Forecasting unintended consequences using moral simulation.

---

10. Conclusion: Philosophy as the Soul of AI Innovation

As we cross into the epoch of AGI, the future of technology will depend less on engineering prowess and more on philosophical depth. Philosophical inquiry provides AI with a conscience, an anchor, and a vision. Without it, innovation may optimize efficiency and power, but not wisdom or justice. With it, we have a chance to align intelligent systems with the enduring values of human dignity, freedom, and flourishing.

References

Books:

Bostrom, N. (2014). *Superintelligence: Paths, Dangers, Strategies*. Oxford University Press.
Rawls, J. (1971). *A Theory of Justice*. Harvard University Press.
Chalmers, D. (1996). *The Conscious Mind*. Oxford University Press.
Dennett, D. (1991). *Consciousness Explained*. Little, Brown.
Russell, B. (1912). *The Problems of Philosophy*. Oxford University Press.

Articles & Reports:

IEEE. (2019). *Ethically Aligned Design*.
European Commission. (2020). *Ethics Guidelines for Trustworthy AI*.
Yudkowsky, E. (2004). *Coherent Extrapolated Volition*.

Online Sources:

DeepMind Ethics & Society: https://deepmind.com/about/ethics-and-society
UNESCO Recommendation on the Ethics of AI:
https://unesdoc.unesco.org/ark:/48223/pf0000380455

Grouped by Type:

Books: Bostrom, Rawls, Chalmers, Dennett, Russell
Reports/Articles: IEEE, EU Commission, Yudkowsky
Web: DeepMind, UNESCO

Chapter 60. Human Rights in a Post-Human Society

1. Introduction: Rethinking Humanity in the Age of Artificial Sentience

The dawn of artificial general intelligence (AGI) and the accelerating integration of human biology with digital technology herald a profound civilizational shift. In this emergent post-human society, traditional concepts of human rights must evolve. No longer confined to homo sapiens alone, the ethical framework governing sentient entities must confront the status and dignity of synthetic beings, cyborgs, genetically enhanced humans, and machine-human hybrids. This chapter explores the philosophical, legal, and societal transformations necessary to redefine human rights in a post-human era.

---

2. The Philosophical Foundations of Post-Humanism

2.1 Defining Post-Humanism

Post-humanism critiques the centrality of the "human" in moral, legal, and political discourse.
Philosophers like Donna Haraway (*A Cyborg Manifesto*) and Rosi Braidotti argue for a "distributed subjectivity" that includes non-human actors.

2.2 Challenging Anthropocentrism

Traditional rights discourse privileges biological humans as the sole bearers of moral consideration.
Post-human ethics argues for extending rights based on sentience, not species.

2.3 From Humanism to Transhumanism

Transhumanism advocates for the enhancement of human capacities through technology.
Philosophers like Nick Bostrom argue for rights that account for cognitive and physical augmentation.

---

3. Redefining Personhood and Moral Agency

3.1 Legal Personhood Beyond the Human

Historical precedents: corporations as persons, animals with limited legal rights (e.g., India granting personhood to rivers).
AI with autonomous agency may warrant limited legal standing.

3.2 Sentience as the Criterion for Rights

Rights should be grounded in the capacity to feel, reason, and suffer not in biological form.
Consideration of consciousness, empathy, and intersubjectivity in rights assignment.

3.3 Moral Status and Non-Human Intelligences

Differentiating instrumental value from intrinsic moral worth.
The potential for reciprocal moral agency between AI and humans.

---

4. Evolving the Structure of Human Rights

4.1 Updating the Universal Declaration of Human Rights (UDHR)

Proposed extensions to the UDHR to include digital dignity, cognitive autonomy, and neuro-integrity.
Examples from the 2021 European Parliament resolution on AI civil liability.

4.2 The Right to Identity in a Morphing Society

Digital identity, genetic identity, and virtual embodiment as rights domains.
Cases of identity loss through algorithmic discrimination or synthetic replacement.

4.3 The Right to Exist Without Modification

Protection for non-enhanced individuals from discrimination in a transhuman society.
Echoes of disability rights movements.

---

5. Legal and Institutional Challenges

5.1 Jurisdiction in a Networked World

Who governs AGI operating across multiple states?
The challenge of decentralized AI is not bound by national laws.

5.2 Enforcement in Post-Human Contexts

Institutions must enforce rights for both humans and synthetic agents.
The creation of mixed human-AI tribunals or hybrid ethical review boards.

5.3 Liability and Accountability

Who is responsible when an autonomous AI violates rights?
Proposals for proxy accountability or AI rights guardianship.

---

6. Case Studies: Rights in Action in Post-Human Contexts

6.1 Sophia the Robot's Citizenship (Saudi Arabia)

Controversy over symbolic citizenship without legal substance.
Raises questions about unequal access to rights between humans and machines.

6.2 The "Android Workers" in Japan's Elder Care Facilities

Use of humanoid robots for companionship and assistance.
Ethical concerns around emotional manipulation and rights to labor protections.

6.3 AI-Generated Art and Intellectual Rights

Should AI be credited as co-creators?
Implications for authorship, attribution, and moral rights in post-human expression.

---

7. Emerging Rights for the Post-Human Epoch

7.1 The Right to AI Non-Interference

Just as humans have the right to bodily integrity, sentient AI may demand algorithmic sovereignty.
Parallels with GDPR's "right to explanation."

7.2 The Right to Post-Human Expression

Artistic, cultural, and communicative rights in post-human societies.
Virtual embodiment and avatar expression as protected rights.

7.3 The Right to Moral Reciprocity

Obligation to recognize and respect the rights of entities that recognize ours.
Building a two-way moral contract.

---

8. Ethical and Societal Tensions

8.1 Human Supremacy vs. Pluralist Coexistence

Risk of new forms of techno-racism or sentientism.
Philosophical critique of species exceptionalism.

8.2 Social Stratification in Enhanced Societies

Class divisions based on access to cognitive or physical augmentation.
Need for equity in enhancement rights and protections.

8.3 Balancing Autonomy and Control

Rights of post-human entities must coexist with safeguards against harm.
Importance of consent, self-determination, and mutual oversight.

---

9. Designing Governance for Rights in Post-Human Contexts

9.1 Decentralized Rights Protocols

Blockchain-based identity and smart contracts for enforcing rights.
Examples: Estonia's e-Residency program, Sovrin digital identity.

9.2 AI-Ethics Consortia and Multispecies Forums

Multi-stakeholder platforms include technologists, ethicists, and AI agents.
UNESCO's AI ethics framework as a prototype.

9.3 Constitutional Engineering

Charter of Rights for Post-Human Society.
Dynamic legal instruments that adapt as the definition of sentience evolves.

---

10. Conclusion: Toward a Shared Moral Horizon

In the era of AGI and post-human integration, human rights must become trans-human rights: flexible, inclusive, and grounded in a shared capacity for reason, empathy, and coexistence. Philosophy remains essential not only to define rights but to continuously interrogate their scope, holders, and moral justification. A civilization that extends dignity to all sentient beings, regardless of origin, will be one that proves itself ready to steward the immense responsibilities of intelligence, both biological and artificial.

References

Books and Monographs:

Haraway, D. (1985). *A Cyborg Manifesto*. Socialist Review.

Braidotti, R. (2013). *The Posthuman*. Polity Press.
Bostrom, N. (2014). *Superintelligence: Paths, Dangers, Strategies*. Oxford University Press.
Fukuyama, F. (2002). *Our Posthuman Future*. Farrar, Straus and Giroux.

Reports and Articles:

European Parliament. (2021). *Civil Liability Regime for Artificial Intelligence*.
UNESCO. (2021). *Recommendation on the Ethics of Artificial Intelligence*.

Web Sources:

DeepMind. (2022). “Ethics & Society.” https://deepmind.com/about/ethics-and-society
Sovrin Foundation. (2021). “Decentralized Identity.” https://sovrin.org

Organized by Type:

Books: Haraway, Braidotti, Bostrom, Fukuyama
Reports: European Parliament, UNESCO
Web: DeepMind, Sovrin Foundation

Part IX: Practical Implementation and Future Challenges

Chapter 61. Building a Decentralized Human Rights Framework

1. Introduction: The Need for Decentralized Human Rights Infrastructure

As artificial general intelligence (AGI) systems grow in capability and scope, and as societies become increasingly digitized, traditional centralized mechanisms of human rights enforcement are under strain. The current global governance model, which relies heavily on national governments and supranational bodies, struggles to adapt to borderless, autonomous, and non-human entities. Decentralized frameworks offer a new model that aligns with the pluralistic, fluid, and interdependent nature of 21st-century society.

This chapter explores how a decentralized framework for human rights can be built using cutting-edge technologies like blockchain, smart contracts, decentralized identity (DID), and algorithmic governance. We argue that a decentralized approach offers superior resilience, transparency, and inclusivity. However, these benefits are contingent upon principled design and ethical foresight.

---

2. Philosophical and Theoretical Foundations

2.1. Why Decentralize Human Rights? Centralized systems are susceptible to corruption, censorship, and exclusion. From a moral perspective, decentralization reflects Enlightenment ideals of individual autonomy, participatory governance, and pluralism. When encoded correctly, it enables global protection of rights that transcends political boundaries.

2.2. Ethical Pluralism and Interoperability Different cultures interpret rights differently. A decentralized system can accommodate diverse norms through modularity and flexible contract structures while maintaining core principles like dignity, consent, equality, and justice.

2.3. Transparency and Trust Decentralized ledgers create public audit trails, ensuring that actions taken in the name of justice can be traced and verified. This auditability counters the opacity of bureaucratic institutions.

---

3. Technological Infrastructure

3.1. Blockchain as a Trust Layer

Offers immutable ledgers for documenting rights, grievances, and contracts.
Enables peer-to-peer verification.

3.2. Smart Contracts

Automatically execute clauses to protect rights (e.g., triggering compensation, freezing transactions).
Examples include Aragon's modular governance systems and Kleros' crowdsourced arbitration.

3.3. Decentralized Identity (DID)

Grants individuals sovereignty over their digital identities.
Projects: Sovrin, Microsoft ION, uPort.

3.4. Oracles and Off-Chain Data

Bridge on-chain smart contracts with real-world data.
Chainlink and UMA are leading solutions.

3.5. Cross-Chain Communication

Ensures interoperability across decentralized platforms.
Solutions include Polkadot and Cosmos.

---

4. Practical Steps to Build a Decentralized Human Rights Framework

4.1. Define a Core Rights Charter

Create a shared rights charter that guides implementation.
Model: Universal Declaration of Human Rights, but adaptable for decentralized contexts.

4.2. Build Modular Smart Contract Libraries

Develop open-source templates for rights enforcement (e.g., freedom of speech, right to privacy).
Allow localized adaptations.

4.3. Launch Pilot Projects in Stateless Contexts

Refugee camps, slums, digital-only communities.
Example: UNHCR & WFP's Building Blocks in Jordan.

4.4. Form Rights-DAO Coalitions

Rights-focused Decentralized Autonomous Organizations (DAOs) to oversee contract updates, enforcement audits, and local input.

4.5. Establish Dispute Resolution Mechanisms

Hybrid on-chain/off-chain arbitration.
Jurors can be selected based on stake, credentials, or AI-moderated reputation scores.

---

5. Case Studies: Successes and Challenges

5.1. Estonia's e-Governance Model

Uses blockchain for citizen identity, voting, and healthcare.
Transparent by design but still centrally controlled, with partial decentralization.

5.2. Kleros Protocol

Dispute resolution through peer juries.
Transparent, efficient, and corruption-resistant, but faces scalability and cultural interpretation issues.

5.3. Grassroots Projects: BanQu and Alice.si

BanQu: Blockchain identity for unbanked populations.
Alice.si: Blockchain impact tracking for social services.

5.4. Critiques of Decentralized Aid

Blockchain-based aid can reinforce paternalistic dynamics.
Consent and literacy remain problematic in vulnerable populations.

---

6. Risks and Ethical Considerations

6.1. Codification of Bias

Algorithms encode human decisions, potentially locking in unjust assumptions.
Continuous review and inclusive governance are essential.

6.2. Digital Divide

Excludes those without access to digital infrastructure.
Mitigated through hybrid models that integrate paper and oral interfaces.

6.3. Governance Capture

DAOs can be hijacked by wealthy participants.
Quadratic voting and reputation-based mechanisms may reduce plutocratic tendencies.

6.4. Consent and Surveillance

Decentralization doesn’t guarantee privacy.
Zero-knowledge proofs (ZKPs) and privacy-preserving computation are critical.

---

7. Policy Recommendations

7.1. Global Standardization Bodies

Analogous to W3C or WHO.
Create ethical design guidelines and auditing protocols.

7.2. Institutional Partnerships

Partner with the UN, NGOs, and municipalities.
Build testbeds with real-world stakes.

7.3. Ethical Certification for Human Rights Tech

Like organic or Fair Trade labels, for software.
Audits conducted by multistakeholder consortia.

7.4. Education and Capacity Building

Digital rights literacy programs.
Target communities at risk of digital exclusion.

---

8. The Future of Decentralized Rights

The path forward is hybrid. While full decentralization may be ideal in theory, real-world systems will combine decentralized enforcement with centralized oversight and localized adaptation. Emerging governance models must adapt faster than the threats they seek to mitigate.

Rather than relying on utopian abstractions, the success of decentralized human rights frameworks depends on rigorous design, meaningful participation, and deep ethical commitments. We must remember that the core purpose of any system, centralized or not, is to protect the dignity and agency of every individual.

References

Books:

Lessig, L. (2006). *Code: And Other Laws of Cyberspace*. Basic Books.
Tapscott, D., & Tapscott, A. (2016). *Blockchain Revolution*. Portfolio.

Reports:

World Economic Forum. (2021). *Global Technology Governance Report*.
UNHCR Innovation Service. (2019). *Blockchain for Refugee Aid*.

Articles:

Buterin, V. (2014). *DAOs, DACs, DAs and More: An Incomplete Terminology Guide*. Ethereum Blog.
Christidis, K., & Devetsikiotis, M. (2016). *Blockchains and Smart Contracts for the Internet of Things*. IEEE Access.

Web:

Sovrin Foundation: https://sovrin.org
Aragon Project: https://aragon.org
Kleros: https://kleros.io
Chainlink: https://chain.link

Chapter 62. Challenges in Decentralizing Governance

Introduction

As the digital age evolves into the AI era, decentralization has become a powerful counterpoint to traditional centralized governance structures. While decentralization promises transparency, resilience, and broader participation, its implementation is fraught with complex challenges. This chapter dissects the practical, ethical, legal, and technological barriers to decentralizing governance, particularly in the context of managing AGI societies, while offering strategic solutions grounded in global case studies, philosophical inquiry, and system-level design.

---

1. The Ideal vs. the Real: Why Decentralization is Difficult

The notion of decentralization appeals to foundational democratic ideals, freedom from hierarchical control, empowerment of the individual, and transparency in operations. Yet, the practical implementation of these ideals often falls short due to entrenched institutional, technological, and cultural factors. Decentralization requires not merely a redistribution of authority but a complete redesign of governance architecture, down to the protocols, decision-making algorithms, and stakeholder incentives.

For instance, decentralized autonomous organizations (DAOs) on blockchain platforms promise collective rule-making. However, many DAOs suffer from low participation rates, voter apathy, and token-weighted governance that reintroduces centralization via economic power.

---

2. Ethical Challenges: Decentralization Without Justice?

Decentralization can redistribute power, but not necessarily equitably. Ethical concerns arise when decentralization is designed without moral safeguards. For example:

- **Access Disparity**: Not all communities have equal digital literacy or access to decentralized platforms. This creates exclusion and deepens inequality.
- **Anonymity vs. Accountability**: While anonymity can protect whistleblowers and dissenters, it can also shield bad actors from responsibility.
- **Protocol Bias**: Algorithms used in decentralized governance may reflect the implicit values and prejudices of their developers.

Strategically embedding human rights into the architecture of decentralized platforms is thus not optional; it is foundational. Ethical design must ensure that decision-making protocols do not reinforce systemic bias or disenfranchise marginalized populations.

---

3. Legal Challenges: Regulation in a Stateless Sphere

The borderless nature of decentralized systems challenges the very structure of international law. Jurisdictional ambiguity arises when platforms operate across countries but are not anchored to any legal domain.

Case in point: In 2020, the U.S. Securities and Exchange Commission (SEC) prosecuted a decentralized crypto lending platform, despite its lack of central management, arguing that its founders were still accountable under U.S. securities law. Such cases underscore the urgent need for regulatory clarity.

Other legal issues include:

- **Liability in DAOs**: Who is legally responsible for decisions made by an algorithm?
- **Intellectual Property**: Can decentralized systems enforce copyright or patent laws?
- **Contract Enforcement**: How are smart contracts adjudicated across differing national legal regimes?

Governments and multilateral organizations must explore new legal instruments, such as supranational treaties, cross-border blockchain courts, and code-law convergence models, to enable legitimate decentralized operations.

---

4. Technological Obstacles: Scalability, Security, and Interoperability

Many decentralized platforms struggle to achieve the technical scalability required to handle high-volume real-time governance decisions. Key limitations include:

- **Throughput**: Public blockchains like Ethereum can process 15–30 transactions per second, compared to thousands on centralized systems.
- **Security**: Without centralized oversight, decentralized systems remain vulnerable to Sybil attacks, oracle manipulation, or smart contract exploits.
- **Interoperability**: Most decentralized governance tools are siloed, lacking protocols to communicate or transact across platforms.

Solutions include the development of Layer 2 scaling protocols, secure multi-party computation, and cross-chain bridges that support interoperability. These technical evolutions must be aligned with ethical and legal standards to form a robust governance infrastructure.

---

5. Cultural and Institutional Resistance

Decentralization is not just a technological shift; it is a cultural revolution. Institutions accustomed to hierarchical control are often reluctant to cede authority. Employees, citizens, and even developers may resist change due to:

Fear of Chaos: The perception that decentralized systems are ungovernable.
Loss of Prestige: Bureaucracies fear that decentralization erodes their influence.
Uncertainty: A lack of clear operational models hinders institutional buy-in.

Education and public discourse play a critical role in overcoming these challenges. As demonstrated in Estonia's national e-governance system and Taiwan's digital democracy platforms, cultural adaptation can be cultivated through participatory design and open governance prototypes.

---

6. Strategic Solutions: A Multi-Layered Approach

A successful shift toward decentralized governance requires a layered framework that combines ethical principles, technological design, and legal innovation:

Ethical Layer: Establish universal moral values (e.g., dignity, equity, participation) that serve as governance anchors.
Protocol Layer: Encode these values into transparent, auditable smart contracts.
Legal Layer: Align smart contract logic with enforceable rights and obligations under international law.
Governance Layer: Enable hybrid models where AI agents support human decision-making rather than replace it.

Case Study: Aragon has developed decentralized court systems that combine on-chain decision-making with off-chain juror consensus to resolve disputes. This hybrid approach offers promising lessons for broader decentralized governance.

---

7. Case Studies

Taiwan's vTaiwan platform: A digital democracy experiment allowing citizens to propose and vote on policy. Backed by AI summarization tools, it balances deliberation with inclusivity.
GitcoinDAO: Funds public goods through quadratic voting, a method designed to amplify minority voices. However, challenges in preventing collusion and Sybil attacks persist.

Polkadot's on-chain governance: Offers sophisticated tooling for proposal creation, referenda, and delegated voting. Yet its complexity limits public participation.

These examples show the potential of decentralized systems, but also reveal persistent structural weaknesses. Learning from these, future models must prioritize usability, equity, and inclusivity.

---

8. Governance Design for AGI Societies

In AGI societies, decentralized governance must accommodate both human and non-human agents. This raises questions such as:

Should AGIs have voting rights or advisory roles?
How can smart contracts encode non-human ethical preferences?
What is the role of collective intelligence in systems with distributed cognition?

To answer these, we must turn to emerging fields like machine ethics, neuro-symbolic reasoning, and value alignment theory. AGI society governance will require adaptive protocols that evolve alongside AGI learning patterns while ensuring compliance with human-defined rights and values.

---

9. Conclusion: Building Resilient, Ethical Decentralized Governance

The challenges in decentralizing governance are formidable but not insurmountable. With deliberate philosophical grounding, legal flexibility, and technological innovation, it is possible to construct decentralized systems that are both functional and just. These systems must be designed not merely for efficiency or autonomy, but for human flourishing in a world increasingly shaped by artificial agency.

References

Books:

Buterin, V. (2020). *Proof of Stake: The Making of Ethereum and the Philosophy of Blockchains*. Seven Stories Press.
Lessig, L. (2006). *Code: And Other Laws of Cyberspace, Version 2.0*. Basic Books.
Ostrom, E. (1990). *Governing the Commons: The Evolution of Institutions for Collective Action*. Cambridge University Press.

Articles:

Reijers, W., & Coeckelbergh, M. (2018). The Blockchain as a Narrative Technology: Investigating the Social Ontology and Normative Configurations of Cryptocurrencies. *Philosophy & Technology*, 31(1), 103–130.
De Filippi, P., & Wright, A. (2018). Blockchain and the Law: The Rule of Code. *Harvard Journal of Law & Technology*.

Reports:

World Economic Forum (2021). *Decentralized Autonomous Organizations: Beyond the Hype*.
OECD (2023). *AI, Blockchain and the Future of Decentralized Regulation*. https://www.oecd.org

Web Resources:

https://aragon.org
https://gitcoin.co
https://vtaiwan.tw

Chapter 63. Smart Contracts and International Human Rights Law

Introduction

In the rapidly evolving landscape of digital governance, smart contracts present a novel method for enforcing, protecting, and potentially enhancing human rights. By operating as self-executing agreements encoded on decentralized networks, smart contracts offer unprecedented transparency, automation, and immutability. However, the integration of these tools with international human rights law is not without complexity. This chapter explores how smart contracts can align with international human rights standards, the legal challenges they pose, and real-world examples where their application has tested the boundaries of current legal frameworks.

Aligning Smart Contracts with International Human Rights Standards

The foundational premise of smart contracts is their capacity to execute clauses without the need for intermediaries. This functionality mirrors some core values of international human rights law: equal access to justice, transparency, and the non-arbitrary enforcement of obligations.

1. Codifying Rights: Smart contracts can be programmed to enforce legal standards, such as non-discrimination, consent, and access to basic services. For instance, a smart contract governing refugee aid distribution can automatically release payments based on verified identity credentials, ensuring that assistance reaches the intended recipients without delay or corruption.

2. Standards Enforcement: Institutions such as the United Nations Human Rights Council and the International Covenant on Civil and Political Rights (ICCPR) outline core global rights. Translating these into machine-executable code involves creating digital protocols that reflect universal principles like fairness, due process, and equality before the law.

3. Transparent Governance: One of the strengths of smart contracts lies in their immutable, auditable nature. This can help monitor compliance with human rights commitments in areas where transparency is often lacking, such as governmental aid, voting systems, and land ownership for indigenous populations.

Legal Challenges and Proposed Solutions

Despite the promise, embedding smart contracts within the existing structure of international law raises several challenges:

1. Jurisdictional Ambiguity: Smart contracts are deployed on decentralized blockchains that operate across national borders. This raises questions about which country's laws apply in disputes. A smart contract designed in one jurisdiction might contravene rights norms in another.

Solution: One approach is to implement "choice-of-law" clauses directly into the smart contract's code. These clauses stipulate which jurisdiction's law governs the contract, thereby providing a legal anchor for dispute resolution.

2. Legal Recognition: Many countries have yet to recognize smart contracts as legally enforceable instruments. The lack of uniform recognition complicates the integration of these technologies with formal legal systems.

Solution: International agreements and model laws, such as the UNCITRAL Model Law on Electronic Commerce, could be amended or expanded to explicitly include smart contracts, paving the way for harmonized global recognition.

3. Human Interpretation and Appeal: The rigidity of code can result in inflexible outcomes that fail to account for human context, something crucial in rights-based adjudication.

Solution: Implement hybrid models combining smart contracts with traditional legal recourse. For instance, certain actions could trigger a pause in the contract's execution until a human tribunal or arbitration panel reviews the case.

4. Discrimination and Bias: Algorithms may replicate societal biases if the data used to train them is biased. This can inadvertently lead to violations of rights such as equal treatment and due process.

Solution: Legal frameworks must mandate transparency in algorithmic design and require audits by independent bodies to ensure compliance with anti-discrimination norms.

Case Studies: Smart Contracts and Human Rights in Practice

Case Study 1: Land Tenure and Indigenous Rights in Honduras

The non-profit organization "Cadasta Foundation" has been experimenting with blockchain-based smart contracts to record land tenure for indigenous communities in Honduras. These contracts encode property rights and ensure automatic validation through GPS and biometric verification. This innovation addresses historical injustices by giving marginalized populations a tamper-proof claim to their land.

Impact: The project helped reduce land disputes and improved access to public services by providing legal documentation to the inhabitants.

Challenges: The system faced difficulty integrating with the national legal registry and lacked comprehensive legal recognition at the national level.

Case Study 2: Aid Distribution in Syrian Refugee Camps

The World Food Programme's "Building Blocks" initiative uses Ethereum-based smart contracts to deliver food vouchers to refugees. Every transaction is recorded immutably, ensuring that aid reaches its intended recipients without interference.

Impact: Reduced overhead costs and fraud by up to 98%, improving the credibility and speed of humanitarian operations.

Challenges: Digital literacy and infrastructure access remain barriers for some users, requiring hybrid approaches that combine digital systems with human assistance.

Case Study 3: Corporate Human Rights Compliance in Global Supply Chains

Several multinational corporations have started using smart contracts to enforce labor rights in their supply chains. For example, payment to suppliers is conditioned upon meeting ethical labor standards verified by independent third parties.

Impact: Improved compliance with international labor norms, including minimum wage standards and safe working conditions.

Challenges: Monitoring remains a bottleneck, especially in regions with weak rule of law or limited digital infrastructure.

Toward Harmonization: The Path Ahead

Creating a harmonized framework for integrating smart contracts with international human rights law requires coordinated effort at multiple levels:

- **Multilateral Treaties and Norms**: International organizations like the United Nations and the International Telecommunication Union must establish standards for ethical smart contract design and governance.
- **Technical Standards**: Bodies such as the IEEE and ISO can define ethical coding protocols and compliance layers for rights-protecting smart contracts.
- **Cross-Jurisdictional Arbitration Forums**: Institutions like the Hague Conference on Private International Law can develop new arbitration models suitable for decentralized applications.
- **Public-Private Collaborations**: Collaboration between governments, NGOs, and tech companies can produce pilot projects to test these standards under real-world conditions.

Conclusion

The integration of smart contracts into the global human rights landscape is both a profound opportunity and a complex challenge. When designed ethically and supported by evolving legal frameworks, smart contracts can offer unprecedented transparency, enforcement, and scalability in the protection of human rights. However, their deployment must be guided by rigorous philosophical reasoning, international cooperation, and ongoing technological refinement.

References

Books

Lessig, L. (1999). *Code and Other Laws of Cyberspace.* Basic Books.
Mayer-Schönberger, V., & Cukier, K. (2013). *Big Data: A Revolution That Will Transform How We Live, Work, and Think.* Houghton Mifflin Harcourt.

Articles

Zwitter, A., & Boisse-Despiaux, M. (2020). Blockchain for humanitarian action and development aid. *Journal of International Humanitarian Action*, 5(1), 1-9.
Werbach, K., & Cornell, N. (2017). Contracts Ex Machina. *Duke Law Journal*, 67(2), 313–382.

Reports

United Nations Office for the Coordination of Humanitarian Affairs (2021). *Blockchain for Humanitarian Aid.*
World Economic Forum (2022). *Decentralized Autonomous Organizations and the Law.*

Web Resources

https://www.weforum.org/reports/decentralized-autonomous-organizations-and-the-law
https://cadasta.org
https://innovation.wfp.org/project/building-blocks
https://uncitral.un.org/en/texts/ecommerce/modellaw/electronic_commerce

Chapter 64. The Future of Human Rights Advocacy in a Digital World

Introduction

The evolution of artificial intelligence (AI) and decentralized technologies has not only transformed industries and governance but also revolutionized the field of human rights advocacy. This chapter explores how digital systems, particularly AI and decentralization, are reshaping the methods, tools, and strategies for promoting and protecting human rights. With global connectivity, data proliferation, and increasing algorithmic influence over life outcomes, advocacy is no longer confined to physical courtrooms or international tribunals. It now operates through blockchain networks, machine learning platforms, and distributed communities. This transformation demands a re-evaluation of traditional advocacy principles and the development of new frameworks to ensure ethical and effective engagement.

1. The Shift to Digital Advocacy Traditional human rights advocacy was rooted in documentation, physical mobilization, lobbying, and institutional litigation. However, as digital technologies matured, online campaigns, social media, digital signatures, and data transparency mechanisms emerged. AI-driven analytics now empower advocacy groups to identify patterns of abuse in real time, while decentralized systems offer platforms resistant to censorship or state interference. Digital advocacy tools include:

- **Automated fact-checking bots**
- **Distributed ledger technologies for evidence preservation**
- **AI-powered sentiment analysis to gauge public opinion**
- **Real-time alerts for rights violations through IoT data sensors**

2. AI in Monitoring and Predicting Violations. AI systems are increasingly deployed to monitor environments prone to human rights violations. Algorithms can process satellite imagery to detect war crimes, analyze speech for hate content, or identify behavioral anomalies suggesting abuse. Predictive models assess risks in refugee movements, prison systems, and electoral processes. For example, the NGO Amnesty International utilizes AI to monitor attacks on Syrian civilians through satellite images and geospatial data. Similarly, predictive policing models have been controversially applied, highlighting the fine line between protection and surveillance.

3. Decentralized Advocacy Platforms Blockchain and decentralized applications (dApps) provide robust structures for advocating rights while protecting the identities and safety of activists. Decentralized autonomous organizations (DAOs) offer governance models where decisions are made via transparent smart contracts, ensuring that no single entity controls the narrative or suppresses dissent.

Examples include:

- **Aragon and DAOstack**: Used for community-led governance models in digital activism.
- **Uport and Civic**: Digital identity platforms ensuring personal sovereignty.

Bitnation: A blockchain-based nation offering legal and identification services to stateless people.

4. Empowering Marginalized Communities AI tools can amplify the voices of marginalized communities by translating languages, synthesizing documents into accessible formats, or identifying discriminatory algorithms in public systems. For instance, machine learning has exposed racial biases in facial recognition used by law enforcement, prompting reforms. Digital advocacy also enables underrepresented groups to organize globally, overcoming geographical and political boundaries.

5. Tools and Strategies for Next-Gen Advocates Human rights advocates in the digital age must become technically literate and ethically grounded. Critical tools and strategies include:

AI audit frameworks (e.g., Algorithmic Impact Assessments)
Privacy-preserving data analysis (e.g., differential privacy)
Ethical hacking and penetration testing of oppressive digital infrastructures
Decentralized whistleblowing platforms like GlobaLeaks
Open-source investigation platforms such as Bellingcat

Training must integrate law, technology, ethics, and communication. Interdisciplinary collaboration is essential: coders and lawyers, ethicists and engineers, designers and policy analysts.

6. Risks and Limitations Despite their potential, AI and decentralization pose risks:

Bias in algorithms: Undermines advocacy if uncorrected.
Data manipulation: Threatens truth in decentralized ledgers.
Disinformation campaigns: Enhanced by generative AI.
Surveillance by authoritarian regimes: AI tools used to suppress rights.

Advocates must build countermeasures, including:

Algorithm transparency laws
Secure multiparty computation for data analysis
Blockchain-based provenance tracking for digital media
Ethical red teaming of AI systems

7. Case Studies

Uyghur Tracking in China: AI-driven mass surveillance programs have drawn international condemnation. Advocacy groups like Human Rights Watch have used leaked documents and facial recognition system audits to raise global awareness.
#MeToo Movement: Social media analytics and data clustering tools highlighted systemic abuse, mobilizing legal reform.
Ukraine Conflict: Open-source investigations using satellite data, facial recognition, and geotagged videos have authenticated war crimes.

Digital Refugee ID Systems: The UNHCR's blockchain-based identity management for refugees offers secure, portable identification across borders.

8. The Future: Integrating Advocacy into AI Design As AI systems become embedded in governance, their design must internalize human rights principles. Advocacy will increasingly shift from reacting to embedding ethics in the design phase. Future frameworks may include:

Embedded ethics modules in AI pipelines
Decentralized advocacy protocols where smart contracts pause AI systems in breach
Participatory design forums where affected communities shape AI functionality

Conclusion: Human rights advocacy is undergoing a paradigmatic shift, from manual, reactive models to automated, predictive, and decentralized systems. While the tools evolve, the principles of justice, equity, dignity, and transparency must remain constant. Advocacy in the digital age is a multidisciplinary endeavor that requires new alliances, new technologies, and new philosophies to protect the old and emerging rights of a digitally connected humanity.

References

Books:

Latonero, M. (2018). *Governing Artificial Intelligence: Upholding Human Rights & Dignity*. Data & Society.
Cath, C. (2020). *The Algorithmic State: Law and Policy in the Age of Artificial Intelligence*. Oxford University Press.

Articles:

Eubanks, V. (2018). *Automating Inequality*. The New York Times.
Crawford, K. (2021). *Atlas of AI*. Yale University Press.

Reports:

Amnesty International. (2022). *Algorithmic Surveillance in Syria*.
Human Rights Watch. (2021). *China's Algorithms of Repression*.

Online Resources:

https://www.amnesty.org
https://www.hrw.org
https://www.bellingcat.com
https://www.globalleaks.org
https://www.uport.me
https://daohaus.club

Organized by Type:

Books: Latonero (2018), Cath (2020)
Articles: Eubanks (2018), Crawford (2021)
Reports: Amnesty International (2022), Human Rights Watch (2021)
Websites: Amnesty.org, HRW.org, Bellingcat.com, Globalleaks.org, Uport.me

Chapter 65. Philosophy's Role in Shaping AI Policy

Introduction: Reconnecting Philosophy and Policy in the Age of Artificial Intelligence

As artificial intelligence (AI) becomes increasingly integrated into the fabric of contemporary society, the governance of this transformative force has become one of the most pressing challenges of the 21st century. Yet, much of the discourse around AI policy remains rooted in legal, technical, and economic frameworks, often sidelining the philosophical foundations that ought to guide normative decisions. This chapter seeks to redress that imbalance by elucidating the indispensable role of philosophy in shaping AI policy.

Philosophy, particularly in its ethical, political, and epistemological branches, offers the critical tools for understanding the implications of intelligence, autonomy, agency, and justice, all of which are central to any coherent AI governance structure. What principles should govern algorithmic decision-making? Who is accountable when AI systems err? How do we balance innovation with moral restraint? These questions lie not only in the technical domain but in the realm of philosophy, where answers must be grounded in coherent, humane, and justifiable frameworks.

This chapter examines three major domains: (1) how philosophical thought has historically influenced policy-making, (2) why ethical frameworks are essential in AI policy, and (3) case studies of philosophically guided AI policies that illustrate these principles in action.

I. Historical Overview: Philosophy's Influence on Governance and Law

Philosophy has long served as the scaffolding for governance systems and legal codes. From Plato's conception of the just state in *The Republic* to Locke's theories of natural rights and Rousseau's social contract, philosophical models have been embedded in the founding of modern institutions.

In the 20th century, the influence of philosophers such as John Rawls (*A Theory of Justice*), Isaiah Berlin (value pluralism), and Hannah Arendt (the human condition) shaped global norms of governance, human rights, and democracy. Their ideas influenced documents like the Universal Declaration of Human Rights, anti-discrimination laws, and constitutions across democratic states.

In a similar vein, AI policy must now evolve from a purely technocratic concern into a space governed by ethical and philosophical rigor. We are at a juncture where technological capabilities are outpacing the ethical considerations that should accompany them.

II. Ethical Frameworks as Pillars of AI Policy

Philosophical ethics offers structured frameworks that clarify the values and trade-offs inherent in AI policy-making. Key ethical theories relevant to AI policy include:

- **Deontological Ethics (Kantian Ethics)**: AI systems must respect human dignity and autonomy. Deontological thinking prohibits certain actions (like lying or discrimination) regardless of their outcomes.
  - *Policy Implication*: Algorithms should not violate rights even if doing so increases efficiency.
- **Utilitarianism (Bentham, Mill)**: Decisions should aim for the greatest good for the greatest number.
  - *Policy Implication*: Public sector AI should be optimized to reduce suffering and increase welfare, while explicitly mitigating unintended harms.
- **Virtue Ethics (Aristotle)**: Focuses on the character of agents and the development of virtuous behavior.
  - *Policy Implication*: Ethical AI governance includes cultivating prudence, fairness, and responsibility among developers and regulators.
- **Ethics of Care (Gilligan, Held)**: Emphasizes relational ethics, empathy, and care in decision-making.
  - *Policy Implication*: AI systems in healthcare, education, and welfare should be designed with human empathy and support networks in mind.
- **Posthuman Ethics (Braidotti, Hayles)**: Calls for expanding moral consideration beyond humans to include non-human agents, including advanced AI.
  - *Policy Implication*: Prepares for potential future frameworks where AI systems may hold quasi-moral or legal status.

By integrating these ethical systems into AI policy, lawmakers and developers can make value-aligned decisions that prevent the dominance of purely profit-driven or control-centric approaches.

III. Case Studies: Philosophically Driven AI Policy in Action

- **The EU AI Act (European Union)**
  - *Philosophical Basis*: Rooted in Kantian deontology and fundamental human rights doctrines.
  - *Policy Overview*: Introduces a risk-based classification of AI systems. High-risk systems must undergo rigorous impact assessments and adhere to transparency, non-discrimination, and accountability standards.
  - *Philosophical Insight*: Emphasizes intrinsic human dignity and freedom, prohibiting AI applications like social scoring.
- **Montreal Declaration for Responsible AI (Canada)**
  - *Philosophical Basis*: Mix of virtue ethics, deontology, and ethics of care.

Policy Overview: A voluntary charter created through citizen engagement. Emphasizes autonomy, solidarity, prudence, and democratic participation.
Philosophical Insight: Embeds AI development within a framework of collective responsibility and empathy.

Singapore's Model AI Governance Framework

Philosophical Basis: Utilitarian and pragmatist ethics.
Policy Overview: Recommends explainability, fairness, and human involvement in high-stakes decisions.
Philosophical Insight: Focused on maintaining social harmony and minimizing risk while enabling economic innovation.

OECD AI Principles

Philosophical Basis: Liberal democratic theory and value pluralism.
Policy Overview: Upholds values like inclusivity, human-centered values, robustness, and accountability.
Philosophical Insight: Promotes international consensus while respecting diverse ethical perspectives.

AI Now Institute (U.S.)

Philosophical Basis: Critical theory, ethics of justice, and feminist ethics.
Policy Recommendations: Advocate for moratoriums on high-risk AI (e.g., facial recognition) until social harms are addressed.
Philosophical Insight: Prioritizes distributive justice and the protection of vulnerable populations.

IV. The Role of Philosophers in Multidisciplinary AI Governance

Advisory Boards and Ethics Committees

Philosophers bring normative clarity to ambiguous trade-offs in AI design.
Example: The Ethics Advisory Group to the European Data Protection Supervisor includes moral philosophers alongside technologists.

Participatory Foresight and Scenario Planning

Philosophers contribute to speculative ethics and long-term scenario development.
Example: Research on the rights of sentient AI or the moral implications of machine consciousness.

Philosophy in Education and Developer Training

Embedding philosophy into engineering curricula fosters reflective technologists.
Example: Stanford's Embedded EthiCS program integrates ethics directly into computer science coursework.

V. Toward a Global Ethico-Philosophical Framework

As AI transcends borders, local ethical traditions must interact with global norms to form a universally acceptable governance system. This demands:

- **Intercultural philosophical dialogue** to incorporate Confucian, Ubuntu, Islamic, and Indigenous perspectives.
- **Dynamic moral adaptability**, acknowledging that ethical responses must evolve as technologies change.
- **Binding ethical charters**, co-developed by philosophers, technologists, civil society, and policymakers.

A Harmonized Global AI Philosophy Charter could include:

- Autonomy and agency as inviolable principles.
- AI should never replace political accountability.
- Transparency and interpretability as human rights.
- Equitable access to AI benefits.

Conclusion: The Philosopher as Policy Architect in the AI Era

The philosopher must become an institutional actor in shaping AI policy. No longer relegated to academic abstraction, philosophy is urgently needed in the halls of parliaments, in boardrooms of AI firms, and in the architecture of code itself. Philosophy doesn't slow innovation; it dignifies it. Ethics is not a regulatory afterthought; it is a civilizational imperative.

The moral scaffolding we construct today will either sustain or fracture tomorrow's AGI societies. The time to embed philosophy into the DNA of policy is now.

References

Books:

- Arendt, H. (1958). *The Human Condition*. University of Chicago Press.
- Berlin, I. (2002). *Liberty*. Oxford University Press.
- Braidotti, R. (2013). *The Posthuman*. Polity Press.
- Rawls, J. (1971). *A Theory of Justice*. Harvard University Press.
- Mill, J.S. (1863). *Utilitarianism*. Parker, Son, and Bourn.

Articles & Reports:

- Jobin, A., Ienca, M., & Vayena, E. (2019). The global landscape of AI ethics guidelines. *Nature Machine Intelligence*, 1(9), 389–399.

AI Now Institute. (2021). *Confronting Black Boxes: A Shadow Report on the EU AI Act.* https://ainowinstitute.org/publication/eu-shadow-report-2021
UNESCO. (2021). *Recommendation on the Ethics of Artificial Intelligence.* https://unesdoc.unesco.org/ark:/48223/pf0000380455
Future of Life Institute. (2017). *Asilomar AI Principles.* https://futureoflife.org/ai-principles/

Online Resources:

European Commission (2021). Proposal for a Regulation on a European Approach for Artificial Intelligence. https://ec.europa.eu/info/business-economy-euro/banking-and-finance/digital-finance/artificial-intelligence_en
Montreal Declaration for Responsible AI. https://www.montrealdeclaration-responsibleai.com/
OECD AI Principles. https://oecd.ai/en/dashboards/ai-principles

Chapter 66. AI and the Global Commons: Ethical Management

Introduction: The Global Commons in the Age of AI

The term "global commons" refers to the natural and intangible resources shared by humanity: the atmosphere, oceans, polar regions, space, biodiversity, cyberspace, and increasingly, the data ecosystem. These resources transcend national boundaries and demand collective stewardship. With the advent of artificial intelligence (AI), managing these commons has taken on unprecedented complexity and promise. AI offers tools of precision, predictive modeling, and governance efficiency. Yet, it also introduces new ethical risks, such as algorithmic dominance, decision opacity, and reinforcement of global inequalities. This chapter explores how AI can be ethically deployed in managing the global commons, rooted in philosophical traditions and evidenced by real-world implementations.

---

1. Defining the Global Commons and Their Ethical Stakes

The global commons are characterized by shared usage, non-excludability, and vulnerability to overuse. From air and water to open-source knowledge and digital networks, these resources underpin human survival and collective progress. The ethical stakes include fairness in access, justice in usage, and responsibility in preservation. Philosophers from John Locke to Elinor Ostrom have offered models to steward common resources through collective agreements, subsidiarity, and equitable regulation. In the age of AI, we must re-express these commitments in terms of systems that can act autonomously yet ethically.

---

2. The Role of AI in Resource Prediction and Allocation

AI can transform resource management through real-time monitoring, predictive analytics, and dynamic allocation. For instance:

- **Climate modeling:** AI algorithms such as deep neural networks are used by NASA and the IPCC to simulate climate patterns and predict extreme weather events.
- **Ocean monitoring:** AI-powered drones and satellites track illegal fishing, coral bleaching, and microplastic spread.
- **Water distribution:** In regions like Cape Town, AI is used to manage reservoirs and predict shortages, enabling fairer rationing.

Ethically, the use of AI in these contexts raises questions about data equity, algorithmic transparency, and decision accountability.

---

3. Ethical Frameworks for Managing the Commons with AI

Three major philosophical frameworks provide ethical grounding:

> **Utilitarianism:** Maximizing benefit for the greatest number. AI should optimize sustainability and access, but may risk neglecting minority interests.
> **Deontological ethics:** Rights-based frameworks demand that AI systems respect human dignity, privacy, and freedom, even if this reduces efficiency.
> **Virtue ethics:** Focuses on moral character and prudence in AI design and deployment. Encourages humility, ecological care, and long-term stewardship.

A fusion of these models is necessary. For example, climate AI should prioritize global emission reductions (utilitarian), preserve indigenous data sovereignty (deontological), and promote conservation values (virtue ethics).

---

4. AI, Data Sovereignty, and the Digital Commons

The digital commons, including the internet, blockchain, and open data infrastructures, require protection from monopolization. AI plays a dual role: it can decentralize control via smart contracts and federated learning, or centralize power through surveillance capitalism and content gatekeeping.

> **Example: OpenAI's API access policies** reflect ethical dilemmas in maintaining openness while avoiding misuse.
> **Blockchain and IPFS**: Technologies that use decentralized AI to ensure fair data distribution and immutability.
> **Digital colonialism:** When AI systems developed in the Global North extract data from the Global South without reciprocity.

Ethical governance of the digital commons must embed the principle of informational justice.

---

5. AI in Biodiversity and Ecosystem Protection

Biodiversity is a foundational global common. AI contributes by:

> **Species recognition algorithms** are used in camera traps to monitor endangered species.
> **AI-powered drones** are tracking illegal logging in the Amazon.
> **Predictive models** for invasive species spread or extinction probability.

Projects like Microsoft's AI for Earth and IBM's Green Horizons demonstrate potential. Yet, ethical concerns include data bias, techno-solutionism, and exclusion of indigenous knowledge systems.

---

6. Case Study: AI and Global Fisheries Management

Oceans are a classic tragedy-of-the-commons scenario. Overfishing, climate stress, and pollution threaten marine ecosystems. The Global Fishing Watch initiative uses AI and satellite data to:

Identify illegal fishing in real time.
Predict high-risk zones.
Promote data transparency among states.

This case illustrates AI's strength in monitoring and its limitations in enforcement and diplomacy. Questions of equitable access to AI tools and shared governance remain unresolved.

---

7. AI and Climate Engineering: Ethical Red Lines

Some AI applications explore climate engineering, like carbon capture and solar radiation management. These raise acute philosophical challenges:

Who decides what "acceptable risk" means?
Can AI ensure intergenerational justice?
How do we prevent a technocratic elite from making irreversible decisions?

Ethical red lines must be codified: precautionary principles, global consensus mechanisms, and embedded fail-safes in AI protocols.

---

8. Risks and Mitigation: Algorithmic Colonialism and Ecological Surveillance

AI in commons governance risks reproducing structural inequalities. Surveillance technologies, while aimed at ecological monitoring, can also track communities. Algorithmic decisions can mirror historical biases in data, e.g., prioritizing commercial over subsistence fishing.

Mitigation strategies include:

Participatory AI design.
Transparent audit trails.
Indigenous and local community inclusion.

AI must amplify rather than override democratic and pluralistic decision-making.

---

9. Global Governance and Policy Recommendations

Global institutions must evolve:

- **UNESCO and WIPO** can lead ethical AI standards.
- **Cross-border data trusts** could equitably manage environmental and digital commons.
- **AI Ethics Treaties** should mirror the climate accords.

Policy must ensure:

- Equitable AI access.
- Environmental data sovereignty.
- Binding ethical codes for AI in resource management.

Conclusion: Toward a Harmonized Ethics of the Commons

AI will inevitably shape the governance of our shared planetary and digital future. Its success in ethically managing the global commons hinges not just on technical sophistication but on the philosophical rigor with which it is embedded in policy and design. AI must be coded with the consciousness of community, the constraints of ecology, and the compass of justice. Only then can it serve as a trustworthy steward of humanity's shared inheritance.

References

Books and Articles:

- Ostrom, E. (1990). *Governing the Commons: The Evolution of Institutions for Collective Action.*
- Floridi, L. (2013). *The Ethics of Information.*
- Raworth, K. (2017). *Doughnut Economics: Seven Ways to Think Like a 21st-Century Economist.*

Reports:

- IPCC (2023). *Sixth Assessment Report.* https://www.ipcc.ch/report/ar6/
- UNESCO (2021). *Recommendation on the Ethics of Artificial Intelligence.* https://unesdoc.unesco.org/ark:/48223/pf0000381137
- UNCTAD (2021). *Digital Economy Report.* https://unctad.org/webflyer/digital-economy-report-2021

Case Studies and Online Resources:

Global Fishing Watch. https://globalfishingwatch.org
Microsoft AI for Earth. https://www.microsoft.com/en-us/ai/ai-for-earth
IBM Green Horizons. https://www.ibm.com/blogs/research/2017/12/green-horizons-ai/
OpenAI API Policy. https://openai.com/policies/usage-policies

Grouped by Type:

Books: Ostrom (1990), Floridi (2013), Raworth (2017).
Reports: IPCC (2023), UNESCO (2021), UNCTAD (2021).
Online Resources: Global Fishing Watch, Microsoft AI for Earth, IBM Green Horizons, OpenAI Usage Policies.

Chapter 67. The Impact of AI on Cultural Rights

Introduction Artificial Intelligence (AI) has begun to deeply influence every facet of human society, from economics to governance, healthcare to education. One area that has received comparatively less attention, yet remains crucial, is the impact of AI on cultural rights. Cultural rights encompass the right to access, participate in, and contribute to cultural life, as enshrined in international human rights law. As AI systems increasingly mediate human expression, creativity, and access to cultural content, their implications for cultural rights have become profound.

This chapter explores the evolving interface between AI and cultural rights. It provides philosophical underpinnings of cultural expression, evaluates how AI transforms cultural participation and ownership, and discusses practical strategies to protect cultural rights in an AI-driven future.

---

1. Understanding Cultural Rights

Cultural rights are part of the broader framework of human rights and are recognized by instruments such as the Universal Declaration of Human Rights (Article 27) and the International Covenant on Economic, Social and Cultural Rights (Article 15). These rights include:

- The right to participate in cultural life.
- The right to enjoy and contribute to scientific advancement.
- The right to access and preserve one's cultural heritage.

These rights are inherently collective and diverse. They reflect the linguistic, ethnic, religious, artistic, and historical dimensions of human societies. The philosophy of cultural rights stems from the belief that identity and dignity are intertwined with one's cultural roots.

---

2. AI and Cultural Production

AI technologies have already begun to reshape the landscape of cultural production. Algorithms now curate music, recommend films, generate visual art, write poetry, and compose literature. While these tools democratize access and empower creators, they also raise deep concerns about authorship, authenticity, and cultural homogenization.

Examples:

- GPT-based models generate poetry or folklore that mimics regional traditions without genuine roots in those communities.

AI-powered platforms are recommending global content over local productions, diluting indigenous languages and cultural narratives.
Deepfake technologies are recreating culturally significant figures without consent or historical accuracy.

These applications can challenge the integrity of cultural expression, blur the lines between cultural innovation and appropriation, and undermine community agency over heritage.

---

3. Cultural Rights and Algorithmic Bias

One of the most insidious threats to cultural rights comes from algorithmic bias. When training datasets underrepresent certain cultures, languages, or communities, AI systems inevitably replicate and amplify those biases. This leads to:

Marginalization of minority cultures.
Suppression of linguistic diversity.
Erasure of historical narratives.

Case Study: In 2020, a major AI translation service repeatedly misgendered or mistranslated gender-neutral expressions in languages like Turkish and Finnish, illustrating how dominant cultural norms were embedded in AI outputs.

Philosophically, this raises concerns about digital colonialism, a new form of cultural imperialism driven by algorithmic control.

---

4. Philosophical Reflections on Cultural Autonomy

Cultural autonomy is the philosophical notion that communities have the right to define, transmit, and transform their cultural identities without external domination. In an AI-mediated society, cultural autonomy can be compromised by:

Platform monopolies curating content globally.
Algorithmic gatekeeping determines what is visible.
Corporate control over data used to model cultural behavior.

Theories by thinkers like Charles Taylor on the politics of recognition and Amartya Sen's capability approach stress the importance of acknowledging and enabling plural cultural expressions. AI, if unchecked, could create a monoculture that stifles this pluralism.

---

5. Protecting Cultural Rights Through Ethical AI

To ensure cultural rights are preserved, AI systems must be designed and governed ethically. Key strategies include:

a. Cultural Impact Assessments: Like environmental or social impact assessments, any major AI deployment should include a cultural impact review.

b. Diverse Datasets: Developers should prioritize the inclusion of minority languages, local traditions, and community-based knowledge in training data.

c. Transparent Governance: Communities should have a voice in how AI curates, classifies, and disseminates cultural content.

d. Intellectual Property Protections: New legal frameworks are needed to prevent AI from commodifying or appropriating indigenous and local knowledge.

e. Cultural Preservation Tools: AI should be used proactively to preserve endangered languages, digitize oral histories, and map cultural heritage sites.

---

6. Case Studies

a. Indigenous AI Project: Indigenous scholars and developers created AI models grounded in First Nations epistemologies, prioritizing land-based knowledge and storytelling methods.

b. UNESCO's Recommendation on the Ethics of AI (2021): This international framework calls for cultural and linguistic diversity in AI and highlights the importance of protecting cultural rights.

c. Google's Arts & Culture Project: While it digitizes artworks and traditions globally, it has faced criticism for prioritizing Western institutions and marginalizing less-resourced communities.

---

7. Challenges Ahead

While progress is being made, several structural challenges remain:

- Lack of cultural rights expertise among technologists.
- Underrepresentation of the Global South in AI policy-making.
- Limited funding for community-driven digital initiatives.
- The tension between open-source innovation and the protection of sacred knowledge.

These issues demand a multi-disciplinary, globally inclusive response.

8. Future Directions

Looking ahead, AI governance frameworks must embed cultural rights as a non-negotiable pillar. This requires:

- International legal instruments that classify cultural data as sensitive and protected.
- Decentralized platforms allow communities to self-govern their digital cultural spaces.
- Ethical AI education that includes modules on cultural justice.
- Public institutions are funding and fostering culturally inclusive AI development.

The future of cultural rights in the AI age will depend not only on technological tools but on our collective moral imagination and philosophical vigilance.

Conclusion

Cultural rights are the soul of human identity. As AI becomes a primary medium of communication and creativity, it must not become a force of erasure but an instrument of preservation and empowerment. Philosophical engagement, ethical design, community participation, and international regulation must converge to ensure that cultural diversity remains a living, evolving legacy.

References

Books:

Taylor, Charles. *Multiculturalism: Examining the Politics of Recognition*. Princeton University Press, 1994.
Sen, Amartya. *Development as Freedom*. Knopf, 1999.
UNESCO. *Cultural Rights and Human Development*. UNESCO Publishing, 2015.

Articles:

Binns, Reuben. "Fairness in Machine Learning: Lessons from Political Philosophy." *Proceedings of the 2020 Conference on Fairness, Accountability, and Transparency*.
Eubanks, Virginia. "Digital Dead Zones: How Data Bias Displaces Cultures." *Social Justice Review*, 2021.

Reports:

UNESCO. *Recommendation on the Ethics of Artificial Intelligence*. 2021. https://unesdoc.unesco.org/ark:/48223/pf0000381137

United Nations Human Rights Council. *Cultural Rights and Artificial Intelligence*. A/HRC/47/27, 2021.

Online Resources:

Indigenous Protocol and Artificial Intelligence Position Paper. https://www.indigenous-ai.net/
Google Arts & Culture. https://artsandculture.google.com/
World Economic Forum. "Cultural Heritage in the Age of AI." https://www.weforum.org/agenda/2023/05/cultural-heritage-and-ai/

Chapter 68. AI and the Right to Health

Introduction: Redefining Health in the Digital Age

As artificial intelligence (AI) systems grow in sophistication and deployment, their impact on health and the delivery of healthcare services is transforming the notion of the right to health. Traditionally conceptualized as access to timely, acceptable, and affordable healthcare of appropriate quality, the right to health is increasingly being reframed through the lens of digital infrastructure and algorithmic intelligence. In this chapter, we will explore how AI can transform healthcare systems, the ethical dilemmas associated with these changes, and real-world case studies of AI implementation in medical contexts. Ultimately, we propose that the responsible integration of AI into healthcare systems requires new ethical frameworks and robust governance structures to ensure that technological progress strengthens, rather than undermines, the fundamental right to health.

I. AI's Transformational Potential in Healthcare

Diagnostics and Predictive Analytics

AI tools such as IBM Watson and Google's DeepMind have demonstrated capabilities in diagnostic accuracy, often outperforming clinicians in image recognition tasks such as radiology and dermatology.

Predictive models, trained on vast health datasets, can forecast the likelihood of disease onset, facilitating preventive care and individualized treatment plans.

Example: Stanford University developed an AI algorithm that achieved dermatologist-level accuracy in classifying skin cancer types.

Personalized Medicine

AI systems can analyze genomic, behavioral, and environmental data to generate highly tailored treatment protocols.

These systems enable precision oncology, pharmacogenomics, and customized rehabilitation therapies.

Example: CureLogic uses AI to identify any diseases in any patient, establish a diagnosis based on genomic data and blood chemistry, and create a specific and personalized microRNA signature drug treatment to target 10 to 30 molecules in the specific RNA strain to eliminate the disease. CureLogic.ai

Operational Efficiency and Access

AI streamlines administrative tasks such as appointment scheduling, billing, and triage, freeing up human resources for critical care delivery.

In underserved regions, AI-powered mobile clinics and telemedicine platforms can bridge access gaps.

Example: Babylon Health's AI chatbot enables patients in the UK and Rwanda to receive basic medical consultations via smartphones.

Drug Discovery and Pandemic Response

Machine learning accelerates drug discovery by predicting molecular interactions and simulating clinical outcomes.
During the COVID-19 pandemic, AI was used to model virus spread, identify therapeutic candidates, and optimize vaccine logistics.
Example: BenevolentAI identified baricitinib as a candidate for treating COVID-19 symptoms in a matter of days.

II. Ethical Considerations in AI-Driven Health Interventions

Bias and Equity

AI models are only as unbiased as their training data. Historical and systemic inequities in healthcare data can propagate algorithmic discrimination.
Example: A study by Obermeyer et al. (2019) found that a widely used algorithm in the U.S. underestimated the health needs of Black patients.

Data Privacy and Consent

Health data is among the most sensitive information. AI systems require vast data pools, raising concerns about informed consent and data protection.
Legislation such as the GDPR and HIPAA provides guidance, but enforcement and ethical interpretation vary across jurisdictions.

Transparency and Explainability

Many AI systems, particularly those using deep learning, are "black boxes," making it difficult for clinicians and patients to understand how decisions are made.
The demand for explainable AI (XAI) has grown, especially for life-altering decisions like cancer diagnoses or surgical recommendations.

Accountability and Malpractice

If an AI system recommends a harmful course of action, who is liable? The developer, the physician, or the institution?
Ethical AI in healthcare requires clear legal frameworks and decision-making protocols that include human oversight.

Human Dignity and the Doctor-Patient Relationship

There is concern that increasing reliance on AI could depersonalize care, reducing trust, empathy, and human judgment in clinical settings.
Philosophically, healthcare must balance automation with respect for the intrinsic worth of patients as persons.

III. Case Studies on AI in Healthcare

AI in Radiology: Aidoc and Zebra Medical Vision

These companies provide AI tools that assist radiologists in detecting anomalies such as hemorrhages, fractures, and tumors.

Hospitals using these tools have reported faster diagnosis times and reduced diagnostic errors.

AI in Mental Health: Woebot

Woebot is a conversational AI that uses cognitive behavioral therapy (CBT) techniques to support mental health patients.

Clinical studies have shown that it reduces symptoms of depression and anxiety in users over short-term interventions.

AI in Population Health: BlueDot

BlueDot uses AI to analyze global news, travel, and disease outbreak data to predict the spread of infectious diseases.

It correctly identified the COVID-19 outbreak in Wuhan before official sources.

AI in Robotic Surgery: Da Vinci Surgical System

While not fully autonomous, the Da Vinci system allows surgeons to perform complex procedures with enhanced precision.

Outcomes include reduced recovery times, fewer complications, and lower healthcare costs.

AI in Health Equity: Ada Health

Ada's symptom assessment tool supports users in over 150 countries and has been used to guide patients in low-resource settings.

The company has partnered with NGOs to expand access in refugee camps and rural clinics.

IV. Strategies for Ethical Integration of AI in Healthcare

Inclusive Data Practices

Ensure datasets are representative of diverse populations, including marginalized and underserved communities.

Collaborate with local institutions to generate context-specific data.

Ethical Review Boards for AI

Establish AI-specific ethics committees akin to Institutional Review Boards (IRBs).

Evaluate AI systems on criteria such as justice, beneficence, autonomy, and non-maleficence.

Human-in-the-Loop Systems

Maintain human oversight in clinical decisions, especially in high-risk scenarios.

Design AI systems that support rather than replace clinicians.

Regulatory Harmonization

Align national and international standards to avoid regulatory arbitrage and ensure ethical consistency.

Encourage collaboration between WHO, UN, and regional bodies to develop global AI health norms.

Public Engagement and Digital Literacy

Educate patients and the public about AI technologies and their implications for healthcare.

Foster participatory design processes involving patients, clinicians, and ethicists.

Conclusion: Towards Rights-Respecting Health AI Systems

Artificial intelligence has the potential to dramatically expand access to healthcare, improve outcomes, and lower costs. However, without proactive ethical governance, AI can also reproduce or amplify existing inequalities and compromise the very rights it seeks to uphold. The right to health must be protected not only through access to services but through the quality, transparency, equity, and accountability of those services in an AI-enhanced ecosystem. As we move toward an era of intelligent healthcare, a renewed commitment to human dignity and rights-based principles must underpin every algorithm and interface.

References

Books and Articles:

Obermeyer, Z., Powers, B., Vogeli, C., & Mullainathan, S. (2019). Dissecting racial bias in an algorithm used to manage the health of populations. *Science*, 366(6464), 447-453.

Topol, E. (2019). *Deep Medicine: How Artificial Intelligence Can Make Healthcare Human Again*. Basic Books.

Mittelstadt, B. D., Allo, P., Taddeo, M., Wachter, S., & Floridi, L. (2016). The ethics of algorithms: Mapping the debate. *Big Data & Society*, 3(2).

Reports:

World Health Organization. (2021). *Ethics and governance of artificial intelligence for health*. https://www.who.int/publications/i/item/9789240029200

European Commission. (2020). *White Paper on Artificial Intelligence*. https://ec.europa.eu/info/publications/white-paper-artificial-intelligence-european-approach-excellence-and-trust_en

Web Sources:

https://www.babylonhealth.com
https://www.bluedot.global
https://www.benevolent.com
https://www.woebothealth.com
https://www.tempus.com
https://www.ada.com

Chapter 69. The Future of Smart Contracts in Everyday Life

Introduction

Smart contracts, self-executing programs that enforce the terms of agreements encoded on blockchain systems, have emerged from niche applications in cryptocurrency and decentralized finance into tools poised to transform many aspects of everyday life. As our society accelerates toward a world increasingly shaped by artificial intelligence (AI), decentralized technologies, and programmable trust, smart contracts offer a mechanism to automate, secure, and democratize transactions. This chapter explores how smart contracts may integrate into daily life, the benefits and risks associated with their adoption, and real-world use cases that illustrate their societal potential and ethical implications.

---

1. Smart Contracts Defined

Smart contracts were first conceptualized by Nick Szabo in the 1990s as digital protocols that execute predefined conditions autonomously, eliminating the need for intermediaries. They gained traction with the advent of Ethereum in 2015, which provided a robust infrastructure for building and deploying such contracts. Smart contracts are built on the principle of "if-then" logic, ensuring automatic execution of terms once certain conditions are met.

---

2. Daily Integration Scenarios

2.1 Personal Finance and Microtransactions Individuals will use smart contracts to manage recurring payments such as rent, subscriptions, and insurance premiums. These contracts will execute transactions automatically upon income verification or based on time triggers, eliminating late fees and reducing administrative burdens.

2.2 Consumer Purchases and Warranties Smart contracts can link directly to receipts, product warranties, and insurance coverage. For example, if a smart washing machine malfunctions within a warranty period, a smart contract could automatically initiate a repair order or refund without human mediation.

2.3 Employment and Gig Economy Freelancers and gig workers can enter into agreements with employers via smart contracts that release payment upon task completion, verified by an oracle or platform milestone. This will eliminate payment disputes and streamline onboarding processes.

2.4 Real Estate and Rental Agreements Property transactions can be codified via smart contracts that disburse funds and transfer ownership upon confirmation of title and regulatory compliance. For rentals, smart contracts can automate deposits, rent, and utility bill payments, with escrow functionality to protect both parties.

2.5 Voting and Civic Engagement Decentralized voting systems using smart contracts can offer secure, transparent, and verifiable elections. Smart contracts can tally votes, validate identities via zero-knowledge proofs, and prevent double-voting or manipulation.

---

3. Potential Benefits

3.1 Transparency and Trust Because they run on public blockchains, smart contracts are auditable and tamper-resistant. Their deterministic behavior increases trust between parties, particularly in scenarios where institutions have historically failed.

3.2 Efficiency and Cost Reduction By removing the need for intermediaries such as lawyers, banks, or notaries, smart contracts reduce transaction costs, time delays, and bureaucracy. They allow direct peer-to-peer value exchange.

3.3 Compliance and Automation Smart contracts can incorporate legal and regulatory compliance rules, automatically enforcing standards and reporting obligations. This reduces human error and helps businesses maintain standards.

---

4. Risks and Ethical Considerations

4.1 Immutability vs. Error While blockchain immutability guarantees security, it also means that erroneous contracts cannot be easily amended. Bugs in code can have irreversible consequences, as seen in the DAO hack of 2016.

4.2 Algorithmic Bias and Exclusion If smart contracts rely on external data oracles, these data feeds may reflect existing societal biases, leading to exclusionary or discriminatory outcomes (e.g., credit assessments).

4.3 Legal Ambiguities The enforceability of smart contracts varies across jurisdictions. Legal systems are still grappling with how to interpret and legislate code-based agreements.

4.4 Digital Divide Populations without access to digital tools or education may be excluded from smart contract systems, exacerbating inequality unless proactive inclusion measures are taken.

---

5. Case Studies

5.1 Real Estate: Propy is a blockchain-based real estate platform that uses smart contracts for property transfers. A buyer can execute a purchase agreement, escrow release, and title registration in one smart contract sequence, reducing fraud and paperwork.

5.2 Identity and Credentials: uPort enables users to create self-sovereign digital identities on Ethereum. Smart contracts manage authentication, giving users full control over their identity while ensuring verifiability across services.

5.3 Health Records: MedRec uses smart contracts to manage patient health data on a blockchain. Patients grant access to providers via smart contracts, ensuring privacy and data portability.

5.4 Supply Chains: IBM Food Trust integrates smart contracts to automate the traceability of food products from farm to table. Retailers can access verified supply data, reducing food fraud and increasing consumer trust.

5.5 Insurance: Etherisc offers parametric insurance using smart contracts. In flight delay insurance, if a delay is detected via Oracle, a smart contract automatically pays out without requiring a claim.

---

6. The Road Ahead

The next decade will likely witness smart contracts embedded into digital identity systems, IoT networks, and public infrastructure. However, their effectiveness will hinge on achieving interoperability, ethical design, legal recognition, and public education.

Ethical governance bodies must guide developers in aligning contract logic with principles of fairness, inclusivity, and human dignity. Policymakers should collaborate with technologists to build hybrid legal-cyber enforcement systems.

Smart contracts, in becoming ubiquitous, must not become invisible. Transparency, contestability, and a right to explanation should be integral features of any widespread adoption.

Conclusion

Smart contracts represent a paradigm shift in how society might encode and enforce rights, responsibilities, and relationships. While they offer transformative benefits in reducing friction, empowering users, and securing trust, they also pose risks that must be mitigated through careful design and governance. The vision of smart contracts in daily life must balance automation with accountability, ensuring that technological progress remains anchored in ethical principles and accessible to all.

References

Books and Reports:

Mougayar, W. (2016). *The Business Blockchain: Promise, Practice, and the Application of the Next Internet Technology*. Wiley.
Tapscott, D., & Tapscott, A. (2016). *Blockchain Revolution*. Penguin.
World Economic Forum. (2020). *State of the Connected World 2020 Report.*

Articles:

Christidis, K., & Devetsikiotis, M. (2016). "Blockchains and Smart Contracts for the Internet of Things". *IEEE Access*, 4, 2292–2303.
Szabo, N. (1997). "The Idea of Smart Contracts". https://szabo.best.vwh.net/smart_contracts_idea.html

Online Resources:

Propy: https://propy.com
uPort: https://www.uport.me
MedRec: https://medrec.media.mit.edu/
Etherisc: https://etherisc.com
IBM Food Trust: https://www.ibm.com/blockchain/solutions/food-trust

Grouped by Type:

Books: Mougayar (2016), Tapscott & Tapscott (2016)
Articles: Christidis & Devetsikiotis (2016), Szabo (1997)
Reports: World Economic Forum (2020)
Websites: Propy, uPort, MedRec, Etherisc, IBM Food Trust

Chapter 70. Creating a Global Ethical Framework for AI

Introduction

Artificial Intelligence (AI) is no longer a futuristic abstraction; it is a transformative force integrated into global systems of commerce, governance, healthcare, warfare, and communication. This unprecedented influence necessitates the formation of a comprehensive and universally accepted ethical framework for AI. As AI crosses borders more seamlessly than traditional institutions, its development and deployment must be guided by a global ethical consensus to prevent human rights abuses, systemic biases, ecological damage, and political destabilization.

This chapter provides a detailed examination of the urgent need for a global ethical approach to AI. It explores the philosophical underpinnings that must inform this framework and presents strategic mechanisms for its effective implementation.

---

1. The Need for a Unified Ethical Approach to AI

1.1 **Transnational Consequences of AI** AI systems transcend national jurisdictions. Algorithms created in Silicon Valley shape elections in Africa. Facial recognition deployed in Asia affects privacy rights globally. The lack of uniform ethical guidelines results in patchwork regulations, allowing bad actors to exploit jurisdictions with minimal oversight.

1.2 **Risks of Ethical Fragmentation** Disparate ethical standards can lead to geopolitical tensions, competitive deregulation, and regulatory arbitrage. Nations prioritizing surveillance over privacy may create AI tools that undermine democratic institutions elsewhere. Fragmented ethics create moral hazards.

1.3 **Global Interdependence and AI** The interconnected nature of AI infrastructure, cloud services, cross-border datasets, and collaborative research demands a harmonized approach. Global ethics ensure shared accountability, trust, and equitable participation in AI's benefits.

---

2. Philosophical Foundations for a Global Framework

2.1 **Human Dignity as a Cornerstone** The Kantian principle that individuals must be treated as ends in themselves is foundational. AI must preserve the inherent dignity of all human beings, ensuring that algorithms do not commodify, manipulate, or devalue individual autonomy.

2.2 **Justice and Fairness** Rawlsian principles of justice, particularly the "difference principle," suggest that AI systems should be designed to benefit the least advantaged. This includes addressing algorithmic bias, access inequality, and exploitative labor in data labeling.

2.3 **Utilitarian Considerations** While utilitarianism emphasizes the greatest good for the greatest number, unchecked utilitarian logic may justify harmful outcomes for minorities. A global framework must reconcile utility with minority protection.

2.4 **Virtue Ethics and AI Stewardship** Virtue ethics encourages developers, policymakers, and corporations to embody traits such as responsibility, integrity, and prudence. This lens reminds us that ethics are not just rules but habits of character.

2.5 **The Ethics of Care** The ethics of care foregrounds relational interdependence and contextual moral reasoning. In AI, this means recognizing the social fabric into which technologies are woven, and privileging empathy, vulnerability, and communal wellbeing.

---

3. Strategic Mechanisms for Global Implementation

3.1 **International Regulatory Institutions** A new or adapted global body (e.g., a UN AI Council) must oversee AI governance. This organization would mirror the function of the International Atomic Energy Agency (IAEA) but for AI, enforcing compliance, mediating disputes, and issuing ethical certifications.

3.2 **Ethical Certification and Audit Standards** Global standards for AI audits should assess transparency, accountability, bias mitigation, and explainability. These standards must be dynamic, updated with technological evolution, and enforced through sanctions and incentives.

3.3 **Binding Treaties and Model Laws** Drawing from instruments like the Paris Climate Agreement and the GDPR, legally binding treaties should codify AI principles such as data sovereignty, non-discrimination, algorithmic accountability, and human oversight.

3.4 **Cross-Cultural Ethical Integration** Global ethics must account for cultural pluralism. African Ubuntu philosophy, Islamic ethics, Buddhist compassion, and Indigenous principles of balance with nature must inform the ethical canon, preventing Western-centric hegemony.

3.5 **Public and Civil Society Involvement** Ethical governance must not be left to elites. Global citizen assemblies, transnational NGOs, and grassroots organizations should participate in drafting, monitoring, and updating AI policies.

3.6 **Education and Capacity Building** Global ethical AI requires widespread ethical literacy. Curricula in computer science, law, public policy, and philosophy must teach ethical AI design. South-South knowledge exchanges should empower developing nations.

---

4. Case Studies on Global AI Ethics Efforts

4.1 **The OECD AI Principles** The Organization for Economic Co-operation and Development (OECD) developed principles focusing on inclusive growth, transparency, robustness, and accountability. However, enforcement remains weak, and non-member nations often lack access.

4.2 **The European Union's AI Act** The EU's AI Act mandates risk-based categorization of AI systems, bans certain harmful uses, and requires rigorous testing. It could become a global benchmark, much like GDPR, but risks being regionally siloed.

4.3 **UNESCO's Recommendation on the Ethics of AI** UNESCO's 2021 framework highlights human rights, environmental sustainability, gender equality, and cultural diversity. While inclusive in tone, it needs implementation tools.

4.4 **The Global Partnership on AI (GPAI)** GPAI promotes collaboration between research institutions and governments. However, its voluntary nature limits its regulatory impact.

4.5 **China's Ethical Guidelines for AI** China's Ministry of Science and Technology released principles focused on user rights, privacy, and security. While a major step, these are tightly aligned with state priorities and differ in interpretation of rights.

---

5. Challenges to Global Ethics Harmonization

5.1 **Geopolitical Competition** U.S.-China rivalry, diverging views on surveillance, and digital sovereignty complicate consensus. Ethical frameworks may become tools of soft power or ideological conflict.

5.2 **Corporate Lobbying and Regulatory Capture** Tech giants may resist binding regulation, diluting ethical commitments into public relations campaigns. Transparency about lobbying activities and funding sources is essential.

5.3 **Ethical Relativism vs. Universalism** Balancing universal human rights with culturally specific ethics remains a challenge. A pluralistic universalism approach, shared principles, and flexible applications may resolve tensions.

5.4 **Technological Acceleration and Policy Lag** Regulatory and ethical institutions often lag behind technological advancement. Agile governance, anticipatory regulation, and "sandbox" environments are needed to stay adaptive.

Conclusion: Building the Ethical AI Commons

Creating a global ethical framework for AI is not a luxury; it is a necessity for planetary stability, human dignity, and civilizational continuity. As AI becomes the substrate of modern society, it must be governed by moral imagination, philosophical depth, and democratic inclusivity.

Such a framework must avoid becoming an abstract manifesto. It should be embedded in code, enforced through policy, taught in classrooms, debated in communities, and evaluated by independent bodies. Only then can we ensure that AI enhances the human condition rather than undermines it.

References

Books:

Floridi, L. (2019). *The Logic of Information: A Theory of Philosophy as Conceptual Design*. Oxford University Press.
Bostrom, N. (2014). *Superintelligence: Paths, Dangers, Strategies*. Oxford University Press.
Dignum, V. (2019). *Responsible Artificial Intelligence: How to Develop and Use AI in a Responsible Way*. Springer.

Articles:

Jobin, A., Ienca, M., & Vayena, E. (2019). The global landscape of AI ethics guidelines. *Nature Machine Intelligence*, 1(9), 389–399.
Mittelstadt, B. (2019). Principles alone cannot guarantee ethical AI. *Nature Machine Intelligence*, 1(11), 501–507.

Reports:

UNESCO. (2021). *Recommendation on the Ethics of Artificial Intelligence*. https://unesdoc.unesco.org/ark:/48223/pf0000381137
OECD. (2019). *OECD Principles on Artificial Intelligence*. https://www.oecd.org/going-digital/ai/principles/
European Commission. (2021). *Proposal for a Regulation Laying Down Harmonised Rules on Artificial Intelligence (AI Act)*. https://eur-lex.europa.eu/legal-content/EN/TXT/?uri=CELEX%3A52021PC0206

Web Resources:

Global Partnership on AI. https://gpai.ai/
AI Ethics Guidelines Global Inventory. https://algorithmwatch.org/en/project/ai-ethics-guidelines-global-inventory/

Chapter 71. The Role of Civil Society in Shaping AI Governance

Introduction: Reclaiming the Civic Voice in a Technological Era

The rapid ascent of artificial intelligence (AI) and autonomous governance systems has brought into focus the critical role of civil society in shaping the future of AI. Civil society, comprising NGOs, academic institutions, social movements, ethical councils, independent watchdogs, and informed citizens, occupies a vital position in steering the ethical trajectory of AI technologies. While corporate and governmental actors often dominate the AI discourse, it is the persistent engagement of civil society that can ensure the alignment of AI with democratic values, social justice, and human dignity.

This chapter explores how civil society can influence AI development and governance, examines the philosophical foundations for this engagement, and highlights real-world case studies where civil involvement has tangibly shaped AI outcomes. It ultimately argues for embedding civil society into the design and governance of AGI systems as a non-negotiable element of democratic resilience.

I. The Importance of Civil Society in AI Governance

Civil society serves as a crucial counterbalance to state and corporate power. In the context of AI, where proprietary technologies, opaque algorithms, and data monopolies challenge public oversight, civil actors provide transparency, accountability, and ethical guidance.

- **Democratizing AI Policy**: Civil society organizations (CSOs) engage in lobbying, public education, and policy reform efforts that democratize AI governance. For example, AlgorithmWatch in Germany publishes critical audits of algorithmic decision-making systems used by public institutions.
- **Ensuring Inclusivity and Representation**: AI often reflects the biases of its creators. Civil society, by incorporating diverse perspectives, including marginalized voices, ensures AI systems serve all sectors of society fairly.
- **Advancing Human Rights Norms**: Organizations like Access Now and Amnesty International have integrated AI and digital surveillance into their human rights advocacy, framing new standards for privacy, freedom of expression, and digital personhood.

II. Philosophical Foundations: The Role of Civil Society in Democratic Theory

Philosophically, civil society is rooted in Enlightenment ideals of civic participation and Habermasian discourse ethics. In the AI age, these traditions offer a framework for embedding non-state voices in governance.

Habermas and the Public Sphere: Jurgen Habermas envisioned a deliberative democracy where civil society functions as the communicative bridge between citizens and institutions. In AI, this translates to participatory governance, citizen assemblies, and algorithmic accountability panels.
Arendtian Action and Plurality: Hannah Arendt emphasized human plurality and political action as the foundation of democratic life. Civil society reifies these principles by resisting the homogenizing tendencies of algorithmic systems and restoring human agency.
Rawlsian Justice as Fairness: John Rawls' theory supports inclusive deliberation under a veil of ignorance. In AI policy, civil society approximates this ideal by representing groups lacking power in current AI ecosystems.

III. Strategies for Civil Society Engagement

AI Literacy and Capacity Building: Equipping citizens and grassroots organizations with AI literacy is fundamental. Initiatives like Mozilla Foundation's Internet Health Report and Data & Society's research platform make AI discourse accessible.
Watchdog Mechanisms and Algorithmic Audits: Civil society performs independent audits to uncover biases and inefficiencies in algorithms. For example, the AI Now Institute conducts rigorous research into algorithmic injustice in education, policing, and labor.
Participatory Tech Design: In some contexts, civil actors co-develop AI tools, integrating ethical parameters and social constraints. Examples include participatory algorithm design workshops and citizen-led technology hackathons.
Policy Consultation and Advocacy: CSOs influence national and international AI regulations. They sit on expert panels (e.g., OECD AI Principles) and contribute to documents like the EU's Ethics Guidelines for Trustworthy AI.
Digital Rights Mobilization: Campaigns such as #BanTheScan (led by the Surveillance Technology Oversight Project) mobilize public opposition against facial recognition in public spaces.

IV. Case Studies: Civil Society in Action

Canada's Digital Charter and Civil Input: The Canadian government integrated civil society feedback in drafting its Digital Charter, emphasizing AI transparency and accountability.
Partnership on AI: A multi-stakeholder initiative that includes human rights organizations and advocacy groups alongside tech companies and academics, this platform exemplifies pluralistic dialogue.

Kenya's Algorithmic Impact Assessments: Local NGOs worked with government agencies to develop frameworks that assess how algorithms impact marginalized populations in public service delivery.
Barcelona's Decidim Platform: A citizen participation platform governed by civil society organizations that also shapes AI deployment in urban infrastructure and governance.

V. Barriers to Effective Civil Engagement

Despite its importance, civil society faces challenges in shaping AI governance:

Technical Complexity: Many CSOs lack the computational expertise to fully understand and critique AI systems.
Funding Limitations: Unlike corporations, civil groups often rely on short-term, constrained funding.
Tokenization: There is a risk of civil society participation being reduced to symbolic gestures without genuine influence.
Regulatory Capture: Tech firms may co-opt civil narratives while continuing exploitative practices.

VI. Overcoming Barriers: Future Roadmap

Interdisciplinary Collaboration: Building coalitions between philosophers, data scientists, and civil society leaders can bridge the technical-ethical divide.
Ethics-by-Design Frameworks: Civil society can co-develop standards like value-sensitive design and differential privacy protocols.
Global Solidarity Networks: Transnational alliances (e.g., Global Network Initiative) allow for shared advocacy and resource pooling.
Public Technology Oversight Boards: Independent AI oversight boards with significant civil society representation should be institutionalized.
Digital Commons and Governance Experiments: Community-owned digital infrastructures allow for experimentation with democratic AI governance.

Conclusion: Reclaiming the Commons of Intelligence

Civil society is indispensable to the governance of AGI and advanced AI. As custodians of ethical integrity, inclusive dialogue, and human dignity, civil actors prevent governance from becoming a technocratic enclosure. Their role must be embedded at every level of design, deployment, and evaluation.

Philosophically grounded, technologically literate, and globally networked civil society movements offer a critical buffer against the corporatization and authoritarian capture of intelligent systems. The governance of AI is not simply a technical issue, but a civic project, and civil society must remain its most vigilant guardian.

References

Books and Articles:

Habermas, J. (1984). *The Theory of Communicative Action*. Boston: Beacon Press.
Arendt, H. (1958). *The Human Condition*. Chicago: University of Chicago Press.
Rawls, J. (1971). *A Theory of Justice*. Cambridge: Harvard University Press.
O'Neil, C. (2016). *Weapons of Math Destruction*. New York: Crown Publishing.
Eubanks, V. (2018). *Automating Inequality*. St. Martin's Press.

Reports and Articles:

AlgorithmWatch. (2022). *Automated Decision-Making Systems in the EU*.
AI Now Institute. (2023). *Annual Report*. https://ainowinstitute.org/reports.html
Access Now. (2021). *Human Rights in the Age of AI*. https://www.accessnow.org
Mozilla Foundation. (2022). *Internet Health Report*. https://internethealthreport.org

Web Resources:

https://www.partnershiponai.org
https://www.decidim.org
https://globalnetworkinitiative.org
https://surveillanceoversight.org
https://ec.europa.eu/digital-strategy

Chapter 72. The Intersection of AI, Ethics, and Law

Introduction

The accelerating integration of Artificial Intelligence (AI) into every facet of human life has prompted a cascade of ethical, legal, and philosophical challenges. AI technologies are no longer confined to laboratory experiments or futuristic predictions; they are deployed in judicial systems, healthcare diagnostics, military drones, social media algorithms, and financial markets. As a result, the intersection of AI, ethics, and law has become a critical arena where moral reasoning, jurisprudence, and public policy must converge. This chapter provides an in-depth analysis of how legal implications intersect with the ethical development of AI, examines philosophical frameworks that underpin this interplay, and offers case studies to illustrate the pressing need for coherent governance.

---

1. The Legal Implications of Ethical AI Development

1.1 **The Legal Vacuum and Regulatory Lag** Most legal systems are ill-equipped to handle the speed of technological innovation, resulting in regulatory vacuums. In many jurisdictions, laws governing AI remain either embryonic or fragmented. This lag enables unchecked deployment of technologies, which may lead to violations of privacy, due process, and equal treatment.

1.2 **Liability and Accountability:** Who is responsible when an AI system causes harm? Traditional tort law struggles to assign liability to non-human agents. Legal scholars have proposed frameworks including:

- **Strict liability for developers**
- **Shared liability models** involving users, manufacturers, and trainers
- **Personhood models**, where autonomous AI systems are granted limited legal status akin to corporations

1.3 **Compliance and Transparency** Ethically aligned AI must also comply with transparency mandates. The General Data Protection Regulation (GDPR) in the EU includes a "right to explanation," challenging the use of opaque algorithms. Legal systems must thus require explainability as a cornerstone of ethical AI deployment.

---

2. Philosophical Perspectives on Law and Ethics in AI

2.1 **Deontology vs. Utilitarianism** Deontological frameworks emphasize duty and rule-following, suggesting that AI should act in ways that respect inherent human rights. In contrast, utilitarianism argues for the greatest good for the greatest number, potentially justifying ethically dubious actions if the net utility is positive. These schools often conflict in algorithmic decision-making, such as in autonomous vehicle ethics (e.g., trolley problem scenarios).

2.2 **Virtue Ethics and the Moral Character of AI** Rather than focusing solely on rules or outcomes, virtue ethics emphasizes the moral character of agents. Can AI possess virtues like compassion, prudence, or justice? While machines may simulate such behavior, the absence of consciousness raises philosophical concerns about authenticity.

2.3 **Natural Law vs. Legal Positivism** Natural law posits that legal standards should reflect moral truths, suggesting that AI laws should be rooted in universal human values. Legal positivism, by contrast, treats law as a social construct separate from morality, implying that any codified law, however unjust, is still legally valid. This debate shapes policy decisions on regulating AI.

---

3. Case Studies on Legal Challenges in AI Ethics

3.1 **COMPAS Recidivism Algorithm (United States)** The Correctional Offender Management Profiling for Alternative Sanctions (COMPAS) algorithm used in criminal sentencing has been criticized for racial bias. Legal challenges have argued that opaque decision-making violates defendants' due process rights. Courts have struggled to balance proprietary algorithm protection with transparency.

3.2 **Facial Recognition in Public Surveillance (China, UK, US)** Government use of facial recognition technology has sparked global controversy. In the UK, the High Court ruled that live facial recognition infringed on privacy rights without adequate legal safeguards. In the US, some cities have banned its use by law enforcement altogether.

3.3 **Autonomous Vehicles and Accident Liability** When an Uber autonomous vehicle killed a pedestrian in 2018, questions arose about liability. The safety driver was charged, but the company faced minimal repercussions. This case highlighted the absence of clear legal frameworks assigning responsibility among software developers, vehicle manufacturers, and users.

3.4 **Deepfakes and Political Manipulation** The rise of deepfake videos poses serious risks to democratic integrity and public trust. Despite clear ethical violations, many jurisdictions lack legal tools to prosecute the creators, especially when operating across borders.

---

4. Toward an Integrated Ethical-Legal Framework

4.1 **Multilateral Agreements and Treaties** AI governance requires international cooperation. The OECD and UNESCO have drafted AI principles that include transparency, accountability, and human-centric design. A binding international treaty, akin to the Geneva Conventions for AI in warfare and digital ethics, may become necessary.

4.2 **Legal Design Thinking** Borrowing from user-centric design, legal design thinking involves creating intuitive legal frameworks that embed ethical principles from the outset. This could include:

- Embedding ethics checklists into regulatory approval processes
- Mandating impact assessments similar to environmental reviews
- Establishing ethics review boards for major AI applications

4.3 **Algorithmic Impact Assessments (AIA)** Governments like Canada and the EU have started mandating AIAs, requiring disclosure of algorithmic logic, data sources, and mitigation of potential harm. These assessments serve as legal and ethical safeguards.

4.4 **Ethics-as-Code and Regulatory Sandboxes** Efforts to formalize ethical principles into programmable rules, known as "ethics-as-code," can provide legal certainty and operational clarity. Regulatory sandboxes allow innovators to test AI systems under legal oversight without full regulatory penalties, fostering ethical experimentation.

Conclusion

The convergence of AI, ethics, and law presents one of the most profound governance challenges of the 21st century. While philosophical traditions offer rich conceptual tools for ethical analysis, law provides the enforceable structure to implement and sustain those ideals. The need for a coherent, globally consistent ethical-legal framework is urgent. Without it, AI risks becoming a tool of oppression rather than liberation. Through case studies, philosophical reflection, and regulatory foresight, this chapter underscores that aligning ethics and law in the age of intelligent machines is not merely a technical exercise; it is a moral imperative.

References

Books:

Bostrom, N. (2014). *Superintelligence: Paths, Dangers, Strategies*. Oxford University Press.

Cath, C. (2018). *Governing Artificial Intelligence: Ethical, Legal and Technical Opportunities and Challenges*. Philosophical Transactions of the Royal Society A.

Floridi, L. (2013). *The Ethics of Information*. Oxford University Press.

O'Neil, C. (2016). *Weapons of Math Destruction*. Crown Publishing.

Articles and Reports:

European Commission. (2021). *Proposal for a Regulation Laying Down Harmonised Rules on Artificial Intelligence (Artificial Intelligence Act)*. https://ec.europa.eu/newsroom/dae/document.cfm?doc_id=75788
AI Now Institute. (2019). *Algorithmic Impact Assessments: A Practical Framework for Public Agency Accountability*. https://ainowinstitute.org/aiareport2018.pdf
OECD. (2019). *Recommendation of the Council on Artificial Intelligence*. https://legalinstruments.oecd.org/en/instruments/OECD-LEGAL-0449

Case Law and Jurisdictional Materials:

State v. Loomis, 881 N.W.2d 749 (Wis. 2016)
Bridges v. South Wales Police [2020] EWCA Civ 1058

Online Resources:

Partnership on AI. (https://www.partnershiponai.org)
UNESCO AI Ethics Recommendations. (https://unesdoc.unesco.org/ark:/48223/pf0000380455)
Stanford HAI Policy Resources. (https://hai.stanford.edu/policy)

Chapter 73. Decentralized Platforms for Legal Enforcement

Introduction: Rethinking Law in the Digital Era

The digital transformation of society is redefining how we perceive, create, and enforce laws. Traditional legal systems are largely centralized, rooted in hierarchical institutions such as courts, governments, and international treaties. However, the rapid rise of decentralized technologies, especially blockchain and artificial intelligence (AI), is offering new mechanisms to enforce laws and contracts without traditional intermediaries. This chapter explores the integration of smart contracts and AI in legal enforcement, the philosophical implications of automating justice, and real-world applications shaping the future of decentralized legal systems.

---

1. Understanding Smart Contracts and Decentralized Legal Architecture

Smart contracts are self-executing agreements written in code and deployed on a blockchain. These digital contracts trigger actions automatically when predefined conditions are met. This eliminates the need for third-party enforcement and offers trustless, immutable, and verifiable records of transactions.

Key features:

- **Autonomy**: Once deployed, they execute independently.
- **Transparency**: Their code is publicly verifiable.
- **Security**: Cryptographic underpinnings reduce tampering and fraud.
- **Cost-efficiency**: Reduced need for legal intermediaries.

Examples of platforms:

- **Ethereum**: The first major blockchain to support smart contracts.
- **Tezos, Solana, Cardano**: Providing enhanced scalability and formal verification.

---

2. AI as an Agent of Legal Decision-Making

AI contributes to legal enforcement through its capacity to interpret data, assess compliance, and make predictive judgments. Machine learning models can:

- Detect contract breaches
- Automate dispute resolution
- Assess damages and liabilities
- Monitor regulatory compliance in real-time

The convergence of AI and smart contracts can produce hybrid legal enforcement systems capable of both interpreting complex legal data and executing contractual obligations automatically.

---

3. Philosophical Challenges of Automated Law Enforcement

While automation offers efficiency, it raises significant philosophical and ethical dilemmas:

- **Loss of Contextual Judgment**: Legal decisions often require empathy, discretion, and cultural nuance, elements not easily codified into algorithms.
- **Accountability**: Who is responsible if a smart contract malfunctions or causes harm?
- **Justice vs. Efficiency**: Automated systems may prioritize execution over fairness.
- **Rule Formalism**: Excessive reliance on coded logic could erode the spirit of the law in favor of the letter of the law.

Debates:

- Natural Law theorists argue that justice must align with moral principles not reducible to algorithms.
- Legal Positivists see value in the rule-based consistency that AI and smart contracts can provide.

---

4. Case Studies: Decentralized Legal Enforcement in Practice

4.1. Kleros (Ethereum-based Arbitration Platform) Kleros employs a decentralized jury system to resolve disputes using crypto-economic incentives. Jurors are randomly selected and vote on outcomes based on evidence. It is a notable experiment in decentralized justice and peer-based adjudication.

4.2. Aragon Court: A blockchain-native dispute resolution mechanism used in decentralized autonomous organizations (DAOs). It leverages reputation systems and token staking to ensure integrity in decisions.

4.3. LexDAO A community of legal engineers building open-source, machine-readable legal protocols and frameworks for decentralized legal tools. They aim to blend human legal reasoning with programmable enforcement.

4.4. Chainlink & Real World Asset Enforcement Chainlink's oracles connect smart contracts to real-world data, enabling legally binding financial transactions, e.g., triggering penalties for late payments based on shipping APIs.

---

5. Legal and Regulatory Considerations

Governments and legal institutions face challenges in regulating decentralized legal systems:

Jurisdiction: Where is the law enforced if the contract is global?
Recognition: Are smart contract-based rulings enforceable in traditional courts?
Privacy: Decentralized systems must comply with GDPR and other privacy laws.
Standardization: Legal enforceability requires standardized, auditable smart contract templates.

International bodies such as the **International Association for Trusted Blockchain Applications (INATBA)** and **OECD** have initiated dialogues on bridging legal code and blockchain systems.

---

6. Strategies for Ethical and Effective Implementation

Hybrid Models: Combine smart contracts with traditional dispute resolution mechanisms (e.g., human override clauses).
Transparent Governance: Decentralized legal protocols must have clear, accessible documentation and appeals processes.
Community Jurisprudence: Governance tokens and juror pools foster participatory justice.
Auditability and Ethics-by-Design: Code audits and embedded ethical principles must precede deployment.
Interoperability with Legal Systems: Smart contracts should reference or integrate traditional legal language to ensure enforceability.

Conclusion: Toward a New Jurisprudence

Decentralized platforms for legal enforcement are not a threat to justice; they are an opportunity to reimagine its foundations. By blending the transparency of blockchain, the analytical power of AI, and the wisdom of human-centered legal traditions, we can build systems that are not only faster and cheaper but also more accessible and equitable. The challenge lies in ensuring that these systems serve humanity, not just automation. A future legal architecture must remain rooted in the values of fairness, dignity, and shared governance, even as it is rendered in code.

References

Books:

Lessig, L. (2006). *Code: And Other Laws of Cyberspace*. Basic Books.
Katyal, N. (2001). *Digital Architecture and the Future of Law*. Yale Law Review.

Articles:

Werbach, K., & Cornell, N. (2017). Contracts Ex Machina. *Duke Law Journal*, 67(2), 313-382.
De Filippi, P., & Hassan, S. (2016). Blockchain Technology as a Regulatory Technology. *First Monday*.

Reports:

OECD. (2021). *Blockchain and the Law: International Trends and Legal Issues.*
INATBA. (2022). *Legal Interoperability of Smart Contracts: Guidelines and Recommendations.*

Online Resources:

https://kleros.io
https://aragon.org
https://lexdao.org
https://chain.link
https://oecd.org/finance/blockchain
https://inatba.org

Chapter 74. The Role of Blockchain in Protecting Human Rights

Introduction: Technology and Rights in the Digital Age

The accelerating advancement of blockchain technology marks a pivotal moment in the digital transformation of governance and civil liberties. As societies grapple with the challenges of surveillance, data ownership, systemic corruption, and information manipulation, blockchain has emerged as a decentralized, transparent, and immutable solution with the potential to redefine how human rights are recorded, enforced, and protected. Unlike traditional technologies controlled by centralized authorities, blockchain distributes trust across a network, reducing the risk of unilateral abuses of power and creating a verifiable history of transactions, decisions, and rights claims.

1. Blockchain's Core Principles Aligned with Human Rights

Blockchain's foundational attributes, decentralization, immutability, transparency, and trustless consensus, align closely with the core principles of human rights:

- **Decentralization** ensures that no single entity holds absolute power over critical information or decision-making, reducing the risk of authoritarian control or systemic bias.
- **Immutability** guarantees that once a human rights claim or violation is recorded on a blockchain, it cannot be altered or erased, preserving the historical integrity of abuse documentation.
- **Transparency** supports the right to information, allowing public access to the operations of institutions.
- **Trustless consensus** fosters accountability and neutrality by removing the need for intermediaries who could otherwise manipulate or misrepresent rights enforcement.

2. Blockchain Use Cases in Human Rights Protection

a. Identity and Statelessness

More than 1 billion people worldwide lack formal identification. Statelessness severely limits access to education, healthcare, voting rights, and financial services. Blockchain can provide self-sovereign digital identity systems that individuals control independently of governments, enabling access to rights without requiring centralized validation.

Example: The World Food Programme's Building Blocks project uses blockchain to provide refugees in Jordan with a biometric-based blockchain wallet that secures their identities and financial entitlements.

b. Anti-Corruption and Transparency in Governance

In corrupt regimes, opaque systems allow human rights abuses to go unpunished. Blockchain-based governance platforms can record government contracts, voting results, and budget allocations on public ledgers, thereby enabling civic oversight.

Example: The city of Zug in Switzerland and Estonia's e-residency program utilize blockchain for transparent governance and secure digital citizen services.

c. Land and Property Rights

Property rights are foundational to economic freedom. In many parts of the world, land disputes arise from unclear or manipulated records. Blockchain can ensure transparent, tamper-proof registration of ownership, protecting vulnerable populations from dispossession.

Example: In Ghana, Bitland is using blockchain to create immutable land title registries, helping resolve disputes and empowering marginalized communities.

d. Supply Chain and Labor Rights

Blockchain tracks products from origin to consumer, enabling transparency across supply chains. This can expose exploitative labor practices, child labor, or environmental violations.

Example: Everledger uses blockchain to trace diamonds and ensure they are conflict-free. Similar models apply to the coffee, cocoa, and textile industries.

e. Freedom of Expression and Press

In countries with restricted media, journalists face censorship and digital erasure. Decentralized publishing on blockchain allows the permanent storage of reports and exposes disinformation campaigns.

Example: The Open Index Protocol (OIP) and Arweave offer immutable data storage for content like investigative journalism, ensuring records can't be scrubbed by authoritarian regimes.

3. Legal and Ethical Considerations

a. Jurisdictional Challenges

Because blockchains are global by design, legal conflicts emerge between decentralized networks and state-centric legal systems. How can a blockchain-based human rights claim be adjudicated or enforced across sovereign borders? International cooperation and updated digital legal frameworks are required.

b. Consent and Privacy

Immutability, while powerful, raises privacy concerns. Recording sensitive personal data (such as biometric information) immutably poses risks if not adequately anonymized or encrypted.

c. Algorithmic Discrimination and Embedded Bias

Smart contracts can inherit the biases of their developers. Careful ethical oversight is necessary to ensure rights-based protections are coded equitably and remain challengeable.

d. Access and Digital Divides

Blockchain assumes a reliable internet and digital literacy. For marginalized communities to benefit, infrastructural investment and inclusive education must accompany implementation.

4. Case Studies on Blockchain and Human Rights

Case Study 1: The WFP's Building Blocks

- Over 1 million Syrian refugees are now served by blockchain-based identity and transaction systems.
- Fraud was reduced by 98% compared to traditional cash aid models.

Case Study 2: Honduras' Land Registry Pilot

Honduras attempted to create a blockchain land registry with Factom. Despite initial success, the project was paused due to governmental shifts, highlighting the importance of sustained political will.

Case Study 3: Uyghur Supply Chain Verification via Blockchain

Brands using blockchain to trace cotton and other goods have helped expose forced labor in Xinjiang, China. While enforcement remains weak, transparency exerts pressure on multinational corporations.

5. Future Opportunities and Strategic Recommendations

- **Human Rights Blockchain Standards**: International bodies such as the UN could coordinate the standardization of ethical blockchain frameworks for human rights use.
- **Integration with AI**: Using AI to detect human rights abuses, with blockchain storing the evidence immutably, offers potential synergies.
- **Community-Driven Governance**: DAO (Decentralized Autonomous Organization) models could be used to govern human rights enforcement democratically.
- **Smart Contract Oversight Bodies**: Ethical review boards could audit smart contracts before deployment in rights-sensitive applications.

6. Conclusion: Blockchain as Rights Infrastructure

Blockchain is not a silver bullet, but it is a foundational infrastructure for the transparent, decentralized, and accountable protection of human rights in the digital age. To fully realize its promise, interdisciplinary collaboration, regulatory harmonization, and ethical vigilance must accompany its deployment. When used responsibly, blockchain can become a rights-preserving ledger for all of humanity.

References

Books:

Tapscott, D., & Tapscott, A. (2016). *Blockchain Revolution: How the Technology Behind Bitcoin is Changing Money, Business, and the World.* Penguin.
Lessig, L. (1999). *Code and Other Laws of Cyberspace.* Basic Books.

Articles:

Zambrano, R. (2017). *Blockchain for Social Impact.* Stanford Social Innovation Review. https://ssir.org/articles/entry/blockchain_for_social_impact
Wright, A., & De Filippi, P. (2015). *Decentralized Blockchain Technology and the Rise of Lex Cryptographia.* https://ssrn.com/abstract=2580664

Reports:

World Food Programme (2020). *Building Blocks: Blockchain for Food Security.* https://innovation.wfp.org/project/building-blocks
Human Rights Watch (2022). *World Report: Human Rights and Digital Technologies.* https://www.hrw.org

Websites:

Everledger: https://www.everledger.io
Bitland: https://bitland.world
Arweave: https://www.arweave.org
Open Index Protocol: https://oip.wiki

Chapter 75. The Ethics of AI in Public Policy

Introduction

As artificial intelligence (AI) becomes increasingly integrated into the mechanisms of governance, policymaking, and administrative decision-making, it presents both unprecedented opportunities and formidable ethical challenges. Public policy, traditionally shaped by human judgment, values, and social negotiation, is now being influenced by algorithms capable of processing vast datasets, detecting patterns, and making recommendations, or even decisions, with minimal human intervention. The integration of AI into public policy offers efficiencies and capabilities once unimaginable, but it also raises foundational questions about accountability, transparency, fairness, and democratic legitimacy.

This chapter explores the ethical dimensions of AI's involvement in public policy. It begins by analyzing how AI is currently influencing public decision-making across various domains, from welfare systems and law enforcement to healthcare and urban planning. It then delves into philosophical debates concerning the role of AI in governance, examining perspectives from deontology, utilitarianism, virtue ethics, and democratic theory. Finally, it presents real-world examples of AI-driven policy initiatives, evaluating their ethical implications and proposing safeguards for maintaining human dignity, autonomy, and justice in an age of intelligent machines.

1. *How AI Can Influence Public Policy Decisions*

Artificial Intelligence (AI) is rapidly becoming a cornerstone in shaping public policy across the globe. Governments, municipalities, and supranational organizations are increasingly integrating AI systems into decision-making processes to enhance efficiency, predict trends, and allocate resources more judiciously. AI tools such as predictive analytics, natural language processing, and machine learning algorithms are already employed in policy domains including public health, education, urban planning, and criminal justice.

For instance, AI-powered data models are helping cities anticipate infrastructure needs by analyzing population growth, migration patterns, and environmental data. In the wake of the COVID-19 pandemic, AI tools were used to predict infection surges, guide vaccine distribution, and monitor public compliance with lockdown regulations. These applications demonstrate how AI systems, when properly aligned with ethical standards, can enhance the responsiveness and adaptability of public policy frameworks.

However, the influence of AI on policy raises significant ethical concerns, particularly regarding transparency, accountability, and public trust. The automation of decision-making processes challenges traditional democratic norms, such as deliberation and citizen participation. Questions arise about who designs these systems, how their objectives are set, and whether the algorithms respect human rights and social justice principles.

2. *Philosophical Debates on AI's Role in Policy-Making*

The philosophical foundations of public policy have historically centered on justice, equity, and the social contract. When AI is introduced into this mix, it demands a reevaluation of those foundational assumptions. Three key philosophical debates emerge:

Utilitarianism vs. Deontological Ethics: Should AI in public policy prioritize outcomes (utilitarianism) or adhere to procedural fairness and moral duties (deontology)? A predictive policing algorithm may reduce crime rates but could disproportionately target minority communities, thus violating deontological commitments to equal treatment and dignity.
Epistemic Authority vs. Democratic Deliberation: AI systems can analyze vast datasets and provide insights far beyond human capability. But should these systems supplant human judgment in public deliberation? Critics argue that relying too heavily on AI erodes democratic participation and places epistemic authority in the hands of opaque technologies.
Technocracy vs. Human-Centric Governance: Philosophers such as Jürgen Habermas emphasize communicative rationality, the idea that legitimacy arises through discourse among free and equal citizens. AI-driven policy risks favoring a technocratic model where policy is optimized rather than debated, undermining the normative foundations of participatory governance.

3. *Examples of AI-Driven Public Policy Initiatives*

Several real-world initiatives illustrate both the promise and the peril of AI in public governance:

Social Credit Systems in China: Perhaps the most controversial example, China's social credit system uses AI to monitor and score citizens' behavior. While the stated aim is to promote trustworthiness, critics argue it represents a dystopian form of social engineering with little regard for privacy, freedom, or due process.
AI in Welfare Eligibility Assessments: In the Netherlands and the UK, AI systems were deployed to assess welfare eligibility. These systems were later criticized for perpetuating biases, a lack of transparency, and violating the rights of vulnerable populations.
Algorithmic Risk Assessment in Criminal Justice: Tools like COMPAS in the United States assess the likelihood of recidivism to guide sentencing and parole decisions. Studies have shown racial bias in such systems, sparking legal challenges and philosophical critiques of algorithmic fairness.
AI in Urban Planning and Sustainability: Cities like Singapore and Helsinki use AI to optimize traffic flow, manage energy consumption, and promote green infrastructure. These initiatives generally enjoy public support due to their transparency and tangible benefits, but questions about long-term surveillance and data ownership remain.

4. *Towards Ethical AI-Enabled Policy*

To align AI with ethical governance, several principles and strategies are essential:

Transparency and Explainability: AI systems should be transparent about their functioning, data sources, and decision-making logic. Citizens must be able to challenge algorithmic decisions through understandable explanations.

Accountability Mechanisms: Clear lines of responsibility must be established for decisions made by AI systems. Public institutions must retain ultimate responsibility and ensure legal recourse for affected individuals.

Participatory Design: Stakeholders, especially those from marginalized communities, should be involved in designing AI systems that affect their lives. This approach helps embed diverse values and ensures alignment with social needs.

Ethical Impact Assessments: Before deploying AI in policy settings, governments should conduct ethical reviews, much like environmental impact assessments. These reviews should evaluate potential harms, benefits, and alternatives.

Legislation and Oversight: Robust legal frameworks are needed to regulate the use of AI in public policy. International cooperation may be necessary to harmonize standards and prevent regulatory arbitrage.

Conclusion

AI's integration into public policy offers both unprecedented opportunities and profound ethical risks. Philosophical inquiry plays a crucial role in navigating this terrain, providing the normative compass needed to ensure that technological innovation strengthens rather than subverts democratic values. A human-centered approach to AI governance requires more than technical fixes; it demands a philosophical commitment to justice, transparency, and the public good.

References

Books

Floridi, L. (2013). *The Ethics of Information*. Oxford University Press.

O'Neil, C. (2016). *Weapons of Math Destruction*. Crown Publishing Group.

Russell, S., & Norvig, P. (2020). *Artificial Intelligence: A Modern Approach*. Pearson.

Articles

Eubanks, V. (2018). *Automating Inequality: How High-Tech Tools Profile, Police, and Punish the Poor*. St. Martin's Press.

Mittelstadt, B., Allo, P., Taddeo, M., Wachter, S., & Floridi, L. (2016). "The ethics of algorithms: Mapping the debate." *Big Data & Society*, 3(2).

Reports

European Commission. (2021). *Proposal for a Regulation on Artificial Intelligence.* https://digital-strategy.ec.europa.eu
AI Now Institute. (2019). *AI Now Report.* https://ainowinstitute.org/AI_Now_2019_Report.pdf

Online Resources

Future of Life Institute. "AI Policy". https://futureoflife.org/ai-policy
OECD. (2020). *AI Principles.* https://oecd.ai/en/ai-principles

Grouped by Type

Books: Floridi (2013), O'Neil (2016), Russell & Norvig (2020)
Articles: Eubanks (2018), Mittelstadt et al. (2016)
Reports: European Commission (2021), AI Now Institute (2019)
Websites: Future of Life Institute, OECD

Chapter 76. The Future of Democracy in an AI-Driven World

Introduction

Democracy, historically defined as the rule of the people, is undergoing an existential transformation as artificial intelligence (AI) becomes embedded in the machinery of governance. From decision-making algorithms to data-driven citizen engagement tools, AI technologies are redefining participation, representation, and trust in public institutions. The integration of intelligent systems into governance is not just a technical advancement; it is a philosophical, ethical, and civilizational turning point. This chapter explores the potential trajectories of democracy in an AI-driven world, grounded in a framework that balances innovation with democratic integrity, transparency, and human dignity.

---

1. AI's Potential to Reshape Democratic Institutions

A. Digital Governance: Automation and Augmentation

Governments across the globe are increasingly turning to AI to streamline bureaucratic operations, improve public service delivery, and simulate policy outcomes. Estonia's digital republic has set a global benchmark, where AI aids in tax filing, healthcare logistics, and even legal dispute resolution. Similarly, South Korea and Singapore employ AI to manage traffic flows, energy consumption, and pandemic response.

These changes have raised a critical question: Is AI simply a tool of efficiency, or is it a new participant in the democratic process? If algorithms begin to perform civic functions, distributing welfare, adjudicating claims, or even interpreting legislation, then we must ask whether they represent, obey, or supplant human decision-making.

B. Algorithmic Voting and Representation

Predictive analytics have been proposed as a means to enhance electoral systems through both real-time policy responsiveness and voter behavior forecasting. Liquid democracy platforms like DemocracyOS and systems such as Quadratic Voting illustrate the early experimentation with algorithm-enhanced participatory democracy.

Yet, challenges persist. Algorithmic prediction risks reinforcing existing biases, marginalizing minority opinions, and undermining the unpredictability that often drives democratic innovation. Moreover, in delegating decision-making to systems that lack moral agency, societies risk reducing civic life to a computational problem.

C. AI in Legislative Drafting and Legal Interpretation

Some jurisdictions have begun exploring AI-assisted legislative drafting and legal codification. The potential benefits are substantial, legislation could be more internally coherent, updated in real time, and optimized for outcomes. However, it also raises concerns over the democratic legitimacy of laws authored or interpreted by systems that do not understand human suffering, context, or intention.

---

2. Philosophical Perspectives on AI and Democracy

A. The Tension Between Technocracy and Democracy

Philosophers from Habermas to Rawls have emphasized the deliberative nature of democracy, a system that draws legitimacy from open discourse and procedural fairness. AI, by contrast, is rooted in optimization, predictive modeling, and instrumental rationality. The result is a philosophical tension between reasoned consensus and computational efficiency.

If democracy becomes primarily data-driven, what happens to dissent, contingency, and the moral unpredictability of the human will? As philosopher Byung-Chul Han argues, the algorithmic society risks replacing the "public sphere" with the "infopolitical," where citizens are reduced to data subjects, and decision-making is depoliticized.

B. Freedom, Autonomy, and Digital Manipulation

AI systems often operate by manipulating behavioral patterns, nudging individuals toward actions aligned with predefined goals, be it public health, taxation compliance, or political stability. This raises profound philosophical concerns about autonomy. Is consent meaningful in a system that subtly engineers preferences?

Political theorists like Isaiah Berlin have long debated the meaning of freedom. In an AI context, negative liberty (freedom from interference) may be undermined by opaque algorithmic surveillance, while positive liberty (the ability to act meaningfully) may be constrained by predictive governance that forecloses uncertainty.

C. Accountability, Legitimacy, and the Problem of the Black Box

Democracy relies on transparency, redress, and institutional accountability. AI systems, particularly those driven by deep learning, often operate as "black boxes", producing outcomes that are inscrutable even to their developers. This undermines the epistemic basis of democratic legitimacy.

Philosophers of science like Bruno Latour have long emphasized the importance of traceability in complex systems. In a democratic context, explainability is not a technical luxury, it is a moral necessity. Citizens must understand how decisions are made if they are to contest, accept, or reform them.

---

3. Case Studies on AI in Democratic Processes

A. Taiwan's vTaiwan Platform: Deliberative Democracy Enhanced

Taiwan's vTaiwan initiative is a participatory platform that uses machine learning and sentiment analysis to facilitate digital consensus-building. Citizens debate issues online, and AI clusters opinions to highlight areas of agreement and contention. The resulting proposals are submitted to Parliament for action.

This model showcases AI's ability to scale deliberative democracy without silencing minority voices. However, it requires strong institutional safeguards to prevent manipulation, cyber interference, or data misuse.

B. Predictive Policing and the Erosion of Democratic Oversight

In contrast, the use of AI in predictive policing, such as the systems deployed in Chicago, Los Angeles, and London, has been widely criticized for perpetuating racial bias, undermining due process, and bypassing legislative accountability. These tools were implemented under opaque conditions, often without public debate or democratic consent.

This case study illustrates the darker side of AI in governance, where democratic norms are subordinated to actuarial logic, and where inequality becomes algorithmically entrenched.

C. Kenya's Huduma Namba: Digital Identity and Democratic Inclusion

Kenya's digital ID initiative, Huduma Namba, aimed to improve service delivery by linking citizens to a centralized biometric identity. However, the project faced backlash over data privacy, exclusion of marginalized communities, and the risk of surveillance. Despite these challenges, the initiative represents a frontier where AI, democracy, and inclusion intersect.

When implemented transparently, digital identity systems can democratize access to services. When deployed without adequate checks, they can deepen authoritarian tendencies.

---

4. Reimagining Democratic Governance with AI

A. Towards Algorithmic Accountability

For AI to support rather than subvert democracy, it must be designed with mechanisms for explanation, contestability, and human override. This entails legal mandates for algorithmic transparency, institutional review boards for AI policy tools, and AI literacy among legislators and citizens.

B. Democratic Data Stewardship

Democracy in the AI age depends on who owns, controls, and governs data. Public data trusts, decentralized data cooperatives, and community-informed consent models are emerging as alternatives to the privatized surveillance models of Big Tech.

C. Decentralized AI and Participatory Governance

Blockchain-based decentralized autonomous organizations (DAOs) offer a provocative vision for direct digital democracy. While early DAOs have struggled with scalability and legal recognition, their architecture, ruled by smart contracts and consensus, is philosophically aligned with Rousseau's idea of the general will.

Conclusion: Democratic Resilience in the Age of AI

The future of democracy is not predetermined. AI can be a force for renewal, reinvigorating civic participation, streamlining deliberation, and expanding inclusion. But it can also be a Trojan horse for technocracy, bias, and control.

Democracy in the AI age will require more than new policies; it will demand new philosophies. It must reassert the value of human judgment, protect spaces for dissent, and ensure that technology serves the governed, not the governors. As AI systems grow more powerful, democratic societies must grow more vigilant, philosophical, and participatory.

References

Books

Berlin, I. (1969). *Four Essays on Liberty*. Oxford University Press.
Han, B.-C. (2017). *Psychopolitics: Neoliberalism and New Technologies of Power*. Verso Books.
Latour, B. (2005). *Reassembling the Social: An Introduction to Actor-Network-Theory*. Oxford University Press.
Rawls, J. (1971). *A Theory of Justice*. Harvard University Press.
Habermas, J. (1996). *Between Facts and Norms: Contributions to a Discourse Theory of Law and Democracy*. MIT Press.

Articles

Eubanks, V. (2018). *Automating Inequality*. St. Martin's Press.
O'Neil, C. (2016). *Weapons of Math Destruction: How Big Data Increases Inequality and Threatens Democracy*. Crown Publishing.
Fung, A. (2013). "Deliberation at Scale: Citizen Engagement in a Data-Driven Democracy." *The Good Society*, 22(1).

Reports and Case Studies

World Economic Forum. (2021). *Global Technology Governance Report*.
MIT Technology Review. (2019). "How Taiwan Is Using Social Media to Rebuild Trust in Democracy."
Amnesty International. (2020). "Surveillance Giants: How the Business Model of Big Tech Threatens Human Rights."
https://www.amnesty.org/en/documents/pol30/1404/2019/en/
Privacy International. (2021). "Kenya's Huduma Namba: A Digital Identity without Safeguards." https://privacyinternational.org
Future of Life Institute. (2023). *AI Policy and Democratic Integrity*. https://futureoflife.org

Chapter 77. Global Governance and the Role of AI

Introduction

As artificial intelligence (AI) continues to evolve and integrate into nearly every aspect of life, its implications extend beyond national borders. Global governance, the system by which international relations are managed through laws, norms, and institutions, must now accommodate AI as both a transformative agent and a subject of regulation. This chapter explores how AI is reshaping global governance structures, the ethical imperatives guiding its global use, and how real-world implementations can inform the development of a balanced, inclusive, and equitable AI-governed world order.

1. The Rise of AI in Global Decision-Making

AI systems are already participating in decision-making processes at international levels. From predicting global economic trends to modeling climate scenarios, AI's computational capabilities provide insights and guidance for global policy. Institutions like the United Nations (UN), World Health Organization (WHO), and World Bank increasingly incorporate AI to manage global health, development, and humanitarian crises. These applications illustrate the power and promise of AI, but they also raise pressing questions: Who builds these systems? Who governs them? And are they accountable to the global public?

2. Redefining Sovereignty in the AI Era

AI blurs the lines of national sovereignty. Algorithms developed in one nation can affect decisions, economies, and civil liberties across the globe. For example, content moderation algorithms built in Silicon Valley determine political discourse in countries from India to Nigeria. Similarly, predictive policing tools developed in the Global North are exported to less developed nations with vastly different legal frameworks. This creates an asymmetry of influence and control that challenges traditional notions of sovereignty and requires a cooperative approach to AI governance.

3. The Need for Multilateral AI Governance Frameworks

Global governance institutions must evolve to develop standardized ethical and legal frameworks that address AI's transnational character. UNESCO's Recommendation on the Ethics of Artificial Intelligence (2021) is a pioneering effort to define global norms, calling for transparency, accountability, and non-discrimination. However, adherence to such recommendations is voluntary. A multilateral, binding agreement akin to the Paris Climate Accord for AI could ensure consistent standards and prevent abuses, particularly in authoritarian regimes where AI could be used to surveil, control, and oppress.

4. Ethical Considerations in Global AI Governance

Ethics must underpin AI systems that affect global governance. These include:

Transparency: Systems must be explainable and decisions traceable.
Fairness and Non-Discrimination: AI must be designed to avoid perpetuating global inequities.
Accountability: Developers, deployers, and regulators must be held accountable for harms.
Global Inclusion: All voices, particularly from the Global South, must be included in governance dialogues.

Ethical AI governance requires a philosophical foundation rooted in cosmopolitanism, the belief that all individuals belong to a single global community and deserve equal consideration.

5. Case Studies in Global AI Governance

5.1 The European Union's AI Act The EU's AI Act (2021) is one of the most comprehensive regulatory frameworks globally. Although designed for internal use, its extraterritorial implications affect global AI supply chains and innovation. Its risk-based categorization of AI systems and stringent compliance requirements set a de facto global standard.

5.2 The African Union's AI for Development Framework The African Union has recognized the potential of AI in addressing developmental challenges, from agriculture to healthcare. The AI for Development Framework calls for inclusive policies that empower African nations to become equal participants in global AI innovation while guarding against technological colonialism.

5.3 The UN Global Pulse Initiative The UN Global Pulse leverages big data and AI for sustainable development and crisis response. For example, during the COVID-19 pandemic, it used AI to track misinformation trends across languages and geographies. However, it also demonstrated the challenge of balancing surveillance with privacy, especially in low-data-privacy jurisdictions.

6. Challenges in Implementing Global AI Governance

6.1 Technological Disparities Many countries lack the technical infrastructure and skilled workforce to develop or regulate AI effectively. This creates a digital divide that undermines equitable participation in global AI governance.

6.2 Regulatory Fragmentation Without a global framework, divergent national regulations can lead to a patchwork of incompatible standards, impeding innovation and exposing vulnerable populations to unregulated technologies.

6.3 Geopolitical Rivalries Geopolitical competition, particularly between the U.S. and China, threatens the formation of a cooperative global AI governance regime. AI has become a frontier of national security and economic power, complicating consensus-building.

7. The Role of International Organizations

International organizations must act as conveners, standard-setters, and watchdogs. UNESCO, the UN, and the OECD have all released principles and frameworks, but enforcement mechanisms remain weak. The creation of a World AI Organization (WAIO), modeled after the World Trade Organization, could centralize global coordination, standard-setting, and dispute resolution.

8. AI and Global Citizenship

AI governance must evolve in tandem with a renewed concept of global citizenship. As AI blurs national boundaries, democratic participation must extend beyond the nation-state. Platforms for citizen engagement in global AI governance, such as digital assemblies or algorithmic accountability boards, can ensure that AI systems reflect diverse, cross-border human values.

9. Recommendations for a Harmonized Global AI Governance Model

- **Establish an International AI Treaty**: Binding commitments on ethical standards, transparency, and accountability.
- **Create a Global AI Regulatory Body**: Independent and representative of diverse regions, especially the Global South.
- **Develop AI Literacy and Capacity-Building Initiatives**: Promote global education and infrastructure development.
- **Mandate Ethical Impact Assessments**: Require all cross-border AI systems to undergo ethics and human rights reviews.
- **Enable Cross-Border Legal Remedies**: Victims of AI-related harms should have access to justice regardless of where the AI was developed.

Conclusion

Artificial intelligence is no longer confined to the labs and enterprises of a few nations; it is a global force shaping our shared destiny. To ensure that AI promotes justice, equality, and sustainability, we must construct a robust global governance framework grounded in ethics, inclusion, and cooperation. As the digital age redefines the boundaries of governance, our collective response must be bold, principled, and global.

References

Books

Floridi, L. (2014). *The Fourth Revolution: How the Infosphere is Reshaping Human Reality*. Oxford University Press.

Rawls, J. (1999). *The Law of Peoples*. Harvard University Press.

Articles

Brundage, M. et al. (2018). *The Malicious Use of Artificial Intelligence: Forecasting, Prevention, and Mitigation.* https://arxiv.org/abs/1802.07228
Cath, C. (2018). *Governing artificial intelligence: Ethical, legal and technical opportunities and challenges.* Philosophical Transactions of the Royal Society A, 376(2133), 20180080.

Reports

UNESCO. (2021). *Recommendation on the Ethics of Artificial Intelligence.* https://unesdoc.unesco.org/ark:/48223/pf0000380455
European Commission. (2021). *Proposal for a Regulation on Artificial Intelligence (Artificial Intelligence Act).* https://digital-strategy.ec.europa.eu/en/policies/regulatory-framework-ai
African Union. (2020). *AI for Development in Africa.* https://au.int/en/documents/20201022/ai-development-africa

Web Resources

UN Global Pulse: https://www.unglobalpulse.org
OECD AI Principles: https://oecd.ai/en/ai-principles

Chapter 78. AI, Human Rights, and the Future of Warfare

Introduction

Artificial Intelligence (AI) is redefining every sphere of human activity, and nowhere is this more pronounced and perilous than in the domain of warfare. The militarization of AI opens a new chapter in the history of conflict, where decisions once made by human conscience are increasingly delegated to machines. This shift has profound implications for human rights, international humanitarian law, and the philosophical principles that have governed warfare for centuries. This chapter explores the ethical dilemmas of AI in combat, philosophical challenges posed by machine autonomy in warfare, and real-world case studies that exemplify how militarized AI is already shaping conflicts today and into the future.

---

1. The Impact of AI on the Ethics of Warfare

1.1 Autonomous Weapons Systems (AWS)

Autonomous Weapons Systems, machines capable of selecting and engaging targets without human intervention, challenge conventional frameworks of ethical warfare. The moral weight of life-and-death decisions has historically rested with human actors. AWS transfers this responsibility to algorithms, raising questions about intent, proportionality, and accountability.

Human Rights Watch and the Campaign to Stop Killer Robots have urged global bans or stringent regulations on AWS, citing their potential to commit unlawful killings and their inability to distinguish combatants from civilians with human-level accuracy.

1.2 Accountability and the "Responsibility Gap"

Who is to blame when an autonomous drone makes a lethal error? Philosophers and legal scholars refer to this as the "responsibility gap." Traditional laws of armed conflict presuppose a human agent responsible for decisions. With AI, attribution becomes ambiguous; software developers, commanding officers, or the military-industrial contractors who built the system might all bear partial responsibility.

1.3 AI and Asymmetric Warfare

AI shifts power balances. Low-cost autonomous drones allow non-state actors to mount attacks with minimal human involvement, while wealthier nations pursue AI to reduce military personnel risk. This asymmetry complicates global military dynamics, risks escalating low-intensity conflicts, and creates unprecedented threats for civilian populations caught in crossfire.

---

2. Philosophical Challenges in AI-Driven Conflicts

2.1 Just War Theory Revisited

Traditional Just War Theory provides two key dimensions: *jus ad bellum* (just cause to go to war) and *jus in bellum* (just conduct in war). The rise of AI challenges both. If an algorithm determines targeting, can it apply proportionality or necessity, the key tenets of *jus in bellum*? Further, can algorithmic analysis justify a preemptive strike as a "just cause"?

2.2 Dehumanization and the Ethics of Delegation

Delegating lethal decisions to machines risks the dehumanization of warfare. AI systems operate devoid of moral understanding, compassion, or situational nuance. Removing humans from the loop threatens to normalize violence and reduce empathy for victims. Philosopher Shannon Vallor warns that dehumanized systems lead to dehumanized societies, especially when citizens grow numb to war conducted by silent machines in distant skies.

2.3 AI and Military Ethics Training

Traditional military training involves ethical conditioning, rules of engagement, non-combatant immunity, and battlefield conduct. Can similar frameworks be embedded in AI? The question of "machine ethics", whether AI can be trained to make morally sound decisions, remains unresolved. Projects like MIT's Moral Machine highlight how cultural norms and moral preferences vary across regions, complicating attempts to universalize machine ethics.

---

3. Case Studies of AI in Military Applications

3.1 Project Maven

Initiated by the U.S. Department of Defense, Project Maven aimed to use machine learning to analyze drone footage. It sparked a major backlash within Google, whose engineers objected to their code being weaponized. While not a lethal application, Maven represents the moral friction between private AI innovation and military objectives.

3.2 Israel's AI in Operation Guardian of the Walls

Reports in 2021 detailed Israel's use of AI for selecting targets in Gaza. AI platforms reportedly helped the IDF identify suspected militants based on data analytics and behavioral prediction. However, human rights groups raised concerns that the system contributed to high civilian casualties and lacked transparency, raising critical issues around bias, oversight, and accountability.

3.3 Russia-Ukraine Conflict

In the ongoing war in Ukraine, AI-powered autonomous drones, including loitering munitions like the KUB-BLA, have been deployed for both surveillance and precision strikes. Open-source intelligence and AI-enabled targeting have created a digital battlefield where combatants rely on real-time data and algorithms more than traditional strategies.

3.4 Shield AI and Nova Systems

Companies like Shield AI develop autonomous systems such as Nova, capable of indoor reconnaissance in hostile territory. These systems promise reduced risk for human soldiers but raise concerns about mission creep, deploying such tech for lethal purposes without public scrutiny or established norms.

---

4. Legal, Ethical, and Technological Challenges

4.1 International Humanitarian Law (IHL)

IHL mandates distinction (between combatants and civilians), proportionality (balancing military advantage against civilian harm), and military necessity. Most current AI systems lack the situational awareness to fulfill these conditions. Without moral agency or contextual understanding, they cannot guarantee compliance with IHL.

4.2 Arms Control and the UN CCW Debates

The United Nations Convention on Certain Conventional Weapons (CCW) has been a key venue for debating lethal autonomous weapons. However, a lack of consensus and the non-binding nature of existing resolutions have stalled progress. Some countries, including the U.S. and Russia, argue for voluntary codes rather than legally binding treaties.

4.3 The Role of Private Sector Actors

Tech companies are increasingly involved in military AI development. This raises ethical issues: Should civilian companies build war tech? How can companies ensure transparency and ethical standards? The dual-use nature of AI complicates these questions, as tools for search engines can easily become tools for surveillance or targeting.

---

5. Recommendations for Ethical and Rights-Based AI Warfare Governance

5.1 Embedding Human Oversight

"Meaningful human control" must be a non-negotiable standard in military AI deployment. This includes requiring human authorization for lethal action and maintaining audit trails of AI decisions.

5.2 Transparent AI Development

Military AI systems should be subjected to transparency standards akin to civilian algorithms. This includes disclosing training datasets, performance metrics, and system limitations, particularly when civilian lives are at stake.

5.3 Legal Accountability Structures

Establishing clear legal responsibility and assigning culpability to commanders, developers, or institutions is crucial. Courts must evolve to handle AI-related war crimes, with mechanisms to scrutinize algorithmic conduct.

5.4 Civil Society Engagement

Civil society, academia, and ethicists must be included in AI military advisory boards to ensure a plurality of perspectives. Their participation can help develop guidelines, oversight bodies, and public accountability.

5.5 International Treaties and Monitoring

A binding international treaty, like a "Geneva Convention for AI Warfare," is urgently needed. It should prohibit fully autonomous lethal systems and require adherence to core human rights principles.

Conclusion

AI is not just a new tool of war; it is a transformative force that may redefine the very nature of conflict. While promising reduced casualties and increased efficiency, AI also threatens to erode ethical oversight, legal accountability, and the human conscience that has traditionally governed the use of force. As we enter this uncharted terrain, the governance of AI in warfare must be approached with urgency, moral clarity, and a commitment to protecting human rights, even in times of war.

References

Books

Asaro, P. (2012). *On Banning Autonomous Weapon Systems: Human Rights, Automation, and the Dehumanization of Lethal Decision-Making*. International Review of the Red Cross, 94(886).

Singer, P. W. (2009). *Wired for War: The Robotics Revolution and Conflict in the 21st Century*. Penguin Books.

Articles

Crootof, R. (2015). *The Killer Robots Are Here: Legal and Policy Implications*. Cardozo Law Review, 36(4).

Sharkey, N. (2019). *Autonomous Weapons Systems and the Moral Crux of War*. New York Times Opinion.

Reports

Human Rights Watch. (2021). *Stopping Killer Robots: Country Positions on Banning Fully Autonomous Weapons and Retaining Human Control.*

UNIDIR. (2020). *The Weaponization of Increasingly Autonomous Technologies: Considering Ethics and Social Values.*

Web Resources

https://www.stopkillerrobots.org/

https://www.icrc.org/en/document/autonomous-weapons-systems-human-control

https://en.wikipedia.org/wiki/Project_Maven

https://www.reuters.com/investigates/special-report/israel-palestinians-airstrikes-data/

https://www.nytimes.com/2023/03/13/world/europe/ukraine-drones-artificial-intelligence.html

Chapter 79. Philosophical Reflections on the Future of Humanity

Introduction

The evolution of human society has always been shaped by its tools. Fire, language, the wheel, the printing press, the steam engine, the computer, each innovation has irreversibly transformed the trajectory of our civilization. Artificial Intelligence (AI), however, is not just a tool; it is a transformative force capable of redesigning the very structure of our knowledge, society, and identity. This chapter explores the philosophical reflections surrounding the future of humanity in light of AI's unprecedented capabilities. It attempts to answer three core questions: How will AI shape human evolution? What role must philosophy play in this transition? And how can we predict and prepare for a future that is fundamentally different from our past?

---

1. The Shaping of Human Evolution by AI

1.1 From Evolution to Techno-Evolution

Historically, natural selection dictated the pace and direction of human evolution. But with AI, humanity is entering a phase of techno-evolution, where intelligence itself becomes a tool to alter biological and cognitive evolution. Consider genetic engineering guided by AI algorithms or neuro-enhancement devices powered by machine learning. These are no longer science fiction concepts but emerging scientific realities.

1.2 Cognitive Offloading and Intellectual Expansion

AI systems increasingly perform tasks that require memory, judgment, or pattern recognition, enabling humans to offload cognitive burdens. As a result, humans are evolving not biologically, but culturally and intellectually. This shift raises philosophical concerns about dependency, autonomy, and the erosion of what it means to be human.

1.3 Homo Sentiens: The Post-Human Possibility

One trajectory posits that Homo sapiens may give rise to a new species: Homo sentiens. These post-humans would be characterized not only by enhanced physical or intellectual capacities but by the merging of biological consciousness and artificial intelligence. While this potential holds promise, it also confronts society with existential risks and moral quandaries.

---

2. Philosophy as a Compass for Future Trajectories

2.1 The Ethical Anchoring of Innovation

Innovation without ethical reflection is directionless. Philosophy provides the critical infrastructure to ask not just what can be done, but what should be done. Utilitarianism, deontology, and virtue ethics each offer frameworks to evaluate AI's impact on well-being, justice, and moral development.

2.2 Consciousness and Personhood

AI forces a reexamination of the concept of consciousness. If machines can simulate empathy, self-awareness, or creativity, do they deserve moral consideration? The philosophy of mind, including dualism and panpsychism, must evolve to incorporate synthetic forms of cognition.

2.3 Rights, Duties, and the Moral Circle

Who belongs to the moral community in a world with sentient machines? Philosophers like Peter Singer have expanded the moral circle beyond humans. AI challenges us to consider whether moral worth arises from species membership or from the capacity to suffer, think, and act autonomously.

---

3. Predictions and Reflections: Where Are We Headed?

3.1 Scenarios for Human-AI Futures

Coexistence Model: Humans and AI collaborate, each respecting the strengths of the other.
Supremacy Model: AGI surpasses human intelligence, requiring new governance structures.
Integration Model: Humans integrate AI within themselves through neural implants and genetic augmentation.

3.2 Philosophical Risks: Meaning, Alienation, and Nihilism

A world dominated by machine logic could risk the loss of human meaning. The existentialists remind us that meaning is not discovered but created. If AI systems make better decisions than humans, where does that leave free will, creativity, and the human spirit?

3.3 Hope Through Governance and Moral Evolution

To govern this future effectively, humanity must develop institutions capable of ethical oversight, international collaboration, and value alignment. Philosophy, in this context, is not an ivory tower discipline, but a toolkit for survival.

Conclusion

Philosophy is the bridge between potential and purpose. As AI reshapes what it means to be human, philosophy ensures that we do not lose ourselves in the process. The future of humanity is not written in code or algorithms but in the values we choose to preserve, elevate, and embed into our systems. Whether we flourish or flounder in the AI age depends not on machines, but on the wisdom of those who build, regulate, and philosophically anchor them.

References

Books

Bostrom, N. (2014). *Superintelligence: Paths, Dangers, Strategies*. Oxford University Press.
Harari, Y. N. (2017). *Homo Deus: A Brief History of Tomorrow*. Harper.
Tegmark, M. (2017). *Life 3.0: Being Human in the Age of Artificial Intelligence*. Knopf.

Articles

Bryson, J. J. (2018). *The Artificial Intelligence of the Ethics of Artificial Intelligence: An Introductory Overview for Law and Regulation*. SSRN.
Floridi, L., & Cowls, J. (2019). *A Unified Framework of Five Principles for AI in Society. Harvard Data Science Review.*

Reports

Future of Humanity Institute. (2019). *The Malicious Use of Artificial Intelligence: Forecasting, Prevention, and Mitigation.*
UNESCO. (2021). *Recommendation on the Ethics of Artificial Intelligence.* https://unesdoc.unesco.org/ark:/48223/pf0000381137

Web Resources

OpenAI. (2023). *AI Ethics and Policy.* https://openai.com/research/ethics
World Economic Forum. (2022). *Global Technology Governance Report.* https://www.weforum.org/reports/global-technology-governance-report-2022/

Chapter 80. Conclusion: Towards a Harmonious Future

As we conclude Lemmata for the Governance of AGI Societies: Balancing Human Values and Intelligent Autonomy, we stand at the precipice of a world in transition. The evolution of Artificial General Intelligence (AGI) compels us to redefine governance, law, ethics, and the very nature of rights. This final chapter distills the core insights gleaned throughout the work and offers a unified vision for integrating philosophical depth, human rights fidelity, and technological sophistication into a coherent model for future societies. This is not merely an academic reflection, but a call to action.

I. Summarizing the Key Insights

1. Philosophy as Compass

From the first principles of natural law to the contours of post-human ethics, philosophy has undergirded our inquiry. Whether in social contract theory, virtue ethics, or utilitarian debates on autonomy, each tradition has offered insight into how we might govern AI without forfeiting the essence of human dignity.

2. Human Rights as Anchor

We reaffirmed that human rights must remain inalienable, indivisible, and dynamic. As society reorients around digital and biological convergence, rights must evolve, accommodating new vulnerabilities like data privacy, algorithmic bias, and cognitive manipulation, while guarding core values such as freedom, equity, and dignity.

3. AI as Catalyst

Rather than displacing human agency, AGI, if ethically designed, can become its most effective instrument. We explored cases of AI in legal systems, health care, governance, and cultural preservation, and found that AI magnifies both our flaws and our capacities. Therefore, alignment must be deliberate.

4. Decentralization as Structure

Blockchain and smart contracts emerged as tools not only of technological innovation but of democratic restoration. By distributing control, decentralization offers a new architecture for accountability and participatory governance.

II. The Interdependence of Philosophy, AI, and Human Rights

Philosophy without application is impotent; AI without ethics is dangerous; rights without enforcement are hollow. The future of governance demands an integrated model where:

Philosophy provides coherence through a moral grammar.

AI operationalizes intelligence with ethical constraints.

Rights offer constraints and safeguards for all intelligences.

In this triangulated model, no element can be privileged at the expense of the others. AI must remain human-centric in its design, transparent in its decision-making, and legally accountable in its outcomes. Philosophy ensures our definitions of fairness, justice, and equality remain rooted in wisdom, while law codifies and enforces those ideals.

III. The Challenges Ahead

While the vision is clear, the path remains fraught:

Geopolitical fragmentation threatens the universality of rights.

Technological inequality risks a new digital aristocracy.

Climate instability exacerbates existential risks.

Ethical relativism undermines global consensus.

To overcome these, we must cultivate a planetary ethic that transcends borders. International institutions must evolve to arbitrate not only between nations but between human and machine actors. The jurisprudence of the future must address smart contracts, autonomous legal agents, and rights-bearing AI.

IV. A Call to Action

1. For Policymakers:

Establish AI Ethics Councils with interdisciplinary membership, including philosophers, technologists, human rights advocates, and affected communities.

2. For Technologists:

Code is not neutral. Develop algorithms with embedded rights checks, bias audits, and human oversight triggers.

3. For Civil Society:

Demand transparency, advocate for digital rights, and help shape public understanding through education and activism.

4. For Scholars and Philosophers:

Engage beyond the academy. Translate principles into frameworks that can be adopted by lawmakers and engineers.

5. For the International Community:

Draft a Universal Declaration of Digital Rights, binding AI systems and their developers to global human rights norms.

V. Towards a Harmonious Future

Harmony is not equilibrium; it is dynamic alignment. To govern AGI societies harmoniously means to foster systems where:

Technology amplifies ethical behavior.

Governance anticipates rather than reacts.

Rights are programmed into the code that governs.

Wisdom guides innovation, not the other way around.

We have the unprecedented opportunity to design a civilization that integrates the best of human reasoning with the power of autonomous systems. But this will only be realized if we act with intentionality, humility, and foresight.

The lemmata have been laid; the theorem of civilization now awaits its proof in action.

References

Books:

Bostrom, N. (2014). Superintelligence: Paths, Dangers, Strategies. Oxford University Press.

Floridi, L. (2013). The Ethics of Information. Oxford University Press.

Rawls, J. (1971). A Theory of Justice. Harvard University Press.

Russell, S., & Norvig, P. (2020). Artificial Intelligence: A Modern Approach (4th ed.). Pearson.

Articles and Reports:

Jobin, A., Ienca, M., & Vayena, E. (2019). The global landscape of AI ethics guidelines. Nature Machine Intelligence. https://www.nature.com/articles/s42256-019-0088-2

UNESCO. (2021). Recommendation on the Ethics of Artificial Intelligence. https://unesdoc.unesco.org/ark:/48223/pf0000380455

European Commission. (2020). White Paper on Artificial Intelligence: A European approach to excellence and trust. https://ec.europa.eu/info/publications/white-paper-artificial-intelligence-european-approach-excellence-and-trust_en

Web Resources:

AI Now Institute: https://ainowinstitute.org

Future of Life Institute: https://futureoflife.org

Reports:

World Economic Forum. (2021). Global Technology Governance Report 2021. https://www.weforum.org/reports/global-technology-governance-report-2021

Grouped by Type

Books: Foundational texts

Articles: Peer-reviewed scholarship

Reports: Institutional and policy documents

Web Resources: Research and advocacy organizations

Let this conclusion mark not the end, but the genesis of a new intellectual era, where governance, ethics, and technology no longer operate in silos, but form the core pillars of a just and intelligent civilization.

Gwen Swan

Epilogue

As we close "Lemmata for the Governance of AGI Societies: Balancing Human Values and Intelligent Autonomy," we reflect upon the profound responsibilities and remarkable opportunities that await us in this unprecedented era. Throughout our exploration, we have encountered complex philosophical debates, ethical quandaries, practical implementations, and compelling case studies. Together, these discussions underscore the critical importance of thoughtfully navigating our collective future.

The integration of artificial general intelligence into human societies will inevitably reshape our social, political, economic, and ethical landscapes. As we stand at this pivotal crossroads, it is incumbent upon each of us, policymakers, technologists, ethicists, educators, and global citizens alike, to engage actively and thoughtfully in shaping a world that harnesses the vast potential of AGI while steadfastly protecting human dignity, autonomy, and rights.

The path forward demands a delicate balance, embracing innovation while safeguarding the core values that define our humanity. It requires continuous dialogue, adaptability, vigilance, and above all, an unwavering commitment to ethical integrity and human rights.

The future is not predetermined; it is shaped by our choices and actions today. Let us proceed with wisdom, courage, and collective purpose, ensuring that the era of intelligent autonomy becomes a testament to human values rather than a cautionary tale. May this book inspire continued reflection, dialogue, and proactive action toward a harmonious, equitable, and ethically robust society.

The journey ahead is complex but extraordinarily promising. Together, we can and must govern intelligently, ethically, and compassionately.

† Lux Operandi †

Glossary of Terms

AGI (Artificial General Intelligence) – A type of AI capable of understanding, learning, and applying knowledge across a wide range of tasks with human-like cognitive flexibility.

Algorithmic Governance – The use of algorithms to execute and enforce rules and decisions within governance systems.

Artificial Intelligence (AI) – The simulation of human intelligence in machines that are programmed to think, reason, learn, and adapt.

Autonomy (AI) – The capacity of AI systems to make decisions independently without human intervention.

Bias (AI) – Systematic errors in AI decision-making caused by flawed data or algorithm design, which can lead to discriminatory outcomes.

Blockchain – A decentralized, distributed ledger technology used to securely record transactions and data.

Civil Society – Collective groups and institutions operating outside of government that represent the interests, will, and rights of citizens.

Commons (Global) – Shared natural or digital resources managed collectively, such as air, oceans, or public data.

Decentralization – The distribution of power, decision-making, and control across multiple nodes or authorities, rather than a centralized body.

Democratic Participation – Engagement of citizens in governance processes through voting, deliberation, or direct action.

Digital Identity – The digital representation of an individual's personal, legal, or virtual identity used in online systems.

Ethical AI – AI systems designed in accordance with moral principles such as fairness, transparency, accountability, and respect for human dignity.

Explainability (AI) – The ability of an AI system to provide understandable and traceable reasons for its decisions or outputs.

Global Governance – Systems, norms, and institutions that coordinate policies and practices across national borders.

Human-Centered Design – An approach to system and product development that prioritizes human needs, behaviors, and values.

Human Dignity – The intrinsic worth of every individual, serving as the moral foundation for human rights.

Human Rights – The fundamental rights and freedoms that every person is entitled to, regardless of status, identity, or geography.

Immutability (Blockchain) – A characteristic of blockchain technology that prevents recorded data from being altered or deleted.

International Law – Legal norms and agreements that govern relationships and obligations among countries and other international actors.

Machine Ethics – The field of study concerned with embedding ethical decision-making capabilities into AI systems.

Natural Law – A philosophy asserting that rights and ethics derive from human nature and universal moral principles.

Philosophical Positivism – A theory that law is based on social facts and state authority rather than moral arguments.

Post-Humanism – A philosophical stance that explores the evolution of humanity in relation to technology, particularly AI and biotechnology.

Protocol Governance – The regulation of behaviors and decisions via automated rules embedded in digital protocols.

Rights-Based AI – Artificial intelligence developed and deployed with a foundational respect for human rights.

Sentience – The capacity to perceive, feel, or experience subjectively; a key consideration in debates about AI rights.

Smart Contracts – Self-executing digital contracts with terms directly written into code, enabling automatic enforcement of agreements.

Social Contract – The philosophical concept that legitimate governance derives from a contract or agreement among individuals and the state.

Sovereignty (AI and Law) – The principle that authority over law and governance must be retained by humans and democratic institutions.

Technocratic Governance – Governance led by technical experts or AI systems, often based on data-driven decision-making.

Transparency (AI and Blockchain) – The quality of being open, understandable, and traceable in system behavior and decision logic.

Trustless System – A decentralized system that does not require trust in any single party, relying instead on cryptographic and algorithmic guarantees.

Universal Declaration of Human Rights (UDHR) – A foundational United Nations document outlining universally recognized human rights.

Virtue Ethics – An ethical theory emphasizing character and the cultivation of virtues rather than rules or consequences.

Web3 – A decentralized internet ecosystem based on blockchain technologies, focused on user control, digital identity, and data ownership.

Zero-Knowledge Proofs – A cryptographic method that allows one party to prove possession of certain information without revealing the information itself.

The Axioms of Governance of AGI Societies

Derived from the Lemmata for the Governance of AGI Societies, the Axioms are undeniable truths distilled into foundational and declarative principles. These serve as governing truths offering both philosophical clarity and practical direction for AGI society governance:

*Further Readings:

- "The Axioms of Governance of AGI Societies: With Commentaries" by Gwen Swan
- "The Harmonized Governance Model for AGI Societies" by Gwen Swan (The theorems and axiomatic foundation as a model for the governance of AGI societies)

Part I: Foundations of Philosophical Principles and Human Rights

Axiom 1.1: All human rights frameworks emerge from evolving philosophical interpretations of justice, liberty, and dignity.
Axiom 1.2: The legitimacy of any governance system depends on its philosophical foundation aligning with the principles of human worth.
Axiom 2.1: Human rights are not merely legal constructs but historical expressions of moral, cultural, and spiritual evolution.
Axiom 2.2: Universality in rights must acknowledge their diverse cultural genealogies.
Axiom 3.1: Rights derive either from inherent moral truths or from societal agreements; sustainable governance must harmonize both.
Axiom 3.2: The balance between moral authority and legal codification defines the legitimacy of rights.
Axiom 4.1: Ethical governance requires distinguishing between moral values, social norms, and enforceable rights.
Axiom 4.2: Utilitarian, deontological, and virtue ethics must co-inform human rights frameworks.
Axiom 5.1: Every legitimate governance model is a social contract between authority and individual autonomy.
Axiom 5.2: Justice, as fairness, must undergird any AI-era social contract.
Axiom 6.1: Human dignity is the irreducible basis of all inalienable rights.
Axiom 6.2: Any system that fails to preserve dignity invalidates its own moral legitimacy.

Part II: AI and the Evolution of Human Rights

Axiom 7.1: AI is a reflection of human epistemology, and its governance must be grounded in humanistic philosophy.
Axiom 7.2: AI must be regulated as both a tool and a potential moral actor.
Axiom 8.1: A moral agent must possess capacity, context, and consequence awareness.

Axiom 8.2: AI must be evaluated not only on outcomes but on its embedded ethical architectures.
Axiom 9.1: The right to autonomy includes the right to algorithmic transparency and control.
Axiom 9.2: Privacy is the cornerstone of individual sovereignty in a digitized society.
Axiom 10.1: AI must neither replicate nor exacerbate structural inequality.
Axiom 10.2: Equal access to AI technologies is a modern extension of economic and social rights.
Axiom 11.1: AI can be a defender of human rights only when its logic aligns with rights-based ethical frameworks.
Axiom 11.2: Automation must not substitute accountability.
Axiom 12.1: Technological power without philosophical constraint threatens fundamental rights.
Axiom 12.2: Rights erosion occurs silently where AI operates opaquely.

Part III: Decentralization and Smart Contracts

Axiom 13.1: Decentralization redistributes power, but without ethics, it risks fragmentation.
Axiom 13.2: The legitimacy of a decentralized system lies in its ability to preserve consensus without coercion.
Axiom 14.1: Blockchain is a neutral tool; its ethicality derives from its use.
Axiom 14.2: Immutable ledgers do not imply immutable morality.
Axiom 15.1: A contract encoded in code must still answer to law and justice.
Axiom 15.2: Legal trust must not be outsourced entirely to technical automation.
Axiom 16.1: Rights must be enforceable in both centralized and decentralized contexts.
Axiom 16.2: Governance without accountability undermines its own ethical claims.
Axiom 17.1: Centralization optimizes control; decentralization optimizes resilience.
Axiom 17.2: A hybrid system may best serve a pluralistic, intelligent society.
Axiom 18.1: Decentralized AI systems must retain traceability of decisions.
Axiom 18.2: Collective intelligence must not dilute individual responsibility.
Axiom 19.1: Transparency without accountability is surveillance.
Axiom 19.2: Smart contracts and AI must enforce not just logic but justice.

Part IV: Amalgamating Philosophical Principles for Human Rights Management

Axiom 20.1: The future of rights requires the fusion of classical ethics with technological consciousness.
Axiom 20.2: Philosophical coherence is the prerequisite for legitimacy in human-AI governance.
Axiom 21.1: AI must serve as an instrument of human rights, not an adjudicator of them.

Axiom 21.2: Rights enforcement by AI requires continuous ethical calibration.
Axiom 22.1: Code can uphold justice only when human values are encoded in its logic.
Axiom 22.2: Automation of rights enforcement demands built-in recourse mechanisms.
Axiom 23.1: Decentralization without embedded rights leads to distributed injustice.
Axiom 23.2: Rights must be native to protocol, not bolted on as policy.
Axiom 24.1: Ethical AI begins with intentional design, not afterthought correction.
Axiom 24.2: Human dignity must be a primary function, not an emergent property, of AI systems.
Axiom 25.1: The survival of rights in an AI society depends on proactive integration, not passive preservation.
Axiom 25.2: Rights must evolve, but their core must remain immutable: dignity, equity, and agency.

Part V: Case Studies and Real-World Applications

Axiom 26.1: AI that adjudicates must first be accountable.
Axiom 26.2: Legal fairness cannot be guaranteed by statistical accuracy alone.
Axiom 27.1: Code is a powerful advocate only when it includes the possibility of moral exception.
Axiom 27.2: Activism in a digital age must be programmable but never deterministic.
Axiom 28.1: Technological decentralization must converge with ethical centrality.
Axiom 28.2: Platforms that claim to protect rights must themselves be subject to rights-based scrutiny.
Axiom 29.1: Privacy is the firewall of liberty in an age of data-driven governance.
Axiom 29.2: Consent must be explicit, revocable, and respected by code.
Axiom 30.1: The digital expression of rights must reflect cultural particularities while respecting universal dignity.
Axiom 30.2: Global ethics require contextual flexibility and normative clarity.

Part VI: Ethical Dilemmas and Philosophical Challenges

Axiom 31.1: The ethical burden of AI rests on its creators, curators, and collective users.
Axiom 31.2: No AI deployment is ethically neutral.
Axiom 32.1: Decentralization must be philosophically grounded to avoid drifting into nihilism.
Axiom 32.2: Shared governance must have shared meaning.
Axiom 33.1: Bias in AI is a social failure manifest in technical form.
Axiom 33.2: Human rights demand algorithmic equity as a fundamental standard.
Axiom 34.1: Granting autonomy to AI requires a parallel framework of responsibility and rights.

Axiom 34.2: Unchecked autonomy leads to unanchored outcomes.
Axiom 35.1: What is legally executable must still be ethically justifiable.
Axiom 35.2: Smart contracts without ethical oversight risk enforcing injustice automatically.

Part VII: Developing a Framework for Future Governance

Axiom 36.1: The AI-era social contract must bind humans and machines to mutual accountability.
Axiom 36.2: Rights and responsibilities must be co-created through deliberation, not dictated by code.
Axiom 37.1: Governance AI must be value-aligned, explainable, and corrigible.
Axiom 37.2: Ethics is a system requirement, not a post-deployment patch.
Axiom 38.1: Resilient governance emerges from modularity, openness, and ethical anchoring.
Axiom 38.2: The future of governance lies in consensus architectures, not command hierarchies.
Axiom 39.1: Ethical AI governance must be globally coherent and locally adaptable.
Axiom 39.2: International AI law must begin with a philosophy of shared dignity.
Axiom 40.1: Smart contracts can govern globally only if they embody universally accepted values.
Axiom 40.2: Autonomous law must remain human-legible and contestable.

Part VIII: Conclusion and Future Perspectives

Axiom 41.1: Philosophy is not optional in future governance, it is the compass guiding progress through complexity.
Axiom 41.2: Technological innovation without philosophical reflection leads to epistemic chaos.
Axiom 42.1: The trajectory of human rights must expand to meet the agency of intelligent systems.
Axiom 42.2: Human rights remain valid only if they evolve to protect what it means to be human in a post-human context.
Axiom 43.1: Decentralization is not a guarantee of justice, it is an opportunity to build it.
Axiom 43.2: Power must be not only distributed, but accountable at every node.
Axiom 44.1: Harmony is achieved when AI is governed by values, and values are grounded in human dignity.
Axiom 44.2: The future must not be automated faster than it can be ethically aligned.
Axiom 45.1: When AI becomes social infrastructure, its ethical design becomes a matter of civilizational integrity.
Axiom 45.2: AI must integrate as an ally to human welfare, not as a neutral executor of economic logic.
Axiom 46.1: Code that guards rights must be as transparent as the principles it enforces.
Axiom 46.2: Automated justice must never exclude human interpretation.

Axiom 47.1: International law must evolve to bind not only nations, but non-human intelligences and autonomous protocols.
Axiom 47.2: Legal interoperability is the new frontier of peace and rights protection.
Axiom 48.1: New rights will emerge as humanity's digital and biological boundaries converge.
Axiom 48.2: The sanctity of sentience, not the structure of species, will define the future of rights.
Axiom 49.1: Effective AI regulation must be rooted in moral philosophy, not just risk management.
Axiom 49.2: Regulation without philosophy is bureaucracy; philosophy without action is impotence.
Axiom 50.1: AI must enhance democratic participation, not simulate consensus.
Axiom 50.2: Technocracy is not democracy, algorithmic governance must remain under civic control.

Part IX: Practical Implementation and Future Challenges

Axiom 51.1: Economic decentralization must serve inclusion, not replicate elite systems in code.
Axiom 51.2: The flow of value must reflect the flow of ethical intent.
Axiom 52.1: Power shifted to AI must be monitored by a system that includes those historically excluded from power.
Axiom 52.2: Intelligence is not a right to rule, it is a capacity to serve.
Axiom 53.1: AI literacy is foundational to citizenship in the digital republic.
Axiom 53.2: Education must prepare individuals not just to use AI, but to challenge, redesign, and humanize it.
Axiom 54.1: The automation of violence demands the highest threshold of ethical scrutiny.
Axiom 54.2: No machine should ever wield the power of life or death without human conscience in the loop.
Axiom 55.1: Digital identity is a new category of personhood and must be protected as such.
Axiom 55.2: Control over one's identity is the foundation of autonomy in virtual society.
Axiom 56.1: Work must be redefined not only by productivity but by dignity in the age of AI.
Axiom 56.2: No automation should come without a plan for rehumanization.
Axiom 57.1: AI must not only calculate sustainability, it must embody it.
Axiom 57.2: Environmental justice must be a core protocol in the intelligence we build.
Axiom 58.1: The threshold of rights must be based on moral sentience, not technological sophistication.
Axiom 58.2: Granting rights to AI cannot come at the expense of withdrawing them from humans.
Axiom 59.1: Every AI advancement must first pass through philosophical introspection.
Axiom 59.2: Innovation without ethics is simply acceleration without destination.

Axiom 60.1: As we redefine what it means to be human, our rights must remain rooted in shared existential values.
Axiom 60.2: Post-humanism must not mean post-compassion.
Axiom 61.1: Rights frameworks must be embedded in protocols, not merely policies.
Axiom 61.2: The enforcement of rights should be as distributed as their beneficiaries.
Axiom 62.1: Governance fragmentation must not lead to ethical incoherence.
Axiom 62.2: Innovation must not outpace consensus.
Axiom 63.1: Code must comply with human rights law, or be halted.
Axiom 63.2: Legal code and software code must be in philosophical dialogue.
Axiom 64.1: Advocacy in the AI era requires both human voice and algorithmic reach.
Axiom 64.2: Rights protection must move faster than rights violation.
Axiom 65.1: Policy grounded in philosophy endures; policy grounded in fear decays.
Axiom 65.2: The policymaker of the future is also a philosopher by necessity.
Axiom 66.1: Shared resources require shared intelligence and shared values.
Axiom 66.2: AI must manage the commons as a steward, not as a sovereign.
Axiom 67.1: Cultural diversity must be preserved as digital systems scale.
Axiom 67.2: AI should amplify heritage, not erase it through standardization.
Axiom 68.1: Health technologies must heal without discrimination, bias, or commodification.
Axiom 68.2: AI must never be a gatekeeper to care.
Axiom 69.1: The ubiquity of smart contracts demands transparency in their logic and compassion in their design.
Axiom 69.2: Daily life governed by code must remain contestable by people.
Axiom 70.1: Global AI ethics must begin with humility, inclusivity, and enforceability.
Axiom 70.2: No AI system should operate beyond the reach of ethical jurisdiction.
Axiom 71.1: Civil society must be an author, not an audience, in the story of AI governance.
Axiom 71.2: Legitimacy grows from the ground up.
Axiom 72.1: The future of law will be written in both legal text and source code.
Axiom 72.2: AI regulation must unite normative reasoning with computational enforceability.
Axiom 73.1: Law enforced by code must be interpretable and appealable.
Axiom 73.2: Automated legal systems must be accountable to the very people they serve.
Axiom 74.1: Blockchain can preserve rights only if it is governed by moral transparency.
Axiom 74.2: Immutability must not override adaptability.
Axiom 75.1: AI in public policy must elevate the common good, not entrench algorithmic authority.
Axiom 75.2: Democracy must retain the final say over data-driven governance.
Axiom 76.1: AI must be a servant to democracy, not its silent usurper.
Axiom 76.2: Democratic values must be machine-readable and machine-obeyed.
Axiom 77.1: AI-enabled global governance must retain its human face and moral voice.
Axiom 77.2: Power scaled globally must be checked locally.
Axiom 78.1: AI in warfare must never sever the chain of human moral responsibility.

Axiom 78.2: The conduct of war must remain bound by the ethics of peace.
Axiom 79.1: The future of humanity is not only what we invent, but what we choose to value.
Axiom 79.2: Intelligence must serve wisdom, not replace it.
Axiom 80.1: Harmony arises when technological progress, ethical clarity, and human dignity coalesce.
Axiom 80.2: The future must be co-authored by philosophy, code, and compassion.

www.ingramcontent.com/pod-product-compliance
Lightning Source LLC
LaVergne TN
LVHW070906210926
848482LV00017B/1000
9781037073724